LAND GRANTS AND LAWSUITS IN NORTHERN NEW MEXICO

Land Grants and Lawsuits in Northern New Mexico

MALCOLM EBRIGHT

NEW MEXICO LAND GRANT SERIES

JOHN R. VAN NESS, SERIES EDITOR

University of New Mexico Press / Albuquerque

Library of Congress Cataloging-in-Publication Data
Ebright, Malcolm.
Land grants and lawsuits in northern New Mexico / Malcolm Ebright. — 1 ed.
p.   cm. — (New Mexico land grant series)
Includes bibliographical references and index.
ISBN 0-8263-1468-6 (cloth) — ISBN 0-8263-1461-9 (pbk.)
1. Land grants — Law and legislation — New Mexico — History.
I. Title.   II. Series.
KFN4055.E27   1994
343.789'0253 — dc20
[347.8903253]
93-30863
CIP

SECOND PAPERBOUND PRINTING, 1996

An earlier version of the Introduction appeared in Charles L. Briggs and John R. Van
Ness, eds., Land Water and Culture: New Perspectives on Hispanic Land Grants
(Albuquerque: University of New Mexico Press, 1987).
Chapter 3 is a revised version of an essay that appeared in the New Mexico Historical
Review 54 (January 1979): 21–34 and is reprinted by permission.
Chapter 6 is a revised version of an essay that appeared in the New Mexico Historical
Review 57 (January 1982): 5–26 and is reprinted by permission.
Chapter 5 is a revised version of an essay that appeared in The Journal of the West
19 (July 1980): 74–85 and is reprinted by permission.

Chapter opening and cover illustrations by Glen T. Strock.
Illustrations on pp. 164 and 245 by Rini Templeton.
Illustrations on pp. 199 and 270 by Danté Ruiz.

Dedicated to my mother and the memory of my father

One can learn a great deal about something only if he loves it.
LUIS GONZALEZ
San José de Gracia: A Mexican Village in Transition

CONTENTS

PREFACE

The study of New Mexico's land and water history has intensified in the past twenty-five years because of unsettled land claims and, more recently, because of the state's decision to adjudicate water rights on all of its streams and rivers. Because this process involves complex legal issues emanating from both Hispanic and United States law, and because the rights claimed by Native Americans and Hispanics under protection of the federal government frequently clash with rights claimed by the state and guaranties of property protection written into the Treaty of Guadalupe Hidalgo, the issues are often very involved, heatedly debated, and extremely costly to litigate.

All sides seek expert testimony in court, and these "experts" have succeeded in producing a body of information that has considerably improved our understanding of land and water matters in the Southwest. With few exceptions, the scholarship has been impartial, thorough, and imaginative. Unfortunately, much of the written material has not been released for publication. Malcolm Ebright's essays provide information of a kind that has been locked up far too long, and are a result of many years' investigation of land and water problems in New Mexico.

While the essays were not originally planned to be linked together in a book, Ebright has arranged them in such a manner that they can be read sequentially or individually. Each contains at least one of several conclusions. First, the Hispanic descendants of grantees of land under Spain and Mexico have been deprived consistently of their property (land and water) because of the United States' inability and/or unwillingness to recognize the rights of settlers under Hispanic law and custom. This is Ebright's underlying theme. Secondly, as both attorney and historian, he has focused on the need to understand the difference between Hispanic civil law with its emphasis on preservation of community, and Anglo-American common law promoting individualism and a sense of superiority through Manifest

Destiny. The change of sovereignty in 1848, he concludes, brought into conflict two very different social and legal systems. Interpretation of the Treaty of Guadalupe Hidalgo, the work of the surveyor general and Court of Private Land Claims, and the role of Congress and the territory and state of New Mexico can only be understood against the background of competing concepts of social order. Finally, Ebright laments the United States' inability to recognize and honor the Hispanic use of common lands and the role of custom in preserving these lands and their waters. While some of the original grants remain, most have been stripped of the shared wood, water, and pasture that were essential for survival of the Hispanic people prior to 1848.

As with writers John Nichols and Stanley Crawford, both of whom have also raised protests against the government's seemingly relentless attempts to destroy the Hispanic man-land relationship in northern New Mexico, Ebright writes from the perspective of one who works the earth himself. His commitment to scholarship is no less than his love of the Guadalupita valley where he resides. What he says in these essays is as much a product of archival research as it is a personal commitment to what one hundred and fifty years of conflict have meant to neighbors fighting for generations to preserve their way of life against the attacks of speculators, ignorant politicians, and greedy attorneys. The content of these essays will prove illuminating to open- minded readers, and the copious footnotes will provide additional guidance to anyone wishing to follow the stimulating course which Ebright has set.

COLORADO STATE UNIVERSITY   *Daniel Tyler*

FOREWORD

This is the fifth volume in the New Mexico Land Grant Series, which is dedicated to the serious study of New Mexico's Hispanic land grants and the small farming and ranching communities founded on them. Through the series a large body of primary research, that is, work based on exhaustive study of primary documents and other pertinent information, has been made available for the first time to the general reader. Previously, much of the writing on land grants was based on a superficial study of secondary documents, derived principally from the records of the Office of the Surveyor General and the Court of Private Land Claims. It was often assumed that these land grant records told the whole story, and evidence presented in administrative hearings and court cases was uncritically accepted as true. What was not studied was the history of the land grants prior to the 1846 occupation of New Mexico by the United States. This series examines Hispanic New Mexico through primary documents, many of which are from the eighteenth and early nineteenth centuries, and by doing so provides a more complete history.

A principal aim of the series is to establish the place of the ordinary Hispanic and Pueblo Indian people, common men and women, in the history of New Mexico's Spanish and Mexican land grants. This is necessary because the central role that these people played in settling and developing the land grants in New Mexico has frequently been distorted or ignored. To accomplish this goal, the series has brought together the work of outstanding scholars from wide-ranging backgrounds — lawyers, historians, and anthropologists.

The present volume is authored by Malcolm Ebright, whose work will be familiar to readers of the series, for he contributed a chapter to volume four, *Land Water and Culture: New Perspectives on Hispanic Land Grants*. It is particularly fitting and appropriate to present in one place a substantial body of Ebright's extensive writing on New Mexico land grants because of his unique and important place in contemporary land grant research.

I have known Malcolm Ebright for nearly twenty years and have great admiration for his dedication to Hispanic land grant research, public advocacy of the rights of land grant communities to their patrimony, as well as his legal services in representing numerous Hispanic claimants struggling to regain or maintain their property rights. Ebright has shown a remarkable level of commitment to the pursuit of justice for those whose lives have been limited and impoverished as the result of the alienation of land and water resources.

As the reader will soon discover, Ebright is passionately committed to righting these wrongs, wrongs that should shock the conscience of every fair-minded American. These are not wrongs that can be conveniently dismissed as merely the outcome of actions and decisions that affected individuals and whole communities now long dead and gone. This is more than a regrettable episode in American history to be relegated to the dusty shelves of the library and forgotten. On the contrary, as Ebright so cogently argues, these nineteenth-century land and water claims remain major issues in current lawsuits crowding the dockets of New Mexico's courts. In Ebright's words, "by documenting the unfairness and injustices that accompanied land loss in New Mexico, history can be made to bear witness to current policy and legal decisions affecting New Mexico's land and water resources."

Malcolm Ebright brings the special sensitivities of a practicing attorney to the historical records and other relevant data. As a legal scholar he appreciates the contrasts between the Spanish/Mexican and the Anglo-American legal systems and demonstrates that this is one of the basic causes of the unfair treatment that Hispanic claimants experienced in attempting to establish their property rights as American citizens. The essence of fairness in an adversarial system of justice, Ebright contends, depends on a basic equality between the opposing sides attempting to prove their case in court. Because of the differing legal systems and the Hispanics' limited economic and political power, claimants rarely enjoyed equal standing with the U.S. government in court.

One of the principal contributions of these essays is to demonstrate the importance of custom in administering the law on the remote New Mexican frontier during Spanish Colonial and Mexican rule. Ebright shows through specific case studies that unfair decisions were rendered as the result of the failure of American officials and judges to acknowledge the legitimate role of custom in Hispanic New Mexico. These essays also break new ground by treating the events that transpired after decisions made by the Surveyor General and/or the Court of Private Land Claims, for substantial land loss by Hispanic residents also resulted from partition suits initiated following a grant's confirmation.

Ebright's major conclusions represent a dismal assessment of the fairness with which Hispanic land grant claims were adjudicated under United States sovereignty. Further, *Land Grants and Lawsuits in Northern New Mexico* paints an unsavory picture of many of the government officials, judges, lawyers, and land speculators involved in these affairs. Even by the standards of the place and time, the self-dealing, avarice, unethical practices, and dishonesty uncovered by Ebright are shocking.

I commend Malcolm Ebright for bringing the findings of his research to the public through this collection of revealing essays. It takes more than a little courage to challenge cherished American myths regarding equality under the law and the prevalence of fair play in American society. However, the interpretation of history can never be static. Few would doubt that there is still much to revise in our history of "winning the West." Previous generations of American historians have emphasized the rapid and impressive sweep of American civilization across the vast and sparsely populated western territories, bringing American know-how, industriousness, superior technology, and aggressive capitalistic economic development. In popular American culture the theme of Manifest Destiny became a myth of justification for countless injustices perpetrated against those who had occupied the land for many generations.

The purpose of this revisionist history of the West, however, is not to transform the heros of past histories into one-dimensional villains nor is it merely to make the unsung victims new heros. Its purpose is to break down simplistic nationalistic readings of the American past; to enable us to acknowledge and learn to respect the substantial differences in historical experience of the ethnically diverse groups that make up contemporary American society. This is an essential step in shaping a viable identity for our present multiethnic and multicultural nation. "America is a construction of mind," as Robert Hughes has aptly put it (*Time*, February 3, 1992, p. 44). Our nation consists of scores of ethnic groups that have been incorporated into American society through the process of negotiating accommodations with one another. As we have become acutely aware in recent decades, some ethnic groups have enjoyed much greater success than others in this process. We must constantly be reminded that this is an unfinished process, one of the messages conveyed by *Land Grants and Lawsuits in Northern New Mexico.*

This volume will have served its purpose if it is accepted as a contribution to our understanding of an important aspect of the complex, multi-stranded history of a unique region of the American West. It is my hope that this history will also aid those engaged in the process of finding ways to resolve their struggles to regain rights to numerous land grants. These land grants nurtured Hispanic New Mexicans for generations, and this land remains a core component of their distinctive ethnic identity as Americans. Finally, I trust that the reader will find this volume to be stimulating and thought provoking and a useful addition to Western History.

John R. Van Ness
SERIES EDITOR

Introduction:
Land Grants and Lawsuits
in Northern New Mexico

In the late 1960s when I first began to study the history of New Mexico land grants, the subject of land grants and the fairness of their adjudication had received international attention because of the courthouse raid in Tierra Amarilla, New Mexico.[1] During that period land grant activists spoke repeatedly about the loss of land grant land, but anyone interested in the facts of land grant history in New Mexico had little published material to consult. Government attention focused on the subject of land titles within New Mexico land grants when the state of New Mexico sponsored the Land Title Study in the early 1970s.[2] As a coauthor of that study I interviewed scholars, attorneys, government officials, and anyone else with knowledge in the field to determine what was known about New Mexico's land grants.[3] Although much pioneering work had been done,[4] it was apparent then that relatively little was known about New Mexico's land grants. Twenty years later, though much work remains to be done, land grant studies has become a recognized field of inquiry and much new research has been published.[5]

The essays that make up this book follow a pattern of inquiry that mirrors my own quest to research and write some of the history of New Mexico's land grants. They are written in such a way that any one of them can be read independently of the others, if, for example, the reader is interested in a specific land grant, but the chapters are also arranged in a logical progression, and tied together by an overall theme. In order to understand the background of land grants in New Mexico one needs to look at land tenure and law in Spain and Mexico, since many land laws, customs, and procedures followed in New Mexico had their origin in those countries. Accordingly Chapter 1 traces the antecedents of New Mexico's land grants back to Spain and Mexico. It then reviews the obligations assumed by the United States under the Treaty of Guadalupe Hidalgo in regard to land grants in the Southwest and follows the history and adjudication of these grants in New Mexico.

The evidence strongly suggests that U.S. courts and Congress did not fairly meet the obligations assumed by the United States under the Guadalupe Hidalgo treaty.[6] The main reason for this was that the land grants were established under one legal system and adjudicated by another. The Anglo common law system did not sufficiently take into account important elements of the Hispanic civil law system such as customary law, which drove the legal system in New Mexico when the land grants were made.[7] Hispanic customary law was poorly understood in late nineteenth-century New Mexico because the lawsuits and governmental actions that defined and comprised customary law had not yet been documented in any detail. As modern lawsuits continue to adjudicate land and water rights originating in New Mexico's land grants, it is important that New Mexico's Hispanic legal system be better understood.

To understand the legal system followed when New Mexico was part of Spain and then Mexico one must study individual lawsuits as they were fought out in New Mexico before the United States invasion. Chapter 2 reviews some of these lawsuits against the background of New Mexico's legal system during the Spanish and Mexican periods and briefly compares this Hispanic system with the Anglo-American common law system that replaced it. Whereas Chapter 1 deals with abstract law and land tenure, Chapter 2 treats the specifics of the lawsuits themselves.

A lawsuit over water rights in Abiquiú brought by Manuel Martínez, who was later to request the Tierra Amarilla community land grant that was the subject of the courthouse raid in 1967, is the subject of Chapter 3. This detailed examination of one lawsuit reveals how custom became the means of deciding that case and how specific customs were proven in the course of the lawsuit. In addition, we see how the political relationship between the governor in Santa Fe and the local government council (*ayuntamiento*) was of major importance in determining the outcome of the litigation.

Political considerations also had a great deal to do with the outcome of Spanish and Mexican period lawsuits over the Santa Fe Ciénega, a public tract of land northeast of the Santa Fe plaza, dealt with in Chapter 4. The governor who decided these cases had to balance competing interests, and he often found a way to make both sides happy by giving each part of what they wanted. One of these interests was the municipality of Santa Fe, which was trying to protect its ownership of the Ciénega. The city fathers were unsuccessful in holding on to the Ciénega, but the institution of *propios* (property used for municipal purposes), and customs such as stubble grazing documented in these lawsuits, bring into focus another part of the mosaic of customary law.

Chapter 5 examines the institution of common land ownership as it existed prior to the United States' occupation of New Mexico and compares that with common land ownership as erroneously decided by the

United States Supreme Court in the adjudication of the San Joaquín grant. This landmark decision was responsible for the loss of more land grant land than any other by an American court adjudicating land grants under the Treaty of Guadalupe Hidalgo. The pattern followed in this essay and in those dealing with the Embudo, Las Trampas, Las Vegas, Ramón Vigil, and Jacona grants is to trace the history of the settlement of the land grant under the laws and customs of New Mexico prior to 1846, and then to examine the adjudication of that grant by the United States. In the Las Trampas, Las Vegas, and Jacona chapters, the legal history of the grants after adjudication is also studied because the loss of the Las Trampas common lands, the sale of most of the Las Vegas common lands, and the retention of the Jacona grant's common lands were results of activities that took place after the grants were confirmed.

The adjudication of the Embudo grant by the Court of Private Land Claims was another mistaken decision that failed to recognize the system of customary law followed in Hispanic New Mexico. There the Land Claims Court rejected the grant because an official called an *escribano* did not make the copy of the grant document offered to the court, even though such officials were not present in New Mexico at the time the copy was made. In addition, Chapter 6 examines some of the reasons why the Anglo-American legal system often failed to fairly decide land grant issues that arose under the Hispanic system.

Not all land lost from New Mexican land grants was due to the actions of courts set up to adjudicate these grants pursuant to the Treaty of Guadalupe Hidalgo. Chapter 7 traces the history of the Las Trampas community land grant from its beginning as one of the earliest grants established in the mountains north of Santa Fe, through the adjudication process and the subsequent loss of common land use rights, to a modern day lawsuit that sought to restore those rights. Evidence submitted in that lawsuit revealed that the use-rights were lost because Santa Fe Ring members Alois B. Renehan and Charles Catron tricked the settlers with a secret agreement not submitted to the court in 1913. This case study provides an example of Hispanic land loss due to the machinations of lawyer-speculators.

Another land grant history relevant to a current lawsuit is the Las Vegas grant. There the issue is water rights. The settlement pattern of the grant becomes crucial in determining whether the Pueblo Rights Doctrine applies to the grant (if such a doctrine even existed under Spanish or Mexican law). In the search for the history of settlement in and around Las Vegas, a story of conflict over the control of the common lands emerges, in which governmental officials are inextricably involved in the complicated maneuverings. Also illustrated is the difficulty of overturning an erroneous historical doctrine encapsulated in a judicial decision that fails to adequately define the extent of and basis for the doctrine. Chapter 8 tells the story of the Las Vegas grant up until the arrival of General Stephen Watts Kearny in Las Vegas and Chapter 9 takes the story through the Territorial Period when the battle for the common lands continued until finally the grant was placed in the hands of a court-appointed board of trustees.

Several twists in the case of the Ramón Vigil grant discussed in Chapter 10, make that story of land grant speculation different from the others. One of those twists is the discovery that the grant documents submitted for confirmation to the surveyor general of New Mexico were forged. Although the grant itself did exist, the question of who forged the documents and why, opens up the larger question of why the surveyor general's office did not discover the forgery. In addition, we see that not all land speculators were lawyers and politicians belonging to the Santa Fe Ring. Instead we find a priest, Father Thomas Aquinas Hayes, making a larger profit by buying and selling the Ramon Vigil Grant than Thomas B. Catron ever did in his land grant dealings.

All land grant histories are not tales of land loss, although many of them are. In the case of the Jacona grant discussed in Chapter 11, the grant was able to keep its common lands through a unity of purpose among the grant members, organized by an early land grant activist named Cosme Herrera. The grant residents themselves purchased the land grant after it was partitioned and sold by the lawyer for the grant, Napoleon Bonaparte Laughlin. Other land grants have also had success in holding on to their lands, and the Jacona story attempts to find out why some New Mexico land grants have survived in the face of overwhelming odds, while others have been less successful.

I wish to thank the following people who have helped me with this book. Much of what is of value here is due to them, the errors are my responsibility. Robert Torrez read and commented on Chapter 2 "Lawsuits, Litigants and Custom" and Jean Keller, former chairman of the Department of Modern Languages at Albion College, Michigan, helped me considerably with the documents upon which Manuel Martínez's Ditch Dispute is based. William Taylor, Daniel Tyler, and David Weber each read the Ciénega chapter and made helpful comments, and Linda Tigges and

David Snow shared their recent archeological and documentary research on the location of the Ciénega. Estevan Arellano contributed his extensive knowledge of the Dixon area to the Embudo chapter, and Anselmo Arellano read the Las Vegas chapters sharing his considerable knowledge about the Las Vegas area with me. Thomas J. Steele, S. J., Laurie Macrae, and the late Peggy Pond Church provided help with the Ramón Vigil chapter. I received financial support and encouragement from Wilfredo Vigil and Agnes Vigil Martinez in researching their ancestor, Ramón Vigil, although Wilfredo does not necessarily agree with all my conclusions. Lawyer Santiago "Jaime" Chávez provided assistance with the Las Trampas and Jacona chapters, and attorney John Roybal helped with background and documents for the Jacona chapter. Christian Fritz read most of the manuscript and gave me helpful suggestions, sharing his research on land grant litigation in California. Special thanks go to Daniel Tyler who read the entire manuscript providing general comments on the whole and detailed comments on the Ciénega chapter as well as writing the foreword.

The following archival staff at the New Mexico State Records Center and Archives in Santa Fe have been extremely helpful and good humored: Richard Salazar, Al Regensberg, Sandra Jaramillo Macias, Alfred Aragon, and Arlene Padilla. Thanks also to library director Ann Kaiser, Joann Castillo, and the rest of the staff of the Carnegie Library in Las Vegas for patiently processing my inter-library loan requests and allowing me unrestricted use of their excellent Southwest collection. Mary Jane Parker of the Supreme Court Law Library has also earned my gratitude for her assistance. Capable and cheerful secretarial assistance was provided by Kate Jeffries, Shona Jeffries, Pauline Cordova, Greta Ruiz, Dante Ruiz, and Pamela Larson, all of whom eased my relationship with the implacable Macintosh and earned my heartfelt thanks. Pamela Larson provided editorial assistance on Chapter 1 and 2, and Barbara Guth at University of New Mexico Press edited the entire manuscript and more than anyone else, prodded it into print. Many thanks also to Glen Strock for his drawings and to Dante Ruiz and Carrie Arnold for theirs. Additional thanks to Robert Wittwer for the maps. I am also indebted to Martín González de la Vara for negotiating the treacherous Mexico City traffic as we searched for rare books there and for introducing me to the work of his father, Luis González.

From the beginning I have benefitted from the friendly sparring that Emlen Hall and I have engaged in as we each tried to live and write a part of

New Mexico's legal history. Anselmo Arellano, Julián Josué Vigil, Daniel Tyler, Robert Torrez, Stanley Hordes, William deBuys, Robert Shadow, David Benavides, Michael Rock, and I have carried on extensive discussions on the history of New Mexico and her land grants, all of which have inspired parts of this book. To Richard Salazar I owe my greatest debt for his guidance in the close reading of the historical documents coupled with his ability to enter the world of the Hispanic *pobladores*.

Writing about the history of New Mexico land grants requires an understanding of the land itself and why it is so important to those whose lives are tied to it. I have been fortunate in knowing many people who have helped me gain some degree of that intangible quality that develops between the land and those who live close to it. That quality is a source of strength for me. Rather than list the names of those people and record my thanks to them, I choose instead to document my gratitude to the land itself, which continues to sustain us all in spite of the controversy that rages over it. May we learn to better respect the land as we begin to understand the history of the early settlers of Northern New Mexico, and of their land grants and lawsuits.

One

Land Grants and the Law:
Spain, Mexico, and New Mexico

Spanish law was shaped over the centuries when the Iberian Peninsula was beset with successive waves of conquest. When the reconquest of the Moors was completed under Ferdinand and Isabella in 1492, Spanish law became the instrument of Spain's own conquests.[1] One of the main reasons for the successful establishment of the Spanish empire was Spain's mastery of the practice of law and government and the Spanish love for the abstract field of jurisprudence. When Spanish sovereignty was projected into New Mexico by Juan de Oñate in 1598, the theory and practice of Spanish law played a major role in the settlement of that province. In fact, it was the law and its administration that was the cutting edge of royal power. After the *conquistador* conquered, and the priest converted, the *letrado* administered. The *mercedes de tierras* or grants of land made by Oñate and succeeding governors were an important device for establishing control of New Mexico by a handful of Spaniards, and it was a device born out of and maintained by Spanish jurisprudence.[2]

When Columbus first set foot on the island of Española (today's Haiti and the Dominican Republic), he brought with him the baggage of Spain's institutions, including the legal system out of which the land grants were established. By 1492 Spain's legal institutions had been affected by a series of invasions, each bringing a different legal influence into the crucible of Spanish jurisprudence.

To understand the development of law and society in Mexico we must first look at these early invasions of Spain. First came the Romans, then the Visigoths, and finally the Moors. But even before these waves of conquest there was a body of Spanish customary law that formed the core of Spanish jurisprudence. This system was characterized by a combination of individual and communal property rights, common pastures and woodlands, and rural councils in charge of common land usage. These councils also regulated the use of arable lands, community works, gleaning and pasture in left-over stubble, and distribution of irrigation water.[3] These concerns are very similar to those found centuries later in the records of New Mexico's land grants and lawsuits.

The Romans brought the first formal legal system to Spain, when in 38 B.C. Emperor Augustus declared Spain a province of Rome, though it was not the system centered around the famous Justinian Code, which came later. The Romans were quite flexible in their tolerance of existing customs, a pattern later followed by Spain in Mexico. Roman law at the end of the Roman Period in A.D. 476 consisted of the writings of the great lawyers and the legal codes issued by the Roman rulers of the fourth and fifth centuries. Of major importance were the municipal codes of Rome, which served as a model for other cities in the Roman Empire. These codes often reinforced existing Spanish customary law, such as the law relating to municipal ownership of lands and other property. For example, rent paid to the city of Rome for municipal property was used to help finance public works and the costs of government.[4] This concept of municipally owned property used as a partial substitute for taxes is also found in the later Spanish concept of *propios* property, which is examined in Chapter 5 on the Ciénega of Santa Fe.

The invasion of Spain by the Visigoths in A.D. 476 was the culmination of a series of attacks on Spain by various barbarian tribes beginning in the year 409. The Visigoths were also tolerant of existing Spanish law and custom, and did not attempt to impose their own Germanic laws on Spain. By the seventh century the Visigoths promulgated a code called the *Fuero Juzgo*, which was an amalgam of Roman and Visigothic law. Germanic law placed a greater emphasis on custom than did Roman law, and this first major Spanish code thus gave formal sanction to the continuing power of customary law. The *Fuero Juzgo* was to remain Spain's principal code of laws until it was replaced in 1255 by *Las Siete Partidas*. The latter code met with less than universal acceptance, however, and customary law continued to have major importance.[5]

The third major wave of conquest of the Iberian peninsula took place in 711 with the coming of the Moors, who were finally repelled from Spain in 1492. Formal Moorish law left little imprint on Spanish law, but the effect of Moorish custom is still being felt in places that inherited the Spanish legal system. Moorish irrigation practices had a particularly powerful influence on Spanish customs,[6] evident in the Moorish origin of many words connected with irrigation in New Mexico, such as *acequia* (irrigation ditch), *noria* (well), *atarque* (diversion dam), and *zanja* (feeder ditch).[7]

The beginnings of legal unification under the *Fuero Juzgo* were disrupted by the Moorish invasion and by the ninth century the *Fuero Juzgo* was effective only in the kingdom of Leon. The Spanish monarchy struggled to unify Spain under one set of laws with little success until the reign of Ferdinand and Isabella. Each region had its own set of customs and special

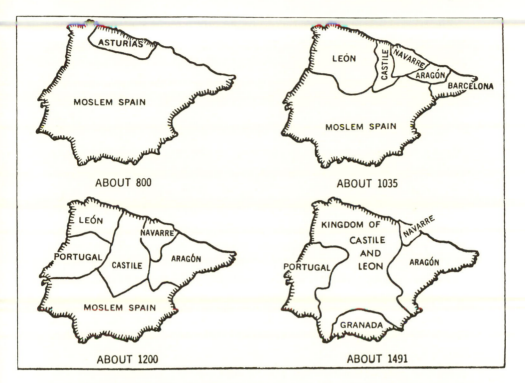

1.2. The Reconquest of Spain from Moorish occupation: 800–1492. Map drawn by Iris W. H. Engstrand and Robert Wittwer.

judicial privileges known as *fueros*, granted to municipalities and social groups by successive rulers. The nobles, the cities, the military, and the church were each jealous of their *fueros* and resisted attempts by the crown to impose legal unity on Spain.[8]

During the reconquest of Spain from the Moors, two practices developed that shaped the future of the institution of land grants in Mexico generally and in New Mexico in particular. The first was the practice of rewarding individual *conquistadores* by giving them land. Since the Catholic monarchs lacked funds to finance the Reconquest, they compensated privately financed soldiers with land, noble titles, and special privileges such as exemption from taxes. These land grants were a means of raising ones social status, much as community grants to *genízaros* in nineteenth-century New Mexico gave those Indians *vecino* status. These grants made during the Reconquest were the forerunners of the private land grant in New Mexico.[9]

The second practice reveals the probable origin of the community land grant on the Iberian peninsula. During the long period of the Reconquest, from the eighth to the fifteenth centuries, the Spanish *pueblos* assumed a strategic importance, both as fortified centers holding the land against further attack by the Moors and as colonizing centers from which new settlements were planted. This importance made it possible for individual pueblos to gain control, usually by grant from the king, of the land surrounding the *pueblo*, which was administered according to local custom rather than codified law. These outlying lands were generally used in common. The Spanish *pueblo* with its common lands was the counterpart of today's community land grant in New Mexico. The lessons learned from the experience of the Reconquest were applied when Spain was formulating her land policies for the New World, and when the Americas were colonized, the institution of common lands was transplanted in New Spain.[10] In New Mexico these lands were sometimes called *ejidos* or *montes*, while other land grant documents describe the common lands by the uses to which they were put or the resources found there: *pastos* (pastures), *abrevaderos* (watering places), *leña* (firewood), *arboles frutales* (fruit-bearing trees), *caza* (hunting), and *pesca* (fishing).[11]

Another Spanish institution of great importance to the settlement of the New World was the *encomienda*. An *encomienda* was a grant to a Spaniard of the fruits of Indian labor, which initially was collectible either in material tribute or in personal service, but soon became tantamount to slavery. By holding an Indian town in *encomienda*, a Spanish *conquistador* had the right to collect tribute from the town and sometimes to require personal service from the Indians. Although the *encomienda* by itself did not give the Spaniard a right to the land of the Indians, often *encomenderos* came to believe that they did own this land.[12]

The institution of the *encomienda* grew out of the Moorish conquest in Spain that entailed the same problems faced by Cortés in Mexico: rewarding conquerors, defending conquered lands, and protecting conquered peoples. Cortés made *encomienda* grants knowing that they had been misused in Cuba and realizing that he had no authority to make them. In 1522 Cortés told the king that he had made *encomienda* grants and requested their approval. The king replied that royal policy forbade them and ordered Cortés to revoke all *encomienda* grants. Cortés did not follow this order, but tried instead to persuade the king that *encomiendas* were necessary to induce colonists to settle in Mexico.[13] This argument was later used as a justification for the system of land grants that soon developed in New Mexico. Debate over the *encomienda* raged in the Spanish royal court for many decades until the crown issued new laws forbidding the requirement of personal service as an incident of the *encomienda* in 1542. Actual practice often deviated from the letter of the law however, especially on remote frontiers like New Mexico. Although the *encomienda* was introduced in New Mexico with Oñate, it was abolished after the 1680 Pueblo Revolt.[14]

The theory of Spanish law at the time that Spain was formulating its policy toward the Americas had developed from a point during the middle of the thirteenth century when royal justice was a personal matter resting in the hands of the king and his advisors, whose decisions were often based more on whim than rule of law. Alfonso X, the sponsor of *Las Siete Partidas*, was the first monarch to establish a court, thereby creating an institutional framework for the administration of justice independent of the king. Although this royal tribunal composed of twenty-three *alcaldes de corte* lapsed with Alfonso's death, it was revived as the *audiencia* during the reign of Henry II.[15] But it was Ferdinand and Isabella who reorganized the court system in the same way they had consolidated Spain under a unified set of laws. In the fateful year 1492 the Catholic monarchs established an *audiencia* in Valladolid and later ones in Granada and Galicia.[16] This auspicious year also marked the end of the expulsion of the Moslems from Spain and the beginning of the famous Columbus voyages. Ferdinand and Isabella had united their kingdoms through their marriage, reconquered all of Spain, and established a centralized legal system at the same time that Columbus planted the Spanish flag in the Americas.

After the establishment of legal codes, and courts to administer them, it was important to the crown to recruit a group of lawyers and bureaucrats to administer the lands won for the Castilian monarchs in the Americas. The crown hoped to establish absolute control of the Indies by limiting the power of overseas officials. The Spanish monarchs liked the Roman law enshrined in codes like *Las Siete Partidas* and the *Leyes de Toro* because Roman law favored absolute royal power and viewed judges as receiving their power as representatives of the king. These kings also liked the confusion caused by multiple, often contradictory, laws because they were not hampered by one rule of law but could pick and choose among several possible rules.[17] They also preferred the overlapping jurisdictions that they intentionally conferred on the legal and administrative branches of government in the Americas. For example, the *audiencias* in the New World had both judicial and administrative functions and sometimes served as the only government in a region. As a member of the *audiencia*, the *viceroy* presided over court procedure and could vote on substantive questions if he was a *letrado*. On the other hand, the *audiencia* advised the *viceroy* on governmental matters. These interdependent jurisdictions checked the power of the *viceroy* and the *audiencia*, and the endless disputes that resulted kept the king informed of their activities.[18]

Thus the Spanish monarchs kept a tight rein on their overseas possessions, steering a middle course between a patrimonial system where all judicial functions were derived from the power of the monarch and an independent legal system where justice was administered in a corporate capacity regardless of changes in personnel. Under the latter system, which became the norm in the nineteenth century, the legal bureaucracy acted in accordance with legislative regulation rather than royal fiat.[19] The *letrados* sent to the Indies to administer these laws were ideally fitted to royal absolutist designs. Having disciplined themselves through years of academic study, they generally had the traits called for in the classic bureaucrat: "they were all well educated and zealous, but also generally impecunious, somewhat inhuman, and eager to sell their services to the highest bidder."[20]

In 1542 the need for a special body in Spain to govern the Spanish colonial empire resulted in the establishment of the Council of the Indies. Unique conditions in the Americas called for specific laws tailored to conditions there. For a century and a half the king and the Council of the Indies issued their *cedulas* without organizing them into any kind of comprehensive code. Finally in 1681 the monumental *Recopilación de las Leyes de los Reynos de las Indias* was published to fill this need. The *Recopilación* directed that its laws were the primary ones to apply to the Indies, but in cases where the *Recopilación* was silent on a particular question, the laws of the kingdom of Castile were to apply.[21] The *Recopilación* has an ad hoc flavor since most of the royal *cedulas* from which these laws were derived were directed at a specific problem in a particular place. The Castilian monarchs found that the very fact of the *Recopilación*'s publication meant that they were more encumbered by binding precedent than they would have liked. But the overlapping and sometimes contradictory nature of the compilation, coupled with the gap between the law and its observance, still provided some flexibility to those governed by Hispanic law.[22]

Although the *Recopilación* was quite specific in delineating the procedures

RECOPILACION DE LEYES

DE

LOS REYNOS

DE

LAS INDIAS.

CON EL INDICE GENERAL.

TOMO QUARTO.

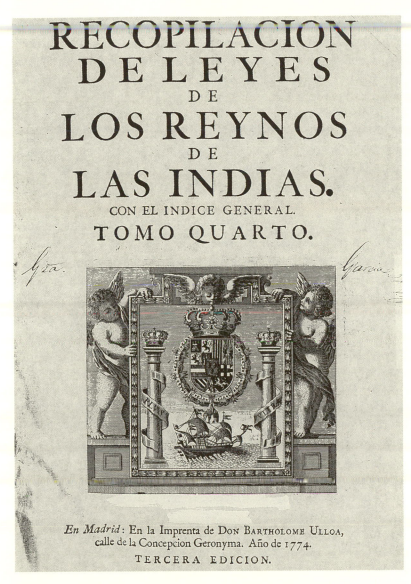

En Madrid: En la Imprenta de DON BARTHOLOME ULLOA,
calle de la Concepcion Geronyma. Año de 1774.

TERCERA EDICION.

1.3. Title page of the 1774 edition of the Recopilación de Leyes de los Reynos de las
Indias, *printed in Madrid.*

for forming new settlements, many of its provisions did not apply to New Mexico. The laws regarding new settlements are found in Book 4 and are rather utopian in nature. They provide that towns should only be established where there was a healthy environment with pure air, moderate weather without extremes of heat and cold, land suitable for farming and ranching, mountains with a supply of stone and wood for building, and a sufficient water supply for irrigation and drinking. Most of these conditions were present in New Mexico, though extremes of hot and cold weather are found throughout the state today and were even more prevalent then, causing Governor Alberto Maynez to blame the sorry state of New Mexico's agriculture in 1815 on the extreme cold.[23]

The Spanish land-holding towns established in New Spain were based upon the Castilian agricultural villages with which the conquerors were familiar as well as the rules for establishing settlements found in the *Recopilación*. The 1555 grant to the town of San Miguel in Central Mexico was fairly typical; each head of a family (*vecino*), received a building lot (*solar de casa*), usually fifty square varas,[24] a garden plot (*suerte*), and one or two *caballerías* of land for field crops (a *caballería* contained approximately 105 acres). In addition, each *vecino* received a sheep pasture located within a six-mile square surrounding the town. Finally, most towns owned an *ejido* for common usage. The settlers were required to reside on the land for a minimum period (at San Miguel it was initially ten years, later reduced to six) before they received title to the private tracts, and they had to maintain a horse and weapons. These conditions were similar to those imposed on some New Mexico land grants. The communal property associated with an Hispanic municipality like San Miguel gradually disappeared, leaving Indian common lands as the only type of communal property in Mexico just prior to the revolution.[25]

In addition to these grants made to communities, individual private land grants were also made in Mexico. Often these were grazing lands varying in size, depending on whether the grant was for cattle (a *sitio de gañado mayor* of 4,316 acres) or for sheep (a *sitio de gañado menor* of 1,918 acres).[26] These private land grants, often supplemented with lands acquired by other means, comprised large landed estates known as *haciendas*. *Haciendas* devoted to the raising of livestock were known as *haciendas de ganado*. Those devoted primarily to the rasing of crops, with the incidental production of livestock, were called *haciendas de labor*, and those operated in connection with mining activities were called *haciendas de beneficio*. A *mayordomo* was usually appointed to administer each *hacienda*, which was often divided into smaller *ranchos*. In some cases, individual families controlled vast stretches of land combining several *haciendas* into a larger estate called a *latifundio*. For example, the *latifundio* of the Sanchez Navarro family covered more than half of the state of Coahuila and included the most productive areas of the state. One of the aims of the 1910 Mexican Revolution was to end the dominance of these large landed estates and provide a more equitable distribution of land.[27]

Earlier official attempts at land reform met with limited success. In 1535 large land grants were not in favor and instructions were issued not to distribute lands to excess. The Hapsburg kings believed large land holdings to be inimical to colonial progress and they initiated several plans designed to induce small- to medium-sized land tenure. Later the Bourbon monarchs issued laws emphasizing land reform between 1805 and 1820, showing the monarchy's determination to redistribute land in New Spain, while the Cortes of Cádiz also passed several laws aimed at land redistribution, particularly of common lands.[28]

Several methods were employed to circumvent the policy of encouraging small- to moderate-sized landholdings. One method was to simply purchase grants made to others, in spite of the standard provision that grants were to be settled or stocked with animals by the grantee himself and that the grant could not be sold for a minimum period of time (generally from four to ten years). Often those selling the grant were in fact mere straw men, who were paid to apply for the grant with the understanding that they would transfer it as soon as they received it. Another common method of increasing the size of one's holdings was to simply appropriate unused land adjacent to land lawfully granted. Often the land that was seized in this manner was Indian land.[29]

The Indian land-holding system that Cortés encountered was similar to that of the Spanish, and was changing at the time of the Spanish arrival toward a greater emphasis on private property. For example, land whose harvest was used to support local *caciques* (chiefs), but which was owned by the Indian community, came to be considered as the property of the *cacique*. This arrangement made it easier for Spaniards to acquire Indian land, such as the land of a *cacique* who was in debt.[30] Similar methods of land acquisition by speculators took place later in New Mexico in the nineteenth century.

A problem often encountered in Central Mexico that was later repeated

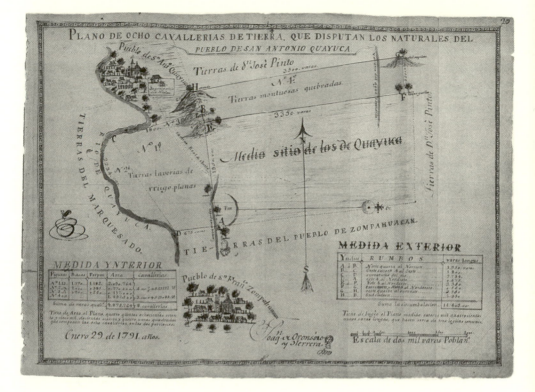

1.4. Survey map drawn by Joaquín de Oronsoro y Herrera, used as evidence in a lawsuit between the Indians of San Antonio Quayuca and José Pinto del Aguila in the Mexican state of Puebla. The map describes the boundary between the lands of the pueblo and lands of José Pinto, as well as those of a neighboring pueblo. From Cartografía Mexicana Tesoros de la Nación siglos XVI a XIX *(Mexico, D.F.: Archivo General de la Nación, 1983). Courtesy Guillermo Margadant.*

in New Mexico was that of Spanish stock overrunning and damaging Indian fields. This concern was not limited to the Indians, however, for Spanish farmers also filed numerous complaints with the Viceroy concerning damages to their crops by sheep and cattle owned by Spaniards.[31] Indian crop-damage cases, heard by a General Indian Court, were probably more numerous than cases involving Spanish farmers because of the greater area covered by Indian farms and because of an attitude on the part of some Spanish ranchers that they had a right to graze their cattle on Indian fields. For example, in 1551 an *estanciero* named Alonso de Villaseca complained to the *audiencia* that the Indians of Toluca had maliciously fenced off their cornfields to keep his cattle out! The rancher was ordered to remove his cattle from the Indians' land during the growing season, but from December to March, the Indians had to allow the Spaniard's cattle to graze on their land.[32] This ruling was in accordance with the ancient Castilian custom of *derrota de mieses* or stubble grazing. According to this custom, which was followed in New Mexico as well as Central Mexico, every owner of private farmland had to open his fields to the livestock of the town where he lived from after harvest until spring planting.[33]

In the course of the Spanish legal history briefly traced here, there were numerous occasions when a clash of cultures caused a change in the rules societies used to guide the actions of individuals, communities, and the state. What we have seen and will see in the following pages is a series of deaths and rebirths of legal concepts, at the same time that men and women were fighting and dying over these concepts and the realities they symbolized. When the Iberian peninsula was invaded, then when Spain invaded Mexico, and finally when the United States invaded Mexico, the conquerors found a different legal system than the one they were familiar with, and in each case the existing system was one where customary law and common property predominated. The conquered people tended to resist the imposition of formal legal systems with which they were not familiar, clinging instead to their customary law which was rooted in the popular conscience. This customary law often outlived the formal system of law and was even tolerated by several of these conquering nations.[34]

As we look at the aftermath of the American invasion of Mexico in the light of the earlier cycles of conquest, it seems proper to ask how the United States dealt with the problems of an unfamiliar legal system containing legal concepts long out of favor under its laws.

Land Grants in New Mexico

 The themes found in the history of land tenure and law in Spain and Mexico are repeated in New Mexico: the importance of custom in Spanish law, the varying emphasis on private and communal land, and the continual battles between the Spanish colonists and the Indians over choice land, and for a short time the *encomienda*. The *encomienda* disappeared in New Mexico, but the other themes continued, each with its own array of problems.[35]

During the early years of the first permanent settlement of New Mexico, the faithful followers of Juan de Oñate were rewarded for their loyalty with *encomiendas*. For example, Captain Juan Martínez de Montoya, who was named by the viceroy as interim governor when Oñate resigned, but was rejected as governor by the Cabildo of San Gabriel, received one of the Jémez Pueblos in *encomienda* for three generations in 1606.[35] Although *encomenderos* were forbidden by law from living on the lands granted to them in *encomienda* (generally an Indian Pueblo or part of it), most ignored this law. There was a great deal of encroachment on Indian lands, and *encomenderos* often levied excessive tribute on the Indians.[36]

As in Central Mexico, this soldier-citizen upper class was not interested in farming initially, preferring instead to live off Indian labor and tribute. Eventually the *encomenderos* asked for and received grants of land for farming and/or stock raising. As they had done in the Mexican heartland, the Spaniards grew wheat to supplement beans and corn, the staples of the Pueblo Indian diet. The Pueblos resisted foreign foods, and when in 1680 they rebelled against the Spanish and forced them to retreat to El Paso, some Indian leaders demanded that all seeds other than corn and beans be burned.[37]

Since abuses connected with the *encomienda* were a major reason for the Pueblo Revolt, this practice was not followed after the Revolt,[38] and a era of improved relations between the Spanish and the Pueblos was born. One aspect of this relationship was better defense against raids by nomadic Indians, because the Pueblos now served as allies of the Spaniards on retaliatory expeditions.[39] Another facet of improved Hispano-Pueblo relations was a different pattern of land use and settlement than had developed in the first part of the seventeenth century. The prerevolt pattern was one of widely scattered large properties worked primarily by Indians; a pattern much like that of the Mexican hacienda. But settlement of New Mexico proceeded along different lines after the end of the *encomienda*. Typical settlements were made up of smaller ranchos strung out along the Rio Grande and its tributaries. Although the Spaniard was traditionally a town dweller, and although royal policy encouraged formation of compact plazas where settlers could gather for defence against Indian raids, it was typical of the independent New Mexican to build his house near his fields, where he could keep an eye out for wild animals or nomadic Indians who might make off with his crops.[40]

Since the archives of New Mexico were destroyed in the Pueblo Revolt, little information has survived concerning prerevolt land grants. The power to make land grants was given to the governor, although lesser officials also granted land to individuals or to groups of settlers.[41] The first land grants in New Mexico of which we have a written record were made by Diego de Vargas after his reconquest of the province in 1692.[42] Many of these grants were made as rewards to followers of Vargas and to individuals who had possessed land grants prior to the revolt and who were willing to resettle them.[43]

Regulation of the granting of land in New Mexico was based as much on custom as on written law, particularly during the Spanish Period. It was not until the Colonization Law of 1824 and the Regulations of 1828 during the Mexican Period,[44] that any detailed land grant laws were enacted for New Mexico, and these generally validated the customary procedure that had developed there over the previous 230 years. One of the main differences between the regulation of 1828 and prior custom was the provision in Article 1 that authorized grants to foreigners. During the Spanish Colonial Period foreigners were generally not welcome in New Mexico.[45] Under 1828 regulations, anyone seeking a land grant would address a petition to the governor describing the land sought and their qualifications for receiving a land grant and stating that there were no adverse claims. Then, in most cases, the governor would refer the petition to the local *alcalde* for his recommendations as to whether the grant should be made. The primary considerations were whether the land was being used or claimed by others, the sufficiency of the petitioner's qualifications, and in the case of a community grant, the availability of resources like pasture, water, and firewood.[46] If the governor happened to be personally familiar with the land and with the petitioner, he might himself report on the advisability of making the grant.[47] Frequently neighboring Pueblo Indians and Spaniards would be summoned at this stage and given an opportunity to object to the grant if they thought it would be an encroachment on their land; in other cases this would not occur until the final step in the procedure, or it would not occur at all.[48]

If the recommendation of the *alcalde* was favorable, then the governor would make the grant, directing the *alcalde* to perform the final step — the ceremony of delivery of possession. On an appointed day, the grantee would go to the land to meet the *alcalde*. Also summoned to be present were the neighboring landowners. This was the last chance for anyone to object to the grant, and sometimes the *alcalde* was called upon to settle a protest on the spot. If the *alcalde* found that the grant would not be prejudicial to anyone, he proceeded with the ritual of delivery of possession.[49]

If feasible, the grantees and the *alcalde* would walk the boundaries, together with the neighboring property owners, placing monuments — usually a mound of stones or a cross — on the boundary lines or corners. This practice was designed to prevent future boundary disputes, but it was not always successful. Generally, even the most basic kind of survey was lacking, and boundaries were usually described by natural landmarks, such as an arroyo, a ridge, a river, or a neighbor's property. These vague land descriptions caused myriad problems when land grants were later adjudicated by the United States. When a survey was performed, it was done by means of a *cordel* — a rope varying in length from 50 to 100 varas.[50] Since these ropes were subject to shrinkage or stretching, boundary measurements by means of the *cordel* sometimes provoked heated arguments.[51] To complete the act of possession, the *alcalde* took the grantees by the hand and walked them over the land, while the grantees plucked up grass, threw stones to signify their dominion over the land, and shouted "Long live the King!"[52]

The documents evidencing these steps — the petition, the *alcalde*'s report, the grant by the governor, and the act of possession — were assembled into one document called an *expediente*, a copy of which was given to the grantee as his evidence of title. This copy was the *testimonio*. Many problems later faced by American courts concerned the adequacy, by United States standards, of these documents. Often originals became worn with handling, and certified copies were made by *alcaldes*. But United States courts held that these copies were invalid, even though there was no other method at the time of preserving these important documents.[53]

Land grants in New Mexico fell into two main categories, which were determined more by custom that by written law. A private grant was made to an individual who would own the entire grant and could sell it after the possession requirement was met. In the eighteenth century, more land grants in New Mexico tended to be private grants, probably an outgrowth of the seventeenth-century *encomienda* practice. Community grants became more prevalent in the nineteenth century.[54]

In the case of a community grant, individuals in a group of settlers would each receive an allotment of land for a house (*solar de casa*), an irrigable plot (*suerte*), and the right to use the remaining unallotted land on the grant in common with the other settlers for pastures, watering places, firewood, and logs for building, as well as for hunting, fishing, gathering herbs, and rock quarrying, among other uses.[55] Depending on the lay of the land, these allotments were often combined into one plot—usually a strip of land running from the river to the foothills.[56] A settler would own his allotment free and clear after four years, and could sell it as private property.[57] But the common lands were owned by the community and could not be sold.[58] Between the classic private grant and the classic community grant there were many hybrid grants containing aspects of each type. Often as settlement progressed on a private land grant, its character would become more like a community grant. Since the grant documents did not define a grant as either private or community, the classification of land grants became another problem for U.S. courts.

Not only were there several kinds of land grants in terms of their legal classification, but actual settlements on these grants also varied from a physical standpoint. Eighteenth century governors like Tomás Vélez Cachupín and Pedro Fermín de Mendinueta tried as legalists to follow the laws regarding settlements, and as practical men they saw the defensive value of a compact settlement built around a central plaza.[59] Houses built wall-to-wall in a square, without windows on the outside, formed a protective fortress—sometimes with a circular watchtower (*torreón*) at one or more corners. Although villages like Truchas, Chimayó, Córdova, and Las Trampas were built along this pattern, the tendency of other New Mexican settlers was to build their houses along streams and rivers against the specific orders of the governors. Even the three largest settlements in the province, designated as *villas*, were built at random instead of following the orderly plan called for in the *Recopilación*.[60] After the establishment of Santa Fe in 1610, the *villa* of Santa Cruz de la Cañada was founded in 1695 near present-day Española, and in 1706 the *villa* of Albuquerque was reported by Governor Cuervo y Valdez to have been established. Santa Cruz and Albuquerque followed the helter-skelter make-up of Santa Fe, and Albuquerque did not even meet the minimum requirements set forth in the *Recopilación* for a *villa*.[61]

The primary means of subsistence on New Mexican settlements was agriculture and stock raising. In addition an artisan class grew up in Albuquerque and Santa Fe by the late 1700s.[62] The pattern of land use for settlements on community land grants involved more intense usage of the land near the watercourses for agriculture and homes, and less intense uses, such as grazing, as one progressed farther from the rivers on to the common lands. New Mexico documents reveal that grazing animals intruding on planted fields was as much of a concern there as it had been in Central Mexico.[63]

Although few records have survived concerning the use of common lands in New Mexico, documentary evidence does exist for Santa Fe on the practice of stubble grazing. Under that system, every local citizen's animals were allowed to graze on harvested private fields before the next planting, giving these fields the character of common lands during this period. Also in Santa Fe, there are records of a plot of swampy land called the Ciénega that was used by Santa Fe residents as common lands in the 1700s, when its lush grass could be mowed by any Santa Fe resident to feed his animals.[64]

Raids by the Comanche, Apache, Ute, and Navajo hampered the expansion of settlements beyond the Albuquerque, Santa Fe, and Santa Cruz population centers, but intrepid settlers continued to start new settlements in spite of the danger. Abiquiú was settled by 1734, Ojo Caliente by 1735, Tomé in 1739, Valencia in 1740, Ranchos de Taos by 1744, Belén in 1750, and Las Trampas in 1751.[65] Repeated Indian raids caused the Ojo Caliente settlers to withdraw to more secure settlements. Time after time the governor of New Mexico ordered these settlers to return to their village, but many preferred to forfeit their lands rather than risk their lives again, after they had already lost members of their families during Indian attacks. These forfeited lands would then be granted to new *pobladores* (settlers).[66]

The settlement that is now Ranchos de Taos on the Cristóbal de la Serna grant suffered so much from Indian attacks that by the 1770s the settlers moved in with the Indians of Taos Pueblo for mutual protection. But Ranchos de Taos was soon reestablished, and the population began to increase there and elsewhere in the Taos Valley after the Comanche Peace Treaty was achieved by Governor Anza in 1786 and maintained into the 1800s by his successor, Governor Fernando de la Concha.[67] After the turn of the century, land grants were made more frequently, not only in the Taos Valley, but also in the Mora Valley, along the Chama River, and on the high plains east of Santa Fe, as settlements began to increase dramatically.[68]

Spanish policy before Mexican independence in 1821 prohibited trade with *extranjeros* (foreigners), who were not allowed to receive land grants. The Mexican colonization regulations of 1828 changed this by authorizing grants to be made to both Mexicans and foreigners. With the inception of the Santa Fe Trail in 1821, Anglo merchants and trappers began to settle in New Mexico, marry Hispanas, and even become naturalized Mexican citizens. Many of them sought and received land grants, either alone or in partnership with Hispanos.[69]

The most notorious land grants during the Mexican period were made by Governor Manuel Armijo in the 1840s, mostly to partnerships of Anglos and Hispanos. Grants such as the Beaubien-Miranda (Maxwell) and Sangre de Cristo grants clearly violated the Mexican Colonization Law of 1824, which limited the amount of land that one person could receive. Since these two grants were both made to two persons, they were limited by that law to 96,000 acres. Yet the Sangre de Cristo grant was patented at 998,764 acres and the Beaubien-Miranda grant at a whopping 1,714,764 acres. Ironically, these two highly questionable grants were among the first to be confirmed by the United States, and their combined area of 2,713,545 acres exceeds the total acreage of New Mexico grants confirmed by the Court of Private Land Claims, thus calling in question the entire process of land grant adjudication.[70]

During both the Spanish and the Mexican Periods, disputes over land and water were settled primarily according to the customs followed in the remote frontier province that was New Mexico. Records of litigation reveal once again that local custom was more often the basis for decision than were the formal rules of Spanish law.[71] Local government and the administration of justice acquired a great deal of autonomy in New Mexico during the Mexican Period, to the point where *alcaldes* and *ayuntamientos* would sometimes defy orders from the governor when they believed them to be unjust,[72] or they would simply delay for years the execution of an unpopular directive.[73] The legal system was composed of local *alcaldes* and *ayuntamientos* and the governor, with occasional appeals made to higher authorities in Central Mexico.[74] The decisions produced by this legal system often dealt with the same questions United States courts would soon face: land and water rights and the validity of land grants under Spanish and Mexican law. These decisions would have been extremely valuable as an aid and touchstone for U.S. land grant adjudication, but even today they remain a largely untapped resource. Instead of attempting to learn how Hispanic

New Mexico's authorities dealt with land grants, the United States imposed its own view of Spanish and Mexican law on the adjudication process — a view that was colored by the bias of a completely different legal system.

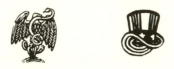

The Treaty of Guadalupe Hidalgo

Changes in New Mexico brought about by the opening of the Santa Fe Trail paved the way for the invasion by United States forces led by General Stephen Watts Kearny in August 1846. Kearny promised the people of New Mexico that their property would be protected by the United States.[75] However, it became a matter of international negotiation to determine what form this guarantee would take.

The negotiations leading up to the Treaty of Guadalupe Hidalgo took place in the autumn of 1847. Nicolas Trist, representing the United States in these negotiations was truly a man caught in the middle. Trist attempted to hammer out a fair treaty in spite of the inflexible policy of his government on many issues. The exact terms of the property guarantee given by Kearny with regard to land grants were the result of protracted negotiations. In August 1847 when General Winfield Scott's army was in position to advance on Mexico City, the Mexican government appointed four commissioners to meet with Trist. Both sides had draft treaties that their respective governments had given them as bases for negotiation.[76]

The first draft treaty suggested by the United States contained no mention of a land grant guarantee, although Trist was instructed not to object if the Mexican commissioners requested one. The Mexican commissioners did request a series of articles on land grants to the effect that all grants made by Mexican authorities were valid and would be recognized as such by the United States. Trist objected to these provisions because they validated all land grants. He said that those grants whose conditions had not been fulfilled should not be respected, nor should those made after the cut-off date of 13 May 1846, the day hostilities began between the United States and Mexico. Trist suggested wording to establish a test of the validity of land grants; only those grants found to be valid by this standard would be respected by the United States. This test, embodied in Article 10 of the treaty, said that land grants would be considered valid to the extent that they were valid under Mexican law.[77]

Article 10 provided a fair standard for adjudicating land grants; unfortunately it was deleted from the treaty by the U.S. Senate prior to ratification. This caused innumerable problems in the subsequent adjudication of land grants. Without a standard by which to test the validity of a land grant, Congress and the courts were free to make their own rules, which they did, and the results were not always just.

A Mexican historian has labeled the Treaty of Guadalupe Hidalgo "one of the harshest in modern history."[78] It was imposed on Mexico — not fairly negotiated. The war began mainly because the United States wanted to fulfill its "manifest destiny" to expand its territory across the entire continent.[79] With the U.S. Army advancing on and finally occupying Mexico City, Secretary of State James Buchanan called the draft treaty "a carefully considered ultimatum."[80] Nicolas Trist negotiated the treaty after ignoring orders from his government to return to Washington. President Polk urged the deletion of Article 10 in his message to the Senate, claiming that Trist did not have the authority to include it. But when Secretary of State James Buchanan explained the deletion of Article 10 to the Mexican government, he objected only to that portion providing additional time within which grantees could fulfill the conditions of their grants.[81] Why then, one might ask, was the entire article deleted, instead of deleting only the objectionable parts?[82] The latter course would have kept in the treaty a standard for later use in land grant adjudication, but apparently U.S. authorities did not want such a clear standard. This cynical position is illustrated by the story of the protocol to the treaty.

The two American commissioners who replaced Trist were asked by the Mexican government to sign, an explanation known as the Protocol of Querétaro, in order to allay the concern of the Mexican government over the deletion of Article 10, as well as the deletion and modification of several other articles. The Protocol stated that the United States did not intend to annul legitimate grants by deleting Article 10, and that legitimate titles were those that were valid under Mexican law before the cut-off date of 13 May 1846. With this written assurance to the government of Mexico, ratifications of the Treaty of Guadalupe Hidalgo were exchanged on 30 May 1848.[83]

While the government of Mexico considered the Protocol binding, the

U.S. State Department refused to recognize its validity. Rumor had it that the Protocol had revived Article 10, but Secretary of State John M. Clayton, who had succeeded Buchanan, made the United States' position crystal clear when he stated:

> It is believed that the Mexican government was not less prodigal in donations of its domains in New Mexico and California than it had been in disposing of Texas lands. . . . Could it however reasonably be expected that this government, in addition to the treasure and blood expended in prosecuting the war, would engage to pay fifteen millions of dollars for lands, the title to the most valuable part of which had been extinguished?[84]

In other words, the United States looked at the treaty as an enormous real estate deal; it expected to get clear title to most of the land it was paying for regardless of the property rights of Mexicans. Because of substantial errors in the map by which the new boundary between Mexico and the United States was to be determined under the Treaty of Guadalupe Hidalgo, it was impossible to locate that boundary. Therefore it was necessary to negotiate the Gadsden Treaty in 1853 by which the United States purchased twenty-nine million more acres of land for another ten million dollars, establishing the present boundaries between Mexico and the states of Arizona and New Mexico. Named after former minister to Mexico James Gadsden, this treaty can be seen as an amendment to the Treaty of Guadalupe Hidalgo in regard to land grant adjudication.[85] One provision in the Gadsden Treaty did place a greater burden on the claimants of land grants within that territory than was the case with the Treaty of Guadalupe Hidalgo. Article 6 provided that only grants whose boundaries were located on the ground and whose documents were recorded in the archives would be recognized by the United States. This provision was to cause problems for a few land grants in this area.[86] It is not surprising that subsequent adjudication of land grants by the United States was often unjust when one considers the vague and conflicting standards of the two treaties and the U.S. goal of acquiring additional territory unencumbered by Mexican claims.

To assess the fairness of land grant adjudication under the Treaty of Guadalupe Hidalgo, a comparison with the experience under earlier United States treaties involving Spanish land grants proves helpful. Spanish

1.5. A portion of the Disturnell map of Mexico showing the seal of the Mexican federation of states. The map was cited in the Treaty of Guadalupe Hidalgo to establish the new boundary between Mexico and the United States. However, the location of El Paso on the map, over 300 miles too far north and 100 miles too far east of its actual location, made protracted negotiations necessary to establish the boundary. Hunter Miller, Treaties and Other International Acts of the United States of America *(Washington, D.C.: Government Printing Office, 1937).*

land grants were adjudicated in Louisiana under an 1803 treaty and in Florida under an 1819 treaty.[87] In each state, land grant claims were filed with a board of commissioners that investigated them and then reported its recommendations to Congress for final action. A majority of these claims were confirmed, partly because the amounts of land in question were relatively small—most claims did not exceed 640 acres.[88] But another factor of importance was the liberal nature of U.S. Supreme Court decisions on questions of land grant adjudication.

The treaty between the United States and Spain covering land grants in Florida contained a clause similar to those proposed by the Mexican commissioners negotiating the Treaty of Guadalupe Hidalgo. Article 8 of the

Florida treaty stated that land grants "shall be ratified and confirmed to those in possession of the lands . . ."[89] Claimants argued to the U.S. Supreme Court that this language meant that the treaty itself confirmed land grants in Florida that met the requirements of Article 8, and that the land grant board did not have the power to reject grants, only to determine which grants were valid. But in 1829 Chief Justice John Marshall rejected that argument and decided that Article 8 of the Florida treaty did not confirm grants by its own terms.[90] Then in a landmark case in 1833, Marshall reversed his earlier decision, giving the same clause of the same treaty a completely different interpretation. The latter case was *United States v. Percheman.* Marshall changed his mind because the attorney representing claimant Juan Percheman focused on the Spanish version of Article 8 which stated that land grants *"quedarán ratificadas y reconocidas a las personas que estan en posesión de ellas . . ."* The verb *quedarán* had been mistranslated, said Perchemen's attorney. It should have been translated, "[land grants] *remain* ratified" instead of "[land grants] *shall be* ratified," thus clearly signifying confirmation by the treaty itself. Accordingly, Justice Marshall held that the land grant board did not have the power to reject land grants but could only recommend confirmation of a grant by congress, or not act at all. By reassessing Article 8 of the Florida treaty, Justice John Marshall reversed his earlier decision regarding the effect of the treaty on the power of the land grant board.[91]

The *Percheman* decision also holds that both the English and the Spanish version of a treaty must be looked at to determine its meaning. It also provides a clue as to why the U.S. Congress deleted Article 10 from the Treaty of Guadalupe Hidalgo. Since the language of Article 8 of the Florida treaty was quite similar to Article 10 of the Treaty of Guadalupe Hidalgo, it is likely that the United States did not want to be fettered with the liberal precedent of *Percheman's* construction of Article 8 of the Florida treaty in the Guadalupe Hidalgo treaty. The Supreme Court took an extremely liberal approach to land grant adjudication in the *Percheman* case, but its decisions under the Treaty of Guadalupe Hidalgo became progressively more conservative.

The first test of how the U.S. Supreme Court would treat the ill-defined obligation of the United States to protect the property rights of Mexicans under the Treaty of Guadalupe Hidalgo came after a board of land commissioners was established in California to adjudicate land grants there. Pressure on Congress to deal with the land title problem came first from

California because of the discovery of gold there and its early admission as a state into the United States. The population increase due to the Gold Rush made land more valuable, and statehood gave California more leverage in Washington than was enjoyed by New Mexico.[92]

Before establishing the California Board of Land Commissioners, Congress attempted to learn something about the nature and extent of that state's land grants. In 1849 the Secretary of the Interior appointed William Carey Jones to make a detailed investigation, the results of which astounded many Congressmen. Jones reported that a number of grants were made to the extent of the eleven-square-league limit (48,000 acres) of the Mexican Colonization Law of 1824. This was a far cry from the 640-acre grants the lawmakers were familiar with from Florida and Louisiana. Other problems with California land grants foreseen by Jones were "the loose designation of their limits and extent" and the likelihood of simulated grants. Jones was right about boundary problems, size limitations, and fraudulent grants, problems that later plagued those trying to settle land grant titles both in California and New Mexico.

William Carey Jones concluded that most California grants were perfect titles, however, and should be confirmed automatically without any further legislation. Even in the case of grants where all the formalities had not been met Jones still believed that most were valid because under Mexico "the law of custom, with the acquiescence of the highest authorities overcame . . . the written law." In those cases where a grant was suspected of being invalid, Jones recommended that the United States bring suit to annul the grant. Jones's conclusion left open the question of how the government would determine which grants might be invalid. Besides this inherent flaw, his recommendations were tainted by the fact that Jones himself had purchased at least three grants — one of them over fifty-three thousand acres — before submitting his report to the government.[93] In another report concerning Mexican land grants in California, Captain Henry Halleck urged a more critical examination of all grants, but recommended that grants by *alcaldes* in San Francisco be summarily confirmed. But Halleck, who was California's military secretary of state, also lacked the attribute of disinterestedness since he owned a dozen of these lots that later became quite valuable.[94]

The California Board of Land Commissioners was highly controversial when it was first proposed. Critics argued that the legislation establishing the board was in violation of the property rights guarantee remaining in the

Guadalupe Hidalgo treaty after the deletion of Article 10.[95] The only part of the treaty protecting land grant property rights after the Senate amendments was Article 8, which provided that "property of every kind now belonging to Mexicans . . . shall be inviolably respected."[96] Questions were left unanswered by Article 8 that had been resolved by Article 10, like the standard to be used in land grant adjudication, but debate over the California law centered on the question of what procedures should be followed in implementing the property rights guarantees of Article 8. The California law placed the burden on the land grant owner to file a claim with the land board by 1853 or have his or her property declared public domain of the United States. This burden of initiating and proving a claim required the claimant to hire an attorney and to gather all the documents and testimony needed to support that claim. After the initial hearing, the land board's decision could be appealed to the federal district court where a new trial would take place. The district court's decision could also be appealed to the U.S. Supreme Court. If the claimant was finally successful there, they still had the burden of paying the cost of surveying their land and defending their survey before the Surveyor General's office.[97]

This procedure transformed land grant owners into claimants who had to jump through numerous costly hoops before their property rights under the treaty were recognized. It was a drastic change from the liberal treaty doctrine Justice Marshall had announced in the *Percheman* case. As Marshall interpreted the Florida treaty, the government had the burden of proving the invalidity of a land grant and had to take the initiative in doing so. This was what William Carey Jones had recommended for California but the situation there was reversed with the claimant shouldering the burden of proof. The U.S. Supreme Court had to decide whether the procedural burdens imposed by the California Act violated the promise of the United States to "inviolably respect" Hispanic property rights.

The test case was *Botiller v. Dominguez* involving the Rancho Las Virgenes grant made by the Mexican government in 1834. The grant was conceded to be a perfect grant in that all its conditions had been fulfilled. California Supreme Court decisions had held that such grant claims did not have to be submitted to the land board since "titles, such as were perfect under the former government, did not need any action of the new government for their protection."[98] This view was very much like Marshall's liberal treaty doctrine. In the *Botiller* case the California Supreme Court decided that the Rancho Las Virgenes grant did not need to be submitted to the land board, and to the extent that the 1851 California Act required this, the act was in violation of the Treaty of Guadalupe Hidalgo.[99] The government appealed this decision and the stage was set. Would the Supreme Court follow its earlier decision in the *Percheman* case?

The answer was a resounding no. The *Botiller* decision showed that the U.S. Supreme Court had changed its position dramatically since *Percheman*. In *Botiller* the court side-stepped the issue of what the treaty required of the United States in the way of land grant adjudication under the property rights guarantee. It simply held that if the 1851 California statute conflicted with the treaty, then the statute must prevail. In the words of the court: "if the treaty was violated by this general statute . . . it was a matter of international concern, which the two states [Mexico and the United States] must determine by treaty, or by such other means as enables one state to enforce upon another the obligations of treaty."[100] In other words, the judicial branch of the government was washing its hands of any responsibility for interpreting and enforcing the treaty. If the treaty was violated, said the court, it was up to Mexico to press the issue with the United States.

Although this was a harsh Supreme Court decision in relation to the earlier liberality of *Percheman*, the actual decisions under the California Act were relatively fair. It was the prospective effect of the *Botiller* decision that was so damaging. Having said that Congress was not bound by the Treaty of Guadalupe Hidalgo in its enactments of land grant adjudication schemes, the door was left open for more restrictive statutes in the future. In fact, the Court of Private Land Claims legislation for New Mexico and Arizona was considered more restrictive than the California Act, and the decisions by that Land Claims Court were even more limiting than was called for by the law establishing the court. Finally, without the regulating effect of the treaty, land grant decisions by the U.S. Supreme Court in the late 1800s circumscribed the property rights of claimants even more than lower court decisions had done.

The deletion of Article 10 and the disregard for the Protocol weakened the Treaty of Guadalupe Hidalgo from the very beginning; after that it was ignored altogether. Since the courts have been unwilling to determine whether land grant adjudication was carried out in accordance with the treaty's requirements, the public must make its own judgement on this issue. Looking first at California and then at New Mexico, one might well ask the question: did the government "inviolably respect" land grants in those states?

Early U.S. Supreme Court decisions on California cases gave hope that a fair and just solution would be forthcoming for the land grant problem. These decisions, handed down before *Botiller*, contained magnanimous rhetoric:

> . . . the United States have bound themselves by a treaty to acknowledge and protect all bona fide titles granted by the previous Government, and this court [has] no discretion to enlarge or curtail such grants to suit our sense of propriety, or defeat just claims, however extensive, by stringent technical rules of construction to which they were not originally subjected,

and

> They [the United States] have not desired the tribunals to conduct their investigations as if the rights of the inhabitants to the property which they claim depended upon the nicest observance of every legal formality.[101]

However, these high-sounding intentions were generally not followed in land grant adjudication. Especially in New Mexico in the 1890s, adjudicatory bodies were influenced by the size of grant claims, and they often held claimants to "the nicest observance of every legal formality" even when the land grants claimed were perfectly valid under Spanish and Mexican law.

The swing from the liberal approach of Justice Marshal in the 1833 *Percheman* case to the strict approach of *Botiller* in 1888 was a broad trend that overshadowed other fluctuations in the supreme court's views about land grants over this fifty-year period. In California, Federal District Judge Ogden Hoffman, who heard most of the appeals from the land board, conscientiously tried to follow supreme court decisions in existence as of the early 1850s. Cases such as *Kingsley* and *Boisdore* required that the grants claimed be located on the ground, that any conditions imposed on the grantee be met, and that the grantee have taken possession of the land. So Hoffman rejected many claims that were insufficient by these standards, until he was reversed by the supreme court in the notorious *Fremont* case.[102]

John C. Fremont, whose topographical explorations had laid the foundation for U.S. occupation of the Far West, had purchased the claim of a grantee who was required to occupy his grant within a year but had been unable to do so. For this reason Hoffman rejected the claim but was reversed by an 1855 supreme court opinion by Roger Taney, author of the infamous *Dred Scott* decision two years later. Taney treated the issue as one of vesting of title and found in favor of the Fremont claim, saying that when the grant was first made title was vested even though the condition had not been performed. This was a typical Anglo-American way to view the problem, not a Hispanic one. The *Fremont* case was liberal for the wrong reasons and resulted in a backlash of stricter supreme court decisions regarding California land grants. Ironically, a similar pattern occurred later in supreme court decisions dealing with New Mexico land grants: liberal decisions favoring speculators initially, yielding to overly strict rulings later that hurt legitimate grantees living on the land.[103]

In any case, the record of land grant adjudication in California was better than that in New Mexico. Statistics tell most of the story. In California approximately 12 million acres were claimed, of which 8.8 million were confirmed for a 73 percent confirmation figure. In New Mexico this percentage was only 24 percent confirmation for both the Surveyor General and the Court of Private Land Claims; for the Claims Court alone it came to a surprisingly small 6 percent confirmation rate.[104]

Why were these percentages so minuscule for New Mexico? To answer this question we must follow the winding path of land grant adjudication in New Mexico from the appointment of the first surveyor general in 1854 to the conclusion of the work of the Court of Private Land Claims in 1904.

The Surveyor General of New Mexico

 California's status as a state with representation in Congress helped insure that the land grant adjudication system established there would be relatively fair, though the California system was not without its critics. New Mexico, in contrast, did not become a state until 1912, and so was not able to vote on the method chosen by Congress to adjudicate land grant titles in New Mexican territory. Being a much poorer state than California, New Mexico found that Congress tended to minimize the importance of settling their land grant titles, so much so that the procedure first set up in New Mexico was wholly inadequate to deal with this vast and complicated problem.

Unlike California's situation, land grant adjudication in New Mexico was not undertaken promptly. By the time Congress established the office of

Surveyor General of New Mexico in 1854, six years had passed since the signing of the Treaty of Guadalupe Hidalgo. This delay created uncertainty about New Mexican land grant titles that the surveyor general system never completely resolved. Moreover, when William Pelham was appointed the first surveyor general of New Mexico he found that he had many other responsibilities in addition to land grants, making it virtually impossible for him to deal adequately with the land grant problem.

The surveyor general's primary duty was to extend the federal public land survey system that provided for a checkerboard of townships, each containing thirty-six 640-acre sections.[105] Once public land had been surveyed under this system, ownership could be obtained under the homestead and other laws that the surveyor general administered.[106] The boundaries of land grants were not to be surveyed until after they were confirmed; even today large areas within land grants have not been surveyed.[107] The American surveying system did not fit the arid Southwest, and Anglo property law was not understood by most Hispanos. Corruption of public officials and dishonesty of claimants under the United States land laws were additional factors preventing Hispanic land grant heirs from obtaining title to the land grants they occupied under the homestead and other similar laws. It was not unusual for enterprising Anglos to wrest from Hispanos their land grant property through fraud or manipulation of the land laws.[108]

In addition to these problems, the scheme for adjudicating land grants under the surveyor general system was badly flawed. Hispanos did not understand or have any trust in the American system of land ownership. Although written evidence of title was not without importance under the Spanish and Mexican land systems, for Hispanos, possession was indeed nine-tenths of the law. Their use of the land was more important in establishing their ownership than were any documents. When called upon to bring their documents to Santa Fe and file claims with the surveyor general, most Hispanos demurred.[109] Some feared that they would lose their documents if they turned them over to the surveyor general, while others felt they were adequately protected by the Treaty of Guadalupe Hidalgo and didn't need to file a claim. Most Hispanos never conceived of the possibility that the common lands of their community grants were in jeopardy because under their laws and customs, the common lands could never be sold. Since filing a claim entailed considerable expense, it was the questionable claim held by the speculator that was often filed first.

The surveyor general's responsibility concerning land grants was to report to Congress his recommendation as to whether claims should be confirmed or rejected by that body. In making this recommendation however, the surveyor general was severely hampered as to the investigation he could make. Surveyor General Pelham had at first taken the position that his responsibility to "ascertain the origin, nature, character and extent of all claims"[110] authorized him to tour the territory and investigate all land grant titles. But he was instructed by his superior that he was limited to dealing only with those claims filed in his office. Moreover, he had no staff with which to attempt to corroborate a claimant's testimony, and though he was directed to summon witnesses, he had no funds for this purpose either.[111] Thus the surveyor general was merely a passive agent of the government, and the procedure before his office was not really an adjudication at all.

This was surely the most serious defect in the surveyor general procedure: it lacked the essential element of all true adjudication — due process of law. To adjudicate land titles is to determine land ownership judicially, and the Constitution of the United States mandates that no one be deprived of property without a judicial determination meeting the requirements of due process of law. Due process requires that there be a hearing at which interested parties can present evidence and cross-examine opposing witnesses and that actual notice of the hearing be given to those whose property rights might be affected.[112] The failure to require a hearing with an adversarial procedure meant that most claims were decided solely on self-serving affidavits with no opportunity for cross-examination. Potential adverse claimants were usually not even notified of the proceedings.[113]

Since claims were not surveyed until after they were confirmed, neither the surveyor general nor Congress had any idea how much land was being confirmed. Thus, after the Maxwell and Sangre de Cristo grants were confirmed, the Maxwell grant was found to contain 1,714,764 acres and the Sangre de Cristo grant 2,713,545 acres. These grants should have been limited to about 97,000 acres if the Mexican Colonization Law of 1824 had been applied (48,500 acres for each grantee). In fact, Congress did apply that law to the confirmation of the Las Animas and Río Don Carlos grants, confirming the former at approximately 97,000 acres and the latter at 48,000 acres.[114]

The injustice of applying the eleven-square-league size limitation to some grants but not to others is apparent. Nevertheless, the U.S. Supreme Court upheld the confirmations of both the Maxwell and Sangre de Cristo grants, conceiving a novel theory to justify its action. Since it was obvious that the confirmations were in violation of Mexican law, the Supreme Court held that Congress had made a grant *de novo*, or a new grant, by its confirmation.[115] This was strange reasoning indeed, for under the surveyor general system, land grants were supposed to have been dealt with by the United States precisely as Spain and Mexico would have done. This reasoning would not have resulted in such an unjust result if it had also been applied later by the Court of Private Land Claims in an evenhanded fashion. Instead the courts and congress were excessively lenient when they were deciding the fate of huge private land grants like the Maxwell, that were claimed by a few speculators, but were excessively strict when adjudicating community grants like San Miguel del Bado, claimed by hundreds of families scattered throughout the grant in small villages.

Besides these grievous faults, the surveyor general system in New Mexico had no provision for the orderly determination of overlapping claims. Under the later Court of Private Land Claims, all possible overlapping claims to the same area were supposed to be joined in one proceeding that determined all rights to the disputed land. Not so under the surveyor general system. Since there was no provision for notifying adverse claimants, the surveyor general operated on a first come, first served basis. Often it was the large grant, overlapping several small grants, that came first and was confirmed. Then when the smaller grants sought confirmation, they were met with the answer that the United States had already confirmed the land to someone else.[116]

It was soon apparent that the surveyor general system was woefully inadequate. Surveyor General Pelham told his superiors in his first annual report that "the present law has utterly failed to secure the object for which it was intended."[117] Congress too despaired of a fair solution to New Mexico's land grant problem under the surveyor general system. In 1860 the Committee on Private Land Claims of the House of Representatives reported on a bill to confirm the first series of grants recommended by Surveyor General Pelham. In its report, the committee noted that it did not have time to properly review the proceedings in each case, "nor will it ever be in the power hereafter of this House to make such an examination as will be entirely satisfactory . . ."[118]

Imperfect as it was, the surveyor general system continued for almost four decades, during which time opportunities were plentiful for individual speculators to enrich themselves, usually at the expense of the settlers living on the land grants. Often these speculators included the surveyor general himself. Of the nine men to hold the office, three were blatant land speculators: T. Rush Spencer (1869–1874), James K. Proudfit (1872–1876), and Henry M. Atkinson (1876–1884). Spencer and Atkinson each had land grant holdings while they were in office.[119] These conflicts of interest, coupled with the inherent defects of the surveyor general system, often guaranteed that land grant adjudication would be unfair.

As an example, Surveyor General Henry Atkinson claimed to own most of the Anton Chico community grant at the same time that he was making important decisions about its title. This story illustrates one of the two main methods used by speculators to acquire land grants during the surveyor general period: purchase of the principal settler's interest in a community grant. The second method was the partition suit.

It was often the case that a community grant like Anton Chico was requested at the outset by one or two individuals on behalf of a group of prospective settlers. This individual was the *poblador principal* (principal settler).[120] Often a list of all the proposed settlers would be attached to the petition, but sometimes only the name of the *poblador principal* would appear on the grant documents. In the case of Anton Chico, the petition was lost, but the granting decree of Governor Facundo Melgares referred to "the petition of citizen Manuel Rivera, for himself and in the name of thirty-six men."[121] Thus, the only name of a grantee appearing on the grant document was that of Manuel Rivera.

Anton Chico was clearly a community grant for it was made to a group of settlers and there was provision in the granting decree for the establishment of common lands. Moreover, when the grant was recommended for confirmation by Surveyor General Pelham, it was determined to be a community grant, for Pelham invoked the rule that the existence of a settlement on the grant in 1846 was *prima facie* evidence of a grant to that community.[122] Nevertheless, the fact that only Manuel Rivera's name appeared on the original grant papers created enough ambiguity that the General Land Office was asked to decide whether the patent should be issued to the Town of Anton Chico or to Manuel Rivera and thirty-six unnamed others. It was decided that Manuel Rivera and the thirty-six others should be the patentees and the patent was so issued on 27 March 1883.[123]

By this time Surveyor General Atkinson had purchased all the interests of the heirs of Manuel Rivera in the grant and deeded them to the New Mexico Land Livestock Company, of which he was president. The stage was set for a hearing on 20 April 1883, when representatives of the Anton

Chico grant applied to Surveyor General Atkinson for delivery of the patent. Not surprisingly, Atkinson ruled that the title was vested only in Manuel Rivera, his heirs and successors. In effect, Henry Atkinson was ruling that he himself owned the grant! Fortunately, the Town of Anton Chico was later declared by the courts to be the owner of the Anton Chico grant, and it finally received the patent.[124] Today the grant is still operated as a community grant. But Atkinson's attempt to obtain the grant from its rightful owners illustrates the corruption that prevailed in the surveyor general's office in the 1870s and 1880s.

The Tierra Amarilla grant was similar to the Anton Chico grant in respects that made possible its acquisition by Thomas Benton Catron, just as Henry Atkinson had acquired Anton Chico. This case also illustrates the first method of land grant acquisition used by speculators. The Tierra Amarilla grant was a community grant, but the grant documents mentioned only the name of the *poblador principal*, Manuel Martínez. Because of the due process defects in the surveyor general system, it was an easy matter for Manuel Martínez's son Francisco to seek confirmation of the grant in his name alone, since no notice of Francisco's claim was given to the other settlers.[125] After the grant was confirmed to the heirs of Manuel Martínez, Catron purchased the interests of those heirs and was able to obtain a court decree stating that he owned the grant. He then sold it, causing another community land grant to be dispossessed of its common lands. Although the Tierra Amarilla grant heirs have gone to court five times to regain their common lands, they have been unsuccessful in each case.[126]

The other device frequently used by speculators to acquire land grants was the partition suit. In numerous cases attorneys like Catron took as their fee for representing land grant claimants a portion of the land confirmed, usually one-third of the total acreage but sometimes up to one-half of the land.[127] Once the grant was confirmed, the attorney became a co-owner of the grant along with the heirs. Under the partition statute enacted by the New Mexico territorial legislature in 1876, the lawyer was entitled to ask the territorial courts to divide the grant among its owners or to force a sale of the land. The statute required a sale if the property could not be physically divided without decreasing its value. The courts uniformly found this prerequisite to exist and ordered the grant sold.[128]

The partition law was usually applied to the common lands of community grants, in direct opposition to the Spanish and Mexican systems of land tenure. Under those systems the common lands could not be sold — they were required to remain intact as a perpetual resource for the community.[129] But under the New Mexico partition statute, common lands were sold, often at ridiculously low prices. Sometimes the purchaser was merely a front for the lawyer who forced the sale in the first place. The grantees would receive a small amount of money for their valuable resource, and the attorney who had secured confirmation of the grant would end up owning most of the grant himself.[130]

Lawyers involved with land grant speculation in the late 1800s, joined by judges, politicians, businessmen, and a sympathetic press, were known as the Santa Fe Ring—a network established for mutual gain. Besides the surveyors general mentioned earlier, nearly every governor of New Mexico from the late 1860s to 1885 was a member of the Santa Fe Ring. Other prominent members of the Ring were lawyers Thomas B. Catron, Stephen B. Elkins, and Henry L. Waldo, federal judges Joseph G. Palen, Samuel B. Axtell, L. Bradford Prince, and probate judge Robert H. Longwill. The Santa Fe Ring also dealt in ranching, mining, and railroad interests in addition to land grants.[131] With this network working against their interests, it was no wonder that Hispanic land grant settlers, unfamiliar with Anglo laws and language and often not aware of court proceedings involving their land grants, had little chance of protecting their property.

Land grant speculation was not the exclusive province of Anglos, however. Many Anglo speculators worked through Hispanic middlemen in acquiring land grants. For example, in the 1870s Thomas B. Catron used Nicolás Pino, the son of land speculator Juan Estevan Pino, to help him acquire his interest in the San Cristóbal grant in Santa Fe County.[132] Furthermore, some members of the Santa Fe Ring like Antonio Joseph of Taos, were themselves Hispanos.[133] In fact, land grant speculation by Hispanos was occurring in New Mexico from the time they arrived. By the 1820s there was a tendency among elite Hispanos such as Juan Estevan Pino and Donaciano Vigil "to regard land as an economic asset to be exploited for the capital it would raise, not for the crops it would yield."[134]

While the abuses of the surveyor general system and the machinations of the Santa Fe Ring were occurring in the four decades after the signing of the Treaty of Guadalupe Hidalgo, most land titles in New Mexico were still in an unsettled state. An attempt at reforming the surveyor general system took place in 1885 with the appointment by President Grover Cleveland of George Washington Julian as surveyor general.[135] One of Julian's main tasks was to break up the Santa Fe Ring and other lesser rings operating in

1.6. Sheep threshing wheat in northern New Mexico, using methods similar to those used in Spain over two hundred years earlier. Photograph by T. Harmon Parkhurst, neg. no. 68820. Courtesy Museum of New Mexico.

New Mexico.[136] He set out vigorously to do this, but his zeal to correct the abuses of land grant adjudication under the surveyor general system led him to an overly critical questioning of many perfectly valid grants. In response to instructions from his superior, William Andrew Jackson Sparks of the General Land Office, Julian reexamined thirty-five claims covering more than four million acres of land that had been recommended for confirmation by his predecessors and were pending before Congress for final action. He recommended the rejection of twenty-two of these grants embracing over two million acres. Of those grants he recommended for confirmation, almost every one was recommended for a smaller area than was claimed.[137]

During his reevaluation of land grant claims, Surveyor General Julian revised both the procedural and the substantive rules that had governed land grant adjudication up to that time. The effect was to make confirmation more difficult for the claimant. Singlehandedly, Julian reversed certain presumptions favoring the validity of land grant claims and took the position that claims should be strictly construed against the claimant.[138] He also initiated investigations on substantive legal issues like ownership of the common lands of community land grants. In 1887 he sent investigators to Las Vegas, New Mexico, to search for evidence in the deed books to support his theory that title to the common lands of the Las Vegas grant was retained by the Mexican government.[139] Although this investigation was never completed, it is evident that the restrictive, conservative approach to land grant adjudication later followed by the Court of Private Land Claims began during the tenure of Surveyor General George Washington Julian.

The Court of Private Land Claims

By 1889 the complete breakdown of the surveyor general system was apparent. A backlog of 116 land grants awaited Congressional action, and Congress had not confirmed any grants since early 1879. The confirmation of the Maxwell and Sangre de Cristo grants had caused considerable embarrassment, both because the size of these grants was far in excess of the maximum provided under Mexican law and because fraud had been committed in their survey.[140] All of the surveyors general had recommended that further legislation be passed to provide for the adjudication of New Mexico land grants before a commission or judicial tribunal,[141] but it was not until 3 March 1891 that a law establishing a five-judge Court of Private Land Claims was signed by President Benjamin Harrison.[142] As early as 1879 bills similar to the 1891 Act had passed the Senate but had foundered in disagreements between the Senate and the House over the proper method of adjudicating land grant claims pursuant to the Treaty of Guadalupe Hidalgo. The House preferred a commission similar to the one established in California while the Senate favored adjudication of claims in local New Mexican courts.[143]

The statute setting up the Court of Private Land Claims was not in itself a radical departure from the procedure followed in California to adjudicate land titles there, but differences in language between the two statutes were later used by the courts to justify a stricter, more technical approach under the 1891 Act. For example, the 1891 Act did not specifically mention custom as a factor to be considered by the court in making its decisions although custom would be implied under international law, a factor that was mentioned.[144] Additionally the act required proof that every condition of a grant was performed within the time allowed[145] and only a grant "lawfully and regularly derived from the Government of Spain or Mexico" was entitled to confirmation.[146]

Some congressmen saw the law that led to the establishment of the Court of Private Land Claims as an overreaction to the abuses of the surveyor general system. During the debate in Congress over the predecessors to the 1891 Act, Senator Plumb remarked that "[the bill] is an illustration of the operation of certain mental characteristics which having been aroused upon a suggestion of fraud about to be committed, the result is an immediate loss of balance and a swinging to the farthest point on the other side."[147] This is an accurate description of the effect of the Land Claims Court. The cause of the swing, however, was the procedure followed under the 1891 Act, the adversarial climate of the Court of Private Land Claims, and the judicial climate of the Supreme Court, more than the statute itself. One effect of the movement from a liberal to a conservative approach to land grant adjudication was that the grants most deserving of confirmation were caught in the middle, since many of the large speculative grants had already been confirmed.

The procedure in the Court of Private Land Claims heavily favored the government, resulting in numerous unjust decisions. As with the surveyor general system, the claimant before the land claims court had the burden of proving the existence of the grant and the performance of all its conditions. Previously however, the claimant was aided by certain presumptions that eased that burden of proof, such as the presumption of the existence of a community grant from the existence of a settlement on the grant in 1846, the presumption of regularity of a grant, and the presumption of authority of a granting official. Under the Court of Private Land Claims, all three of these presumptions were eliminated. Surveyor General Julian seems to have been responsible for discarding of the first two presumptions during his overzealous crusade, but the third, the presumption of the authority of the granting official was eliminated in 1898 by the U.S. Supreme Court in the case of *Hayes v. United States*.[148] After that decision, discussed in Chapter 6, concerning the Embudo grant, the claimant had the burden of proving that the officials granting land or making copies of land grant documents had the authority to do so. It would have been fairer for the government to have this burden since it had physical custody and superior knowledge of the Spanish and Mexican archives.

The *Hayes* decision left the land grant claimant still carrying the burden of proof without the benefit of all the presumptions that had made that burden a little less onerous. Added to this situation was a climate in the Court of Private Land Claims that definitely favored the government.

Experts like Will Tipton and Henry Flipper, who were most familiar with the land grant archives and had researched Spanish and Mexican law, all worked for the government, while the claimants lacked such expertise and were often poorly represented. Since the claimants usually did not have the funds to hire experts to research Spanish and Mexican land records or to survey their grant, they were wholly dependent on the skill and honesty of the attorney they hired to represent them. An examination of the records of the Court of Private Land Claims reveals that often this legal representation was inadequate, resulting in severe injustice to the claimants.

A case in point is the representation of the Pueblo Quemado grant by Thomas Benton Catron. Although the claimants did not have any grant documents, there were numerous references to the grant in the Spanish archives, including the Cundiyó grant to the south that mentioned the Pueblo Quemado grant as its northern boundary. Catron filed a petition for confirmation of the grant in 1893 and then took no action on the case for the next seven years, during which time several grants without documents were confirmed.[149] When the case finally came up for trial in 1900, Catron voluntarily dismissed the petition.[150] If he had brought the case to trial sooner the Supreme Court precedents might have been more favorable. As it was, the claimants never had their day in court, because Catron, like many other attorneys, treated the representation of these land grant claimants more like a business than a trust responsibility.

Land grant lawyers were often more concerned with their own interests than with their basic duty to pursue their clients' interests with vigor. They usually handled several land grant cases simultaneously, and since their fee was dependent on winning a confirmation, they tended to neglect or concede the weaker cases. At the same time, the government pursued every case assiduously, appealing many on highly technical grounds. As the government won more appeals to the Supreme Court, new precedents were established in the government's favor, making more of the claimants' cases doubtful. As a result, claimants' lawyers conceded many cases without a trial near the end of the fourteen-year term of the Court of Private Land Claims.[151]

Although the adversarial climate favored the government in the Court of Private Land Claims, the decisions of the land claims court occasionally displayed a balanced approach that yielded a result favorable to the claimant. But in several instances, when the U.S. attorney appealed these decisions, the U.S. Supreme Court reversed, siding with the government and against the claimant. The most famous of these decisions concerned the ownership of the common lands of the San Miguel del Bado grant in San Miguel County. The case of *U.S. v. Sandoval* illustrates the negative judicial climate of the United States Supreme Court in regard to land grants during the late 1800s.[152]

San Miguel del Bado was a community grant of over 300,000 acres, according to a 1879 survey. Prior to United States occupation, seven villages had grown up on the grant in addition to the initial settlement at San Miguel.[153] When the inhabitants of these villages asked the surveyor general for confirmation of the grant, he recommended that the entire grant be confirmed. Later the General Land Office commissioner recommended that only the occupied lands on the grant should be confirmed, which would mean the rejection of the common lands — the bulk of the land within the grant. But when the Court of Private Land Claims took the opposite view and confirmed the entire grant, the government immediately appealed that decision to the U.S. Supreme Court. This was an important test case for the government, for if the common lands of this grant were rejected, hundreds of thousands — perhaps millions — of acres of other community grant common lands not yet adjudicated would also belong to the government, not to the land grant heirs.

In the end, the Supreme Court reversed the Land Claims Court decision, holding that the common lands belonged to the governments of Spain and Mexico when the grant was first made and that title to those lands had passed to the United States in 1848 under the treaty of Guadalupe Hidalgo. It appears that the Supreme Court was in error on this point of Spanish and Mexican law,[154] but the Court of Private Land Claims was forced to confirm only the allotted lands of the San Miguel del Bado grant, determined to be a little more than 5,000 acres.[155] Although some grant residents were able to recover part of the 300,000 acre common lands of the grant through the homestead and small holding claim laws, other land grants were not so lucky.[156]

After the 1897 *Sandoval* decision, the land claims court rejected the common lands of every community grant that came up for adjudication. This vast acreage acquired by the United States now comprises most of the Carson and Santa Fe National Forests in northern New Mexico. But since the Court of Private Land Claims refused to apply the *Sandoval* decision retroactively, community grants confirmed before the *Sandoval* decision were able to retain their common lands.[157]

Several other grounds were used by the Supreme Court and by the Court of Private Land Claims to reject perfectly valid grants. These included requirements that the grant be recorded in the Spanish or Mexican archives

1.7. *The town of Osuna in the Spanish province of Seville, showing a common threshing floor in the foreground. Georg Braun,* Civitatis orbis terrarum *(Cologne, 1576–1618). Courtesy Harry Ransom Humanities Research Center, University of Texas at Austin.*

of New Mexico,[158] that the grant be approved by the territorial deputation if made during the Mexican Period,[159] and that there be strict compliance with each of the procedural steps of the grant: the petition, the grant, and the act of possession.[160] But these technical reasons were seldom if ever the basis for a land grant rejection by Spain or Mexico.[161] One situation in which Spanish or Mexican officials did reject a land grant due to a procedural defect was where notice to adjacent landowners, giving them the opportunity to object to the grant, had not been given. But United States courts rarely looked to see how the Spanish and Mexican governments had treated land grants in Hispanic New Mexico, despite the availability of numerous cases involving land grant disputes in the archives of New Mexico.

There were several grounds that did justify the rejection of land grants by Spanish and Mexican authorities. These included: (1) forgery of the documents,[162] (2) insufficient proof that a grant had been made,[163] (3) failure to notify owners of land adjoining the grant,[164] (4) failure to meet a condition of the grant,[165] (5) revocation of the grant by Spanish or Mexican officials,[166] and (6) failure to settle the land four years after the grant was made, with continuous possession thereafter.[167] These were grounds that would also justify United States courts in rejecting grants. For under international, law United States courts should have adjudicated land grants in the same manner as Spain and Mexico would have done.[168] But instead, these courts often found it more expedient to rely on an obscure Spanish or Mexican law or commentary on Hispanic Law as the basis for a decision rather than seek the benefit of expert testimony on questions of Spanish and Mexican law.

If Article 10 had not been eliminated from the Treaty of Guadalupe Hidalgo, its mandate to confirm all grants to the extent that New Mexico under Spain or Mexico would have confirmed them, would have provided a guide for land grant adjudication. As it was however, the land claims court and the Supreme Court followed no consistent principles, and both were highly erratic in their land grant decisions. Still these courts did render a few well-reasoned decisions that stand out as beacons of fairness, showing how all these cases should have been handled. One such case was *U.S. v. Chaves.*

The *Chaves* case involved a community grant made in 1833 to the town of Cubero in present-day Valencia County. The Court of Private Land Claims confirmed the grant, although the claimants had no grant documents at all. The government appealed, but the Supreme Court affirmed the Land Claims Court in an opinion by Justice George Shiras. The justice must have done a great deal of independent research, because there was no brief or court appearance on behalf of the claimants to aid him. Nevertheless, Justice Shiras examined many important questions addressed in few other cases.

The government's position was that the grant should not be confirmed, under its restrictive interpretation of the 1891 Act, since it lacked grant documents. Justice Shiras reached a different conclusion. His opinion cites Justice Marshall's decision under the Florida treaty that had set a liberal tone for land grant adjudication.[169] He also examines the rules of international law and the terms of the Treaty of Guadalupe Hidalgo, factors seldom mentioned in other decisions, and concludes that Congress did not intend to restrict the powers of the Court of Private Land Claims. With this background, Justice Shiras proceeds to discuss the facts of the *Chaves* case, summarizing the testimony of several witnesses who had lived in the town of Cubero for varying periods of the time since the grant was made in 1833. Many of these witnesses had seen the original grant documents, although they had since been lost. Also, documents concerning a dispute between the town of Cubero and the Pueblo of Laguna were cited as evidence of a grant to the town of Cubero. But most important was the undisputed testimony that the claimants had been in possession of the land continuously since 1833. It was primarily on the basis of this evidence of uninterrupted possession that the lower court's decision confirming the grant was affirmed.[170]

The *Chaves* decision was in accord with the Spanish and Mexican law of prescription (gaining title by continuous possession), but this principle was rarely used as a ground for decision in other cases.[171] If there had been more Supreme Court decisions like *Chaves*, the 6 percent confirmation record of the Court of Private Land Claims would surely have been higher, because there would have been fewer appeals by the government and more liberal opinions by the Court of Private Land Claims. For example, Matthew Reynolds, one of the attorneys who argued the *Chaves* case before the Supreme Court, was in the habit of appealing almost every case the government lost. But after the *Chaves* decision he moderated this stance, at least for a time. In a similar case involving the Doña Ana Bend Colony grant, Reynolds recommended that a previously authorized appeal be dismissed because the Supreme Court was likely to affirm the Doña Ana Bend grant based on the long and continuous possession of that land by the claimants. Reynolds told the U.S. attorney general that this belief was based on *U.S. v. Chaves*.[172]

It seems apparent that the courts and Congress did not effectively discharge the obligations assumed by the United States under the Treaty of Guadalupe Hidalgo. They should have adopted a clear and consistent standard for judging the validity of Spanish and Mexican land grants, one that would have provided for rejection of grants only in cases where Spain or Mexico would have rejected the grant. Because no such comprehensive standard was followed by United States courts in their adjudication of Spanish and Mexican land grants, Hispanic property rights were not adequately protected. Thus the perception of injustice held by many land grant heirs is largely justified. Some have suggested that the Court of Private Land Claims should be judged by the more lax standards of its time.[173] Other scholars have labeled the work of the Court of Private Land Claims as relatively fair,[174] but this judgement seems to have been reached mostly through a face-value acceptance of the courts' reasoning without an independent in-depth analysis of specific land grant cases.

One thing is clear: Hispanic people have not been treated fairly in relation to the land grant issue. But the causes of this unfairness are not as clear. No one individual or group of individuals is solely to blame — not Matthew Reynolds, nor Thomas Catron, nor Henry Atkinson, nor even the Santa Fe Ring. They all played a part in the chicanery of land grant adjudication, but the drama was allowed to proceed by the United States government. The United States government negotiated the Treaty of Guadalupe Hidalgo and then deleted the part that had to do with land grants. The United States government established the Surveyor General and Court of Private Land Claims but rejected many of the valid land grants submitted for adjudication. Yet to be examined, however, is government participation in acquiring land grants by purchase.

During the 1930s the government instituted a policy of acquiring land grants as part of a Hispanic land reform program. The idea was to make land available for the exclusive use of the local villagers, referred to by New Deal bureaucrats as the "dependent, subsistent . . . population."[175] These bureaucrats were part of a cadre of idealistic New Deal planners whose idea of rural rehabilitation included low interest loans and grants, cooperative marketing associations, and land acquisition by the government to allow local residents preferential grazing rights. Land grants owned by the government and used for this purpose included all or part of the Polvadera, Sebastian Martín, Caja del Río, La Majada, Cuyamungue, San José, Gabaldón, Ramón Vigil, Abiquiú, and Ortiz Mine grants in addition to the Juan José Lobato grant.[176]

Juan José Lobato is a land grant whose acquisition by the Forest Service harmed rather than helped village residents within the grant. The north portion of the grant was acquired by the government in 1942 and administered under this program, first by the Farm Security Administration and then by the Forest Service. When the FSA was pressured to transfer its lands to another agency, it deemed the Forest Service to be the agency most likely to honor the purpose for which the lands had been acquired — rural rehabilitation through preferential grazing rights to local residents. Given the legacy of bitterness left from the administration of northern New Mexico land grants by the U.S. Forest Service, it is somewhat surprising that this agency — known by northern New Mexico's Hispanics as La Floresta — would be picked as a champion of rural villagers.

Scholars disagree as to the truth behind the poor image that the Forest Service has acquired. Suzanne Forrest believes that the Forest Service was acting in good faith when it acquired the North Lobato tract in the early 1940s, but she thinks that its policies changed in the 1960s when it began to emphasize profits from timber sales and grazing permits and raised grazing fees on public lands. Forrest recognizes that "many New Mexicans, Hispanic and otherwise, . . . have come to see United States forest rangers as uniformed occupational troopers guarding the spoils of the Treaty of Guadalupe Hidalgo." She sees some justification for this attitude as large livestock and timber operations gradually have displaced local residents as permittees on the North Lobato tract that the Forest Service still administers.[177] William deBuys, on the other hand, finds from his examination of governmental records that Forest Service grazing policy "was to favor local, small operators over large ones." DeBuys argues that if Anglo cattlemen displaced some local Hispanic stock grazers, it was because they purchased their grazing permits from Hispanos, not because of Forest Service policy.[178] A close look at certain Forest Service correspondence files regarding the Juan José Lobato grant tells a different story, however.

In 1947, after administration of the North Lobato land was transferred to the Forest Service, ranger Paul Martínez in Vallecitos suggested to his superior that "the policy [of] giving 'aid' to the poorer dependents is mostly a fallacy."[179] The Assistant Regional Forester in Albuquerque did not disagree, but sounded a prophetic note in his response:

The original intent of the purchase of the Lobato Grant was to extend relief to a submarginal agricultural population. . . . Martínez' proposal . . . throws this consideration out the window in so far as grazing policy is concerned. I wonder if we would not be charged with lack of faith in [not] continuing the policy objective of the Farmers' Home Administration. At least any major changes in policy should be a slow process rather than to suddenly discontinue consideration of the poorer dependents.[180]

This is exactly what happened. A gradual change did take place after World War II, which saw the Forest Service favoring large timber sales to the wood products industry instead of managing its resources for the benefit of the local villagers.[181]

The U.S. Forest Service has often failed to manage former land grant lands with sensitivity to their historic ownership and use patterns or to the responsibility imposed on the service by land grant purchases. We will see an example of this failure in Chapter 7 concerning the Las Trampas grant.

It is necessary to acknowledge the error of earlier court decisions if there is to be any hope for justice in current litigation with the government (state or federal) concerning land and water rights in New Mexico. The U.S. Supreme Court has been wrong before. In 1896, a year before it decided the *Sandoval* case, the Supreme Court upheld racial segregation in public schools in *Plessy v. Ferguson*, a decision that was overruled in 1954.[182] Recently Congress recognized another mistaken Supreme Court decision during World War II upholding the segregation of Japanese-Americans in internment camps.[183] Now similar attention needs to be paid to the Hispanic land loss problem in the Southwest.

The basic injustices of land grant adjudication and wrongheaded Forest Service administration will not be simply forgotten. It is more likely that controversies and disputes will continue to surface. New Mexico is primarily a rural state with many people still living close to the land. To many Hispanic residents, the land grant story is the story of a passionate and continuing struggle for the land their ancestors were promised when they became citizens of the United States in 1848, not simply a fading part of New Mexico's history. May that promise someday be kept.

Two

Lawsuits, Litigants, and Custom in Hispanic New Mexico

The path of the history of New Mexican land grants is marked by controversy and by often heated litigation over rights to land and water. Struggles over these important resources in New Mexico, and before that in Spain and central Mexico, have been characterized by a fierceness and determination that contain all the elements of good drama. The records of this litigation, reveal men locked in elemental struggles over their very survival. Sometimes the outcome of such a battle is taken out of the hands of the parties to the conflict and is determined by providential forces, as in the following Taos case.

Here is what happened. After a decade and a half of controversy over water from the Río Lucero between the settlers of Arroyo Seco, on one side, and Taos Pueblo and the settlers of El Prado, on the other side, matters were coming to a head. In 1838 the Rio Lucero was running particularly low, and when the two factions could not get their problems resolved through New Mexico's legal system, they decided to take matters into their own hands. They agreed on a date for a physical confrontation, whereby the water right issues would be decided in a trial by combat. When the day arrived, each side marched to the Arroyo Seco headgate, armed and ready to do battle. But before the shooting started, an unexpected thunderstorm forced both sides to seek cover from the rain. When it cleared, the two sides discovered that the Rio Lucero had flooded, making moot the issue of how to divide scarce water.[1]

We see in the facts of this case, a drama so tinged with magical realism that it might have sprung from the pen of Gabriel García Márquez.[2] It is as if a higher power, watching over the struggles of the *vecinos* from Arroyo Seco, El Prado, and Taos Pueblo, brought the rain after the traditional ceremonies had failed, because it was apparent that these people were serious, and could hurt one another if left to their own devices.

The study of such lawsuits and of the land grants with which they are connected reveals an important and little-studied part of the historical record. These lawsuits often illuminate social values in a community and contain the means of determining rights to land and water, not only at the time of the lawsuit, but also today. Above all, we see the major importance of custom in the working out of disputes over land and water in New Mexico.

The records of land and water litigation, and of land grants themselves, are one of the richest sources for the history of New Mexico.[3] The historical record is often full of gaps. Although land grant documents may reveal a grant being made at a certain location, knowing when that grant was settled and by whom is often difficult to determine from the grant documents alone. This information can be quite important in water rights adjudications, and many times the testimony in a lawsuit will provide the missing link. For example, the 1837 grant documents for the Guadalupita grant in Mora County do not reveal when and by whom the grant was settled. But testimony in an 1866 lawsuit between Guadalupita residents establishes that the grant was settled in 1837, abandoned in 1842, and resettled in 1851.[4]

Lawsuits relating to land and water can also tell us much about the community where the lawsuit originated. J. A. Pitt-Rivers uses a water rights lawsuit in the village of Alcalá de la Sierra in twentieth-century Spain as a means of showing the dynamics of friendship and authority in action in that community.[5] Another scholar made use of a lawsuit that lasted almost 130 years in fifteenth- and sixteenth-century Toledo, Spain, to explain the social relationships within the Spanish nobility, and the judicial relationships between the king and the nobility. This one case, containing 34,000 pages of transcript filling forty-five bundles of documents in Toledo's municipal archives, generated enough material for a Ph. D. dissertation.[6] Finally, a recent book also based on litigation (this time a charge of transatlantic bigamy) illuminates society in sixteenth-century Spain and her colonies, as it describes the details of complex legal maneuvers of lawyers and their clients, and the decisions of such prestigious courts as the Council of the Indies.[7] Scholars who have studied Spanish and Mexican Period lawsuits and land grants in New Mexico include: Emlen Hall and Daniel Tyler,[8] Janet Lecompte,[9] Rosalind Z. Rock,[10] Ramón Gutiérrez,[11] Robert J. Torrez and Charles Cutter,[12] Michael Meyer,[13] William Taylor,[14] and John Baxter.[15]

The issues decided by Spanish and Mexican period lawsuits are still with us today. What happened two or more centuries ago in a particular case can still determine the outcome of current land and water rights litigation. For example, recent water rights adjudications in New Mexico require the court to establish priority dates (the dates when ditches were first established) for all the *acequias* on a particular stream system. The determination of these dates is based primarily on the historical evidence found in early land and water rights lawsuits, land grant and deed records, actions to probate wills or settle estates, census and church records, and governmental communications.

The chapters that follow discuss two kinds of land grant related lawsuits. The first group are lawsuits that took place under the Spanish and Mexican government before the Americans arrived in New Mexico; these are the lawsuits treated in this chapter. The second group of lawsuits were tried in United States courts after the United States occupied New Mexico and signed the Treaty of Guadalupe Hidalgo and the Gadsden Treaty with Mexico. These include adjudications of land grant claims by tribunals such as the Court of Private Land Claims, as well as lawsuits tried in state and federal courts in New Mexico dealing with land and water rights. These two kinds of lawsuits are often directly connected because those suits decided when New Mexico was governed by Spain or Mexico can be used as a basis for decision in those cases adjudicated in U.S. courts after the Treaty of Guadalupe Hidalgo. For example, when land grants were adjudicated in the middle and late 1800s, one of the questions to be answered was the validity of land grants under Spanish and Mexican law. A Spanish- or Mexican-Period lawsuit might provide the answer to that question.[16]

In frontier New Mexico, Spanish and Mexican law was more often found in New Mexico's lawsuits than in Spanish law books. To understand the procedural aspects of New Mexico lawsuits, it will be helpful to compare them with the lawsuit in sixteenth-century Castile on the eve of the Columbus voyages to the Americas. In Chapter 1 we dealt with the substantive law under which the monarchy attempted to unify Spain. Now we need to look at the courts where this law was applied to resolve disputes and the lawyers who practiced in those courts. We also must examine the regional customs known as *fueros*.

The *fuero* had two meanings in the Spanish judicial context. In the context of substantive law a *fuero* was a set of customs and local usages that applied only to a specific community or region. Often these customs differed from royal law, and the courts had to decide which would prevail.

When judges applied local *fueros* to a dispute they might rule "in favor of the ancient custom of this valley," as opposed to a conflicting statute.[17] In 1598 a noted jurist stated that "customs defeat the statute and have more force than law."[18] The other meaning of *fuero* is a jurisdiction for privileged groups like the military, the church, and the nobility, or for specific areas.

The complex web of customs and laws through which a litigant had to

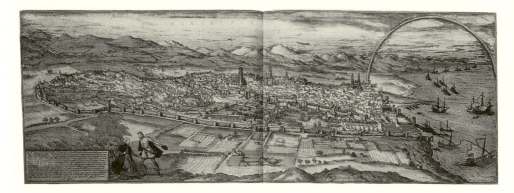

2.2 *The city of Barcelona was the most important port on the western Mediterranean under the Romans and was the capitol of the Visigoths in the fifth century. In 1258 the city issued the* Consulado del Mar, *a maritime code that became the accepted law for European maritime states. John Goss,* Braun & Hogenberg's The City Maps of Europe: A Selection of Sixteenth Century Town Plans and Views *(London: Studio Editions, Ltd., 1991).*

maneuver in Castile was compounded by a court system that was equally tangled and overlapping. In addition to municipal *alcalde* courts and the local *fueros,* the system of royal courts was rather advanced. On the first level were trial courts presided over by the king's *corregidores* and other municipal judges, on the next level were the five regional *audiencias* that heard appeals from the first level, and the top tier consisted of the council of Castile, similar to a royal supreme court. In practice this neat hierarchy broke down as each tribunal tried to increase its jurisdiction at the others' expense.

Lawyers in sixteenth-century Castile made use of this confusion regarding what law to apply, what the law meant, and what jurisdiction the litigants should invoke, resulting in a bewildering array of possibilities that often led to confusion and distrust on the part of the litigant. There were three types of lawyers: the *abogado* (advocate), the *procurador* (attorney), and the *solicitador* (solicitor). Each had different functions, and they often fought among themselves regarding their overlapping duties. The *abogado* researched the law, wrote the briefs required, and orally presented his clients legal arguments to the judge. The *procurador* had direct contact with the client from the time he took the case and was given authority to represent his client in court. This attorney did most of the leg-work in preparing the case, including the interviewing of the witnesses and the preparation of routine documents.[19] Finally there was the *solicitador*, whose functions were not clearly spelled out in the documents. This may have been because some of those duties were illegal, such as arranging for bribes and other payoffs intended to further the client's case. The *solicitador* had to be aware of everything that might affect the case, like changes in royal policy, impending legislation, and just plain court gossip. He was not unlike a modern-day influence peddler whose job was to keep the complex machinery of litigation well oiled, even if he had to grease a few palms to do so.[20] It is not surprising that there was a certain distrust of lawyers in sixteenth-century Spain, as illustrated in the picaresque novel *Lazarillo de Tormes* where lawyers are characterized as "being attracted to money like flies to a honey pot."[21]

In frontier New Mexico where few could afford a lawyer and where the niceties of Roman law were of little use, the legal system was simpler, with similarities to the Spanish system of customary law. With few trained lawyers, and a scarcity of law books, it was the basic skill of persuasive communication that was most effective in New Mexico, and people like don Manuel Martínez, who successfully represented himself in a lengthy ditch dispute in Abiquiú (discussed in Chapter 3), acquitted themselves quite well in this respect.

One of the few lawyers in New Mexico during the Mexican period was Antonio Barreiro who was sent from Mexico City to act as *asesor*, or legal advisor.[22] He played an important role in several lawsuits, including an 1832 dispute involving the San Joaquín grant (discussed in Chapter 5), but he stayed in New Mexico for only three years. The central government in Mexico City notified Governor Manuel Armijo in 1829 that an *asesor* would be sent to advise litigants and judges about the law but the first lawyers assigned to the post resigned and Licenciado Barreiro did not arrive in Santa Fe until 1831. The government in Mexico City sent Barreiro not only as legal advisor but also to provide a check on local authorities for the

Mexico City government.[23] In practice, the opinion of the *asesor* was sought
on a wide range of questions. For example, in a dispute over a house in
Santa Fe in 1832, one of the parties wanted the *alcalde* who had presided
over the *conciliación* proceedings to be summoned to identify his signature.
Asked whether this was proper, Asesor Barreiro said it was. Then, the same
alcalde notified the parties that he would seek Barreiro's advice on how to
decide the dispute. When one side objected, the *alcalde* told the parties that
he planned instead to consult a lawyer in Chihuahua at their expense.
Within a few weeks' time the parties had settled the case.[24]

New Mexico's legal system during the Spanish and Mexican administra-
tions was rudimentary and informal. The closest New Mexico ever got to a
formal legal system during this period was when Juan Estevan Pino recommended to New Mexico's *diputación* in 1829 that a new court of justice be
established that would provide a district judge, an attorney general, a clerk,
and a constable as a skeletal legal system. Even though the Mexican government had provided funds for the salaries of these officials, the plan failed
because no trained lawyers were to be found in New Mexico at this time.[25]
A few lawyers later appeared in New Mexico, but generally, if New Mexican
litigants wanted lawyers to represent them they hired them in Chihuahua
or Durango.

Legal representation was provided to the Pueblo Indians, particularly in
land disputes, by an official called the *Protector de Indios*. The office was
established in Mexico as an idealistic measure aimed at protecting indige-
nous rights. There the protector often had considerable legal training, and
was supported by an annual assessment levied on the Indians. This has been
characterized as an early form of compulsory legal insurance, a kind of
government sponsored legal aid.[26] In New Mexico the office of *Protector de
Indios* was vacant for long periods of time, the officials who did serve lacked
legal training, and there was no assessment imposed upon the Indians.[27]
Nevertheless the protector did provide a valuable service in a litigious, but
almost lawyerless New Mexican society.

The virtual absence of trained lawyers was somewhat compensated for by
the process of *conciliación*. This procedure was required by the law of 23
May 1837 and probably earlier by the constitution of 1836.[28] Instead of
lawyers, each party would appoint an *hombre bueno*, a good man who acted
as a lay representative and whose job it was to recommend a fair settlement
to the *alcalde* hearing the case. Under this simplified procedure, the *alcalde*
would summon the parties to appear, together with their documents if the

2.3. *A portion of the 1771 Nicolas de Lafora map showing parts of Nuevo Mexico, Nueva Vizcaya, and Sonora as redrawn by Ynez Dunnford Haare. Courtesy New Mexico State Records Center and Archives.*

case involved land, at a specific time and place. In some cases additional representatives of the parties, called *apoderados*, would also be present. The *alcalde* would ask each side to state their position and then request the opinions of the *hombres buenos*. If the *hombres buenos* agreed on a settlement then the alcalde would adopt their agreement, but if they disagreed the alcalde had to make the decision himself. If it was accepted by the parties to the dispute that would end the matter.[29] In Mexican-Period California, where *conciliación* was also followed, the *hombres buenos* agreed on a settlement recommendation in almost 90 percent of the cases.[30] If one of the parties did not agree with the decision in *conciliación* the *alcalde* could give the parties more time to accept the proposed settlement. If they still did not agree then they could embark on a more formal procedure, based on written statements rather than on oral argument.

The first step in such a procedure was be the filing of a certificate that *conciliación* had been attempted and failed. After a petition was filed by the plaintiff stating his case, the defendant was given an opportunity to reply in another written statement. This procedure often continued with one or two more statements being filed by each party. In many instances these statements are like well organized legal briefs with arguments persuasively made, but one also finds a good deal of repetition, self-serving statements, and name-calling in these documents. For example, in a 1703 suit between the powerful *alcalde* Diego Arias de Quiros and the sisters María and Juana Griego over land in Santa Fe, Arias argued that he should prevail because of "the loyalty with which I have served his majesty . . . and on account of the good nobility of my blood . . . and of my way of living." On the other hand the Griego sisters said that they should win because

> being poor women and alone, we started out at the time of the insurrec-
> tion of this Kingdom on foot . . . persevering in the face of innumerable
> hardships, awaiting the time to return to our patrimonial land, so that
> there might again be established our Holy Catholic faith . . . at the time
> when the said Capt. Diego Arias . . . probably did not know what was New
> America.[31]

Just as lawyers were rare in New Mexico, so were trained judges. Since there was little formal education in New Mexico at this time,[32] it was difficult enough to find a judge who could read and write, let alone one trained in the law. An 1812 decree of the Spanish Cortes required that judges learned in the law (*jueces letrados*) be available even for small communities.[33] However, this law was not followed in New Mexico — in some cases New Mexico judges were so unlearned that they had to hire someone else to perform part of their duties.[34]

There were also few lawbooks in New Mexico,[35] and specific laws were referred to more often by the litigants than by the judges. In 1828 Domingo Fernandez cited two provisions of the 20 January 1813 decree of the Spanish Cortes,[36] and in 1840 Matías Ortiz cited the *Nueva Recopilación* for the proposition that *regidores* (members of an *ayuntamiento*), could not make land grants without first obtaining a license. Other laws cited were *Las Siete Partidas*, the Novissima Recopilación, the Law of 9 November 1812, the law of 9 October 1812, the law of 4 January 1813, the law of 20 January 1813, the law of 25 March 1813, and the law of 23 June 1813, the constitutions of 1824 and 1836, and the *Bases Organicas*.[37] Though books of procedure did exist in other jurisdictions, there is no evidence that they were used in New Mexico though in at least two estates, law books were listed in the inventories.[38]

In addition to civil courts, provision was made for military and ecclesiastic courts in New Mexico, as in Spain and central Mexico. These *fueros* provided certain privileges for those in the military or those accused of a crime by the church. Under this system the trial would be by a military or ecclesiastic court, but there were few such trials in New Mexico. In 1842 Mexican President Santa Anna reestablished the military *fuero* and Governor Manuel Armijo attempted to prosecute a case in accordance with that law. When several members of the Vera Cruz Squadron, sent to New Mexico to help put down the 1837 Rebellion, were accused of a vicious assault and robbery of Santa Fe merchant Amado Pierotin, the governor attempted to prosecute the case in a military court. But Armijo found that he lacked the number of officers necessary to form the court.[39]

Political officials and bodies—the *alcaldes* and *ayuntamientos*—acted as trial courts, with appeals handled by the governor. From this procedure, however, there was a great deal of deviation.[40] For instance, the question of who had jurisdiction over a lawsuit in the first instance was handled in every conceivable way in New Mexico. Sometimes an *alcalde* would refer a petition directly to the governor for a decision, and on other occasions, when the governor received a petition directly he would refer it back to the *alcalde* for a hearing. On rare occasions, the governor would seek an opinion from a jurist in Chihuahua or elsewhere before deciding a case himself. Pragmatic considerations often determined which procedure would be followed. Sometimes it was apparent that any decision in a particular case would be certain to make enemies for the unlucky official who had to decide the case. Since the official was primarily a politician and secondarily a jurist, the inclination was to "pass the buck."

An example of this was an 1815 lawsuit between Taos Pueblo and the settlers of what is today the town of Taos. The case was started when Taos Pueblo petitioned the local *alcalde* asking him to measure the land that the

2.4. Taos Pueblo with the Rio Pueblo in the foreground, ca. 1925. Lanning Collection #50276. Courtesy New Mexico State Records Center and Archives, Santa Fe

Pueblo was entitled to—four square leagues, or five thousand varas measured in the four directions from the cross in the cemetery (approximately seventeen thousand acres).[41] Since this would include much of the Spanish settlement in the area, the *alcalde* referred the petition to Governor Alberto Maynez, knowing that the Spanish settlers would oppose the request. Governor Maynez decided in favor of the Pueblo's right to their four square leagues, and he referred the case back to the reluctant *alcalde*, directing him to measure the Pueblo's league and then try to work out a settlement.[42] In the end, the governor hedged his final decree by stating that he did not want any more written documents in the case, and that unless a verbal settlement was worked out, he would be forced to refer the matter to the royal *audiencia* "to whom the decision belongs because of its seriousness."[43] This insistence on verbal proceedings is reminiscent of the Spanish monarchs who preferred unwritten laws so they would not be bound by a particular decision.

In a similar 1763 decision by Governor Vélez Cachupín, the governor referred the case to a higher authority, (the magistrate for the villa of Chihuahua), not for decision, but for an advisory opinion, which was adopted by the governor as his decision. By doing this, Governor Vélez Cachupín took some of the pressure off himself, where the explosive issue was the same as in the Taos case: Spanish encroachment on Indian lands.[44] Another example of referring a lawsuit to a higher court was a 1713 murder case where the results were not as successful from the government's standpoint. There the governor decided that the *sala del crimen* (Viceregal Criminal Court) should hear the case. However, the defendant was able to escape while being escorted in chains to Mexico City and received sanctuary in a church in Chihuahua. His escort continued on to Mexico City, delivering copies of the case and a letter to the Viceroy, but not their prisoner.[45]

The New Mexican legal system was not a system based on rigid procedural rules and it sometimes lacked the virtue of consistency. For example, Governor Manuel Armijo often referred petitions back to the local *alcaldes* or prefects for decision, but in some cases he made the requested decision himself.[46] Sometimes Governor Armijo told petitioners who appealed a decision to him that they must first appeal to the local prefect,[47] but in other cases he informed petitioners that they had to appeal to the supreme court, presumably in Guadalajara, Chihuahua, or Mexico City.[48] When an *alcalde* had a conflict of interest, or was related to the petitioner, the governor might appoint another official to hear the case, as in an 1840 Taos dispute involving "el *estranjero* Branch(e),"[49] or he might order the *prefect* to decide which judge should hear the case. The latter course was followed in an Abiquiu case where it was alleged that the complainant and the initial judge were unfriendly on account of quarrels and disagreements.[50] In 1833 the governor told an *alcalde* that the governor did not have the power to advise the *alcalde* on questions about the administration of justice and that he should ask an attorney for the answer.[51] It is apparent from these examples that there was a great deal of flexibility built into the Spanish and Mexican judicial system in New Mexico. In the absence of lawyers, trained judges, and lawbooks, this legal system was one based primarily on custom.

Customary law has a long tradition in Spanish jurisprudence, as we saw in Chapter 1. In Spanish law custom is defined in *Las Siete Partidas* as the usage and practice of the majority of the people in a particular locality over a period of time.[52] Customary law in New Mexico governed both the substantive rules and the procedures followed by judges. Decisions of *alcaldes, ayuntamientos,* and governors seldom mentioned a specific procedural or substantive law, but would often simply state that the particular result was "according to law." In procedural matters custom often dictated the practice followed, as when an *alcalde* was told by the governor in 1833 that in charging fees he should follow the custom most in use as long as it was not contrary to the law.[53]

Governor Manuel Armijo's decrees rendered in the early 1840s provide examples of the use of customary law in the administration of justice in New Mexico at that time. In his directions to local *alcaldes* or prefects, Armijo often orders these officials to "decide whatever he believes to be just," and to "administer prompt and complete justice."[54] Besides these vague pronouncements, Governor Armijo sometimes set forth a legal principle, without citing any legal authority for the principle. Thus he declared in 1841 that, "no person shall be put in jail for not having property," and "none of those contracting matrimony can be compelled to live together if sufficient causes for divorce are set forth."[55] Since no law is cited by Armijo the burden is placed upon the *alcalde* to reach a decision based upon consensus and common sense — that is, upon custom.

When governor Rafael Sarracino was asked by the *alcalde* of Jémez about the proper method of measuring the Jémez Pueblo league, and the amount of fees to charge for doing it, the governor told the *alcalde* to ask an attorney about the measurement and if he did not agree with the answer, the "the only thing to do is to administer perfect justice." As to the fees the *alcalde* was told to follow the custom most in use. In another case involving a complicated probate of an estate, Governor Tomás Vélez Cachupín asked the *abogado de la real audiencia* to review the actions of the co-executors of the estate which were being questioned by the heirs. After reviewing the case the lawyer advised the governor to proceed with equity and moderation instead of applying the full force of the law. Here a lawyer accustomed to the stricter rules of the royal court, in effect waived these requirements for places like New Mexico which, according to the lawyer, "lack all due formalities."[56]

Additional evidence of custom as an important basis for New Mexico legal decisions under Spain and Mexico is the petition on behalf of Isleta Pueblo, objecting to the Ojo de la Cabra grant to Juan Otero. The Pueblo argued in 1845 that "it has been a fully accepted custom . . . with the force of law," for the Pueblo to use the land in question as common pasture, sharing it with other communities. It did not object to the sharing arrangement, but did strongly oppose the privatization of the land. After lengthy litigation that was appealed by Otero to the superior tribunal of justice in Chihuahua, the Ojo de la Cabra grant was annulled. Not only was the customary use of the land upheld, but the *ayuntamiento* was censured for reporting that the land did not belong to anyone, when the grant was first made, and Prefect Francisco Sarracino was suspended "on account of the malice with which he acted."[57]

Civil law uses law codes as the main source of its rules, while Anglo-American common law, on the other hand, looks primarily to the decisions of judges for precedents to govern its jurisprudence. Customary law is found in both systems, but in New Mexico it played a larger role under the Hispanic system. Another important difference between the civil and the common law procedures was the nature of the hearing. Under Anglo-American common law the parties had the right to confront witnesses against them in a trial, usually before a jury, whereas under Spanish and Mexican civil law there were no juries, and most of the proceedings were by written statements presented to the judge. In New Mexico and in California, these differences in procedure, and the perception by foreigners that the administration of justice was corrupt, led to many complaints by foreigners about the Hispanic system.[58]

The problem was due not simply to the differences in legal procedure, but was primarily a conflict between divergent legal and social values of the two cultures. The Anglo common law at this time emphasized individualism displayed in an adversarial struggle between the opposing parties leading to a decisive outcome, with clear winners and losers. In contrast, the Spanish and Mexican system of justice relied heavily on compromise and conciliation as a means of reaching an outcome where each side got something of what they wanted. Under such a system, whether the *alcalde* knew the law was not as important as whether he was considered by the community to be a fair judge. In fact, the *alcalde* was generally a respected member of the community whose decisions were obeyed. Under the Hispanic system of justice, any dispute represented a wound in the community's body politic, and healing that wound was the desired outcome. So the two systems represented a clash between the old society's community values and the new society's individual values.[59] With these sharp differences, it is not surprising that the civil law system and the common law system dealt differently with issues presented to them.

The test of how this conflict would be resolved came when the United States occupied New Mexico in 1846, acquired New Mexico and the rest of the southwest under the Treaty of Guadalupe Hidalgo and the Gadsden Treaty, and adjudicated land grants from 1854 to 1910. As seen elsewhere in this book, the conflict between the Spanish-Mexican and Anglo-American legal systems was an important cause of land loss to Hispanic land grant heirs.

Three
Manuel Martínez's Ditch Dispute:
Mexican-Period Custom and Justice

The year was 1832, the place was Abiquiú, New Mexico, and the subject was water. The month was July, the peak of the growing season and also the rainy season. The Río Chama, which watered the fields of the village, regularly flooded during this time and in so doing it washed out the dam feeding the *acequia* of one of Abiquiú's leading citizens, don Manuel Martínez. When don Manuel attempted to build a new dam and *acequia* on the lands of his neighbor Ramón Martínez, he was forcibly prevented from doing so by Ramón, and a legal battle ensued. The resulting litigation before the *ayuntamiento* or council of Abiquiú and the governor of the province, documented by papers in the Mexican Archives of New Mexico, helps illuminate some dark corners of New Mexico history.[1]

The story of the dispute, as told through the documents, rounds out the character of don Manuel, who is better known as the principal petitioner for the Tierra Amarilla grant. That famous grant was made in the same year, 1832; in fact, it was also in July that don Manuel petitioned Governor Santiago Abreu to make the Tierra Amarilla grant a private rather than a community grant.[2] In the grant papers he urged the governor to overrule the *ayuntamiento*, but in the ditch dispute he tried to get the *ayuntamiento* to overrule the governor, and he said contradictory things to each. His petitions reveal a man determined to use every available legal procedure to obtain what he considered to be justice.

The documents show us the working out of conflict over water through customary legal forms, based more on tradition than legal codes. The path of this tradition is marked by dramas similar to the one here recounted, from fifteenth-century Valencia,[3] to nineteenth-century Taos,[4] to twentieth-century fictional Milagro.[5] The study of Spanish customary law regarding land and water is largely a study of such disputes.

This case study also clarifies the interrelationship between the central government in Santa Fe and the local *ayuntamiento* (town council), during the Mexican Period in New Mexico. The head of the *ayuntamiento* was the *alcalde constitucional*. Prior to the advent of *ayuntamientos*, the *alcalde* exercised all the functions of local government. Although this official combined executive, legislative, and judicial functions, some New Mexico historians like France Scholes have minimized the power of the *alcalde*, and by implication, of the *ayuntamientos* also. Scholes states: "These men were obliged, in the main, to carry out the orders that came to them from Santa Fe. In certain instances, moreover, they were nothing more than tools of the governors."[6] While this may have been generally true for the Spanish period, it appears that by the Mexican period local government, especially in northern New Mexico, had developed strength enough to overrule the governor. Local officials, who were generally in office longer than the governor, became protective of their power, sometimes fighting among themselves over the extent of their respective jurisdictions.[7]

The specifics of don Manuel Martínez's conflict emerge from the documents in fragments. After his dam was destroyed, he went to see the *Alcalde Constitucional* (magistrate judge) of Abiquiú, Pedro Ignacio Gallegos, asking for a new site on which to build his dam. The *alcalde* referred the matter to the *Ayuntamiento* of Abiquiú, which appointed two experts to make an inspection of the dam and of don Manuel's land. The appointment of the experts was in accordance with a custom followed as early as in fifteenth-century Spain, whereby *peritos* (experts) were asked to render an independent report to a judicial body for its consideration in making an important decision.[8] The practice was also followed in Mexican-Period New Mexico.[9] This time the *ayuntamiento* also made its own inspection. After visiting the land, described as "abounding in all seeds and beneficial to the tithe," the inspection party proceeded to the site of the old dam.[10] It had been made of branches and rocks (*rama y piedra*), which had washed into the river making a backwater near the lands of Ramón Martínez. After observing that there was no place downstream from Ramón's land suitable for a dam, the *ayuntamiento* indicated a site for a new dam on Ramón's land, described as a marsh, unplowed and unplanted. They particularly noted "the decision and opinion of the two experts . . . that [it was customary] for *acequias* to pass through the lands of others to irrigate [them]" and that Ramón Martínez would not be harmed by don Manuel's ditch.[11] Ramón Martínez apparently did not agree with this determination, and before don Manuel could begin to build his new dam, Ramón stopped him. Ramón had no liking for don Manuel, as is apparent from statements he made later in this litigation, but what makes this case more than a dispute between neighbors is the repercussions it had in the chambers of the *Ayuntamiento* of Abiquiú and in the governor's palace in Santa Fe.

Don Manuel, was not one to brook opposition easily. Even though he was sick in bed, he fired off the first of many petitions to Governor Abreu on 3 July 1832. This petition was apparently drafted by don Manuel, for it

3.2. *A typical diversion dam and acequia, Pecos River, New Mexico, ca. 1917, neg. no. 5530. Courtesy Museum of New Mexico.*

contains phraseology characteristic of documents signed by him, but it was signed on Martínez's behalf by José María Chávez, a member of the five-man *Ayuntamiento* of Abiquiú. This would seem to be a serious conflict of interest, since the *ayuntamiento* was usually called upon to make an impartial report to the governor regarding the facts claimed by the petitioner and in this instance the *ayuntamiento* essentially determined the outcome of the litigation.[12]

Early in his petition, don Manuel contradicted statements he had made two and a half months earlier in his petition for the Tierra Amarilla land grant. As principal petitioner for that grant, he was not allowed to own a substantial amount of land, so he stated then that his lands were "so worthless, old, and worn out that even the most exquisite care and hard work is not enough to harvest what is necessary." But when he was required to show the importance of his *acequia* in this new litigation, he wrote of his "considerable sown land," which he specified to be five *fanegas* of wheat and two of corn (a little more than 25 acres). In addition he had two or three *fanegas* of land ready for sowing beans. It is apparent that don Manuel had a facility for saying whatever the occasion demanded.[13]

In his first petition, Martínez told Governor Abreu the story related above, adding that before he could complete his dam and *acequia*, his neighbor Ramón destroyed the dam and protested to *Alcalde* Gallegos who then ordered don Manuel to suspend work. Don Manuel ended by asking the governor to order the *ayuntamiento* to allow his work on the dam and *acequia* to continue. The same day, Governor Abreu ordered the *ayuntamiento* to report to him on whether the dam in question would harm Ramón's land and whether there was a more suitable place where the dam might be built without prejudice to Ramón's land.[14]

The next day, the *ayuntamiento* met in the *casa consistorial* and drew up its report, which basically corroborated what don Manuel had said. It was the *ayuntamiento's* considered opinion, as well as that of the experts, that the dam would not harm Ramón's land since it was already a marsh.[15] When Governor Abreu read this report, he ordered *Alcalde* Gallegos to carry out what had been decided by the *ayuntamiento*, and the *alcalde* then ordered that don Manuel could continue work on his dam and *acequia*. It looked like an easy victory for don Manuel, until Ramón's petition of the seventh of July reached the governor, disclosing that he had a few tricks remaining up his sleeve.

Ramón started his petition by flatly denying the finding of the three experts and the *ayuntamiento*. He said that the *acequia* ran through the middle of his field and did in fact harm it. He referred the governor to a decree from an earlier ditch dispute that don Manuel had lost in 1816, which contained some shocking statements about don Manuel. The most damning part of the older document was the accusation that don Manuel had attempted to bribe the judge with two fat cows (*dos bacas gordas*)! This new evidence was enough for Governor Abreu, who voided the *ayuntamiento's* decision of the fourth of July and nullified his decree of the same date, stating that these were rendered without full disclosure of the facts.[16]

Don Manuel must still have been in poor health, for it was nine days before he let fly the first of a battery of petitions, using an arsenal of legal procedures that in the end proved to be too much for his opponent. Although don Manuel's rubric was a bit shaky, the content of these documents show him to have been a skillful litigator. Martínez directed the first of these petitions to *Alcalde* Gallegos asking him to order Ramón to produce the 1816 document and to provide don Manuel with a witnessed copy. He wrote that he intended to prove that Ramón had lied, that he did not attempt to bribe the judge commissioned to decide the earlier lawsuit, and that actually he was never even notified of the action or given the opportunity to be heard.[17] The second part of a two-pronged attack on Ramón's attempted character assassination came in yet another petition to *Alcalde* Gallegos made on the same day, asking him to summon citizen Marcos Delgado before him to answer certain questions (*interrogatorios*) regarding the alleged bribe. Delgado, who listed his occupation as parish choir master, was the one who Ramón claimed had communicated the bribe offer to the judge.[18] The key questions that don Manuel wished Gallegos to ask Delgado were whether or not Martínez had asked Delgado to offer Judge Juan Rafael Ortiz two fat cows if he would decide in don Manuel's favor and, if so, the day, hour, and place that this happened. He mentioned incidentally that Ortiz was a very dear friend of his opponent in that case, Mariano Martín. Mariano was the *alférez* (standard bearer) for the Abiquiú militia and was also Ramón Martín's father.[19] It seems that the Martíns and the Martínezes had been engaged in a long-standing family feud over an *atarque* (dam) and irrigation ditch similar to the one that was the subject of this lawsuit.

July 16 was evidently a day of tremendous activity for don Manuel, for besides these two petitions to *Alcalde* Gallegos he also wrote one to Governor Abreu protesting the earlier report of the *ayuntamiento* in another matter regarding his petition for the Tierra Amarilla grant. This was a long elaborate document making the argument that the Tierra Amarilla grant should be a private grant to don Manuel and his family instead of a community grant as the *ayuntamiento* had recommended.[20] He was not successful in this however, for Tierra Amarilla was declared a community grant by the territorial deputation.[21] Don Manuel must have been sorely disappointed, for much work had gone into that petition, and a large amount of land was at stake.[22]

Don Manuel was not fazed by his output of the sixteenth of July, however, for the next day he prepared another petition to *Alcalde* Gallegos, and presented it to the *alcalde* in person. In an apparent attempt to reopen the 1816 case, he asked the *alcalde* to certify at the foot of the document the procedure used to take don Manuel's ditch from him by *juez comisionado* Juan Rafael Ortiz.[23] Don Manuel seemed to be appealing for *Alcalde* Gallegos, whose "well know integrity" is mentioned, to assert jurisdiction in that case since he had been serving as *alcalde* at that time as well. There is

Valga por el Sello Tercero para los años de 1832 y 33

Sor. Gefe Político.

El C. Manuel Martinez vecino de Abiquiú ante V.S. con el debido respeto me presento y digo: que deseoso de vindicarme como hombre de bien sobre la imputación que se me hace por un papel que se dice hizo Dn Juan Rafael Ortiz como Juez comicionado en el año de 1816. diciendo que yo le habia ofrecido el cohecho de dos Bacas gordas porque desara mi Asequia en donde estaba en aquella fecha é hiciera la justicia á mi favor, cuyo falso testimonio resulta aclarado por el contenido del documento N.º 5.º que reverente acompaño, lo mismo que ejecuto con los numeros 2. 3. y 4 con el fin de manifestar á V.S. segun el literal sentido del N.º 2. q.º el mismo Señor Juez comicionado arriba nombrado puriado mandar fundar una presa en tierras propias de mi hermano Dn Ygnacio Martinez; y que el finado Juan Pedro Durán llevase su Asequia por el medio de mi sementera y por lo mejor de la tierra. Para representar ante V.S. sobre el contenido del papel, que sin mi audiencia y prebia notificacion hizo el referido Juez comicion, me presenté al Sor. Alcalde de mi residencia con la instancia numero 3. constando al calce de ella la negativa del C. Ramon Martin á presentar el espresado documento para que se me diere la copia correspondiente, esperandose mas dho. Martin en comunicional el contenido del oficio numero 4. Todo lo que elevo al superior conocimiento de V.S. para que se siava en su vista decretar lo que creyere de Justicia. Juro no ser de malicia &c. Abiquiú 20. de Julio de 1832.

Manuel Martinez

3.3. Manuel Martínez's petition of 20 July 1831. Courtesy New Mexico State Records Center and Archives.

also a hint of rivalry between the two *alcaldes*, since Ortiz was a prominent Santa Fe citizen and politician, who had been commissioned to judge the 1816 lawsuit within the jurisdiction of *Alcalde* Gallegos.[24]

Though the facts of the 1816 case were extraneous to this one, the document illustrates the role played by local officials in determining what custom was. The questions asked of *Alcalde* Gallegos about custom in the petition and his answers reveal that he was acting as a sort of arbiter of custom. This is particularly apparent in the *alcalde*'s statement that, "the force of custom in this jurisdiction [is such] that all *acequias* that have existed from an early date to the present cross the lands of different owners and no diversion [dam] has been located [solely] on private property."[25] Don Manuel must have realized that the words and prestige of *Alcalde* Gallegos, who also served a term in the territorial deputation,[26] could have a powerful effect in determining the outcome of the contest with Ramón.

Armed with *Alcalde* Gallegos's answers, don Manuel continued his barrage of petitions, addressing one to the full *ayuntamiento* the next day, the eighteenth of July. He attacked the statements made by Ramón concerning the alleged harm accruing to his field from don Manuel's dam and *acequia*. This indeed was the crux of the conflict and don Manuel proved himself to be a master of belittlement when he referred to Ramón's "imaginary field." It was not a field at all, he wrote, for "it is public knowledge that his ranch has gone uncultivated because of irremediable impossibility of having even remote hopes of an *acequia* for farming it."[27] He then reminded their excellencies that they themselves ordered him to build his dam and run his ditch where he did. Don Manuel was clearly playing to the *ayuntamiento*'s sense of honor (as well as his own, which he claimed had been badly injured), and to its sense of jurisdictional power when he stated that under the law of 1813 the *ayuntamiento* was charged with protecting life and property in its jurisdiction.[28]

What don Manuel asked the *ayuntamiento* to do, essentially, was to inform the governor that the statements in Ramón's seventh of July petition were not true. But before they could do so, they had to serve the papers don Manuel had set in motion in his attack of July sixteenth: the interrogatory to Marcos Delgado, and the request to Ramón to produce the 1816 document. Each of these produced some surprises.

On the eighteenth of July, *cantor* Marcos Delgado appeared before Alcalde Gallegos and two witnesses and answered under oath that he knew nothing of the alleged bribe offer he was said to have transmitted to Juan

Rafael Ortiz. He mentioned that after the 1816 lawsuit, don Manuel was compelled to move a dam he had on the lands of Mariano Martínez and (by inference) that it was Judge Ortiz himself who made the allegation about the bribe. Delgado, however, was sure that Ortiz could not prove his charge.[29] Also on the eighteenth of July, Alcalde Gallegos issued a summons directing Ramón to appear and produce the 1816 document.[30] But on the same day Ramón refused to do so, stating that his mother had said that only the governor could make him produce documents,[31] and if don Manuel wanted a copy he could go to the courthouse in Santa Fe and get one![32] The tone of the reply rather clearly demonstrated Ramón's animosity towards don Manuel.

Now that Martínez was cleared of the bribery charge by Delgado's testimony, the *ayuntamiento* had all it needed to make its report to the governor as don Manuel had requested. On the nineteenth of July the *ayuntamiento* met in its official chambers (*sala constitucional*) and considered don Manuel's latest petition regarding the *acequia*. The resulting statement (*manifestación*) had a strongly indignant tone, suggesting to Governor Abreu that he should have asked for another report from the *ayuntamiento* after Ramón's seventh of July petition, "for this step would have resulted in the complete [disclosure of the] deception with which the said Ramón Martín deceived your excellency in everything he stated [to you]."[33] Because the governor relied solely on Ramón's petition regarding a matter already decided by the *ayuntamiento*, that body felt that its honor and decorum had been compromised. The *ayuntamiento* went on to reiterate the key points in the dispute. First, the *ayuntamiento* had already made a determination of where don Manuel's dam should be built, based on the opinion of the three experts. Secondly, the *ayuntamiento* had determined that Ramón's land would not be harmed by the dam and *acequia*. Thirdly, Ramón was told to appear at the time this determination was made to state his motives for preventing don Manuel's *acequia* from crossing his land, and to present any documents he might have relating to the matter. Ramón answered that he had no documents, but simply did not want a ditch of Manuel Martínez's to pass through any part of his land, a very capricious attitude in the opinion of the council. The final and most important point, one that don Manuel completely overlooked because of his outrage at the bribery charge, was that the 1816 document did not "have the slightest connection with the new diversion dam which the *ayuntamiento* of this village, in view of its powers, gave and had power to give," because "by its time, difference in place and circumstance, [it] has not the slightest relation to what the *ayuntamiento* decided."[34] Here again was a strong appeal for the primacy of the decision of the *ayuntamiento*. For all these reasons, Governor Abreu was asked to reverse his decision of the seventh of July, which had been in Ramón's favor.

But before the governor could consider the *ayuntamiento*'s report, don Manuel sent still another petition to Abreu on the twentieth of July, dealing with the bribery charge. Apparently don Manuel felt compelled to bring to the governor's attention the favorable testimony of Marcos Delgado, and the refusal of Ramón to produce the 1816 document, neither of which was mentioned in the *ayuntamiento*'s report. Don Manuel, "desiring to defend himself as an honorable man against the [bribery] charge made against him,"[35] attached copies of each of these documents, and asked the governor to decide the case in view of the new testimony. Governor Abreu answered in the margin of the petition that Martínez should file a complaint in the proper court against the man he claimed had injured his honor.[36] Don Manuel, however, was not satisfied with this answer, so on the twenty-seventh of July, he sent his seventh and final petition in this litigation, again directed to Governor Abreu. This time he simply asked the governor to make a decree in this lawsuit in the space at the bottom of his petition.[37]

Governor Abreu acceded to the Martínez request and on the twenty-eighth of July, in effect terminated the lawsuit in don Manuel's favor by ordering the *ayuntamiento* to "decide [the case] according to what you believe is just and . . . according to the uses and customs which have been observed in that jurisdiction in such cases."[38] Since the *ayuntamiento* had already decided in don Manuel's favor, Martínez had clearly won his victory. Presumably, he could irrigate his fields, protected by the *ayuntamiento*'s decision that *Alcalde* Gallegos stood ready to enforce, and secure in the knowledge that his honor (and that of the *ayuntamiento*) had been vindicated.

The *ayuntamiento*'s forceful petition of the nineteenth of July, which turned the tide in don Manuel's favor, reveals an independence of local government that was just beginning to make itself felt in New Mexico at this time. In contrast, eighteenth century *alcaldes* were appointed by the governor for life, and were accused of being under his control. Instead of disagreeing with the governor, as the *ayuntamiento* did in this litigation, they often simply rubber-stamped the governor's decisions and joined him in illicit enterprises.[39]

Another example of the exercise of local governmental independence is found in the records of the *Ayuntamiento* of Taos. In 1822 Taos was also exhibiting its independence, even to the point of refusing to obey an order from Governor Facundo Melgares. In that year the governor granted the petition of a group of Jicarilla Apaches who wanted to settle at the village of Cieneguilla, near Taos. No report on the petition had been requested from the *Ayuntamiento* of Taos, but when they were summarily ordered to allot land to the Jicarillas, they wrote a strong protest to the governor citing numerous reasons why the village did not want the Indians. The land had already been granted to the Spanish (in 1795 by Governor Fernando Chacón), wrote the Taos council, and this argument was presumably enough to induce Melgares to rescind his order.[40]

The Martínez dispute in Abiquiú and the Taos case show fairly clearly that local government in the north had acquired a substantial amount of autonomy in the Mexican period. Local councils expected to be consulted on matters affecting their jurisdictions, and their procedures had developed to the point where they often appointed special committees to make recommendations to the full *ayuntamiento*.[41] They were a far cry from the one-man local government that existed during much of the Spanish period and were anything but tools of the governor.

Another aspect of local government illuminated by these documents is the administration of justice. No formal legal system was ever established in New Mexico by either the Spanish or Mexican authorities, though one was provided for in 1828. The plan called for a district judge, an attorney general, and other court officials but was never put into effect because of the lack of trained lawyers in New Mexico. Instead, *Licenciado* Antonio Barreiro was sent to New Mexico in 1831 to act as *assessor* or legal adviser to the territorial authorities.[42] Barreiro only stayed three years, but in that time he formed a rather low opinion of the condition of the administration of justice. In 1832 he expressed these views in his famous *Ojeada sobre Nuevo México:* "Whoever has a slight conception of the ignorance which reigns in this country, will not require other colors to paint vividly the deplorable and doleful state in which the administration of justice finds itself."

There was no one in the territory, he believed, capable of preparing legal procedures.[43]

Lic. Barreiro was undoubtedly mistaken in this, given the evidence presented here. There was at least one person, don Manuel Martínez. The variety of legal procedures that he used, including counterparts to pretrial interrogatories and motions to produce documents used today, is surprising, and his skill in arguing his case is impressive.

This litigation also demonstrates how custom was the decisive factor in this case, and how it often took the place of a formal legal system in New Mexico. Custom is the practice followed in a particular place in all things including lawsuits, the "unwritten law that has been introduced by use."[44] Since neither the parties to this dispute, nor the officials deciding it were familiar with the Spanish and Mexican laws concerning the issues at stake here, they determined the dispute by means of custom. With his usual astuteness, don Manuel realized that whoever had custom on his side was likely to win the lawsuit. Thus, in his very first petition, Martínez argued that custom and necessity had established the principle that *acequias* must be able to pass freely over private land. In legal terms, private land was subject to a servitude or easement in favor of the ditch. This rule of law had long been established in Spanish jurisprudence, but significantly, don Manuel refers to custom and necessity as the basis for the rule. Then when the experts give their opinion and *dictamen* (judgement), they not only report on the physical condition of the dam and the *acequia*, they also reiterate the custom of ditch easements. Finally, the *alcalde* expands the principle to apply both to *acequias* and to dams when he describes the "force of custom in this jurisdiction."[45]

One of the reasons for the outrage expressed by the *ayuntamiento* in its July nineteenth report to the governor was that the *ayuntamiento* considered it to be its exclusive task, not only to assess the credibility of the parties and decide the case, but also to determine what the custom was. The governor finally recognized this when he told the *ayuntamiento* to decide the case in accordance with the custom and usage followed in its jurisdiction.

Certainly in Manuel Martínez's time, custom governed the settlement of disputes, and likely also the granting of land, much more than did written law.

Four
The Ciénega of Santa Fe:
A Municipal Commons
Used and Abused

The Ciénega of Santa Fe, like the famous Boston Common, was a tract of land dedicated to public use. Unlike the Boston Common, with its background in Anglo-American law, the Ciénega was grounded in the more complex Spanish legal system of public land ownership. It provides a rare example of how an important and valuable tract of municipal property was managed and mismanaged.[1] The Ciénega's value made it the inevitable target of would-be encroachers in the eighteenth century, and of politicians like Manuel Armijo, in the nineteenth century. These attacks were staved off until the late Mexican Period when the Ciénega was finally wrested from the control of the Santa Fe city council or *ayuntamiento*. This is the story of a paradise lost.

Under Spanish law and custom, public land was owned either by the monarch (*tierras realengas* or *tierras baldías*), or by a town or village (*tierras concegiles*).[2] The *tierras baldías* were available for everyone's use, either in common as grazing land, for example, or by a few individuals who would plant a portion of the *baldías* but whose rights to it depended on continued usage. Royal grants of land to individuals or communities were made from the *baldías*. The *tierras concegiles* of the towns and villages fell into two main categories. One was common property set aside for use by all the heads of families (*vecinos*) in the community. These were the *exidos*, the *montes*, the *dehesas*, and the *prados*, each a different type of common land with a specific purpose.[3]

The other kind of property owned by a community or municipality were the *propios*. These were lands, or other kinds of property, owned by the town or village as private property and usually rented out by the municipal council with the proceeds going toward public works in lieu of taxes. *Propios* were provided for in the great Spanish compilation of laws dealing with the New World, the *Recopilación de leyes de los reynos de las Indias*,[4] and were specifically mentioned in the instruction to Governor Pedro de Peralta from the Viceroy of New Spain regarding the establishment of the Villa of Santa Fe.[5] Similarly, the Plan of Pitic, the founding document of the town of Pitic (now Hermosillo), Sonora, called for eight *suertes* of irrigable land to be set aside as *propios*. The plan specified that a *mayordomo de propios* be appointed to administer the *propios* and make annual accountings of its proceeds. Initially, the *propios* of Pitic were to be plowed and planted by all the settlers, each doing a share of the work. In succeeding years, part of the produce from the *propios* would be used to pay the workers who planted and harvested the *propios*, and the remainder would be used for the public good.[6]

In Northern Mexico disputes over the uses of *propio* funds were not uncommon. For example in Saltillo, a dispute between the *cabildo* and the *alcalde* in 1667 over accounting for these funds became so heated that the *alcalde* froze the funds, began court proceedings against the *cabildo* members, and threatened to put them all in the stocks on public display. A generation later it was the *procurador general* who complained to the governor that the *alcaldes* typically seized the *propios* funds and spent them as they wished, without providing money to celebrate the local feast day or to keep the perpetual light burning before the Holy Sacrament in the parish church — traditional uses of municipal funds. In 1690 the governor gave the *procurador* the right to supervise the *propios* funds, but disputes and recriminations over these funds continued in Saltillo for several years. In Santa Fe, Victoriano Padilla asked the *ayuntamiento* in 1832 to give him the proceeds of the Ciénega to pay his back wages as the *ayuntamiento's portero* (door keeper, sergeant-at-arms). That body refused because they needed the money to buy paper, to rebuild their meeting hall, and to pay their secretary.[7]

The legal difference between *propios* and common property was clear in theory, but in practice the same piece of land could be treated both as *propios* and as common property. This was especially true in Spain, where these customs and practices became fully developed before being transplanted in the Americas. Sometimes a field was common as to the grass, but the acorns and branches of the trees were sold as *propios*. In other cases, property would be common for part of the year but rented out as *propios* the rest of the year. Or property might be used as commons some years and as *propios* in other years. The common lands or *propios* of a municipality could be established at the time of its founding or later through a grant.[8]

The history of the Santa Fe Ciénega provides an example of many of these customary practices regarding the common lands of a community and illustrates how public land ownership, and the disputes that go with it, was transplanted from Spain to New Mexico. The Ciénega was treated as a commons early in its history and later as *propios*. As a municipal commons it was rare for New Mexico but not unique. As *propios*, the Ciénega *was* unique, as no reference to another New Mexico settlement having *propios* has been discovered.

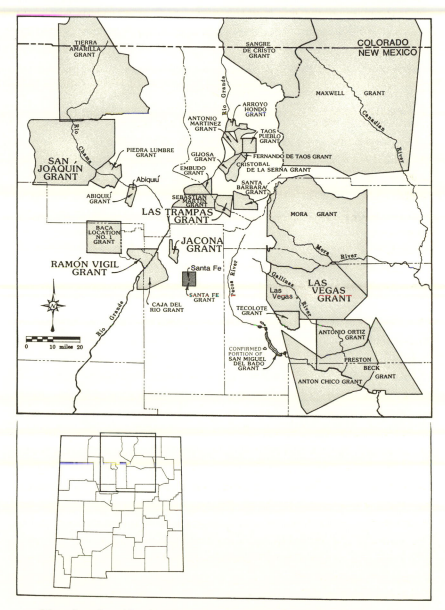

4.2 Map of northern New Mexico land grants with Santa Fe highlighted.

The Ciénega, as its name indicates, was a marshy plot of land east of the Palace of the Governors where grass grew abundantly. Figure 4.3 shows the location of the Ciénega in the early 1700s and the location of the primary *acequias* north of the Santa Fe River.[9]

The earliest use of the Ciénega by the citizens of Santa Fe seems to have been as common lands rather than as *propios*. A decree of Governor Francisco Cuervo y Valdez in 1705 states that it was customary every year to order that no one should drive stock or horses on to the Ciénega so that they "shall not trample or eat the grass that grows there so that anyone who needs it (the grass) can mow it to feed their horses. . . ."[10] Governor Cuervo ordered that anyone, of whatever rank or condition, who violated this order was subject to a sentence of a month in jail for the first offense and for the second, two months of duty guarding the horseherd of the presidio garrison. A similar order issued by Lieutenant Governor Juan Páez Hurtado in 1717 also referred to the annual custom of rounding up loose animals:

> At this time every year a *bando* is promulgated ordering that all the pigs running loose in this Villa of Santa Fe be rounded up, so that no damage is done either to the planted fields, or to the Ciénega of this said Villa, also that the same be done for the horses, cattle, sheep, and other animals, so that these (animals) will not trample or eat their (the Villa's) grass, in order that it may be mowed to feed to the horses of the presidial troops who escort those (residents) who go to the mountains to gather firewood and timber, so that the aforesaid (proclamation) will . . . redound to the common benefit of the residents of this said villa. . . .[11]

By this time the punishment for violation of the decree had been changed to a fine of two pesos for the first offense, and four pesos for the second. The proceeds of these fines were to be applied to "the construction of the holy church" of the villa.[12] This decree was to be proclaimed "at the sound of military instruments in the customary places and posted on the gates of the royal garrison."[13]

This document tells us that the Villa of Santa Fe followed the ancient Spanish custom of stubble grazing, a custom adopted by communities throughout New Mexico. According to this custom, every owner of harvest land had to open his fields to the livestock of the town from after harvest until spring planting. Then the animals were rounded up and kept away from these fields during the growing season.[14] As far as the Ciénega was concerned, however, this round-up was not entirely effective.

In addition to protecting the Ciénega from the incursions of hungry animals seeking its lush grass, the governor took the responsibility of protecting it against the encroachment of powerful individuals who coveted its water more than its grass. One such figure was Diego Arias de Quiros of Santa Fe. Born in Asturias province in Spain, he had been recruited there by Diego de Vargas as a soldier in the Reconquest. In New Mexico he served in the military campaigns of his day and in 1694 was the *real alférez* in Santa Fe.[15] By 1715 he was *alcalde* of Santa Fe and owned a substantial amount of property there, including a tract that ran from the Palace of the Governors east to the Ciénega. He had received this land from Vargas in 1693 as a reward for his military services.[16]

Arias de Quiros had built a pond (*tanque*) on the Ciénega to collect water from one of the springs that kept the area wet and green. Even then, the Santa Fe River was low, especially in August. Thus, there was little water in the *acequias*, and the mayordomo had previously denied Arias de Quiros the use of even that scant flow. So Arias de Quiros used the water stored in his pond to irrigate his fields and orchard. On 23 July 1715 the *Cabildo* of Santa Fe (the municipal council) issued a decree ordering him to remove his pond. The same day Arias dispatched a petition to Governor Juan Ignacio Flores Mogollón explaining the apparent reason for the *cabildo's* action and giving his side of the dispute.[17]

In this petition Arias de Quiros said that the Santa Fe *cabildo* was claiming the Ciénega as its own, but he disputed the *cabildo's* claim. He said that when he built his pond the Ciénega was unappropriated royal lands (*realengas*) and Arias de Quiros claimed both the pond and the part of the Ciénega that he had been using. He asked Governor Flores Mogollón to determine who owned what.[18]

Flores Mogollón answered this petition by ordering the *Cabildo* of Santa Fe to produce any documents it might have showing ownership of the Ciénega. The governor also scolded the *cabildo* for not applying first to him about the offending pond so that he could fashion a remedy.[19] The *cabildo* answered by admitting that the Ciénega had not been granted to the Villa of Santa Fe and that these lands were in fact *realengas* or unappropriated royal lands. It explained its action against Arias de Quiros by saying that the Ciénega was used in common by the residents of Santa Fe for cutting hay for their horses during the summer. If Arias de Quiros used some of the Ciénega's water for himself, it argued, that would mean less water to irrigate the Ciénega as a whole and would constitute an appropriation of part of this common property by one person. The *cabildo* asked the governor to grant the Ciénega to the villa as its *propios*.[20]

The governor responded favorably to this request, making the grant "for *propios* of the villa, so that the community may enjoy the benefit [it has enjoyed] to the present time."[21] Then, Governor Flores Mogollón appointed five men to examine and measure the Arias pond and determine if it diminished the water in the Ciénega as a whole, if it damaged the pond behind the convent by draining it, or if it decreased the amount of water in an *acequia* that had its source in the Ciénega. The five appointed were Lorenzo and Roque Madrid, Miguel Moran, master mason Juan Lorenzo de Medina, and master carpenter Diego de Velasco, all to be assisted by the governor's secretary of government and war, Roque de Pinto.[22] Diego de Velasco was the only master carpenter in New Mexico at the time and had been ordered to remain in Santa Fe and perform various public services for four years as a punishment for his murder of Miguel de Herrera in 1712. This appointment was undoubtedly one of those public services.[23]

After this group had made its investigation the governor asked the crucial question: would the Arias de Quiros pond, if allowed to remain, cause the Ciénega to dry up, either in part or totally? The commissioners answered that the pond would in fact damage the Ciénega, especially the portion towards the Arias de Quiros house. They found this area dry and estimated that it represented about one-third of the Ciénega.[24]

With this report, Governor Flores Mogollón had the information he needed to make a decision. By appointing experts to make a report, the governor was following a custom in water rights cases going back at least to fifteenth-century Spain[25] and followed in Abiquiú in 1832 where experts were appointed in Manuel Martínez's ditch dispute.[26] As to the governor's decision, he may have been influenced by his alleged close friendship with Arias de Quiros, for the governor granted to him the portion of the Ciénega that he was using (the pond), on the condition that he not exceed that amount of land in his future usage — if he did, he would lose the grant. Governor Flores Mogollón also granted Arias de Quiros the spring that filled his pond, after ordering him to reduce the size of the pond to no more than six varas on each side and to close the *acequias* he had opened on the upper part of the Ciénega. The grant of the spring was also subject to a

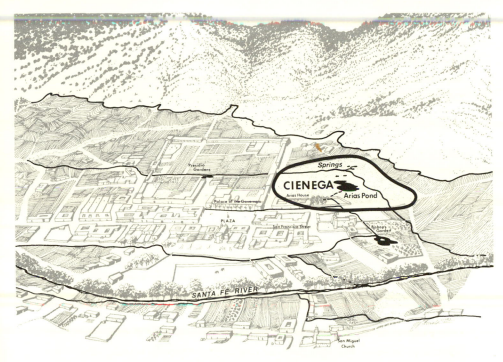

4.3. Birdseye view of Santa Fe, showing the Ciénega's approximate location in the early 1700s. Drawing by Carrie Arnold

condition: if after a year the use of the spring by Arias de Quiros damaged the Ciénega by causing the grass to dry up, the pond would have to be filled in and the grant of the spring would be void.[27]

This type of conditional grant was unusual but not unknown in New Mexico. To be sure, all grants were subject to the conditions that they be continuously occupied, that they not be abandoned without permission from governmental authorities,[28] and that private parcels not be sold within a minimum period (usually four years).[29] Beyond these standard conditions, several grants on the frontier contained the condition that the settlers have firearms within two years of the making of the grant or be subject to expulsion from the land.[30] Then there were grants where the condition was imposed by the grantee himself, as with the Ocaté grant where Manuel Alvarez asked for land in present-day Mora County that he intended to use as pasture for a herd of merino sheep to be brought to New Mexico. Alvarez agreed that if he failed to settle the grant and did not commence raising merino sheep within three years of the making of the grant he would forfeit any rights to the grant. As it turned out he did forfeit his rights.[31] The condition imposed on Arias de Quirós resembles a provision in the *Recopilación* that provided that grants of lands to Spaniards near Indian lands would revert to their rightful owners (the Indians) if they turned out to be encroachments on Indian lands.[32]

Governor Flores Mogollón displayed some creativity by imposing conditions that seemingly satisfied the concerns of both sides. The governor reaffirmed his earlier grant by declaring that the Ciénega (except for the Arias de Quiros pond) belonged to the villa for the cutting of hay. Then he ordered Diego Velasco and Roque de Pinto to go to the Ciénega and measure the Arias pond. Finding that it measured more than the six varas square, Arias de Quiros was ordered to fill the pond to this maximum size.[33]

But on 3 August 1715 an undaunted Arias de Quiros again petitioned his friend the governor stating that because of his poverty he was unable to hire laborers to do the work of filling the pond. His statement must be taken with a grain of salt, however, because Arias de Quiros was anything but poor. Later in the petition he stated his real reason for balking at the governor's order: "because with the six square varas it is not possible to irrigate my garden."[34] He then asked the governor for a grant of the pond as it then existed; six and a half to seven varas wide, sixteen varas long, and one and one-third varas deep. The grant was to be on the same condition as before: if the pond caused the Ciénega to dry up at all within a year, the pond would have to be filled in.[35]

Governor Flores Mogollón gave in to this plea and made a grant to Arias de Quiros of the pond as it then existed on the condition agreed to and on the further condition that the pond not be enlarged in the future. To insure compliance with these conditions, the governor again sent Diego Velasco and Roque de Pinto to the measure the pond. These two individuals found the measurements to be essentially the same as those reported by Arias de Quirós, but significantly, they found that the ditches running into the pond, which were supposed to have been destroyed, were still in operation.[36]

This failure of Arias de Quiros to abide by governor Flores Mogollón's order was a portent of things to come. Approximately one year later the *cabildo* members directed a petition to the new governor, Félix Martínez. They said that the Ciénega was in fact drying up as a result of the Arias de Quiros pond and asked that experts again be appointed to go to the Ciénega and determine for themselves if this was so. If found to be true, they asked that Arias de Quiros be ordered to fill in his pond.[37]

On 16 June 1716, Martínez appointed Diego Velasco, the expert carpenter, Juan Lorenzo de Medina, Andrés Gonzales, and Miguel Durán, all masons and experts in measuring water, to determine whether the Arias pond was causing the Ciénega to dry up in whole or in part.[38] These experts

4.4. Town of Ecija in Andalusia, known for its woolen cloths and flannels, alluded to by the municipal sheep pen in the foreground. John Goss, Braun and Hogenberg's The City Maps of Europe: A Selection of Sixteenth Century Town Plans and Views (London: Studio Editions, Ltd., 1991).

reported back to the governor on the same day. They declared that the Arias de Quiros pond was damaging the Ciénega generally, for not only was the grass around the pond dry, the grass in most of the Ciénega had "little or no vigor."[39] One of the experts estimated that one-third of the Ciénega was damaged and the damage would increase the longer the pond was allowed to remain.[40]

Governor Martínez also ordered his secretary of government and war to take the declaration of Lorenzo Madrid on the question of whether there had been irrigation ponds on the Ciénega in former times. Madrid responded that he was eighty-two years old, and that as long as he could remember there were no ponds on the Ciénega. He did recall a case during the administration of Governor Ugarte y la Concha (1649;n;1653) when one Diego Moraga had begun to make a pond around a spring near his house, but was fined twelve pesos by the governor and was ordered to fill it in. Madrid summed up the situation by saying that before the current ponds were dug, the water from the springs spread out over the entire Ciénega and kept it green.[41]

Now Arias de Quiros had finally come to the end of the line. He clearly had broken the condition on which he had received the grant of the spring and the pond. So Governor Martínez ordered him to fill in the pond and declared his grant to be void (*de ningún valor*).[42] In so doing, Governor Martínez was acting in accordance with a long tradition going back to Spain by which the municipal property of a community was protected from usurpation.[43]

 Later government officials did not act as prudently toward the Ciénega as had governors Flores Mogollón and Martínez. By the Mexican Period, the Ciénega was clearly being used as *propios*: rented to one person with the proceeds presumably used for the common good of the residents of Santa Fe. Its value as a municipal asset became evident by at least the 1830s when it was leased for an average rent of 150 pesos a year.[44] This municipal income was especially important because other sources of revenue were meager or non-existent — the treasury of the villa was consistently empty.[45] About the only other sources of funds for Santa Fe were fines collected by local officials[46] and fees for licenses,[47] so an asset like the Ciénega, which yielded a steady income, was not something to be taken for granted.

It is not clear when the renting of the Ciénega as municipal *propios* began. It was leased out by 1833, for in May of that year, the Santa Fe *ayuntamiento* criticized Antonio Ortiz, a member of that body, for failing to give a report of the funds from the Ciénega. It was rented even earlier, for in 1826 the treasury records for the territory of New Mexico show receipts from the Ciénega, and at their meeting of 28 April 1832, the *ayuntamiento* of Santa Fe noted the application of Victoriano Padilla to lease the Ciénega.[48]

The practice of renting the Ciénega is documented in 1837 in litigation by the American trapper and merchant, John Langham,[49] against the Santa Fe *ayuntamiento*, the successor to the *cabildo*. Langham filed a petition before Governor Albino Pérez on 3 May 1837 complaining that he had leased the Ciénega for 127 pesos for the spring and summer of that year, on the express condition that it be fenced by the *ayuntamiento*. When this condition was not met, he requested the senior *alcalde* of Santa Fe to have the Ciénega fenced according to the agreement. When this was not done,

Langham was forced to fence the south and east sides of the Ciénega himself. He also hired a guard for the north side, while continuing daily to ask the *alcalde* to have the north side fenced. Langham petitioned Governor Pérez to order the senior *alcalde* to immediately fence the Ciénega or return his 127 pesos, plus the salary of the guard who had been on duty for over two weeks.[50]

Governor Pérez responded by ordering the *alcalde* to carry out the agreement to fence the Ciénega, if such an agreement was made, within forty-eight hours, or suffer a fine of fifty pesos.[51] The *alcalde* Juan García, denied any part in the agreement, but agreed to carry out the governor's order. But he did so by passing the buck. *Alcalde* García ordered Manuel Gallegos, (soon to be Padre Gallegos) an adjoining property owner, to complete the fencing within eight days or pay the fifty peso fine and any damages suffered by Langham. The fine would be used to complete the fencing.[52]

When informed of the *ayuntamiento*'s action, Langham was not happy. He sent another petition to Governor Pérez pointing out how *Alcalde* García was attempting to avoid personal responsibility in the matter and asking that damages of one-fifth of the 127 pesos he had paid be assessed against the *ayuntamiento* and paid to him. In justification of his claim, Langham said that he benefitted from his lease of the Ciénega primarily by subleasing it to others for grazing during the five months from mid-April to mid-September. Since he was unable to accept any cattle during the first month of this period for fear of their going astray, he demanded the return of the one-fifth of the rent he had paid.[53]

Governor Pérez again acceded to John Langham's request and ordered the *ayuntamiento* to pay Langham his damages.[54] The final word from the Santa Fe *ayuntamiento* in this litigation was a contumacious response to the governor's order. Instead of paying Langham damages, they returned all the papers of the lawsuit to him saying that he should be satisfied that Gallegos's representatives were about to finish the fence.[55]

Langham again appealed to Governor Pérez for an order directing that he be paid his damages, and again the governor complied, warning the *ayuntamiento* not to evade this order. To do so, he said, would subject the honor of the *ayuntamiento* to ridicule. Whether the *ayuntamiento* continued to defy the governor, is not known. The *alcalde* responsible for the *ayuntamiento*'s intransigent position had retired "on account of his infirmities." Perhaps his replacement, Felipe Sena, was more compliant, but the records are silent. If, however, the *ayuntamiento*'s defiance was due to a lack of funds, then its stance probably remained the same.[56]

This recalcitrance on the part of the Santa Fe *ayuntamiento* was similar to the behavior of the Abiquiú *ayuntamiento* in 1832 when it exhibited remarkable independence by telling Governor Santiago Abreu that he should reverse the order he had made in Manuel Martínez's ditch dispute and conform to a previous decision of the *ayuntamiento*.[57] To be sure, there was an important difference between the *ayuntamientos* at some distance from the capital and the Santa Fe *ayuntamiento*. The governor often served as both president of the *diputación* and president of the Santa Fe *ayuntamiento*.[58] Depending on the personalities of the members of these two bodies, the *ayuntamiento* of Santa Fe was either a docile partner in whatever plan the governor and the *diputación* had in mind, or they were a strongly independent body ready and willing to direct harsh words at the governor and the *diputación*. The final chapter in the history of the Ciénega shows the Santa Fe *ayuntamiento* in both guises.

Between 1826 and 1838, events took place in relation to the Ciénega that culminated in the mortgage of the Ciénega in 1838 and its ultimate loss to the Villa of Santa Fe.[59] To understand these events, we must examine the political and economic relationship between the Santa Fe *ayuntamiento* and the New Mexico territorial deputation.

As the property of the Villa of Santa Fe, the Ciénega and its income should have been the villa's exclusively and should have been beyond the reach of the territorial government. But the territorial treasury was often as empty as were the coffers of the Santa Fe *ayuntamiento*.[60] So territorial officials were continually looking for funds to pay governmental expenses.[61] Any asset of the *ayuntamiento* was a natural object of this quest. The control exercised by the governor and the *diputación* over the affairs of the *ayuntamiento* made it possible for them to eventually pry the Ciénega from the villa's grasp. The *diputación* sometimes paid the salaries of the members of the *ayuntamiento*,[62] and it enacted municipal regulations that determined how much the *ayuntamiento* could collect as license fees and fines.[63] The Santa Fe *ayuntamiento* even participated with Governor Pérez in 1837 in drafting the tax laws that were a prime cause of the uprising that cost Pérez his life. One of these laws imposed a tax of one peso on all wagons and carts entering Santa Fe, which was payable to the municipality.[64] The interconnection between the municipal and territorial (departmental in 1837) economic systems, together with the dire need for funds to run the government of New Mexico, must have caused both the governor and the members of the *diputación* to cast longing glances at the Ciénega as a potential source of those funds.

The first recorded attack on the Ciénega by a government official occurred when Governor Antonio Narbona and the *diputación* questioned whether the Ciénega was a municipal asset or an asset of the territory of New Mexico. In 1826 Narbona notified Agustín Durán, who was responsible for the finances of the territory, that the Ciénega had been declared to be municipal property.[65] Then in 1828 a letter was written to officials in Chihuahua to determine if the Mexican government had any claim on the Ciénega. The officials responded unequivocally that the Ciénega was owned by the Santa Fe municipality, not by the Mexican nation.[66]

After these Mexican officials had disclaimed any interest in the Ciénega, Governor Manuel Armijo and other officials of the department of New Mexico took an extreme step in 1838. To raise badly needed funds, they used the Ciénega as security for a loan from José Chavez to finance the return of the Vera Cruz Squadron to Mexico. This was clearly a departmental rather than a municipal purpose. It is unclear what pressure was brought to bear on the *ayuntamiento* to get them to agree to this arrangement, but later *ayuntamientos* were to complain that the 1838 *ayuntamiento* should have resisted Governor Armijo and the *asamblea* (the successor to the *diputación*). It seems likely that Armijo simply wielded his considerable power to get his way. At the 1838 meeting of the *junta departamental*, (also called the *asamblea*) when the fateful decision to mortgage the Ciénega was made, Armijo agreed to be personally responsible for the loan.[67] Governor Armijo was anxious to find a way to pay for the return of the Vera Cruz Squadron because they had first come to New Mexico in early January 1837 at his request to help put down the 1837 Rebellion. After the Battle of Pojoaque on 27 January the squadron was no longer needed, but neither the Villa of Santa Fe nor the department of New Mexico had the money to finance the return of these troops to Zacatecas. The Chavez loan solved this problem. At the time, the mortgaging of the Ciénega must have seemed like a small risk to take in view of Governor Armijo's promise to pay José Chavez if the Villa was not able to.

Unfortunately however, by 1844 the Ciénega had been lost to the Villa of Santa Fe. The mortgage of the Ciénega to José Chavez had by then been foreclosed, since the *asamblea* did not have sufficient funds to pay the Chavez loan, and Manuel Armijo had not paid the loan as agreed. In 1844 the Santa Fe *ayuntamiento* directed a petition to the *junta departamental* asking that the Ciénega be restored to the *ayuntamiento* and that the *junta* be required to pay José Chavez the amount he had loaned. The *ayuntamiento* bewailed the fact that "something so secure should pass to other ownership."[68] It also mourned the failure of the *ayuntamiento* in 1838 to resist the *junta departamental*, for if it had "it would have stopped an outrage and an uproar."[69] The response of the *asamblea* was predictable. They sympathized with the plight of the *ayuntamiento* but could offer no help "due to the present lack of funds with which to cover the amount for which it (the Ciénega) was conveyed."[70]

So matters stood. The documents do not tell us whether Santa Fe ever got the Ciénega back, but it is unlikely, since the financial condition of the Department of New Mexico was consistently bleak during this period.[71] In 1844 charges were lodged against Armijo in Mexico City for his part in the loss of the Ciénega. And in that same year the *ayuntamiento* of Santa Fe filed one last petition for the recovery of the Ciénega — this time with the president of Mexico.[72]

Manuel Armijo's role in the loss of the Ciénega adds more fuel to the fire of controversy over the governor's place in New Mexico history. Armijo made almost ten million acres of land grants, which were illegal under Mexican law because they exceeded the maximum amount of land authorized to be granted to one or two individuals. In at least one case, Governor Armijo himself received an interest in a grant that he made. This was also clearly illegal, yet some historians have argued that Armijo should not be judged too harshly. The evidence of his leading part in the Ciénega affair will not weigh favorably in the balance of Armijo's reputation, for he did not keep his promise to pay the Chavez loan, and he started the process leading to the loss of the Ciénega.[73]

Aside from the light shed on Governor Armijo and on the interrelationship between the *ayuntamiento* and the *asamblea/junta departamental/diputación*, this legal history of the Santa Fe Ciénega reveals several aspects of the law and custom regarding municipal lands. Early on, the Ciénega was seen as owned by the villa and was protected and administered by the Santa Fe *cabildo*. But as was often true in Spain and New Mexico, there was no clear definition in practice of who the beneficiaries were of the Ciénega as a resource. Initially it was common to all the residents of Santa Fe, then later its grass was used for a common purpose (to feed the horses of the members of the Santa Fe garrison who protected citizens gathering wood in the mountains), and finally it was treated as *propios*, owned by the villa as private property to be rented out with the rent applied to municipal expenses. Nor was the Ciénega's legal classification kept straight in the documents. A 1713 document refers to it as the *exido* of the villa of Santa Fe. The Arias de Quiros documents refer to the Ciénega as the *propios* of the villa, although it is clear from the grant by Governor Flores Mogollón that it was to be used as common lands by all the residents of Santa Fe.[74] Then in the Mexican period it was used as *propios*, abused when it was mortgaged, and then foreclosed upon and lost.

Historian David Vassberg says that: ". . . the *propios*, unlike common lands, were not inalienable goods as such. They were considered to be at the free disposition of their owners . . . but in practice municipalities did not sell their *propios* except under extraordinary circumstances."[75]

The story of the Ciénega of Santa Fe, whose only remaining vestiges are the block-long Ciénega street and many shovels-full of black muck found in recent archaeological excavations,[76] reveals a glimpse of such extraordinary circumstances.

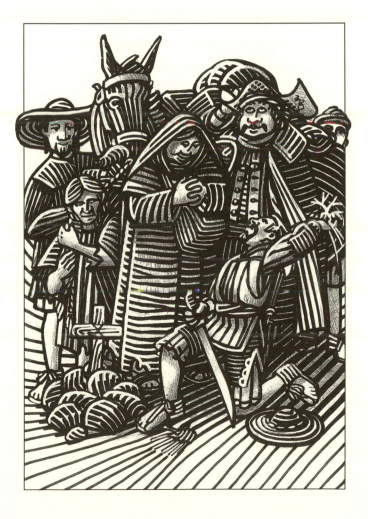

Five
The San Joaquin Grant:
Who Owned the Common Lands?

No question has so perplexed both historians and lawyers as the one addressed in this chapter: under Spanish and Mexican law who owned the common lands of a community land grant? In 1897 the United States Supreme Court decided a landmark case involving the San Joaquín land grant in Rio Arriba County and determined that the Spanish government owned these lands.[1] The Supreme Court's decision was based on scanty Spanish legal authorities and did not take into account either the long history of the Castilian land-owning pueblo or Mexican Period New Mexico cases concerning common land ownership. This and other legal and historical authority not brought to the Supreme Court's attention, indicate that the New Mexico community land grant itself owned its common lands.

The New Mexico community land grant was a direct descendant of the Spanish pueblo, which in turn can be traced back to Roman times. The word *pueblo* as used in Spain (and to some extent New Mexico) has multiple meanings. In New Mexico its primary usage was in reference to the villages of sedentary Indians. In Spain, however, the word refers both to a place (a village together with its outlying lands) and to the people who live at that place. Thus it has both geographical and human connotations. A man born in a pueblo is referred to as a "son of the pueblo" (*hijo del pueblo*.)[2]

As Spain regained control of her land from the Moors during the Reconquest, the pueblos achieved a strategic importance that made it possible for them to gain control of areas surrounding the pueblo by grant from the king.[3] These lands of the Spanish pueblo were divided into several classes according to their use. The *monte* (Latin *montis*, mountain) was used primarily for gathering wood and acorns since it was low quality pasture land covered with trees and brush. The *prado* (pratum, meadow) was high quality pasture, often irrigated. The *dehesa*, (*defensa*, enclosed) was fenced pasture land. The *ejido* (*exitus*, exit) was a multipurpose piece of land just outside the pueblo (at its exit), which was used as a threshing floor, a garbage dump, or for keeping stray animals. These lands of the pueblo were called *tierras concegiles* (lands of the council) and were usually used in common.[4]

The *tierras concegiles* provided the means for maintaining a self-sufficient community; these lands were the life blood of its economic and social life. When the Americas were colonized, the institution of common lands was transplanted in New Spain.[5] In New Mexico these lands were often simply called ejidos[6] or — as in the case of the San Joaquín grant — *pastos* (pastures) and *abrevaderos* (watering places).[7] Other New Mexican land grant documents refer to *montes* and *aguas* as additional names for common lands, in accordance with the resources obtained there.[8]

Besides the right to use the common lands, the settlers on a community land grant in New Mexico received allotments of land for a house lot and an irrigable garden plot. These were treated as private property and could be sold after the four-year possession requirement was satisfied.[9] The San Joaquín grant followed this pattern of a New Mexico community land grant.

In recent history the San Joaquín grant has had more than its share of controversies and contradictions. When land grant activist Reies López Tijerina occupied Echo Amphitheater near Ghost Ranch in October 1966, his stated purpose was to force the U.S. government to prove in court its ownership of the land which was once part of the San Joaquín land grant.[10] Then retired State Historian Dr. Myra Ellen Jenkins was quoted in February 1979 as saying that no genuine title papers existed for the San Joaquín grant and that the copies of these records were very suspect.[11] But in March 1979 Dr. Jenkins discovered the title papers for the San Joaquín grant misfiled in another land grant file.[12] Finally, in July 1979 heirs of the original settlers of the grant set up a roadblock to stop logging trucks from hauling timber from what is now the Santa Fe National Forest and was once the common lands of the grant.[13] As a result of that action, a bill to establish a commission to study the San Joaquín grant and recommend solutions to the many problems that had arisen throughout the grant's history was introduced in Congress by Congressman Manuel Lujan.[14] The bill died in committee.

Even the name of the grant has been open to question. The name San Joaquín is used here because the people living in the villages on the grant have always referred to it by this name. But in the official records of the United States Court of Private Land Claims the grant is called the Cañon de Chama grant. Ironically, this name presaged the fate of the grant, which was held by that court in 1894 to include only allotted lands in the Chama River canyon, surveyed in 1901 as containing a mere 1,422 acres. (The entire community grant, including the common lands, embraced almost half a million acres.)[15]

The confusion as to the name of the grant starts with the original grant documents. When Francisco Salazar petitioned for the grant in 1806 —

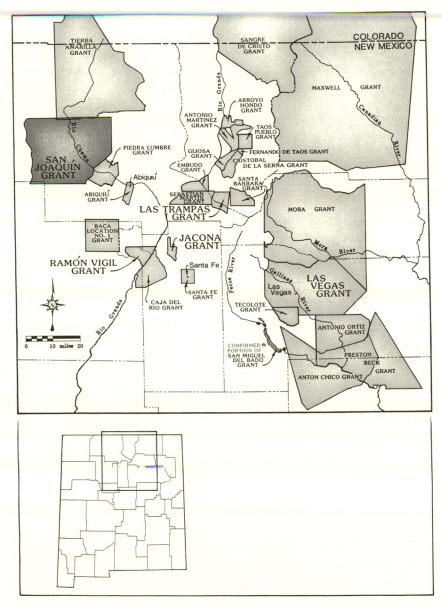

The following labels appear on the map:

TIERRA AMARILLA GRANT

SANGRE DE CRISTO GRANT

COLORADO
NEW MEXICO

MAXWELL GRANT

Rio Grande

ARROYO HONDO GRANT

ANTONIO MARTINEZ GRANT

TAOS PUEBLO GRANT

Canadian River

Rio Chama

PIEDRA LUMBRE GRANT

GIJOSA GRANT

FERNANDO DE TAOS GRANT

CRISTOBAL DE LA SERNA GRANT

SAN JOAQUÍN GRANT

EMBUDO GRANT

Abiquiú

SANTA BARBARA GRANT

ABIQUIÚ GRANT

SEBASTIAN MARTIN GRANT

LAS TRAMPAS GRANT

MORA GRANT

BACA LOCATION NO. 1 GRANT

JACONA GRANT

Mora River

RAMÓN VIGIL GRANT

Santa Fe

Pecos River

Gallinas

LAS VEGAS GRANT

Las Vegas

River

CAJA DEL RIO GRANT

SANTA FE GRANT

Rio Grande

TECOLOTE GRANT

ANTONIO ORTIZ GRANT

N

0   10 miles 20

CONFIRMED PORTION OF SAN MIGUEL DEL BADO GRANT

PRESTON

BECK GRANT

ANTON CHICO GRANT

5.2. Map of northern New Mexico land grants with the San Joaquín grant highlighted.

along with thirty other prospective settlers—he referred to it as "el Cañon del Rio de Chama." *Alcalde* Manuel García de la Mora also used this name in his report to the governor on the propriety of making the grant. But when Governor Joaquín Real Alencaster made the grant, he provided that the first settlement on the grant be called San Joaquín del Rio de Chama, presumably in honor of his name saint. This name stuck, for in 1808 when Alcalde García de la Mora made his report on the ceremony in which he delivered possession of the land to the grantees (whose number had now increased to thirty-nine), he stated: "I proceeded to the Chama River canyon, called San Joaquín."[16]

In response to Salazar's petition, Governor Alencaster ordered *Alcalde* García de la Mora to investigate the extent of the land requested and whether a grant to Salazar and the other petitioners would prejudice the grazing rights of neighboring communities. The *alcalde's* reply did not say precisely how much land was being requested, but did indicate that two leagues of irrigable land surrounding the proposed settlement was available as farm land, and that the rest of the land within the proposed grant was available for pastures, which were abundant. Governor Alencaster's granting decree made it clear that this was to be a community grant with individual private allotments and common lands used jointly by the settlers for grazing and watering their animals and for gathering wood, herbs, and other resources of the land. The granting decree provided that each settler receive a plot of land "capable of being planted with the equivalent of three *cuartillas*[17] of wheat [approximately one-tenth acre] . . . one and a quarter *almudes*[18] of corn [about one acre], and another three of beans [approximately two and one quarter acres], and having erected on them a small house with a garden." The remaining lands were designated as common lands. Alférez Salazar[19] received a double allotment of land as *poblador principal*[20] and was appointed justice for the community.

Although Governor Alencaster was fairly specific in his designation of the size of the private tracts of farm land, he was not as precise when describing the land to be encompassed within the San Joaquín grant. Alencaster left it up to *Alcalde* García de la Mora to place the settlers in possession of the tract of land that he had reported on. The boundaries that García de la Mora designated to enclose the pastures and watering places were: the Cebolla River on the north, the Capulin [mountain] on the south, the boundary of the Martínezes on the east, and the *cejita blanca* (little white ridge) on the west.[21] The boundary of the Martínezes referred to the Piedra

5.3. *Copy of the 1806 grant by Governor Joaquín Alencaster of the land known as the San Joaquín grant. Courtesy New Mexico State Records Center and Archives.*

Lumbre grant, a private grant made to Pedro Martín Serrano in 1766,[22] and the boundaries on the north and south were clearly defined natural landmarks, but the western boundary call was not as clear and was destined to cause a great deal of controversy after the United States occupation of New Mexico.

There was never a serious question as to the validity of the San Joaquín grant nor as to its nature as a community grant. The main question that U.S. officials asked in connection with its adjudication was about its size. In 1861, when approximately four hundred of the grantees and their heirs petitioned the surveyor general of New Mexico for confirmation of the grant, it was estimated at over 184,000 acres.[23] But when surveyed in 1878, it turned out to contain almost 473,000 acres.[24]

Surveyor General George Washington Julian[25] rendered the first report recommending rejection of the common lands of the San Joaquín grant in 1886.[26] Before that, the grant had been recommended for confirmation twice, once by Surveyor General James K. Proudfit in 1872, before the grant had been surveyed,[27] and again in 1880 after the official survey showed how much land was encompassed within the boundaries.[28]

The latter recommendation for approval was unusual, for prior to the establishment of the Court of Private Land Claims, the government official authorized to investigate the validity of land grants was the surveyor general. Thereafter, Congress either confirmed, rejected, or failed to act regarding the surveyor general's recommendation. But in the case of the San Joaquín grant the House Committee on Private Land Claims requested more information from the secretary of the interior concerning the grant.[29] Commissioner J. A. Williamson replied in a letter dated 20 May 1880 in which he recommended that the grant be confirmed in its entirety.[30]

The first inkling of the government's position opposing the confirmation of the San Joaquín common lands is found in Julian's supplemental report of 1886. Until Julian arbitrarily reversed the presumptions that had favored land grant claimants,[31] a community land grant, including its common lands, was presumed to be valid if there was a town or community within the grant as of 1846.[32] In his report on the San Joaquín grant, Julian did not provide any theory to support his opinion regarding the ownership of the common lands, but merely stated that the boundaries called for in the act of possession were too indefinite.[33] Since these boundary calls were no different than those found in every other New Mexico land grant[34] Julian needed a more substantial basis to justify the rejection of millions of acres of common lands in New Mexico's community land grants.[35]

In 1887 Surveyor General Julian set about establishing his theory that the Spanish government retained title to the common lands. He sent investigators to Las Vegas in San Miguel County to search for evidence in the deed books to support his view in connection with the Las Vegas grant.[36] Although funds for this investigation ran out before Julian's theory could be documented, Matthew Reynolds, the United States attorney for the Court of Private Land Claims, picked up the thread when he prosecuted the government's case against the San Joaquín grant before the United States Supreme Court.

The U.S. government did not assert Julian's theory that title to the common lands was retained by the government of Spain until after the Court of Private Land Claims had limited its confirmation of the San Joaquín grant to the allotted lands in the Chama River Canyon. Until the appeal to the Supreme Court, the government's attack on the grant was limited to contesting the location of the boundaries. The Land Court's rejection of the common lands was not supported by any legal theory — the issue was not even raised or argued before the Court of Private Land Claims.

Even before Julian submitted his report of 1886, a protest against the 1878 survey was filed in his office by a group that claimed that the survey of the grant had improperly included their lands. Apparently the seventeen individuals who signed the protest knew that the grant had been sold out from under them.[37] The United States government was in a delicate position regarding this survey because one of the United States attorney's key assistants, Will M. Tipton, was a member of the survey crew. Later Tipton prepared a memorandum stating that he had not agreed with the survey and had refused to sign the required oath, although he had supervised the chaining (measuring) of most of the land and had written rough notes. Tipton then made the shocking statement that the affidavits of the witnesses who pointed out the landmarks serving as boundaries were forged.[38]

These witnesses had been furnished by the speculators who had purportedly acquired the San Joaquín grant. One wonders whether some of the transactions upon which their claim to ownership was based were not also suspect. Instead of pursuing this inquiry, however, the government investigators set about procuring witnesses to testify to what the United States considered to be the true boundaries. While the questions of the bound-aries and the size of the grant were being contested in New Mexico, land speculator William Blackmore was trying to sell the grant in England, although he had not purchased all the interests in the grant, and did not know its size.[39]

On the ground, the most questionable boundary was the western one, the *cejita blanca*. Apparently there were two such landmarks: one was the continental divide, which was used in the survey of 1878; the other was in the Chama River canyon near the San Joaquín settlement of 1808, some fifteen miles to the east of the continental divide. When the San Joaquín grant was adjudicated by the Court of Private Land Claims, most of the testimony at the trial centered on the question of which *cejita blanca* was called for in the original grant.[40] This point was considered so important by the government that it took the deposition of two witnesses before Chief Justice Wilbur F. Stone prior to the trial, a procedure seldom followed in the Land Claims Court. Ninety-two year old General José María Chavez, who had lived on the grant as a young man, testified that the continental divide was the true western boundary of the grant and that a monument had been erected upon it, but Chavez was not called by the claimants to testify at the trial. Thomas B. Catron, who represented some of the speculators, asked the court to grant him a continuance so that General Chavez's testimony could be introduced, but his motion was denied.[41]

The testimony about the location of the boundaries of the San Joaquín grant is important because the case was argued by the government on the theory that if the grant was valid, its extent should be determined by the locations of these boundaries, not by the location of the allotments, as the court eventually decided. This was how the court understood the issues at the trial, for the only questions the judges asked were about the exterior boundaries; no testimony was taken concerning the location of the allot-ments. Thus the decision of the Land Claims Court limiting the size of the grant to these individual allotments was entirely an afterthought.[42]

The United States Supreme Court affirmed the decision of the Court of Private Land Claims on two grounds. First, the decision of Justice Fuller reviewed the title papers and concluded, in language reminiscent of Sur-veyor General Julian's report of 1886, that the *alcalde* did not intend to transfer title to the common lands to the grantees. Fuller wrote that "reference is indeed made to the use of the lands within the outboundaries for pastures and watering places, but this did not put them out of the class of public lands, and . . . no title was conveyed." He then cited the Sandoval case,[43] which was decided on the same day as the San Joaquín grant case, and stated that "we have just held . . . that as to all unallotted lands within exterior boundaries where towns or communities were sought to be formed, as in this instance, the title remained in the [Spanish] government for such disposition as it might see proper to make."[44]

The theory of Matthew Reynolds and of the U.S. Supreme Court was that the Spanish — and then the Mexican — government owned the common lands, so the United States (and not the heirs of the San Joaquín grant) inherited that ownership as successor sovereign. The question of the ownership of the common lands has both legal and historical implications. Because the Supreme Court decided this question without the necessary historical facts and Spanish legal authority before it, a legal and historical distortion resulted. Unfortunately, historians like Ralph Emerson Twitchell have perpetuated this error by quoting these and other similar cases in their writings about Hispanic land tenure, instead of engaging in independent research on the ownership of the common lands of a community land grant.[45]

 Such research would have revealed the legal history of the Castilian land-owning pueblo that took root in New Mexico,[46] of which the Supreme Court was not made aware. The lands owned by the Castilian pueblo were generally distinguished from the lands owned by the king. Crown lands that had not been granted to individuals or communities were called *tierras realengas* or *tierras baldías*. In sixteenth-century Castile, the monarchs followed a policy of protecting the lands of the pueblos — the *tierras concegiles*. Numerous laws were enacted to safeguard the *tierras concegiles* from usurpation by the nobility, by municipal officials, or by ordinary citizens.[47]

The common lands of a New Mexican community land grant were like the *tierras concegiles* in Spain. While both the *tierras baldías* and the *tierras concegiles* fell into the broad classification of public domain, civil law countries like Spain had two classes of public domain: the public domain proper, which was owned by the sovereign, and the private domain, which was owned by communities and municipalities. The former was the *tierras baldías* and the latter was the *tierras concegiles*. The importance of this distinction is that under international law, which the Land Claims Court

was supposed to follow, the public domain passes to a successor state
when there is a change of sovereignty (as when New Mexico was occupied
by the United States), but the private domain is retained by the communities and municipalities just as private property of individuals is retained
by its owners.[48] This well-established rule could have disposed of the
question of ownership of the common lands of the San Joaquín and other
community land grants. But it was overlooked, by both the lawyers and the
judges charged with deciding the important question of common land
ownership.

Also overlooked were three types of Spanish law germane to this issue:
codified law, commentaries on codified law, and Spanish custom. The
foremost Spanish law code, which was still in effect at the time of the
United States invasion of New Mexico, was *Las Siete Partidas. Partida* 3,
título 28, *ley* 9, spells out the ownership of pueblo lands by the community:

> [the things which] belong separately to the commons of cities or towns
> are . . . the *exidos*, . . . forests, and pastures, and all other similar places
> which have been established and granted for the common use of each city
> or town.[49]

This would appear to negate ownership of the commons by the King.

5.4. The village of Cartama in the Spanish province of Málaga in 1564, showing sur-
rounding fields, grasslands, and wooded areas, all patrolled by municipal guards. Georg
Braun, Civitatis orbis terrarum *(Cologne, 1576–1618). Courtesy Harry Ransom Hu-*
manities Research Center, University of Texas at Austin.

The *Recopilación de Leyes de Reynos de las Indias* dealt with the procedural problems of forming settlements in the Americas but had little to say about the substantive law concerning ownership of property; these matters were covered in earlier codes like *Las Siete Partidas*, which the *Recopilación* specifically made applicable to the Americas.[50] The Mexican Colonization Law of 1824 and the regulations issued under that law in 1828 were the first comprehensive legislation regarding New Mexico land grants. Article 2 of the 1824 law recognized the traditional ownership of the common lands by the pueblo when it stated: "the object of this law is those lands of the nation, not being private property *nor belonging to any corporation or pueblo*, and can [therefore] be colonized" [emphasis added].[51]

There were numerous Spanish law codes, but none was truly comprehensive. Instead of providing that later ones would supersede earlier ones, Spanish officials allowed them to overlap and duplicate one another. For this reason it was necessary for legal scholars to synthesize and summarize the authorities on various points of law. The works of Mariano Galván-Rivera are often cited and he is considered one of the leading authorities in the field of land and water law.

Galván-Rivera's primary work, *Tierras y Aguas*, which was attached as an appendix to Escriche's authoritative *Diccionario Razonado de Legislación y Jurisprudencia*, aptly summarizes the situation regarding the ownership of the common lands of a community land grant:

> they [the kings] had to cede to the settlements of America and to their councils . . . a certain portion of lands which they could use for their subsistence and betterment, making use of the pastures and farming lands. . . . These lands they immediately named according to their kind, ownership, and use: *concegiles* or *propios*. . .[52]

The third type of Hispanic law, custom and usage, is the most important for New Mexico. As we have seen, since there were few law books or lawyers in New Mexico prior to American occupation, disputes about land ownership were settled in traditional ways, which were considered binding and accepted by all sides.[53] Though falling under the classification of customary law, this litigation was usually written down and was characterized by a formality somewhat amazing considering the frontier setting in which it took place. The parties were often adept at the use of persuasive techniques and legal procedures generally reserved to trained lawyers.[54]

In the case of the San Joaquín grant such a dispute occurred at a time when New Mexico had the closest thing to a formal judicial system prior to the United States invasion.[55] The details of this litigation are of interest historically, showing how the traditional system of customary law operated and shedding light on the history of the San Joaquín grant. Also of interest is the legal effect of this lawsuit on the question of ownership of the common lands. For under the international law doctrine of acquired rights, a determination by a former government of the validity and nature of the property of its citizens is binding on the successor government (the United States).[56] The Mexican government made such a determination as a result of this litigation, which should have been honored under the Treaty of Guadalupe Hidalgo.

The dispute began in 1828 when *Alcalde* José María Ortiz gave a group of settlers possession of allotments along the Gallina River, at its confluence with the Río Chama. Apparently *Alcalde* Ortiz realized that since the allotments of 1828 on the Gallina were within the boundaries of the San Joaquín grant and were without the sanction of those grantees, they could be justified only by attacking the original allotments made by *Alcalde* García de la Mora in 1808. This Ortiz did by deciding on his own that a provision in the San Joaquín grant for returning the original papers to the governor for deposit in the archives, had not been complied with.[57]

Alcalde Pedro Ignacio Gallegos, the head of the *Ayuntamiento* of Abiquiú who we met in connection with Manuel Martínez's ditch dispute, sided with the San Joaquín settlers and ordered the Gallina settlers off the land. Then, in 1832 José de Jesús Chacón, leader of the Gallina group (he was the son of one of the original grantees who had sold his interest in the grant),[58] petitioned Governor Santiago Abreu, seeking a declaration that the order of *Alcalde* Gallegos ousting the Gallinas settlers was illegal. Chacón appealed to the governor as one "who knows the alcaldes of the territories very well and that many times they avail themselves of our ignorance to commit arbitrary acts . . ." Chacón stated that he and his fellow settlers had raised crops on the land they were claiming, a fact he said he could prove by the tithe collector.[59] The governor referred the petition to the *asesor* (attorney general), Antonio Barreiro, the lawyer whom the central government in Mexico City had sent to New Mexico to act as a one-man judicial system for the province of New Mexico.[60] Barreiro notified Abreu that he had already been approached by *Alcalde* Gallegos and had told him to form an *expediente*, as he could not decide the matter on the basis of a simple

5.5. *The San Joaquín grant and surrounding area.*

communication.[61] So the governor conveyed the wishes of the *asesor* to *Alcalde* Gallegos for the second time.[62]

Again Gallegos tried to circumvent Barreiro's request. Instead of forming an *expediente*, he purported to decide the controversy himself, stating: "I declare that the possession having been given by don José María Ortiz of the lands on the Gallina River without the production of any document approved by the governor nor any approval nor certification of petition is not legal." Another reason he gave was that the title papers had not been certified by the *alcalde*, copies given to the parties, and the original returned to the governor in Santa Fe to be deposited in the archives.[63]

But this attempt by *Alcalde* Gallegos to decide a question that had been submitted to the *asesor* was unsuccessful. Again Barreiro patiently but firmly explained in detail what he meant by his order to the *Alcalde* Gallegos to form an *expediente:*

> Salazar, Chávez and the other complainants [leaders of the San Joaquín settlers], must present you a written statement in which they should set forth plainly and simply the facts relating to their possession and the right which they believe they have to the lands which they claim; of this statement you will give a copy to Chacón, Durán, and Contreras [leaders of the Gallina settlers], in order that they also may give an idea of the right which they claim, basing it upon whatever they believe to be right, but they must express it clearly and briefly . . .

A copy of the Gallina reply statement was to be given to the San Joaquín settlers, who were to respond to it within six days. This statement was to be delivered to the Gallina settlers, who then had another six days to reply. *Alcalde* Gallegos was then asked to assemble these statements, two from each side, and forward them to *Asesor* Barreiro for his decision, which ultimately would determine the validity of the San Joaquín grant.[64] Barreiro's minute specificity as to what he required as a proper *expediente* did not leave room for any further evasions by *Alcalde* Gallegos and it tells us what a Mexico City lawyer thought was the proper way to handle a lawsuit.

The first statement of the San Joaquín settlers argued that their possession was legal and that the possession given by *Alcalde* Ortiz to the Gallina settlers was not legal because it was within the limits of the San Joaquín grant and had not been approved by the Territorial Deputation.[65] The first statement of the Gallina people raised two new points: that the allotments made by *Alcalde* Ortiz were made with the knowledge of the governor, José Antonio Chávez, and that the San Joaquín grantees should have protested in 1828 when the allotments were made. They close their brief with a bit of hyperbole, charging that the San Joaquín settlers "want to enjoy our property without having to reclaim these far off lands which we have improved with the blood in our veins . . . notwithstanding that we are so poor that to acquire an axe or a hoe we would have to hire out [as servants] . . ."[66]

The second statement of the San Joaquín group focuses on this last remark. It singles out Mateo García as not being as poor as stated but rather owning land in Abiquiú sufficient to support a large family and a fertile tract in El Rito. Next it says, as to the work done by the Gallina group on the land, that it is "nothing more than to yoke a pair of oxen and go along planting their seeds." As to the delay in making their protest, it states that two of their group did in fact protest to *Alcalde* Ortiz at the time of the Gallina allotment of 1828, but he would not listen to them. Finally, the San Joaquín settlers reveal that their work in digging the ditch to obtain water for irrigating the San Joaquín fields, when they were put into possession in 1808, was very great, notwithstanding the fact that their efforts were unsuccessful. This probably explains why some of these settlers joined the settlement on the Gallina. Another explanation is that devastating Indian raids had forced the temporary abandonment of San Joaquín in 1819.[67]

At this point in the proceedings much of the argument advanced had degenerated into name calling and flowery rhetoric in spite of Barreiro's admonition to both sides to express themselves plainly, simply, and briefly. The final statement of the Gallina settlers complains that "now we see only rights usurped, justice delayed, and ourselves burdened with costs we can ill afford to bear."[68]

Barreiro now had the *expediente* he had requested. He was acting as a sort of Supreme Court of New Mexico when he rendered his decision, which cut through the verbiage of the *expediente* to the heart of the matter. That the original grant document was not in the archives, he said, did not make the grant invalid. In Barreiro's words, [concerning the legality of] "the possession given at the Cañon de San Joaquín del Río de Chama, even if there be any requirement lacking, it is not essential requirement, but one of pure formality."[69]

The final step in this litigation was taken when *Alcalde* Gallegos executed this decision on 10 May 1832. He announced that anyone who considered himself to have any right to an allotment of land on the Gallina should appear on that day. Three citizens chose not to: Mateo García, Tomás Chacón, and Tomás Salazar. José María Chávez, senior *regidor* of the *ayuntamiento* of Abiquiú, who testified in the Land Claims Court about the grant's boundaries,[70] was appointed to notify these three that by failing to appear they forfeited any right they might have to an allotment. *Alcalde* Gallegos pointed out in his report that neither García nor Chacón would have been entitled to an allotment anyway because García had sold interest in the grant, and Chacón's father had sold their rights.

Those who did appear at Gallina that day in May received *suertes* of 150 varas — fifty varas of irrigable land and one hundred varas of uncultivated land. Many of the eighteen settlers who received allotments at Gallina in 1832 had also received allotments in 1808 at the village of San Joaquín.[71] Among those receiving allotments in 1832 were the children of the deceased Francisco Salazar.[72]

The allotments in 1832 at Gallina, less than five miles from the original village of San Joaquín, demonstrate that the Mexican government viewed the ownership of the San Joaquín grant differently than did the United States Court of Private Land Claims and the Supreme Court, which held that only the allotments of 1808 were valid and that the rest of the land within the grant belonged to the U.S. government.

But the historical as well as the legal facts show that the lands outside the village of San Joaquín were as much a part of the grant as were the allotments of 1808. *Alcalde* Gallegos's report on the *repartimiento* proceedings makes this clear:

> having caused the grant made by the governor, Don Joaquín de Real
> Alencaster, to be read in the presence of all, . . . I ascertained that the lands
> of the Gallina River are within the said grant, and that the lands that were
> not partitioned at the time when possession was [first] given remained for
> the benefit of the children of the [initial] settlers.[73]

The epilogue to this litigation was a decision by a commission of the Territorial Deputation in 1833, based on a claim by those dispossessed by the 1832 allotments, led by Mateo García. The committee reaffirmed the decision of *Asesor* Barreiro when it refused to even hear the claim, stating that the land in question had already been the subject of litigation.[74] It is significant that the commission of 1833 found that the lands on the Gallina River, outside the area confirmed by the Court of Private Land Claims, were not public lands, as held by the Land Court, but were private property. Mateo García was not daunted by this second decision upholding the San Joaquín grant in its entirety. In 1834 he arranged a trade with ex-*Alcalde* Pedro Ignacio Gallegos for the land that Gallegos had received as his fee for performing the *repartimiento* of 1832.[75]

This litigation indicates that the Mexican government considered the entire San Joaquín grant — not just the allotments of 1808 — to be owned by the settlers and not by the government. The common lands, like the Castilian *tierras concegiles*, belonged to the community, and the fact that the Mexican government still exercised some control over them by making additional allotments did not mean that this land was public domain. Even in the case of private land grants, *alcaldes* often made allotments and partitions, dividing the land among heirs upon the death of a previous owner, for example.[76]

Under the acquired rights doctrine, Barreiro's decision and that of the commission of 1833 should have determined the question of the ownership of the common lands because Mexican law was controlling. These decisions, added to the long history of community land ownership in Spain and in New Mexico, suggest that the traditional view of common land ownership, as expressed by Twitchell, needs to be revised. Recent scholarship has all but effected such a revision for New Mexico. After studying all of New Mexico's community land grants, Daniel Tyler came to the conclusion that: "the *ejido* (common lands) belonged to the community to which it was appurtenant." In two of the grants he studied the *alcalde* promised the settlers a title to their *ejidos*, leaving no doubt that these common lands were owned by the community.[77] Moreover, other community land grand documents show that when the private tracts were transferred to the individual grantees, this land carried with it the right to use the common lands. Hispanic settlers received title to their house lots and farm lands as individuals and title to the common lands as a group (*de mancomún*).[78] This connection between the private tracts and the common lands is seen in the granting decree for the Las Trampas grant where title to the grant was transferred "to all in common and to each one in particular, in their private lands *and the rest which is attached [to the private tracts]*."[79] Then when the individual tracts were distributed, the settlers received their private land together "with corresponding water, pastures, and watering places . . ."[80] Again in the Tierra Amarilla grant after the grant was confirmed by Congress, each settler received an *hijuela* (deed) that described the private tract

*5.6. Typical scene of sheep grazing on common lands in northern New Mexico, ca. 1935.
Photograph by T. Harmon Parkhurst, neg. no. 68901. Courtesy Museum of New Mexico.*

conveyed as well as the rights in the common lands: "said *varas* of land
retain the right to pastures, water, firewood, timber for building, and roads,
free and common."[81] These specific instances indicate what the custom was
in other community land grants like San Joaquín.

In contrast to this picture of what Spanish and Mexican custom tells us
about common land ownership, Matthew Reynolds said in his San Joaquín
brief to the supreme court in 1896, that *Alcalde* García de la Mora "delivered possession to each individual of the land to which he was entitled . . .
(but not) to all of them in common or any one individual of a large tract of
land, but simply designated outboundaries . . . the title to the unallotted
portions remaining in the Government." The U.S. Attorney was not reti-
cent about making this statement without giving any authority under

Spanish or Mexican law to back it up.[82] Even in the Sandoval opinion, which purported to provide a more detailed examination of Hispanic law, the only authority cited that was right on point was one Frederic Hall, whose book on the laws of Mexico was published just one year before the San Joaquín case was being argued in the supreme court.[83] Again, the language quoted from Hall was not supported by any reference to Spanish or Mexican law.[84] Knowing what we do now, it is somewhat appalling to contemplate the injustice that resulted from the United States Supreme Court's blanket acceptance of what Mr. Reynolds and Mr. Hall told them about the Hispanic law of New Mexico.

Unfortunately this does not reverse the erroneous Sandoval decision. Today most former common lands of community land grants in northern New Mexico are owned by the federal government as parts of the Carson and Santa Fe National Forests. The Forest Service has shown little sensitivity to the needs and concerns of local residents, and legislation designed to study the effects of the loss of the San Joaquín grant's common lands has failed to pass in Congress.

Six
The Embudo Grant: Justice and the Court of Private Land Claims

An earlier version of this essay appeared in The Journal of the West 29 *(July 1980):* 74–85.

The rejection of the Embudo grant by the Court of Private Land Claims in 1898 was one of the most unjust decisions rendered by that tribunal in its thirteen-year history. To comprehend why this is true, one must understand the history of the Embudo grant, as well as the meaning of fairness in the context of the Court of Private Land Claims, which adjudicated the Spanish and Mexican land grant titles in Arizona, Colorado, and New Mexico. My opinion of the court's record of fairness runs counter to the view expressed by historian Richard Bradfute that "the decisions of the court were relatively fair."[1] I think the Embudo case shows why Bradfute's assessment needs to be revised.

The story of the Embudo land grant starts in 1725, when three men — Juan Márquez, Francisco Martín, and Lasaro de Córdova — appeared before New Mexico governor Juan Domingo de Bustamante with a petition for a *pedazo de tierra* (piece of land) at Embudo de Picuris.[2] The triangular-shaped tract they sought was bounded on the northwest by the Río Bravo del Norte (Río Grande), on the east by a dry *arroyo*, and on the south by the Sebastián Martín grant, which had been made twenty years before.[3] The place was called Embudo because it is there that the Embudo river flows through a narrow pass which resembles a funnel.[4]

The request of the three petitioners, who lived at the Puesto del Rio Arriba, was granted the same day, subject only to the condition that the grant cause no injury to third parties or to the native Indians. The *alcalde* of Santa Fe, Miguel José de la Vega y Coca, was commissioned to examine the land and make the grant if no one appeared to object.[5] Unfortunately, Vega y Coca was not told what to do if the proposed grant was protested, for that is exactly what happened.

In July 1725 Vega y Coca went to Embudo and showed the governor's decree to the *alcalde* of that jurisdiction, Miguel Enríquez. Enríquez signed it after declaring that he would obey the decree, which he placed on his head as a symbolic act of submission to higher authority. Then the two *alcaldes* went to the land, accompanied by the petitioners, two witnesses, the Indians of the Picuris Pueblo and their *alcalde*.

The land was described in the petition as being outside the boundaries of the Pueblo of Picuris by three leagues (approximately eight miles). Mention was also made of some cornfields cultivated by the Indians that were

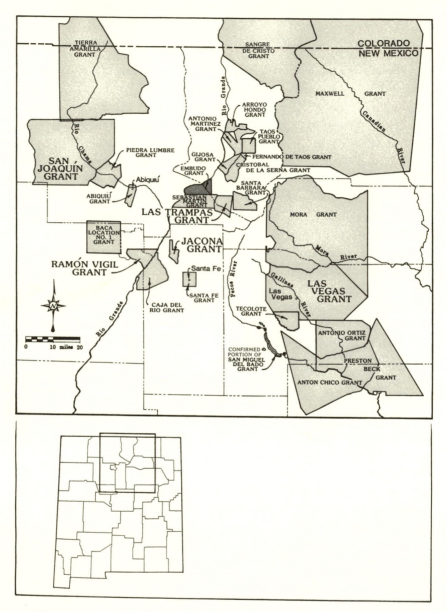

6.2. Map of northern New Mexico land grants with the Embudo grant highlighted.

closer to, if not actually on, the proposed grant. These were to be a source of dispute between the proposed settlers and the Picuris. It is not surprising that the Picuris did not want the Hispanos living near them, for forty-five years earlier they had united with the Taos Indians to lead the other pueblos in the revolt against the Hispanos. After the reconquest, the Picuris had rebelled again in 1694 and 1696.[6]

The Picuris objections to the Embudo grant were that they had grazed their horses and cultivated some fields on the land requested by the Spaniards. *Alcalde* Vega y Coca settled each objection on the spot, each time in favor of the Spanish. He determined that the tracts the Pueblos claimed to have planted were unplowed (*eriases*). Whether his commission from the governor empowered him to make this judgment is not clear from Bustamante's decree, but the *alcalde's* handling of the protest shows him to have been less than objective and somewhat self-righteous. He made the Picuris a final offer to reserve a part of the Embudo tract for their use, but stated in his report that:

> . . . the result of this generous proceeding was that they become arrogant and contended for more land than ever, whereby they clearly manifested [the desire] to prevent the settlement of the Spaniards.

The Picuris were no more successful in preventing the Spanish from settling next to their *pueblo* than they had been in keeping them out of New Mexico in the first place. *Alcalde* Vega y Coca proceeded to perform the traditional final ceremony while the grantees "as upon their own [property] and as a token of ownership, cast stones, plucked up weeds and shouted."[7]

The land was first settled by eight families at the present site of Dixon, New Mexico, then called San Antonio del Embudo. Because of constant danger of attack by the Comanche and other Plains Indians, these first Hispanic settlers built their homes around a *plaza*, with two *torreones* or watch-towers near the corners of the compound. Remains of these *torreones*, where early settlers gathered to battle the Indians, are still standing.[8]

Indian attacks caused the temporary abandonment of the settlement by 1750, for in that year Governor Tomás Veléz Cachupín stated in a decree:

> . . . upon my entrance into this government I found several places deserted and abandoned which had been occupied by different families to whom land had been given . . . in the jurisdiction of the Villa de la Cañada, called Abiquiú, Ojo Caliente and Embudo.[9]

6.3. Winnowing wheat, Picurís Pueblo, New Mexico, ca. 1935. Photograph by T. Harmon Parkhurst, neg. no. 22697. Courtesy Museum of New Mexico.

All of these vulnerable outposts were soon resettled, however, for they provided an essential zone of protection around the settlements at Santa Fe and Santa Cruz de la Cañada. By 1776, when Domínguez made his census, fourteen families totaling sixty-nine people lived at Embudo. Later, other settlements were formed on the grant at Anconcito, La Ciénega, La Junta, La Bolsa, Rinconada, El Bosque, Apodaca, Montecito, and Cañoncito.[10]

By 1786 the copy of the title papers given to the original grantees had become torn from frequent handling, so the heirs of Francisco Martín, one of the grantees, appeared before the *alcalde* of Santa Cruz de la Cañada — José Campo Redondo — asking him to make a certified copy of these papers. Because there were no official notaries (*escribanos*) in New Mexico, Campo Redondo copied the document in his elaborate and distinctive handwriting and signed a certification that the copy agreed with the original. It was this document that would later cause the United States to reject the Embudo grant in its entirety.

Continuous occupation of the grant is attested to by numerous references in the Spanish colonial and Mexican archives.[11] In 1776, for example, one member of the Domínguez-Escalante expedition, Antonio Lucrecio Muñis, was listed as a citizen of the *puesto* of Embudo.[12] In 1795 Governor Fernando Chacón recognized the Embudo grant by implication when he made another grant next to it that had as its western boundary "the surplus lands of those of Embudo."[13] The *alcalde* of Taos put twenty settlers in possession of that grant, which became known as the Town of Cieneguilla grant. It had several things in common with the Embudo grant besides a boundary: both relied on a certified copy of their grant papers for documentary evidence and both were later rejected by the Court of Private Land Claims because these papers were held to be insufficient and not admissible into evidence.[14]

How was it that these two grants, among the oldest in the Rio Arriba (the northern part of New Mexico), could be held invalid by the United States? To answer this question requires some traveling down the twisted paths of legal theory, which sometimes lead into the realm of the absurd.

 The Embudo grant was filed for confirmation with Surveyor-General John Clark in 1863, but for some reason Clark made no investigation or recommendation at that time.[15] Thirty years later Antonio Griego and three others filed suit in the Court of Private Land Claims, for themselves and the other grant heirs, for recognition of their title to the estimated twenty-five thousand acres in the grant.[16] Attorney Napoleon Bonaparte Laughlin represented the plaintiffs, and his handling of the case was less than inspired. It was five years before the case was brought to trial, during which time the U.S. Supreme Court decided the *Hayes* case (to be discussed later), which greatly weakened the position of the Embudo claimants. Laughlin and Eugene Fiske represented the claimants in both the Embudo and Cienequilla cases and in each case the only time when the issue of the validity of an *alcalde*'s certified copy is discussed is after the Land Claims Court had ruled against them and they asked the court to reconsider.[17] At the Embudo trial Laughlin offered the copy of the grant papers, made and certified by *Alcalde* José Campo Redondo, as evidence. William Pope, the attorney for the government, objected because: ". . . there being no proof offered of the correctness of this copy, or of the power of an *alcalde*, by virtue of his office, to make a copy that would be binding on the Government of Spain."[18]

Although no evidence was introduced at the trial regarding the power of an *alcalde* to make a certified copy, this question became the basis for Justice William Murray's majority opinion rejecting the Embudo grant. On its face the opinion seems a model of impeccable logic, demonstrating that because of certain U.S. Supreme Court land grant cases, the Court was compelled to reject the grant. But when viewed in relation to the history of the grant, and to Spanish law as it was practiced in New Mexico, the decision is outrageous.

6.4. Certification by José Campo Redondo that his was a verbatim copy of the Embudo grant title papers. Courtesy New Mexico State Records Center and Archives.

The unstated major premise of the decision is that under Spanish law, the only public official authorized to copy and certify legal documents was the *escribano,* not the *alcalde.* According to this argument, the Embudo copies were invalid since they were certified by an *alcalde.*[19] In Spain, an *escribano* was a professional like a lawyer; to practice he had to pass an examination similar to today's bar examination in the United States. *Escribanos* were qualified to give legal advice and to decide legal questions, and since they were appointed by the king they were considered officials of the government.[20] They were held in such high esteem that Spanish law provided any person killing an *escribano* should be put to death.[21] With but a couple of exceptions, however, Spanish Colonial authorities did not provide for *escribanos* in frontier New Mexico, and they were conspicuously absent in the late eighteenth and early nineteenth centuries.[22] As with all the other functions of local government, the duties of the *escribanos* in New Mexico fell to the *alcaldes.* It was customary for an *alcalde* making a certified copy of a document to state that he was doing so "for lack of a public or royal notary, there being none in this province."[23]

Since it was the custom for *alcaldes* to make certified copies, the practice was legal under New Mexico's legal system. Under Spanish law if a written law does not apply to a specific situation in practice, then custom has the force of law.[24] As New Mexico historian Marc Simmons has pointed out: "In legal proceedings, little attention was paid to any code of laws, since, in fact, the magistrates had no law books or written statutes to guide them. Many were perhaps unaware that such existed. . . . By and large, judgement of the *alcaldes*, when it was not corrupted by personal interest or sheer malicious obstinacy, conformed to the prevailing customs of the country."[25]

In New Mexico prior to United States occupation, evidence of custom was found in the decisions of the *alcaldes, ayuntamientos*, and the acts of the government.[26] Since English common law is also composed of decisions in actual cases, it should not have been difficult for Anglo-American lawyers and judges to understand Hispanic customary law. The problem, then as now, was that these decisions were never translated, organized, and studied the way common-law cases are. The United States government had the expertise to do this, but as we shall see, it was not in its interest to do so.

From a review of some of these documents, indications are that when New Mexico was under Spain and Mexico, the decisions of *alcaldes*, governors, and the Mexican *asesor* on land grant issues emphasized settlement and continuous occupation of the land as the most important factors in land grant validity.[27] Least important were the formalities in making the grant.[28] Ironically, technical defects in land grant documents were often used by the Court of Private Land Claims to reject perfectly valid grants. There were a few notable exceptions where the Land Claims Court applied customary law and confirmed grants where there was continuous settlement even though not all the technical requirements were fulfilled. The Santa Teresa grant, for instance, was made by the lieutenant governor instead of the governor and the claimants also relied on an *alcalde's* certified copy of the grant documents, but the grant was confirmed based on evidence of continuous possession since 1790.[29] In another case, surveyor-general William Pelham recommended confirmation of the Town of Mora grant because:

> It is not to be presumed that the (Mexican) government would allow the richest and most fertile portion of its territory to be usurped and taken over by a party of men without the color or shadow of law. There certainly was a grant or they would not have been allowed to remain unmolested from 1836–1846 . . .[30]

The same could be said for the Embudo grant, where there was a time span of 121 years instead of 10, between the making of the grant and the United States occupation of New Mexico.

Specific evidence of recognition of the Embudo grant by the Spanish Colonial government provided another ground upon which its confirmation could have been based. First, the 1750 decree of Governor Veléz Cachupín reflected the government's concern that Embudo, Abiquiú, and Ojo Caliente be resettled, for these settlements formed a crescent across a favorite raiding corridor of the Kiowa and Comanche and the governor wanted to keep settlers there as a first line of defense for Santa Fe and Santa Cruz.[31] Without these settlements, Spanish government did not even exist in these areas.

Secondly, the making of the certified copy of the Embudo title papers by *Alcalde* José Campo Redondo in 1786 implied recognition of the grant, because if he had disapproved of the grant he could have simply refused to make the certified copy when requested to do so.[32] Since the *alcalde* was the only government official with whom most people had contact, the act of making the certified copy implied approval of the grant by the government. Once having made the copy, *Alcalde* Campo Redondo would be likely to recognize the grant as valid.

The power exercised by *alcaldes* in the grant-making process can be seen from the way *Alcalde* Vega y Coca handled the protest of the Picuris, a matter that probably should have been decided by the governor.[33] *Alcaldes* usually reported to the governor on each petition for a land grant, and their recommendations were almost always followed. In the case of the Embudo grant, this step was eliminated completely; the *alcalde* was ordered to put the petitioners in possession immediately after completing his investigation, if his recommendation was favorable.

The third instance of Spanish recognition of the Embudo grant occurred in 1795 when Governor Chacón made the Cieneguilla grant, designating as its western boundary "the surplus lands of those of Embudo." With all this evidence of approval of the grant by the Spanish and the Mexican governments, added to the continuous possession of the land since 1750, it would take a finely spun technicality of Anglo jurisprudence to cause the rejection of the Embudo grant.

By 1898 the United States Attorney for the Court of Private Land Claims, Matthew Givens Reynolds, had acquired an arsenal of such technicalities, together with several procedural advantages, to aid him in the task of defeating land grant claims, which was the primary responsibility of his position. He also had assembled a superb team of experts to assist him in fashioning a defense to each claim. Although the claimants were U.S. citizens whose property was guaranteed to them by the Treaty of Guadalupe Hidalgo, the adversary system of the Court of Private Land Claims required them to establish their claim, while the United States Attorney tried to defeat it.

Reynolds's most valuable man, Will M. Tipton, had worked sixteen years in the office of the Surveyor General of New Mexico as a translator and custodian of the archives, where: "he had ample opportunity to examine the Spanish and Mexican archives and to familiarize himself with the contents of the records and the signatures of the governors and other officials. . . . His knowledge of the archives enabled him to locate documents which showed revocation of the grant."[34] However, it was not Tipton's job to produce documents showing recognition and approval of a grant — this was the task of the attorneys for the claimants. But since none of the private attorneys representing land grant claimants was as familiar with the archives as was Tipton, they seldom produced archival evidence other than the title papers. In fact, these attorneys often had to rely on Tipton to authenticate documents they wanted to introduce into evidence by having him identify the signatures of the officials who signed them.

Added to Tipton on Reynolds's team of experts was Henry Ossian Flipper, the first African-American to graduate from West Point. He was a handwriting expert, but his main contribution to the government's effort was researching and writing much of the compilation of Spanish and Mexican land laws published under Reynolds's name in 1895. This book became the primary authority for both the Court of Private Land Claims and the Supreme Court of the United States on Spanish and Mexican law.[35]

It was to be expected that this compilation would emphasize codified rather than customary law, since evidence of custom usually favored the claimant. The compilation has a substantial bias, both in the selection of the laws included and in the summary of those laws in the prefatory "historical sketch." No mention is made of laws making custom applicable to a particular situation or laws defining custom.[36] And no mention is made of the important subject of the rules of evidence and presumptions under Spanish and Mexican law.[37] When the courts accepted Reynolds's book as the definitive statement of Spanish and Mexican law, they adopted these biases, giving the government another substantial edge over land grant claimants.

In addition, the land grant claimant was subject to procedural burdens which gave the United States an even greater advantage. From the time when Spanish and Mexican land grants were first adjudicated under the Treaty of Guadalupe Hidalgo in California, the burden of proving title to a land grant was on the claimant, but it was not always so. Land grants made by Spain in Florida and Louisiana had been adjudicated under treaties prior to the 1848 treaty,[38] and Supreme Court decisions on appeals from these cases had established a body of land grant law that was quite liberal compared to later decisions. As we have seen, in 1833 Chief Justice John Marshall decided that the Florida treaty had the effect of confirming valid grants by the force of its terms alone.[39] This placed on the government the burden of instituting a lawsuit and proving the claimed invalidity of a grant. But when land grants were adjudicated in California beginning in 1851, the burden of proof was placed on the claimant, although debate in Congress and at least one law review article had suggested that this was in violation of the Treaty of Guadalupe Hidalgo.[40] By 1889, when the U.S. Supreme Court heard the test case attacking the California legislation, the views of the justices concerning land grants had become much more conservative than those expressed by Chief Justice Marshall, and they held that the procedure followed in California did not violate the treaty.[41]

In land grant adjudications in California and New Mexico between 1851 and 1891, the claimant's burden of proof had been eased immeasurably by certain creatures of the law called presumptions. One was the presumption of a valid grant from proof of the existence of a city, town, or village on the land.[42] This meant that proof of such a settlement on a land grant constituted *prima facie* evidence of the validity of that grant. It was then up to the government to prove any claimed invalidity of the grant with specific evidence. This presumption made practical sense because of the government's superiority in archival expertise. Since it was custodian of the Spanish and Mexican archives, any documentary evidence of land grant invalidity was more readily accessible to the United States. However, this presumption was eliminated by the Court of Private Land Claims. Thus continuous settlement of a grant, which was the primary requirement for validity under Spanish and Mexican law, became less important in the eyes of the Land Claims Court than the strict observance of all the procedural steps in making a land grant, which were of minimal importance under Spanish and Mexican law.

After the loss of this procedural equalizer, one presumption remained that could have made all the difference in the Embudo case: the presumption of authority. With the benefit of this presumption, a claimant need prove only that a grant was made by a government official, and it was presumed that the official had the authority to make the grant. If the United States disagreed, it was then up to the government to produce specific evidence that the official did not have that authority. This also made practical sense in view of the custom of *alcaldes*,[43] *ayuntamientos*,[44] and prefects[45] of making land grants. If this presumption was extended to the authority of an *alcalde* to make a certified copy, it would mean that the government had the burden of proving that José Campo Redondo did not have the authority to make certified copies valid under Spanish law.

In the case of *Hayes v. United States*,[46] Supreme Court Justice Edward D. White demolished the presumption of authority, which was first applied to land grants in 1832 by Chief Justice Marshall.[47] Justice White seized upon the following phrase in the 1891 act establishing the Court of Private Land Claims: "No claim shall be allowed that shall not appear to be upon a title lawfully and regularly derived from the Government of Spain or Mexico."[48] Matthew Reynolds argued that this requirement prohibited the court from applying the presumption of authority, and the Supreme Court agreed, although the above language does not appear so restrictive in its plain meaning as to eliminate grants lawfully derived under customary law.

Now Matthew Reynolds had his finely spun legal technicality. It was only a short step from the Hayes doctrine of requiring strict proof of the authority of the official making the grant, to requiring strict proof of the authority of an official making a certified copy of grant documents. But this was a step into the absurd, for it bore no relation to the conditions or the law of New Mexico prior to U.S. occupation. After the Hayes case, valid grants like Embudo would be rejected on similar technicalities with the apologetic statement that the court was forced to do so by the restrictive provisions of the 1891 Act. Some historians of the Court of Private Land Claims have erroneously taken such statements at face value in arriving at their favorable evaluation of the court's fairness.[49]

In the Embudo case, three of the five Land Claims Court justices accepted Reynolds's argument, but two of the justices registered a rare dissent from the majority opinion. Justices Reed and Stone may have remembered the testimony about the 139 families living on the land who, together with their ancestors, had been there for 148 years.[50] The dissent referred to an earlier Court of Private Land Claims decision in which the Town of Bernalillo grant was confirmed based on a certified copy of the grant papers like Embudo's. Chief Justice Reed's words in the Bernalillo case are perhaps the most cogent statement of the unfairness of the Embudo decision:

> We know from our examination of the many claims under Spanish grants . . . that the practice of perpetuating in this manner the evidences of title . . . was common. Indeed, that was the only way that evidence of title in the hands of the people could be perpetuated . . . The papers were passed from hand to hand as the ownership of the property changed and necessarily in the lapse of time, they became mutilated. It is true that public records of the proceedings relating to the grants of lands were required to be made. But the sovereignty over the country has twice been changed, once by revolution and once by military conquest and in addition to that it is a matter of history that there have been times of turmoil in which all civil government in the country has been endangered. In view of these facts, it is not remarkable that the ancient records should now be found in an unsatisfactory and imperfect condition. It has also many times been proven before us that spoliations of the records have occurred since our own government acquired jurisdiction over the country. It is manifest that if claimants should now be held to the strictness of proof which would be required in the establishment of a title of American origin, great injustice would be done, and the measures established by the government for the purpose of carrying out its treaty stipulations, would be made the instrument of defeating that purpose.[51]

 Ultimately, everyone makes his or her own judgment about the fairness of the decisions of the Court of Private Land Claims. In doing so, not only must the decisions of the court be weighed, but also the entire adjudication process must be scrutinized to assess its fairness.

The essence of fairness in an adversary system of justice is a basic equality between opposing sides each attempting to prove their case. As we have seen, this did not exist in the Embudo case. Instead, the scales were tipped against the claimants from the beginning by the distortion of Spanish law, by the U.S. monopoly on archival expertise, and by the elimination of the presumptions that had helped claimants overcome their burden of proof. The Embudo and other claimants faced an almost insurmountable burden. Accordingly, the decisions of the Court of Private Land Claims were often unfair. Valid grants should have been confirmed as property, which the Treaty of Guadalupe Hidalgo promised would be "inviolably respected" by the United States.[52] Generally speaking, a grant was valid under Spanish and Mexican law if conditions such as settlement of the land had been met, if the grant had not been revoked,[53] and if the grantees had some title papers.[54] The acreage rejected by the Court of Private Land Claims for legitimate reasons under Hispanic law was small compared to that rejected for the alleged lack of authority of the granting official, some formal insufficiency in the grant documents,[55] or the ruling that the common lands of a community were not part of the grant but were public domain.[56] The court used these reasons, urged upon them by Matthew Reynolds and his assistants, to reject valid grants.

The question of the fairness of the Embudo decision would be of only academic interest if it were not for the fact that the United States still owns most of the Embudo grant, and still must deal with the families who remain on the land. These families could rightfully expect that the U.S. government take full responsibility for the questionable manner in which it acquired this land. One way of doing this would be to regard the land as subject to a trust obligation dictating that it be managed primarily for the benefit of residents of communities on the grant. This is just the opposite of what has happened.

The Embudo grant is administered by the Bureau of Land Management, and on B.L.M. maps it is all colored yellow indicating that it is B.L.M. land.[57] Until 1974 the B.L.M. recognized as private land, property that was improved and occupied or cultivated. Most of this land had been acquired as small holding claims after the rejection of the grant. In 1974, however, the B.L.M.'s "color it yellow" philosophy began to spread. The Bureau, as part of its program of surveying federal lands, began notifying residents of Apodaca, Cañoncito, and Montecito that land on which their homes, churches, and cemeteries were located was B.L.M. land. When the people protested, they were told that they could buy the land back from the government at current market value. Residents of Apodaca, believing they

6.5. Scene of a typical Hispanic village in the summer. Painting by Glen Strock.

had no alternative, paid the United States for the very land on which they had always lived. A public outcry resulted from publicity of the B.L.M.'s action and the agency canceled plans to require residents of Montecito and Cañoncito to buy back their lands.[58]

Now, however, the B.L.M. is again contesting titles of Embudo grant residents. While many people have applied for patents from the government, only about 15 percent have received them, and of those the majority paid the government full value (in 1993, $7,000 per acre for irrigated land, $5,000 per acre for other land). Only about 4 percent of the applicants have qualified for a patent upon payment of a lesser amount under the terms of the federal color of title act.[59]

The B.L.M. has been niggardly in granting patents under the color of title program partly because of the restrictive nature of the regulations, but especially because of the narrow manner in which they are applied. Local B.L.M. offices construe the statute strictly, sometimes creating impediments not found in federal case law. For example, some claims have been rejected because the claimant knew that the land in question was owned by the United States and therefore, according to the government's reasoning, lacked good faith. The "knowledge of government ownership test" is applied, not only when the property was acquired by the claimant (which is reasonable and accords with state law), but throughout the twenty years the property is required to be held. Thus, claimants who purchased property in good faith and then used and improved the property for a twenty-year period, are still barred from receiving a color of title patent if at any time during that period they knew the U.S. owned or claimed the land. This interpretation penalizes those who cooperate with the B.L.M. and those with the most knowledge of the legal history of the Embudo grant.[60]

The B.L.M.'s policy is particularly unfair because the B.L.M. itself has actively engaged in a publicity campaign to advise Embudo area residents that they do not have clear title because of government ownership, and then has used this information to deny *bona fide* claims. In fact, the literature distributed by the B.L.M., which causes claimants who read it to have fatal knowledge of the infirmities of their title and infects them with bad faith, actually tells the claimant that good faith *purchase* is all that is required.[61]

When one contemplates the unfairness of the decision of the Land Claims Court under which the United States acquired title to the Embudo grant, the current policy of the B.L.M. is remarkably insensitive. This can be seen in the cavalier bureaucratic jargon found in the brochure explaining the federal rules:

Q: Can the BLM refuse to give me title and "kick me off their land?"
A: Possibly. Each parcel of land will be considered for retention by the government or disposal. The decision will come from a process called "The Bureau Planning System." This system considers all values to the public from the resources on each parcel of public land. If a piece of public land is more valuable to the general public in federal ownership, you will have to move.[62]

Imagine how this must sound to someone who has a chain of title going back before the turn of the century on land they purchased, farmed, and raised their families on without any opposition from the government.

This latest chapter in the Embudo history suggests a definition of unfairness that could be used as a standard for assessing all the decisions of the Court of Private Land Claims: is this a decision which shocks the conscience? If any land grant meets this test, it is Embudo. In fact, the audacity of the federal government in the Embudo situation is amazing. First it took the land upon which the villagers depended for their subsistence — farming, grazing, hunting and gathering land. Then the government tried to make the villagers pay for the land on which they had built their homes and churches and even the earth where they had buried their dead. And it is still trying.

The Embudo decision was not unique in the annals of the Court of Private Land Claims. The court rejected 91 percent of the acreage claimed before it,[63] and preliminary studies indicate that the majority of these rejections were, like Embudo, unfair.[64] These figures generally, and the Embudo case in particular, raise doubts about the opinions of scholars who state that the court fairly and effectively discharged the obligations assumed by the United States under the Treaty of Guadalupe Hidalgo.[65]

The truth is better expressed in the following excerpt from a study of the Land Claims Court by Sandra Grisham and Jay Ortiz: "The court sat during the period of American history in which the nation sought to impose its concept of Manifest Destiny upon the Spanish-speaking world. Perhaps it was inevitable, therefore, that the court would view as a national service the releasing of vast areas of New Mexico to the federal government. . . ." Perhaps it was inevitable that the United States would acquire this land [and] that the interests of Spanish-speaking peasants would not prevent such acquisition. Perhaps it was inevitable, but somehow that does not seem to render it less wrong."[66]

Seven

The Las Trampas Grant:
A Case of Duplicity and Legal Traps

The Las Trampas grant is one of the oldest continuously occupied community land grants in Northern New Mexico. It survived against incredible odds on the periphery of Spanish settlement in the Rio Arriba, until it was faced with an assault by Anglo lawyers in the early 1900s. It survived both Comanche attacks and the merciless land grant confirmation system, but the common lands of the Las Trampas grant finally fell under attack by three members of the Santa Fe Ring: Alonzo B. McMillan, Alois B. Renehan, and Charles Catron, son of Thomas B. Catron. These men used the double edged sword of duplicity to accomplish their ends, telling the villagers one thing and the courts another. This is the story of common land use–rights sliced to pieces by sharp practices.

Spanish settlement at Las Trampas resulted from the progressive movement of settlers northward from the relatively secure population centers of Santa Fe and Santa Cruz de la Cañada. In 1695 after the Diego de Vargas reconquest of New Mexico following the Pueblo Revolt, the Villa of Santa Cruz de la Cañada was established near present-day Española.[1] Soon settlements were strung out along the Santa Cruz River as far as Chimayó, and by 1725 the area was becoming crowded.[2] The village of Cundiyó was settled by 1754, and we know that the Pueblo Quemado grant (site of present-day Córdova) was at least partially settled by 1748, for in that year the Pueblo Quemado inhabitants asked Governor Codallos y Rabal for permission to abandon the grant because of severe Indian raids.[3] Then in 1749 the settlers requested that they be allowed to plant and harvest their crops at Córdova, though they did not feel secure enough to move back there. Governor Cadallos y Rabal granted their request but specified that while working their fields the settlers should post sentries on the hills to warn of Indian attack. At night, they were directed by the governor to gather in one house for optimum protection.[4] By 1750 the Córdova settlers had moved back to their village, but raids by nomadic Indians continued to be a problem.[5] Other settlements in the Rio Arriba area abandoned during the 1740s and early 1750s were Ojo Caliente, Santa Rosa de Lima de Abiquiú,[6] and Embudo.[7]

In order to swing the balance on the northern frontier in favor of the Spanish, Governor Tomás Vélez Cachupín carried into effect a settlement plan involving the establishment of buffer communities to provide a zone of protection around the population centers at Santa Cruz and Santa Fe. These communities were to be built around a central plaza, which was thus completely enclosed, having one gate large enough for wagons to pass through, like Truchas[8] and Cordova.[9] But many other settlements resisted Vélez Cachupín's directions to consolidate into compact communities, preferring instead to live in *ranchos* scattered along the watercourses. These settlers built their homes close to their fields because they placed a higher priority on protecting their crops from raiding Indians and wild animals than they did on personal safety.[10]

In 1750 Governor Vélez Cachupín noted the abandonment of several important frontier settlements and directed the resettlement of Abiquiú, ordering that former settlers who did not return would forfeit their land. Those who did resettle Abiquiú were directed to build their houses contiguously around a fortified plaza, to own firearms and take them when they went to work in their fields, and to go to their fields in one body, working the field of one person at a time until everyone's land had been cultivated. Vélez Cachupín hoped that prompt resettlement under these conditions would demonstrate to "the barbarous enemies . . . the greater effort and valor of the Spanish . . . ," [and] that repeated raids had not broken the resolve of the Spanish to settle the remote areas of the province.[11]

The making of the Las Trampas grant in 1751 by Governor Vélez Cachupín was part of the governor's over-all Indian defense policy. In his granting decree, he pointed out that the settlement would provide a barrier to Indian raids on the interior settlements, and would make agricultural land available to Santa Fe's unemployed, for due to the overpopulation of the villa there was insufficient land and water to support its inhabitants.[12]

The twelve petitioners for the Las Trampas grant came from the Barrio de Analco region of Santa Fe, the area south of the Santa Fe River administered for spiritual purposes by the San Miguel Chapel. The residents of this area were primarily presidio soldiers, Mexican Indian (Tlascalán) servants of the Spanish, and *genízaros*.[13] The Tlascaláns had been traditional allies of the Spanish ever since they aided Cortés in conquering the Aztecs. Settlements of Tlascaláns were founded in Northern Mexico during the second half of the sixteenth century to provide a buffer zone between hostile Chichimecas and the Spanish population and to provide an example to the Chichimecas, whom the Spanish hoped would follow the Tlascalán example and settle down in permanent villages.[14] At Las Trampas a similar policy was being followed, though the defensive value of the barrier com-

munity was more realistic than any hope that the roving Apache and Ute
would settle down and follow the example of the Las Trampas settlement.

Besides Mexican Indians, the Trampas settlers included Melchor Rodríguez, son of Sebastián Rodríguez, Diego de Vargas's black drummer and
herald,[15] Melchor's son, Pedro Felipe, and his daughter, Joaquina, wife of
Juan García, also one of the Trampas twelve. The leader of the group was
Juan de Arguello, who was fifty-seven when the settlement was founded and
died at the age of ninety-five, at which time he was described as the founder
of Las Trampas and its church. Arguello's wife was Juana Gregoria Brito,
who probably had some Indian blood, and at least three of their children
were either settlers or wives of settlers.[16] Thus the Trampas settlers were of
mixed *genízaro*, Tlascalán, African, and Spanish blood.

Genízaros were nomadic Indians whom the Spanish had purchased as
slaves, often as children. Eventually many of them would be granted their
freedom and might even acquire *vecino* status. *Genízaros* were among the
best warriors and had a strong incentive to stick it out at a new settlement,
for this was one of the few ways they could move out of their low social class
and achieve *vecino* status by acquiring land.[17] Las Trampas was similar to the
genízaro settlements at Abiquiú and San Miguel del Bado: in all three cases,
the task of holding frontier outposts against Indian attack fell primarily to
other Indians and mixed-blood Spaniards.

The Trampas petitioners began laying the groundwork for their new
settlement several weeks before the mid-July 1751 granting decree from
Governor Vélez Cachupín by looking to the west of their proposed grant to
the Sebastián Martín grant, where the boundary between the two grants
was the Río de las Trampas. The new settlers induced Sebastián Martín to
deed them 1640 varas of land on the west side of the river in order to obtain
as much irrigable land as possible. It appears that there may have been some
friendly persuasion in high places to get Martín to make this donation, for
his deed referred to "reliable information . . . [that Governor] Vélez Cachupín . . . intends, as good government should do, to settle the place called
Santo Tomás del Rio de las Trampas." Martín, who lived in Nuestra Señora
de la Soledad (present day Villita), stood to gain from the new settlement
with better protection from Indian raids — an added inducement to convey
these farm lands. He made his deed on 1 July 1751 before Alcalde Juan José
Lobato to the twelve heads of families.[18]

The petition for the Las Trampas community grant has not survived.
Governor Vélez Cachupín's granting decree gave 180 *varas* along the river

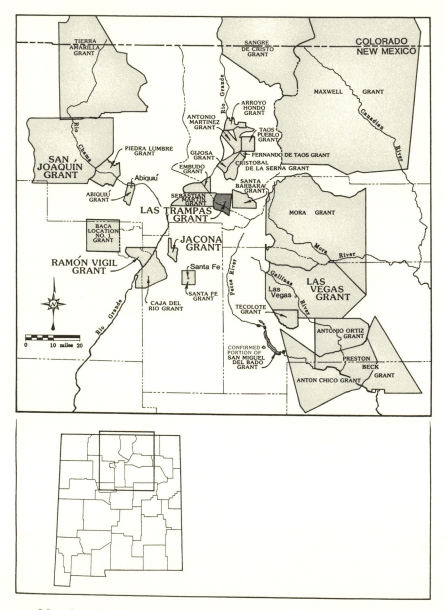

7.2. *Map of northern New Mexico land grants with the Las Trampas grant highlighted.*

of wheat-growing land (*tierras del pan llevar*) to each of the twelve grantees. In addition, he specified that each would receive "corresponding water, pastures and watering places" (*con sus aguas pastos y abrevaderos*), the traditional manner of designating the settlers' rights to common land and water. The governor directed that the grantees could not sell their private tracts for four years and ordered Alcalde Lovato to place the twelve heads of families in possession of the land.[19] Lovato performed the act of possession on 10 July 1751, assigning each family 157 varas of land for dwellings, gardens, and outbuildings, and then distributing the 180 varas of wheat-growing land called for in Vélez Cachupín's decree.[20]

In some cases more than 180 *varas* of land were distributed; for instance, Salvador Baca received 200 *varas*.[21] This measurement was made along the river and, though unstated, the length of the tract was from acequia to acequia. Thus where the river valley narrowed into a canyon, the length of the strip of land would be shorter. To compensate, the width along the river would be increased, as was the case with Salvador Baca's allotment. Although not set forth in the act of possession, the traditional ceremony of plucking up grass, throwing stones, and shouting "Long live the King!" was undoubtedly performed, for no land grant ritual of taking possession of the land would be complete without it. The Trampas twelve now had their community land grant. What remained to be done was to keep the settlement alive in the face of ever present Indian attacks.

One such raid occurred in 1773 when five hundred Comanches are said to have attacked the settlement of El Valle.[22] The resulting battle must have cost the lives of numerous settlers, for the population of the entire grant was only 278 when Fray Francisco Atanasio Domínguez took a census in connection with his well known visitation to New Mexico in 1776.

Domínguez describes the Trampas settlement and its settlers in his usual graphic and gossipy style:

> These settlers do not live in ranchos but in a plaza like a neighborhood house, For the most part they are a ragged lot, but there are three or four who have enough to get along after a fashion. They are as festive as they are poor, and very merry. Accordingly, most of them are low class, and there are very few of good or even moderately good blood. Almost all are their own masters and servants . . .[23]

Domínguez also describes the Las Trampas church, recently called "the most perfectly preserved Spanish Colonial church in the United States," by one architectural expert.[24] Bishop Tamarón licensed the church in 1760 and it was still under construction in 1776, when Domínguez reported that Juan Arguello, then over eighty years old, asked him for alms to support the building project.[25]

A major setback to the Trampas grant settlements occurred in 1781 when a smallpox epidemic that had taken a heavy toll in other parts of New Mexico caused the death of thirty-one adults and twenty-three children.[26] But despite the multiple problems of disease, Indian attack, and basic survival, the Las Trampas grant settlers stayed and even prospered in a modest way. Besides the village of Las Trampas, the villages of Ojo Sarco, Chamisal, Llano, and El Valle had grown up on the grant by the time the United States occupied Mexican New Mexico in 1846.

The Las Trampas grant's first contact with the new Anglo legal system was relatively smooth and did not contain any warning of the legal machinations which were to be the grant's undoing. Cristobal Romero, a justice of the peace for Taos County, took the first step in obtaining U.S. confirmation of the Las Trampas grant in June 1859, when he filed a petition before Surveyor General William Pelham seeking confirmation of the grant on behalf of the heirs and successors of the original twelve settlers. Romero stated that the tract contained the communities of Las Trampas, Chamisal, and [El] Valle,[27] and a later witness estimated the population of Las Trampas to be two hundred souls.[28] Pelham took the testimony of two witnesses who testified that they had known of the Las Trampas grant since their youth, that it was continuously occupied, and that it was in existence in 1846.[29] Pelham then recommended to Congress that the claim be confirmed,[30] basing his report on the fact that the grant documents were properly located in the archives of New Mexico and upon the presumption of a valid community grant when a town is shown to have existed on the grant as of 1846.[31] As a result of this favorable report, Congress confirmed the grant on 2 June 1860 to the Town of Las Trampas, clearly indicating its intention that it be confirmed as a community grant.[32]

The grant was surveyed in June 1876 by Deputy Surveyors Sawyer and McBroom and found to contain more than forty-six thousand acres. However, Commissioner N. C. McFarland of the General Land Office was not satisfied with this survey and advised Surveyor General Henry M. Atkinson that the eastern boundary line was located too far east, causing the Las

Trampas grant to substantially overlap the Santa Barbara grant. On 13 May 1885, General Land Office Commissioner William Sparks set the Sawyer-McBroom survey aside and ordered a resurvey of the southern and eastern boundaries of the Las Trampas grant.[33] Deputy Surveyor Clayton Coleman resurveyed the grant in May of 1891 and found that the grant contained only about twenty-eight thousand acres. A patent based on the greatly reduced acreage of the Coleman survey was issued on 6 January 1903.[34]

Three years before the delivery of the patent, the wheels of that engine of destruction called the partition suit were set in motion, which would ultimately lead to the loss of the grant's common lands. The partition suit, authorized by New Mexico statute in 1876,[35] set up a procedure for either the sale or physical division of jointly owned land, when requested by one of the owners. The right to a physical division was never applied to the common lands of a community land grant, however, for it was the sale of the common lands that was universally desired by those bringing the suit. Often the instigator of a partition suit was the attorney who secured confirmation of the grant, for he could thereby convert his interest in the common lands into cash. These attorneys customarily took a quarter to one-third of the commons as their fee for successfully securing grant confirmation. But lawyers were not interested in owning land in common with a multiplicity of land grant heirs—they wanted hard cash for their efforts. The contingency fee was probably the only way land grant heirs could acquire legal counsel, for under this arrangement the grant did not have to pay the lawyer unless he was successful in obtaining confirmation of the grant. But hiring a lawyer in this way forced the land grant to make a terrible choice between no legal representation at all or the alienation of their priceless common lands. Although the partition and sale of the Las Trampas grant was initiated by a grant heir and not by the attorney wanting to convert his share of the grant into cash, lawyers were required in the long drawn-out legal process that followed the filing of a suit to partition the grant, and it was these lawyers who ended up with the lion's share of the grant.

One of these attorneys was Alonzo B. McMillan, who filed the suit for the partition of the Las Trampas grant on behalf of David Martínez, Jr. who hoped to solve his chronic debt problems by liquidating his interest in the grant. Martínez had defaulted on an unsecured loan of $1,000.00 made by the First National Bank of Santa Fe and he needed money badly. He had written Surveyor General Edward F. Hobart in 1892 to ask when the patent would be issued,[36] but the bureaucracy in Washington had misplaced some papers causing an eleven year delay in issuing the patent.[37] By 1899 the bank had obtained a judgment against Martínez and the partition suit followed within a year.[38]

The suit to partition the common lands of the Las Trampas community land grant was filed in October 1900 by Martínez and four other descendants of the original grantees, and it named only five individual defendants.[39] All the living heirs of the original twelve grantees and all grant residents should have been named as defendants and served with a copy of the complaint to give them notice of the suit and an opportunity to contest it, but Martínez certified under oath that he did not know the names of any of the other heirs.[40] This was absurd. Almost everyone living in the villages on the grant was either an heir of the original Trampas grantees or a purchaser from an heir and thus an owner of the grant's common lands. But land grant partition suits were routinely filed naming only a handful of living defendants and publishing notice of the lawsuit to "unknown heirs" until the New Mexico Supreme Court put an end to this unfair practice.

In 1912, thirty-six years after the partition statute was enacted, the New Mexico Supreme Court required that persons in possession of land sought to be partitioned had to be served personally instead of by publication in a newspaper. The court in *Rodriguez v. La Cueva Ranch Co.* said that if this rule of basic fairness was not followed,

> the plaintiff in a partition proceeding may sit in his office, refrain from all inquiry as to the persons claiming any part of the estate sought to be partitioned . . . (and) proceed against them as unknown owners, and thereby deprive them effectually of all their rights and property . . .[41]

That is exactly what happened with the Las Trampas grant common lands.

By certifying that the heirs and owners of the grant were unknown, the plaintiffs were able to obtain a court order allowing notification of these "unknown heirs" through publication of a legal notice. The notice for the Trampas grant was published in English in the *Taos Cresset* newspaper.[42] Since very few of the heirs could read English, and those few were not likely to read the legal notices, this device allowed the plaintiffs to force the sale of the grant without the knowledge of the other owners. After the legal notice was published, the court appointed Ernest A. Johnson as referee to determine the owners of the grant and their fractional interests in the common

7.3. Aerial photograph of the village of Las Trampas and surrounding lands, showing the Trampas River flowing through the center. The acequias on each side form a clear dividing line between the wooded common lands on one side and the irrigated private tracts on the other. The pattern is typical of many northern New Mexico mountain villages. Courtesy Historic Preservation Division, New Mexico Office of Cultural Affairs.

lands. Just as important, Johnson was to determine how much of the grant was common lands and how much was the private property of the settlers living on the grant.[43] This private property was comprised of the occupied land in the settlements of Ojo Sarco (150 acres), Cañada de los Alamos (50 acres), Las Trampas (150 acres), El Valle (50 acres), Chamisal (50 acres), and El Llano (200 acres). Referee Johnson found that only 650 acres were private land and that the rest was common land subject to partition. He prepared a list of the owners of the grant together with their fractional interests, and submitted it to the court.[44] The 650-acre estimate for private land was not based on any survey and was less than one-tenth the area that an actual survey would later determine the private lands to be. None of the owners of the private lands knew about this ridiculous estimate, but nevertheless the squeeze had begun.

Judge Daniel H. McMillan, substituting for Judge John R. McFie, entered an order of partition and appointed a board of commissioners to physically divide the common lands of the grant, if feasible.[45] The commissioners predictably reported that due to the character of the land and the large number of interests involved (nearly 300), partition of the grant was impossible.[46] Judge McFie, who had returned to the bench, approved the report of the commissioners, and ordered that the common lands of the grant be sold.[47] The only bid at the sale was $5,000 by H. F. Raynolds.[48] Ernest Johnson, who was special master to conduct the sale in addition to being the referee, closed the sale, and Judge McFie confirmed his actions, setting the fees for the commissioners. He determined attorney McMillan's fee as one-quarter of the net proceeds.[49]

Not only did attorney McMillan stand to receive the largest portion of the sale proceeds for performing the unwanted service of forcing the sale in the first place, he also had at least two more fingers in the Las Trampas grant pie. Not content with his attorney's fee for the partition suit, McMillan had been acquiring deeds to one-third and one-quarter interests in the common lands from the grant heirs, including David Martínez who deeded him one-quarter of his interest. By this means McMillan had acquired an additional 10.6 percent of the grant. The only heir with a larger interest was Martínez himself with 18.3 percent. The share of most heirs was substantially smaller (as little as 1/14,000 of the grant).[50]

His second finger in the pie caused lawyer McMillan some embarrassment, and temporarily stalled his plan for cashing in on the Las Trampas grant. After the partition sale had been confirmed, a suit was filed by a creditor of Amado Chavez, the assistant to Referee and Special Master Johnson, to set the sale aside. The suit alleged that Raynolds, the purchaser at the sale, was the law partner of attorney McMillan and that McMillan and Amado Chavez were silent partners who had all conspired to purchase the grant at the sale for 18 cents and then sell it at $1.50 per acre. According to the complaint, prepared by lawyer Alois B. Renehan, Raynolds and McMillan had a contract to sell at the higher price and had bribed Referee and Special Master Johnson to go along with the scheme.[51] Judge McFie must have believed these allegations for he set aside the sale on 1 May 1902 and ordered that a new one be held.[52]

It was not until February 1903 that another sale was scheduled, but David Martínez tried to stop it from occurring. Martínez must have known that the sale price would not be enough to yield him a significant amount of money. Although he told Special Master Ernest Johnson that he knew of prospective buyers who would pay a dollar per acre if the sale could only be delayed a few days, Johnson was unmoved and proceeded with the sale. The high bid was about $17,000 — approximately 60 cents per acre. The high bidder was Frank Bond, an Española merchant and sheepman who had come to New Mexico from Canada in 1883.[53] Bond had prospered in merchandising and sheep raising and he owned other land grants to provide grazeland for his sheep and for speculation.[54]

After the transfer of the grant's common lands to Bond, attorney A. B. McMillan was still able to walk away from the Las Trampas grant partition suit with a fee of over $4,200 — the largest slice of the common land pie — though his dream of owning the entire grant was not to be. David Martínez netted only about $200 after his debt to the First National Bank of Santa Fe was paid, but the villagers received an average of only $25 for their interests in the common lands. They were still unaware of the magnitude of what had happened to them and their grant.[55]

Thus ended the first phase of the Las Trampas grant dismemberment. Still to come was a new group of attorneys who again took advantage of the unsuspecting villagers. Chief among them was Charles C. Catron, the son of New Mexico's land grant tycoon, Thomas B. Catron. Charles was to fail so badly in protecting the villagers that the seeds of his neglect are still bearing the fruit of continued litigation over the Trampas common lands. This all came to pass because the Trampas settlers did not realize in 1903 that the common lands of their grant had been sold. Over the next four years the villagers were still able to use the common lands as they had in the past, but during that period, Frank Bond was trying to sell the grant. Even though Bond had title to the common lands, the settlers' use of the land indicated that they still might have some rights to it.

Bond was attracted to the Trampas grant by more than its rangeland — it was the timber that made the land valuable to an outsider. Shortly after his purchase of the grant at 69 cents per acre, Bond received an offer to sell the grant at a $10,000 profit, but he decided to wait and see if he could get more. No more lucrative offers were forthcoming, however. Instead Bond was compelled to pour an additional $108,000 into the grant in the ten years following his purchase. In 1907 he sold the grant to the Las Trampas Lumber Company, a corporation comprised of four Albuquerque business-men, for an unknown purchase price with a down payment of $16,000. But the new owners soon found out that their title was not secure, for the

inhabitants of the grant had at last discovered that their common lands had
been sold, and they hired attorney Charles Catron to help them get their
land back. Probably it was Catron who notified O. N. Marron, the attorney
for and a principal investor in the Las Trampas Lumber Company, of the
situation.[56]

Then began a new round of litigation. It followed a pattern common to
other land grants which, like Las Trampas, were partitioned and sold in the
early 1900s. These partition suits turned out to be defective because all
parties with a claim to the land were not named. Usually the attorney
handling the suit would do exactly what the court in *Rodriguez v. La Cueva
Ranch Co.* criticized. He would sit in his office and draw up the legal papers
without making any attempt to locate and name as defendants the owners
of the grant who were living on the land. Instead, defendants would be
named as "unknown heirs of the original grantee(s)." Then, instead of
receiving notice of the proceedings by having a copy of the complaint
personally delivered to them, the defendants would supposedly receive
notification by publication in the legal notices of a newspaper in their
county. This did not actually give notice in most cases, and that was why
lawyers preferred this method. If no one knew of the lawsuit, no one would
contest it, and the plaintiff would win by default.

But New Mexico's courts finally put an end to this practice. Besides the
Rodriguez case dealing with partition suits mentioned earlier, a 1911 New
Mexico Supreme Court case held that property owners whose identities
could be determined, must be sued by name and not as unknown heirs. This
was the case of *Priest v. Town of Las Vegas,* a suit to quiet title to the Las
Vegas grant.[57] The *Priest* and *Rodriguez* cases together had a telling impact
on the Las Trampas grant.

The second phase of Las Trampas litigation began with the filing of a
quiet title suit by the Las Trampas Lumber Company, which wanted to find
out exactly what land it owned and clear the title to that land. The common
lands had never been surveyed, but were estimated to include all of the
grant except 650 acres of private land. More precision in the identification
of the privately held lands was necessary in the face of a challenge by the
villagers to the validity of the partition suit. When the quiet title suit was
first filed in 1908, only a few individuals were named and any attempt to sue
all the villagers proceeded very slowly. In 1911, Charles Catron filed an
answer on behalf of a large number of people residing on the grant. Two
years later an amended complaint was filed naming even more individual

defendants.[58] Finally, an attempt was being made to name the real owners of the grant in a suit designed to take most of their land from them. It was probably no coincidence that the amended complaint was filed in 1913 after both the *Rodriguez* and *Priest* decisions had been handed down, The message of those cases — that a person in actual possession of land involved in a partition or quiet title suit must be named and personally served — was finally being heard. Now for the first time the Las Trampas grant settlers had a chance to have their day in court in a suit to determine the ownership of the grant. But the suit was never tried before a court — instead it was settled.

The two lead lawyers in the quiet title suit were Charles Catron, supposedly representing the settlers, and Alois B. Renehan. Renehan was no stranger to the Las Trampas grant for he was the lawyer who sued to have the first partition sale set aside due to the alleged fraud and bribery of Alonzo McMillan and his law partner. Now Renehan was representing Frank Bond, who had sold the grant to the Las Trampas Lumber Company. In his deed to the lumber company, Bond had warranted that he had good title to the land he was selling and that he would defend any title claim made against the lumber company. When the settlers represented by Catron filed their answer contesting the quiet title suit, the Las Trampas Lumber Company formally demanded that Bond fulfill the warranties in his deed to the lumber company.[59] Eventually Bond and the company reached an agreement by which Bond assumed responsibility for clearing the title to the grant and bought half the stock in the lumber company for almost $58,000. This explains why Renehan, as Frank Bond's attorney, took such an active part in the quiet title suit. Surprisingly however, Renehan not only represented the lumber company, but he also acted as attorney for some of the settlers.

Both Catron and Renehan represented different groups of settlers, and between them the two attorneys worked out a settlement of the lawsuit. Renehan had a serious conflict of interest when he acted as lawyer for the Las Trampas Lumber Company in the quiet title suit, at the same time he was representing some of the settlers who were defendants in that suit. He attempted to cover up this conflict by having his partner, E. R. Wright, sign the lumber company's court documents, but it is clear from Renehan's papers that he was the lawyer for the company. In a letter to the lumber company, Renehan explained the settlement in great detail revealing that he and not Wright was the attorney for the company.[60]

As a first step in clearing the title to the grant, Bond hired civil engineer Thomas Hayden to survey and map the private land in the villages. Hayden's survey disclosed that lands in the villages of Ojo Sarco, Cañada de los Alamos, Diamante, Las Trampas, El Valle, Llano, Chamisal, Ojito, and other private tracts along the Santa Barbara River, amounted to almost 7,000 acres, instead of the 650 acres estimated at the time of the partition suit.[61] According to the settlement reached by Catron and Renehan, the villagers received deeds to these private tracts where their houses and fields were located, and right of way easements for their irrigation ditches. And although the settlers executed quit-claim deeds to the lumber company covering what had been the common lands, they retained certain important use-rights in the common lands. These rights were spelled out in agreements that gave the settlers the right to graze their animals on the common lands near the villages, and to take from this forested land "down timber for fuel and unmerchantable standing timber for fence posts and rafters (vigas)."[62] Under this settlement agreement the villagers would still have use-rights for grazing and wood gathering, the two land uses essential to their subsistence, and the lumber company would retain the timber rights for all the merchantable standing timber. It seemed like a deal that would benefit both sides, especially since Catron and Renehan led the settlers to believe that they and their heirs would retain these use-rights perpetually. But unbeknownst to the settlers, Renehan tried to make sure that these rights would last only as long as the Las Trampas Lumber Company owned the grant.

The use-rights were described in an agreement between the lumber company and the settlers represented by Catron and Renehan that was filed with the court. Pursuant to this settlement agreement the villagers signed a deed to the lumber company conveying the common lands to the company, and although this deed was recorded in the county land records it did not mention the use-rights. Those rights were referred to in the master settlement between the Las Trampas Lumber Company and the villagers. Under this agreement the lumber company was to deliver to each of the land grant heirs an individual agreement in his or her name setting forth the wood-gathering and grazing privileges.[63] These individual use-right agreements were on a printed form, signed by the president and secretary of the Las Trampas Lumber Company and stamped with the seal of the lumber company.[64] They looked very official, and the settlers undoubtedly thought that they were fully protected once they had their own copy with their

THIS AGREEMENT, made and entered into this.................day of ...., 1913, by and between Las Trampas Lumber Company, a New Mexico Corporation of Albuquerque, New Mexico, party of the first part, and..

of.., New Mexico, part.......of the second part.

WITNESSETH: That for and in consideration of the sum of one dollar, lawful money of the United States, paid unto Las Trampas Lumber Company by the said part......of the second part, the receipt whereof is hereby confessed and acknowledged, and in the further consideration of the compromise and settlement of that certain controversy existing between the parties hereto, concerning the Las Trampas Grant, situate partly in Rio Arriba County and partly in Taos County, State of New Mexico, entitled Las Trampas Lumber Company v. Juan B. Ortega, et al., and numbered 840 on the docket of the District Court of Taos County, and a certain quit-claim deed given by the par......of the second part unto the said party of the first part to such portion of the Las Trampas Grant as is not included within the segregated tracts around the towns of Ojo Sarco, Canada de Los Alamos, Diamante, Trampas, Valle, Llano, Chamisal, sometimes called Ojito, and the possessions along the Santa Barbara River, which said segregations are to be made under the provisions of a decree to be entered in said cause, the party of the first part hereby grants unto the part......of the second part the following rights within the exterior boundaries of the said Las Trampas Grant, as officially surveyed, to wit:

That the said part......of the second part, and ....heirs shall have the right to graze domestic animals upon the said Las Trampas Grant in proximity to the towns and settlements wherein the said part......of the second part reside......on the said grant, outside of the said segregations in reference to the place of residence of said second part......and shall have the right to take from the said grant down timber for fuel, and unmerchantable standing timber for fence posts and rafters (vigas) for their domestic use, but such grazing and taking of fuel, fence posts and rafters, shall be confined to such parts of the said grant as shall be open and not in use by the said first party, Las Trampas Lumber Company, from time to time, or by its successors, assigns, tenants, servants or employes, nor shall such grazing and taking of fuel, fence posts or rafters be at any time done in such manner as to interfere with the operations of the party of the first part and its privies upon or within the said grant, nor shall the rights hereby granted be construed to permit the said part......of the second part, or ....heirs, to take, have or remove merchantable timber from the said grant for any purpose, outside of said segregations, nor to graze ....domestic animals at any other place or places within the said grant outside of the said segregations, than such as are not operated, occupied or used by the party of the first part, its successors or assigns, from time to time, nor shall it be construed to permit the part......of the second part or...................heirs to take fuel, fence posts or rafters from the said grant outside of said segregations, except such as may be reasonably proper and necessary for their domestic uses; nor shall the said part......of the second part, or ....heirs, have the right hereunder to take, have, use or remove any saw timber or any timber convertible into merchantable lumber, nor shall ....have the right to interfere with, impede or prevent the party of the first part, its successors or assigns, in the occupancy or use of any part of the said grant outside of such segregations from time to time, provided, that the segregations made at and about the towns and settlements, as segregated, under the provisions of a decree in the aforesaid cause, for the benefit of the said towns and settlements, and the inhabitants thereof and the landholders therein, shall be and shall be understood to be, no part of the said grant, and, provided, that, except as herein otherwise stipulated, all timber upon the said grant except that upon the individual holdings of the tenants and landholders within such towns and settlements, as segregated, shall appertain to the plaintiff, Las Trampas Lumber Company.

That the inhabitants and landholders of such town or settlement, as well as of each town and settlement within the said grant, segregated as aforesaid, the private and public ditches thereof, and the owner or owners of such private or public ditches, shall at all times have the right of way for such ditches as are at this time in existence upon the said grant, and the party of the first part, its successors and assigns, shall at all times protect such ditches and their headgates and intakes against destruction from its operations.

In further consideration whereof, the said part......of the second part ....contemporaneously with the execution of this instrument by the party of the first part, made and delivered to it a quitclaim or relinquishment deed for all right, title or interest on the part of the part......of the second part in said Las Trampas Grant outside of such towns or settlements, segregated as aforesaid.

IN WITNESS WHEREOF the party of the first part has caused these presents to be executed by its President and attested by its Secretary, and its corporate seal to be hereto affixed, under and by virtue of authority of its Board of Directors the day and year first hereinbefore written.

LAS TRAMPAS LUMBER COMPANY,

By..

Its President

7.4. Printed form of agreement issued to Las Trampas grant villagers, giving grazing and wood-gathering rights on the common lands in return for conveyance of those lands to the Las Trampas Lumber Company. Courtesy New Mexico State Records Center and Archives.

name on it. But under Renehan's scheme the protection was good only until the lumber company sold the grant.

This was so because Renehan had inserted in his own writing the following stipulation into the settlement agreement: "neither this contract nor any contract delivered pursuant hereto by said company is to be acknowledged or recorded."[65] By adding this language, Renehan planned to trick the settlers out of their use-rights to wood and pasture through an Anglo legal principle unknown to the settlers. Under American law if a document is not signed and acknowledged before a notary, it cannot be recorded,[66] and if these agreements were not recorded, the purchaser of the land from the lumber company would not have to respect the use-rights unless they actually knew about them.[67] Renehan did not want any prospective buyer of the common lands to know about the use-rights agreements, for if a buyer knew of these privileges they would not be willing to pay as much for the land, if they would buy it at all. With the device of preventing the recording of the use-rights agreement, Catron and Renehan were able to have their cake (settling the quiet title suit with the villagers based on "perpetual" use rights) and eat it (sell the grant based on no use-rights).

Renehan and Catron failed to properly represent the settler's interests, and they actively deceived both their clients and the court. Renehan told the settlers that the use-rights agreements would be "carried out to the letter," yet there was no trace of these agreements in the court file. Both lawyers did their best to be sure that the use-rights agreements would not be recorded and that the judge would not know of their scheme. The final decree does not mention the obligation of the Las Trampas Lumber Company to allow the villagers to graze their animals and gather wood on the grant, and the settlement agreement filed with the court does not contain the anti-recording clause that Renehan had added to his copy. As the primary lawyer for the settlers, Catron should have made sure that the villagers' grazing and wood-gathering rights were spelled out in the final decree and that they were recorded in the county deed books. Nevertheless, a decree quieting the title to the Las Trampas grant was signed by Judge Thomas Lieb in early May 1914, ending another phase of the legal history of the Las Trampas grant. Another set of lawyers exited with substantial legal fees for which they did the grant more harm than good.[68] Charles Catron's fee was $5,500 in return for which he left a legacy of misunderstanding, confusion, and continued litigation.

Next comes the third act of the Las Trampas grant's legal drama, which is still going on. Soon after title to the common lands was cleared, Frank Bond put the grant on the market at an asking price of $160,000, almost ten times what he paid for it.[69] But Bond did not receive his asking price, or any other profit from the grant, because the Las Trampas Lumber Company declared bankruptcy over a decade later. As was usually the case with land grant speculation, lawyers made the most money from partitioning and clearing the title to a grant, either by working for the speculator as in Renehan's case, or as in McMillan and Catron's case, supposedly for the

the said Las Trampas Lumber Company shall and will give an

individual contract conforming hereto, on demand, when such tenants

and land holders tender to it the quit-claim deed in said stipulation

and herein mentioned. *But neither this contract nor any contract I delivered pursuant hereto by the plaintiff is to be acknowledged or recorded.*

   IN WITNESS WHEREOF, the said Company has caused these presents

7.5. Portion of the settlement agreement between the Las Trampas Lumber Company, represented by A. B. Renehan, and the Las Trampas grant villagers. By inserting certain language in the agreement, Renehan tried to make sure that the printed agreements issued to the villagers would not be binding on a purchaser from the Las Trampas Lumber Company. The handwritten insertion states, "Neither this contract nor any contract delivered pursuant hereto by said company is to be acknowledged or recorded." Courtesy New Mexico State Records Center and Archives.

heirs. Speculators like Frank Bond who purchased a land grant were usually lucky to get back their investment.

When no takers were found to buy the grant, the Las Trampas Lumber Company was forced to live up to its name. It went into the lumber business. The company built a sawmill in El Valle and opened a shipping station next to the railroad at Velarde. The company's manufacture of boards, poles, pilings, and railroad ties was not a profitable enterprise, however, and in 1926 the Las Trampas Lumber Company declared bankruptcy.[70] A year before filing for bankruptcy the lumber company started negotiating with the United States government for the sale of the grant. Renehan, who was still representing the company, provided an abstract of title for the grant to the Albuquerque office of the U.S. Forest Service,[71] and they sent it to Washington where title was approved in late March 1926.[72] The Forest Service also commissioned logging engineer D. M.

Lang, to report on the value of the grant's timber and the feasibility of running a logging operation on the grant. The results of this study were issued as a Stumpage Appraisal Report, which turned out to be an important document in a 1982 court attempt to compel the Forest Service to respect the villagers' use-rights agreements. In his report, Lang found timber cutting in addition to what had been done by the Las Trampas Lumber Company and other mills. He noted that "promiscuous cutting of house logs, poles and posts and fuel wood has taken place throughout the Grant.... It is an established practice for the settlers on the grant . . . to take whatever material they desire from the grant lands."[73]

Despite this evidence on the ground of the taking of wood from the grant, the United States purchased the grant in 1926 in a three-way transaction whereby the receiver in bankruptcy of the Las Trampas Lumber Company sold the grant for $63,000 to the George E. Breece Lumber Company. The Breece Company simultaneously traded the grant to the United States for $76,000 worth of standing timber in the Zuni Mountains of the Manzano National Forest west of Grants, New Mexico.[74]

Soon after the government acquired the Las Trampas grant the villagers expressed concern to their congressman about whether the government would recognize their use-agreements. In early March 1927 New Mexico Congressman John Morrow sent a copy of House Joint Memorial No. 5, which had recently been introduced in the New Mexico legislature, to the Chief Forester in Washington D.C.[75] The memorial stated that ". . . the United States has lately acquired large tracts of Lands within the State comprising certain Spanish and Mexican Land Grants. . . ," and went on to state "that numerous settlements have existed for several generations and the said settlers have acquired certain vested rights such as the right to take and use from said Land Grants the dead and down timber free of cost, [and] the right to take and use unmerchantable standing timber for building purposes." It closed by asking Congress to enact legislation to protect these settler use-rights.[76]

The Forester in Washington forwarded the memorial to the Albuquerque office for an explanation. The Albuquerque office had done some checking with the attorneys who had been involved in the compromise that had given rise to the use agreements. Attorney Renehan had prepared the abstract containing all the deeds and legal documents that supposedly had any bearing on the title to the common lands, but that abstract had not contained any of the use agreements. Renehan's duplicity is clearly revealed here and it is shocking. After leading the settlers to believe that their use-rights would be passed on to their heirs,[77] he wrote a representative of the lumber company that the printed use agreements were "not intended to be recorded for certain reasons."[78] Those reasons became clear when Renehan represented to the Forest Service that no such agreements existed. This is the kind of unethical conduct that almost got him disbarred a few years later. It must have been quite a surprise to the Forest Service when Congressman Morrow sent them one of the agreements.

When the Forest Service asked Charles Catron about the use-agreements, his statements were just as shocking. Although he had represented the settlers he failed to warn them that unless the use-agreements were acknowledged and recorded they would not be binding on a purchaser from the lumber company. He merely told the Forest Service that he had deposited copies in the court file. However an examination of this file reveals no sign of the use-agreements, and the court's copy of the settlement agreement did not contain the anti-recording clause. After talking to Catron the Forest Service concluded that since the use-agreements were not referred to in the court decree and were not recorded "they are without any effect."

In spite of this conclusion the Acting District Forester in Albuquerque had this to say in reply to the Forester in Washington, D.C.: "On receipt of your letter, we took this matter up with the Forest Supervisor, who secured a copy of one of the deeds said to be held by each of the settlers on the grant." The office then expressed a willingness to abide by the terms of the printed agreements:

> Of course it is unfortunate to have this complication arise, but it is believed that with the cooperation of Attorney Catron and tactful action on the part of the local officers, this can be worked out without any great amount of hardship. Our free use and exempt stock regulation will go far to meet the needs of the settlers and their need for timbers or vegas [sic] for construction purposes is confined to poles usually of about eight inches in diameter. With the heavy growth of young stuff on the Trampas Grant, the administrative thinning will meet this need to a large extent.[79]

Note that the Acting District Forester did not express an opinion as to whether the Forest Service would respect the use-agreements, indicating only that existing Forest Service policy would allow the matter to be "worked out."

But even this Forest Service policy changed. Limits were placed on the number and kinds of animals that could be grazed, and the amount of wood that could be taken from the old Trampas grant common lands, and a different and less benevolent Forest Service attitude emerged towards the rights of the villagers under the use-agreements. Soon the Renehan/

Catron deception would be relied upon by the Forest Service to deny the validity of the use-rights agreements altogether.

The shift from the early more kindly Forest Service attitude was felt all over New Mexico from 1915 to the early 1930s. The Service had legitimate concerns about the depletion of forest resources by excessive logging and grazing, but the limitations put into effect took their toll mostly on the small operator who was least responsible for the problem. Large scale operators, of which Frank Bond was the biggest, were hardly affected by these changes in Forest Service policy, which had been building since the Forest Service was established in 1905.[80] The Forest Service began charging grazing fees, limiting the number of sheep and goats that could be grazed, and requiring everyone who grazed animals on the National Forest to first obtain permits.[81]

The situation for the villagers on the Las Trampas grant worsened in the 1930s when wage labor was difficult or impossible to come by. The Trampero's were hemmed in by a forest that was no longer theirs, and now they had to pay for the forage that their use-agreements said they could have for free. Nor did things improve during the 1940s, 1950s or 1960s. In fact they got worse. More people left the villages, though many of those who stayed held on to their agreements as they held on to the hope that some day these agreements would be recognized.

The 1967 courthouse raid in Tierra Amarilla, which had grown out of unredressed land grant grievances, caused the Forest Service to temporarily adopt a more conciliatory position toward land grant heirs. The regional forester issued a written policy which called for the liberalization of livestock management and wood-gathering policies. Unfortunately there was little implementation of the laudable rhetoric contained in this policy.[82] The raid also brought some action on the state level with a project sponsored by the State Planning Office that set out to study land title problems within the land grants and published the *Land Title Study* recommending solutions to these problems.[83]

In early 1971 at a community meeting held in Peñasco as part of the Land Title Study, local residents produced old copies of the use-agreement and made several complaints against the Forest Service. The State Planning Office forwarded a copy of the use-agreement and a summary of the complaints to the Forest Service for its comments. In response the service took the position that it had no knowledge of the use-rights agreements because the agreements were not recorded and not listed in the abstract that the Forest Service examined. Renehan's deception surfaced when the Forest Service argued that it was not required to recognize the agreements, following the same reasoning that Renehan had put forth in the 1920s. In the end the Forest Service refused to give the villagers any assistance.[84]

So the matter stood until a fall day in September 1981 when Ben F. Dominguez and José Paz López were gathering firewood in the mountains about a mile south of the village of Las Trampas. Ben is the son-in-law of José Paz López, and they had brought along a third man, Ron Maestas. Although the three men were on Carson National Forest land, they claimed the right to take wood under their use-agreements and had not obtained permits from the Forest Service. They had filled two of their three pick-up trucks with mostly dead wood and were cutting trees to fill the last truck, when a forest ranger appeared on the scene and cited them for cutting wood without a permit.

Domínguez and López plead not guilty and were tried in federal court in Santa Fe. Though the charge was not a serious one, it raised the issue of the validity of the use-agreements against the Forest Service. Unfortunately, however, that issue was not determined in this litigation because of a technicality. But during the presentation of evidence about the use-agreements, Judge Santiago Campos indicated that if the question of their validity was squarely presented to him again he might well rule in favor of their validity. This was not quite the victory the villagers had been hoping for, but it was encouraging.

The technicality that kept the issue from being decided was this. While the use-agreements gave the villagers the right "to take . . . down timber for fuel, and unmerchantable standing timber for fence posts and rafters (vigas) . . . ," the defendants admitted that they were cutting some standing timber for firewood. Thus the court did not reach the question of the validity of the use-agreements, for even if they were valid, the defendants were not acting in accordance with their terms, and could not claim their protection. But before this point was decided by the court against the defendants, they presented testimony and legal argument on the question of whether the Forest Service was bound by the agreements or whether it could disregard them even if the villagers were complying with their terms. In other words, would the Renehan deception effectively deprive the villagers of their rights?

Ever since the purchase of the grant in 1926 the Forest Service invoked the legal rule that it was not bound by unrecorded use-agreements of which it did not have actual knowledge. This raised the issue of notice: did the Forest Service know about the use-agreements before it bought the land even if they were not recorded? First and foremost, three of the use-agreements were in fact recorded, despite the provision in Renehan's copy of the master agreement that they were not to be notarized or recorded. At the time of the Forest Service purchase Renehan told the service that these recorded agreements did not affect the title to the grant because they were not entitled to be recorded even though they were in fact recorded.[85]

This was a self-serving argument because Renehan was simply trying to protect his client against the use-agreements that had slipped through the cracks in his scheme. Nevertheless, the fact that the three recorded agreements were on a printed form should have prompted the government to investigate further. The law makes any one buying land responsible, not only for what they know about a possible prior interest in the land, but also for what they would learn upon investigation of any suspicious circumstances that come to their attention. A prospective purchaser is held to know everything an investigation would disclose and must investigate such suspicious circumstances as these printed forms; if they do not, they cannot plead ignorance.[86] As it turned out the government had other knowledge of the villagers' use-rights besides the recorded deeds. The government knew from its 1925 Stumpage Appraisal Report that the settlers were cutting a substantial amount of wood from the former common lands. The report referred to: "promiscuous cutting" and of the "established practice for the settlers . . . to take whatever material they desire[d] from the grant lands."

Both the Stumpage Appraisal Report and the three recorded deeds were introduced into evidence at the trial of Ben Domínguez and José Paz López. Their attorney, Santiago Jaime Chavez, argued that these documents gave rise to a legally mandated suspicion called "inquiry notice." Under this rule, according to Chavez's argument, the government should have had at least a suspicion that the wood-cutting usage was based on agreements similar to those that were recorded and should have investigated. Such an investigation would have disclosed the existence of the other use-agreements.

In the Federal Court prosecution of Domínguez and López, Judge Santiago Campos said as much to Deputy United States Attorney Benjamin Silva:

I would suggest to you, Mr. Silva, that if you are proposing to buy a piece of property . . . and some one is coming on that land to purchase timber . . . or if somebody is grazing animals on that land, that you propose to [buy], you better go find out by what right that person is doing that, and do some investigation on that. And if you turn up a deed, or an agreement . . . such as was presented to the United States Government in this abstract, these three agreements, then that should wave a flag colored red before you, and you better do a lot of investigation.[87]

Judge Campos seemed to be saying that he might uphold the use-agreements in another case against the Forest Service. But in the defense of Ben Domínguez and José Paz López, these agreements were of no assistance, for the actions of the defendants were outside their terms. Domín-guez and López, were found guilty and were fined a modest fifty dollars each. Despite the judge's favorable language in support of the use-agree-ments, no court has yet recognized these agreements and the Forest Service still denies their efficacy.

The legal traps and sharp practices of lawyers Charles Catron, Alois B. Renehan, and Alonzo McMillan caused grave injustice to the descendants of the twelve families who courageously settled the Las Trampas grant. The settlers signed away their common lands in return for use-rights, but these rights have been unfairly denied to the descendants of those settlers. Hope-fully this injustice will someday be corrected if the issue of Renehan's deception in connection with the use-rights agreements is again presented to a court for decision.

Eight

Settlement of the Las Vegas Grant and the Invisible Pueblo Rights Doctrine

When the Las Vegas community land grant was granted in 1835 and permanently settled by 1838, it was the culmination of a gradual movement of Hispanic settlement out of the protection of Santa Fe to the rich but exposed grasslands of the northeastern high plains of New Mexico. The settlement of this area is a complicated story of overlapping land grants and competition between small farmer-ranchers and large-scale sheep and cattle operators for grazing lands. To gain control of these lands, *ricos* like Antonio Ortiz, Santiago Ulibarrí, and Luis María Cabesa de Baca, tried to acquire large private grazing grants or control parts of the common lands of community land grants. Small scale farmer-ranchers like the settlers on the Las Vegas community grant often fought these expansionist efforts with varying degrees of success. The resulting pattern of settlement and land ownership included a complex overlay of private and community land grants, several of which are still operating as community land grants to this day.[1] This settlement pattern is of historic interest in itself and as a model to compare with settlement patterns elsewhere in New Mexico. It is also of importance in determining the water rights of the current residents of the Las Vegas grant, many of whom are direct descendants of the early pioneers who planted the first Spanish settlements in a region where Plains Indians did not welcome their presence.

A water rights doctrine completely discredited by modern historians was applied to Las Vegas by the Supreme Court of New Mexico in 1958. Now that court may reconsider its decision, based in part on the following information about the settlement of Las Vegas.[2] If the New Mexico Supreme Court does overrule *Cartwright v. Public Service Company of New Mexico*, it would be correcting a situation whereby the present day municipality of Las Vegas can take all the water in the Gallinas River and deprive community *acequias* in the area of vital irrigation water.[3] This was never the situation under Spanish and Mexican law and practice. The following is some of the historical evidence not submitted to the New Mexico Supreme Court in the late 1950s.

Permanent settlement of the area north and east of Santa Fe began by at least 1794 when the San Miguel del Bado grant was made by New Mexico Governor Fernando Chacón to Lorenzo Márquez and fifty-one others, including thirteen *genízaros* (ransomed Plains Indians who lived as His-

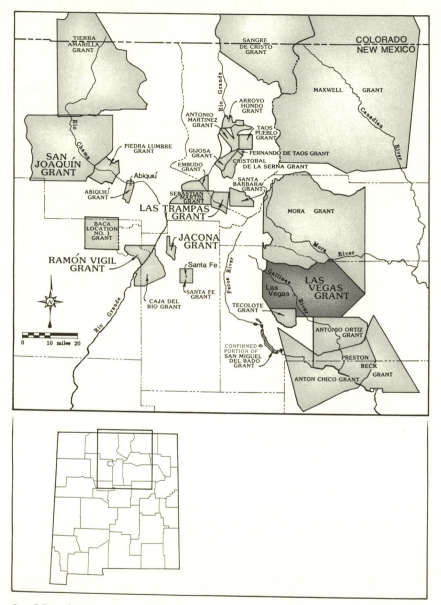

8.2. *Map of northern New Mexico land grants with the Las Vegas grant highlighted.*

panos).[4] San Miguel lies twenty miles downriver from Pecos Pueblo at the place where the trail to the plains, used by *comancheros* and *ciboleros*, crosses the Pecos River. Thus the name San Miguel del Bado.[5] Settlement at San Miguel (then often called simply Bado), took root slowly. It was not until 1798 that a settler from San Miguel del Bado appeared in the marriage registers of the Pecos Pueblo parish, and it is likely that settlement on the grant did not begin until about that time.[6] In 1803 formal allotments were made to fifty-eight families at San Miguel and to forty-seven families at San José, three miles up the Pecos River.[7] By 1811 the San Miguel settlers had finished their church, and in 1812 the priest at Pecos Pueblo received permission from the diocese in Durango to move to San Miguel. By that time San Miguel's population outnumbered that of the once-mighty Pecos Pueblo which was declining in numbers and complaining about Hispanic encroachment on their lands. Soon after Mexico's independence from Spain, San Miguel del Bado elected an *ayuntamiento* and became the administrative headquarters for the entire northeastern plains region of New Mexico.[8]

By 1815 Hispanic settlement had spread beyond the San Miguel del Bado grant, following the Pecos River north to the Los Trigos grant and to what would become known as the Alexander Valle grant.[9] While this movement up the Pecos was going on, three large grants were being made further east on the high plains, in part to provide pasture for increasingly large flocks of sheep owned by wealthy ranchers from Santa Fe and the Rio Abajo region.[10] Two of these were private grants and one was a community grant.

When Santa Fe resident Antonio Ortiz requested a private land grant east of the San Miguel del Bado grant in 1818, it appeared as a threat to *alcalde* Vicente Villanueva of San Miguel, who objected to the grant because it was contrary to the interests of the livestock owners of San Miguel del Bado. The *alcalde* believed that grazing lands in the area previously available to these ranchers would be closed to them if the Ortiz grant was made. In spite of this objection Governor Facundo Melgares granted the land to Antonio Ortiz, who used it to graze his animals.[11] Ortiz's sheep operation was particularly successful; some of his flocks were later herded to California for sale at a healthy profit in San Francisco and at the gold camps.[12]

In 1823 Juan Estevan Pino, the son of the famous Pedro Bautista Pino, received a grant which became known as the Preston Beck grant because of its sale to Beck twenty years later by Pino's sons and their wives. Pino's grant was bounded on the north by the Antonio Ortiz grant, and like the Ortiz grant, it had to be abandoned when Indian raids became too severe.[13] Ironically, Navajo depredations in the Rio Abajo area had been the initial cause of the movement by powerful rancher-merchants to the north and east in search of greener pastures.[14] It is also supremely ironic that fifty years later Thomas B. Catron acquired the Beck and Ortiz grants once again for their prime grazing lands.

The Anton Chico community grant thirty miles southeast of San Miguel del Bado was made to a group of thirty-seven settlers in 1822. Attacks by Comanche and other Indian tribes caused the abandonment of the grant around 1827, but it was resettled in 1834, and this time the settlement took firm root.[15] Since the northern boundary of the Anton Chico grant was also the Antonio Ortiz grant, a substantial overlap between the Beck grant and Anton Chico resulted. This later caused major litigation when both the grants were confirmed by Congress.[16]

Another grant made during this period was Tecolote, northeast of San Miguel and southwest of the later Las Vegas grant. First made in 1824, this community grant followed the pattern of the earlier San Miguel del Bado and Anton Chico grants, with a period of partial abandonment after the grant was first made. The 1824 Tecolote grant was made to six individuals[17] but only two of them remained in 1838 when allotments were made to sixty-nine heads of families at Tecolote and to nineteen at San Gerónimo.[18]

The settlement pattern on the Tecolote grant was different than on the two private grants to Ortiz and Pino, which were grazing grants where sheepherders were the primary occupants. But Tecolote, as well as San Miguel del Bado and Anton Chico, were community grants, where groups of settlers established small communities along the rivers within the grants. These community land grants east of Santa Fe made settlement on the Las Vegas grant feasible by advancing the settled area closer to those large grassy meadows—*las vegas grandes*—so sought after by early land grant petitioners. One of those early pioneers was Luis Mariá Cabesa de Baca, who received the first grant in the Las Vegas area, a short-lived private grant.

Luis María Cabesa de Baca has been described as one of the most notable men of his time.[19] He lived at Peña Blanca where he owned a ranch purchased from Cochiti Pueblo. Cochiti's attempt to annul the sale of that land in 1817 involved Cabesa de Baca in litigation that went all the way up to the *Juzgado General de Indios* in Mexico City, before it was decided by the

Audiencia de Guadalajara.[20] Luis María Cabesa de Baca was no stranger to litigation. In 1792 he was tried for abusing his position as *teniente alcalde* of Santo Domingo and mistreating the Indians there.[21] In his later lawsuit with Cochiti Pueblo it was claimed that Cabesa de Baca had used intimidation and fraud to induce certain members of the pueblo to sell the Peña Blanca land to him. Santo Domingo was also involved in that litigation, asserting that because their boundaries had not been measured accurately they were also entitled to some of Baca's Peña Blanca property. The suit was finally decided in Cochiti's favor in 1819, but Cabesa de Baca did not vacate the Peña Blanca property when ordered to do so.[22]

Cabesa de Baca's experience in these cases may have been the impetus for his seeking a land grant at Las Vegas. His Cochiti lawsuit was consolidated with another land dispute between Santo Domingo Pueblo and Antonio Ortiz, who received the large grant south of Las Vegas mentioned earlier. Antonio Ortiz also appears in the records of Cabesa de Baca's 1792 suit, as *alcalde* of Santa Fe.[23] Cabesa de Baca's acquaintance with Antonio Ortiz may well have alerted the Peña Blanca *ranchero* to the availability of lands north of the Ortiz grant. Moreover, since Cabesa de Baca served for a time as *alcalde* of San Miguel del Bado, the Las Vegas area was within his jurisdiction, so he certainly would have known about the availability of lands there.[24]

Cabesa de Baca may have pastured his sheep and cattle in the Las Vegas area for some time before petitioning for a formal land grant. In January 1821 when he requested a grant of Las Vegas Grandes, he directed the request, not to the governor of New Mexico as was customary, but to the provincial deputation of Durango.[25] It is not clear why Cabesa de Baca followed this unusual procedure, but it may have been that in his travels to Guadalajara to defend the Cochiti litigation he made some connections in Durango that assured him favorable action on his petition. Another more telling reason could be that his position as *alcalde* of San Miguel del Bado in 1820 posed a severe conflict of interest, and he sought to avoid the kind of criticism directed at other large landowners by going to Durango.[26]

In any case, Cabesa de Baca chose Durango as the venue for his solicitations, submitting at least two petitions to the Durango provincial deputation, presenting himself as one of nine petitioners for the grant, all from San Miguel del Bado. The first grant made by the Durango authorities was to all nine, but in his second petition Cabesa de Baca told the *diputación* that none of his eight former companions had any interest in the grant, because each had since acquired other lands. Cabesa de Baca then asked that the grant be reissued to him and his seventeen sons (*hijos varones*; actually several were sons-in-law).[27] After receiving a favorable report on the petition by New Mexico governor Facundo Melgares, the provincial deputation acceded to Cabesa de Baca's second request and revalidated the grant in 1821, with the proviso that if any of his eight erstwhile co-grantees had incurred any expenses in reliance on the first grant (such as building houses), he was to reimburse them.[28] However, it was not until 1823 when another Baca, New Mexico governor Bartolome Baca, signed a decree directing that Cabesa de Baca be placed in possession of the grant by a third Baca, the *alcalde* at San Miguel del Bado, Manuel Antonio Baca. The governor's decree quoted the order of the Durango provincial deputation *verbatim* and determined that the provision about reimbursing the eight companions was not operative because they had not placed any improvements on the land.[29]

It does not appear that *alcalde* Baca actually placed grantee Cabesa de Baca in possession of the land in 1823, for in February 1825 one of his sons, Juan Antonio, petitioned the New Mexico territorial deputation asking that a proper document be issued to his father.[30] The same day the *diputación* agreed to issue the document and again the *alcalde* at San Miguel del Bado was directed to place Cabesa de Baca in possession of the grant.[31] But Luis María Cabesa de Baca's quest to possess the land was to be frustrated for at least two more years. Baca, through his son, stated that on several occasions he had applied to the *alcalde* at San Miguel del Bado asking to be put in possession of his grant at Las Vegas but had been refused.[32] In an earlier statement, *alcalde* Tomás Sena gave what appears to be a lame excuse for not complying with a request by two more of Cabesa de Baca's sons, Miguel and Manuel Baca, that the family be placed in possession. *Alcalde* Sena said that he had been in the middle of an election to determine his successor, and to compound things he had become so sick that he had to send for the priest to hear his confession. He did not explain why he had not performed his duties either before or after his illness and the election.[33] Governor Narbona's response in 1826 to the Cabesa de Baca appeal forms a terse end to the documentation of the first grant at Las Vegas: the governor finally ordered *alcalde* Sena to deliver possession of the grant to Cabesa de Baca.[34]

The reluctance of a series of *alcaldes* at San Miguel del Bado to place Cabesa de Baca in possession of his grant seems to arise from the same motive that caused San Miguel del Bado *alcalde* Vicente Villanueva to object to the Antonio Ortiz grant. Las Vegas Grandes, like the Ortiz grant, was probably being used for grazing by the settlers at San Miguel del Bado who wanted to continue the practice without interference from the Cabesa de Baca family.

The boundaries of the 1821 grant received by Cabesa de Baca were the Sapello River on the north, the San Miguel del Bado grant on the south, the Aguaje de la Yegua and the Antonio Ortiz grant on the east, and the summit of the Pecos mountains (*la cumbre de la sierra de Pecos*) on the west.[35] These are similar to the boundaries given for the 1835 Las Vegas community grant. In 1835 the northern and eastern Las Vegas grant boundaries remained the Sapello River and the Aguaje de la Yegua respectively, but the southern and western boundaries were different. The Antonio Ortiz grant became the southern boundary in 1835 instead of one of the eastern boundaries as in 1821, and the San Miguel del Bado grant became the western boundary in 1835 instead of the southern boundary, as it had been in 1821. These changes in the southern and western boundaries probably meant that the grant to Cabesa de Baca was larger than the subsequent Las Vegas community grant.[36] Thus Luis Mariá Cabesa de Baca had been granted a tract of land probably well in excess of half a million acres on which to graze his herds of cattle and flocks of sheep.[37]

Although Cabesa de Baca had indicated his desire to use the grant for farming as well as cattle raising, no evidence has been found that he or his sons ever irrigated any farmland. The only indication of the settlement of the Baca family on the grant is the testimony of witnesses before the surveyor general and at least one contemporary account. José Francisco Salas, a shepherd for Luis María Cabesa de Baca, testified that he had cared for as many as three thousand sheep on the grant. He said that Cabesa de Baca had built a hut at the Loma Montosa and remained on the grant off and on for ten years before Pawnee Indians finally drove him off. The Cabesa de Baca family is said to have retreated several times to settled areas when the Indians took all their horses, but they returned to the grant when things quieted down. They were forced to abandon the grant in the end, however, and later claimed to have suffered losses totalling $36,000 when six hundred of their mules and horses were driven off by hostile Indians.[38] Historian Charles Cutter says that Cabesa de Baca never left Peña Blanca, because several letters sent during the Mexican Period were posted by Baca from Peña Blanca. Cabesa de Baca is said to have died there in 1833. It is likely that the activity on the grant testified to by Salas was by other members of the Cabesa de Baca family, like the son, Antonio Baca, not Luis Mariá.[39]

The Cabesa de Baca family apparently still occupied the grant by 1831, for in that year Santa Fe Trail chronicler Josiah Gregg reported finding a large flock of sheep grazing near the Gallinas River and "a little hovel at the foot of a cliff [which] showed it to be a rancho. A swarthy ranchero soon made his appearance, from whom we procured a treat of goat's milk . . . ."[40] This was probably Cabesa de Baca's shepherd and his sheep.

While the Cabesa de Baca family was being harried by Indian attacks, similar depredations were occurring south of Las Vegas. In October 1826, three shepherds were scalped by Indians near Tecolote, though they lived to tell their tale. The authorities in San Miguel del Bado sent out an eight man scouting party to search for the offenders, without success.[41] By 1829 a detachment of troops from San Miguel del Bado was patrolling the Las Vegas area, then called "Vegas de las Gallinas." Their commander, José Caballero, reported that his soldiers were complaining about their lack of wages and he made a plea to the *comandante principal* that they be paid forthwith.[42] Instead of being paid, however, this same detachment was called back to San Miguel del Bado by *alcalde* Santiago Ulibarrí in June 1829, because there were insufficient troops and equipment to adequately patrol the area. Although the withdrawal was under orders, the soldiers were charged with cowardice! They answered by stating that their thankless task of protecting settlers without adequate pay or even food made them worse off than the residents themselves, who were herding livestock under military protection at Las Vegas.[43] Thus it appears that some military protection was being afforded and that settlers (probably the Cabesa de Baca family) were still herding sheep in the Las Vegas area in 1829.

Undoubtedly the establishment of a more or less permanent detachment of troops at San Miguel del Bado encouraged the settlement of outlying areas in the years to follow. The detachment of Santa Fe presidio soldiers at San Miguel was carried as a separate company on military records and it assumed major importance beginning in 1827.[44] In that year the Bado company (along with Taos) was allotted almost two thousand pesos and was regularly provided with lances, parts for pistols and carbines, and trinkets as gifts to placate hostile Plains Indians.[45]

The mission of the detachment at San Miguel del Bado was not only to protect settlers against Indian incursions but also to prevent smuggling and import tax evasion along the Santa Fe Trail. Until 1835, when the customs

house was moved from Santa Fe to San Miguel, it was common practice for
Santa Fe residents to meet the incoming caravan from the states and
purchase goods at lower prices than were charged after the merchants had
paid their custom duties. The traders had many ingenious ways of reducing
these import taxes, which were based on the number of wagons in the
caravan. These devices included repacking their goods on fewer wagons or
sending some of them by a different route before they reached Santa Fe.[46]
To prevent these practices, a detachment of troops often escorted the
incoming caravans from some predetermined point to the customs house.
In 1837 that point of contact was near Las Vegas at the Paraje del Puertecito. In June of that year, Vicente Rivera reported that he had encountered twenty carts and three wagons with three or four more coming from
Las Vegas behind them. Rivera reported that he would escort the wagons
until he handed them over to the governor.[47] All this military activity in the
area provided more protection for groups of new settlers, thus encouraging
permanent settlement of the Las Vegas grant.[48]

The first wave of settlement in the Las Vegas area occurred in the mid
1830s, brought about not only by increased military presence but also by
population pressure from San Miguel. The need for new settlements was
explained to the governor in a lengthy petition sent by parish priest José
Francisco Leyba of San Miguel, recommending that the Mexican government take specific steps to establish such communities. Father Leyba was
one of a handful of New Mexican priests who were becoming involved in
political issues in the wake of Mexican Independence.[49] Father Leyba's
1831 petition complained about the population increase at San Miguel del
Bado and recommended that lands in the northeastern part of New Mexico
be settled by those in need of farm land. The priest specifically mentioned
Las Vegas, Sapello, and Ocaté as places where land was available. He
suggested that the government assist prospective settlers by providing them
with oxen and farming tools such as axes and hoes. Father Leyba argued
that settlement of these lands would protect the interior settlements from
Indian attacks by providing a buffer zone, would relieve the population
pressure at San Miguel del Bado, and would provide an outlet for vagrants
whose numbers were increasing there. The San Miguel priest pointed out
that a major inducement for settlement of these northern areas (particularly
Las Vegas), was the ready availability of water from the Pecos River. Father
Leyba contrasted the never-failing water supply of the Pecos with the
inadequate flow of the Rio del Norte (Rio Grande) and the Rio Puerco. He

said that the abundant water would allow agriculture to flourish and the plentiful pastures would sustain vast flocks of sheep and herds of cattle.[50]

In response to Father Leyba's petition a committee was established that endorsed the priest's proposal, recommending that the governor submit a copy to Mexico City requesting the necessary funds to carry out the project.[51] When no action was taken by the governor, the *ayuntamiento* of San Miguel del Bado directed an appeal to the *ayuntamiento* of Santa Fe. In language similar to that of Father Leyba's petition, the San Miguel *ayuntamiento* extolled the virtues of establishing new settlements at Vegas, Sapello, Ocaté, and other places, emphasizing the abundance of pasture and water at these spots, and stating somewhat cynically, that it did not expect an answer from the governor or the *diputación*. Nevertheless, said the San Miguel *ayuntamiento*, the proposed settlements could be established without their help. The Santa Fe *ayuntamiento* agreed suggesting that the *ayuntamientos* themselves make loans to the settlers and that they cooperate with each other, as well as with the governor and the territorial deputation, in enforcing the vagrancy law.[52]

Under the 1828 *Ley de Vagos*, tribunals were to be established to determine who was a vagrant and then to give such a person three choices: to be drafted into the military, to go to prison, or to participate in settling new lands on the frontier.[53] The proposal of the San Miguel *ayuntamiento* was a means of facilitating the third alternative. But there appears to have been no response to its appeal, and eventually the Las Vegas community grant was settled without any government subsidies.[54]

The San Miguel del Bado *ayuntamiento* not only promoted the idea of settling Las Vegas, but some of its members actually joined the settlement there. When the grant was made in 1835, and additional allotments were distributed in 1841, three members of the San Miguel *ayuntamiento* received allotments.[55] This activity by members of the *ayuntamiento* is in marked contrast to the *alcalde* who opposed the making of the Antonio Ortiz grant in 1819 because it would interfere with the grazing rights of the sheep and cattle growers of San Miguel del Bado. Several factors could explain this shift. Once the grant had been made to Cabesa de Baca, the *ayuntamiento* knew that someone would use this land if and when the Cabesa de Baca family abandoned it, and it might as well be the San Miguel del Bado *vecinos*. Also, the severe losses suffered by cattle and sheep growers due to Indian depredations would be curbed if Las Vegas became a permanent settlement with occasional military protection. And finally, as Father

Leyba and the 1832 *ayuntamientos* had pointed out, population pressure was an important motive for expansion. Instead of opposing a grant to an outsider, the *ayuntamiento* members were becoming part owners of the grant themselves.[56]

By 1835 the composition of the *ayuntamiento* had completely changed from that of 1832.[57] In 1835 the secretary of the *ayuntamiento* of San Miguel was José Antonio Casados, who was also one of the petitioners for the Las Vegas grant. Since the petition was directed to the *ayuntamiento*, and Casados was both a petitioner and an *ayuntamiento* member, it is not surprising that the council recommended to governor Francisco Sarracino that the petition be granted. In addition to Casados, Juan de Dios Maese (who later became *juez de paz* at Las Vegas), Miguel Archuleta, and Manuel Durán signed on as the principal settlers, asking for a grant of a tract of uncultivated public land on the Gallinas River for themselves and twenty-five others who were not named. The boundaries requested were the Sapello River on the north, the Antonio Ortiz grant on the south, the Aguaje de la Yegua on the east, and the San Miguel del Bado grant on the west.[58] The petitioners claimed that granting their request would benefit several poor families and would encourage agriculture in general, a theme often repeated in other grant documents. In its report, the San Miguel *ayuntamiento* stated that the land requested was indeed public land (*terreno baldío*), that the grant would not prejudice third parties, and would encourage "the advancement of agriculture and the location of many families without occupation."[59]

The petition was referred to the territorial deputation which made the grant, not only to the petitioners but to all residents of El Bado, and all others who lacked farm lands. The *diputación* also provided that the pastures and watering places would be held in common.[60] On the next day, Governor Sarracino notified the *alcalde* at San Miguel del Bado to select a site for a *plaza*, make allotments to the petitioners, and adopt measures necessary for the security of the settlement.[61] Alcalde José de Jesús Ulibarrí, who was also president of the *ayuntamiento*, distributed private tracts to thirty-six settlers on 6 April 1835, giving them the outboundaries requested in their petition, and providing that the waters and pastures on the land within those boundaries be held in common. As for the security measures ordered by the governor, *alcalde* Ulibarrí ordered the settlers to build a wall around the *plaza* and to provide themselves with arms.[62] These were standard provisions that were often routinely inserted in land grant documents without regard to the different circumstances of grantees. It is not clear whether a wall was ever built at Las Vegas, but one may have been built around the *plaza*.[63]

Although the distribution of lots averaging from 100 to 200 *varas* wide to a group of settlers suggests that Las Vegas was actually settled in 1835, subsequent documents demonstrate that this was not the case. As was true on the San Miguel del Bado, Anton Chico, and Tecolote grants, settlement on the Las Vegas grant was delayed. The Las Vegas grantees were still living on the San Miguel del Bado grant in March of 1836 because in that month, Juan de Dios Maese (one of the four principal settlers), asked Governor Albino Pérez to help him convince the other grantees to settle on the grant. Maese had ordered these individuals to appear at the site of the proposed settlement, named Nuestra Señora de los Dolores de Las Vegas, but no one showed up. There were several reasons for this lack of enthusiasm on the part of the grantees, according to Juan de Dios Maese. He told the governor that he had observed a great indifference toward the land (*mucha . . . desamor a la tierra*) in the would-be settlers, and in addition, many of the grantees were afraid of Indian attacks. The main problem however, was that most of the settlers hoped to receive allotments at Tecolote, closer to the protection of San Miguel del Bado. Maese believed that the lands at Tecolote were inferior to those at Las Vegas because of the scarcity of water at Tecolote, and he asked the governor to order the grantees to take possession of their Las Vegas lands and to notify them that they would not be allotted land at Tecolote.[64]

A review of the Las Vegas grant documents alone could lead one to conclude that after the grant was made and allotments distributed in 1835, a community was established around a plaza following a compact municipal plan, all enclosed by a wall as ordered by Governor Sarracino and *alcalde* Ulibarrí. This conclusion was drawn by the New Mexico Supreme Court in the case of *Cartwright v. Public Service Company of New Mexico*.[65] In fact, the Supreme Court was misinformed about the settlement of Las Vegas and surrounding communities, an error that led to the unfair exaggeration of the water rights of the present day municipality of Las Vegas.

Census, deed, and church records, and records of the nearby Tecolote land grant, indicate that permanent settlement on the Las Vegas grant did not commence until 1838.[66] Furthermore, instead of one compact community, Las Vegas took the form of at least two communities: Las Vegas proper, known as Nuestra Señora de los Dolores de Las Vegas, and upper town, whose patron saint was San Antonio. Rather than compact settlements around a central plaza, these communities were strung out along the Gallinas River running north past the community of Los Vigiles, to Hot Springs, with two plazas for Las Vegas.[67] Initially, the entire settled area was known as the new settlement of Nuestra Señora de los Dolores de Las Vegas.[68] Additional allotments were made in 1841 and 1846, and by August 1846 when the conquering American army arrived in Las Vegas, there were numerous other settlements on the grant. The 1845 Las Vegas census lists eight communities with the following number of heads of families in each: Las Vegas (85), Upper Town (San Antonio) (49), Agua Sarca (5), Valles de Tecolote (San Geronimo) (49), Plaza del Burrito (Santa Ana) (5), Plaza del Torreón (Tecolote) (43), Plaza de los Garcías (Lagunas) (26), and Valles de San Agustín (San Agustín) (35).[69] Other small settlements revealed by deed records are Ojitos Frios, Cañada del Salitre, and Los Ojos (Hot Springs).

Several of these communities were established as part of the Tecolote land grant, most notably San Gerónimo. Since permanent settlement of the Las Vegas grant was closely linked with the Tecolote grant, an examination of the making and settlement of that grant would be useful. And since the Tecolote grant involves an initial private grant and a subsequent overlapping community grant, its early history helps explain the governmental policy that allowed these overlapping grants.

During this period of New Mexico's history, the goal of increasing agricultural production for subsistence was a high priority in Santa Fe. This goal of the central government often caused a power struggle between local governments, on the one hand, and the governor and *diputación* in Santa Fe, on the other. In order to increase agricultural production, a wide distribution of irrigable farm land was necessary, but all too often the *alcaldes* and members of the *ayuntamientos* were monopolizing much of this desirable land. Governor Manuel Armijo expressed this in 1827 when he asked the territorial deputation to report to him concerning "the state of hunger and misery to which the inhabitants of that territory (New Mexico) are reduced on account of the mismanagement of the *ayuntamientos* and the scarcity of lands in which to plant, as a result of a few individuals having appropriated them."[70] It is against this backdrop that the Tecolote and Las Vegas grant overlaps must be examined.

The first Tecolote grant was made in 1824 to Salvador Montoya and five associates by the New Mexico *diputación*. The land encompassed within the requested boundaries was later surveyed at over 48,000 acres, but it was

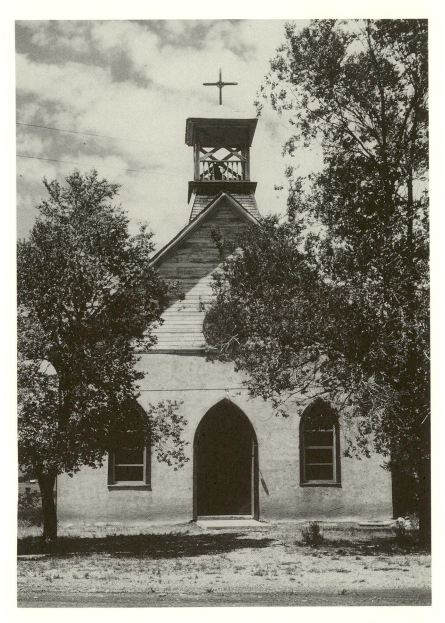

8.3. Church of San Antonio, Upper Las Vegas, ca. 1841. Courtesy Historic Preservation Division, New Mexico Office of Cultural Affairs.

only the agricultural land that Montoya et al. requested.[71] Before the grant was made Governor Bartolomé Baca urged the *diputación* to make the grant to encourage agriculture "whose decline is not due to a lack of lands, but of laboring hands."[72] Here Governor Baca was expressing the opposite view from Governor Armijo's opinion that low agricultural production was caused by unequal land distribution.

According to testimony before the surveyor general, the original Teco-lote grantees were driven off the land by Indians after three or four years, but the land was resettled in the late 1830s.[73] In January 1838 Rafael Benavides and two other individuals requested a grant overlapping the Tecolote grant, for themselves and twenty-four others.[74] The petitioners promised that they would not obstruct the use of the common pastures and waters, and suggested that their petition be forwarded to the *diputación*.[75] *Alcalde* Vicente Rivera referred the petition to governor Manuel Armijo after noting that although the land had already been granted, only two of the grantees had established their rights by cultivating the soil.[76] Governor Armijo referred the petition to the prefect of the first district, Juan Andrés Archuleta,[77] who in turn asked for a report from the *ayuntamiento* of San Miguel del Bado.[78] The San Miguel *ayuntamiento* representatives recommended against the grant because they said the land had already been donated and was being used to pasture animals from the San Miguel area, especially during periods of Indian hostilities. For those reasons, they said, the new grant would be prejudicial to the inhabitants of the area, including presumably the *ayuntamiento* members.[79] It appears that the *ayuntamiento* preferred the land remain open for grazing, instead of being settled by farmers.

The petitioners then decided to start fresh with a new petition that sounded an indignant tone bordering on outrage. How could it be, said the petitioners, that only two individuals with one thousand to four thousand *varas* of land each,[80] could be preferred over a group of more than twenty-five settlers who wanted land to plant in order to support their families. Wasn't this in accordance with the government policy of promoting the development of agriculture? If the land was to remain only as grazing land then shouldn't the 1824 settlers be ousted? For the government to allow two individuals to monopolize Tecolote would mean, said the petitioners, that there was one law for the rich and another law for the poor.[81] In the end Prefect Archuleta decided that the new grant should be made, in language echoing other documents of this period, because the petitioners were asking for agricultural lands, and because the original grantees had been given too much land and had not cultivated it.[82]

The approval of the second Tecolote grant did not end the matter however. Instead there began a dispute between *Juez de Paz* Vicente Rivera and *Juez de Paz* Manuel Antonio Baca over who had jurisdiction and who should place the grantees in possession. It soon became clear that *Juez de Paz* Baca was stalling. He did not want the new grantees put in possession, and he used the jurisdictional question as a delaying tactic.[83] Rivera, on the other hand, felt that the prefect's order should be complied with and suggested a compromise whereby both judges would place the new grantees in possession.[84] Still the two judges could not agree, so the jurisdictional question was submitted to Prefect Archuleta for decision. He decided that the land was within the *Alcaldía* of El Bado, which included San Miguel, Las Vegas, and all the other settlements on the upper side of the Pecos River.[85] This meant that Manuel Antonio Baca was required to put the grantees in possession of land in which he himself claimed an interest. He placed sixty-nine heads of families in possession at Nuestra Señora de los Dolores de Tecolotito (the first village of Tecolote) and nineteen *vecinos* in possession of land at San Gerónimo del Tecolote Grande (present day San Gerónimo on the Las Vegas grant).[86] Both of these settlements are on the Tecolote River.

There is a direct connection between Tecolote's settlement in early 1838 and the actual settlement of the communities around Las Vegas. We know that the 1835 Las Vegas allotments had not been occupied a year later because the Las Vegas settlers hoped to be given land at Tecolote instead. As with other exposed settlements in New Mexico, land grantees northeast of San Miguel wanted some protection from Indian raids before risking their lives on the frontier.[87] Tecolote was closer to the San Miguel del Bado settlements than Las Vegas, so the Las Vegas grantees held out hope that they might receive land at Tecolote until Tecolote was actually settled. The almost simultaneous settlement of the Tecolote and Las Vegas communities is corroborated by the San Miguel County deed books where a substantial number of transfers and allotments at both Tecolote and Las Vegas begin appearing in 1838.[88]

From the early history of the Tecolote grant we learn much about settlement on the Las Vegas grant, about the geographical area of the *alcaldía* of El Bado under whose jurisdiction the Las Vegas settlements fell, and about the power struggles between local officials that centered around

8.4. The village of Tecolote with Hermit's Peak in the background. Drawing by Danté Ruiz.

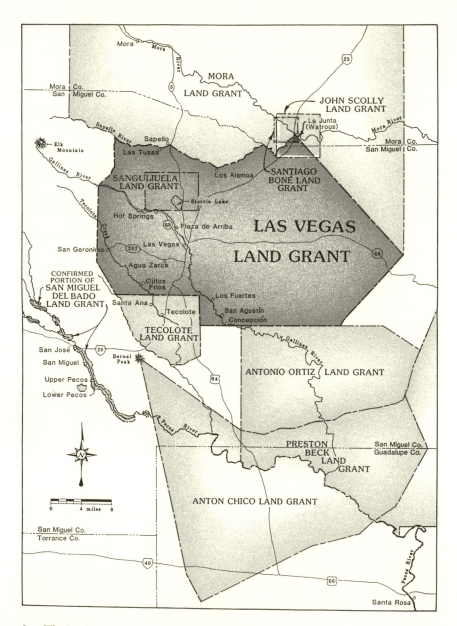

8.5. The Las Vegas Grant and surrounding area.

the major source of wealth in those days — land. *Juez de Paz* Manuel
Antonio Baca is a good example of one such public official who used his
office to further his private ambitions. Baca is the *alcalde* who was ordered to
place Luis María Cabesa de Baca in possession of the first Las Vegas grant
in 1823, but failed to do so, forcing Cabesa de Baca to wage a three year
paper battle to obtain official possession of the land. Manuel Antonio Baca
was temporarily out of office by April of 1825, for in that year he complained as a private citizen to the San Miguel *ayuntamiento* about large
private land grants in the area, particularly a grant made to Juan Estevan
Pino.[89] However, Manuel Antonio Baca was not trying to keep the land
open for the community, but rather for himself, for once back in office he
tried to prevent the second group of Tecolote grantees from being placed in
possession.

Santiago Ulibarrí was another individual who signed the 1825 protest
against the large land holdings of Juan Estevan Pino. Ulibarrí later used his
office to obtain a large private grant within the Las Vegas grant, known as
the Sanguijuela grant. It was one of five grants overlapping the Las Vegas
grant that were later submitted for adjudication to United States forums.
The other four were the Tecolote grant, the Manuelitas grant, the John
Scolly grant, and the Santiago Boné grant. An understanding of each of
these grants, and of several small grants within the Las Vegas grant that
were not submitted for adjudication, is necessary to arrive at a complete
picture of the settlement patterns on the Las Vegas grant.

The Sanguijuela grant was one of two overlaps within overlaps (it was itself
overlapped by the Manuelitas grant),[90] and it involved the Ulibarrí family of
landowners from the San Miguel del Bado area. The patriarch of the family,
Santiago Ulibarrí, lived at San José del Bado along with several other
members of the clan.[91] Early deed records show Santiago buying numerous
parcels of land at San José in the 1820's, where he began to follow the
example of Juan Estevan Pino by controlling as much land as possible,
while at the same time protesting Pino's acquisitions.[92] By 1823 he was

commissioned as a militia captain in the Fifth Cavalry Company, and he later served on the territorial deputation just as Pino did.[93] In the late 1830's and early 1840's, Santiago Ulibarrí was *Juez de Paz* of San Miguel del Bado,[94] and it was in this capacity that he was asked in 1839 for a grant of land at the Arroyo Sanguijuela north of Las Vegas. Two things about that request were highly irregular. First, the four petitioners were all related to Santiago Ulibarrí, either by blood or by marriage: two were his sons and two were married to his daughters.[95] Also unusual was the fact that one of the petitioners, José de Jesus Ulibarrí, was the *alcalde* who had allotted land at Las Vegas in 1835, receiving an allotment there himself. Ulibarrí knew that the Sanguijuela land was totally within the Las Vegas grant, but it appears that the Ulibarrí sons and sons-in-law wanted to stake a more personal claim to the common lands and waters north of Las Vegas and were assured that their petition would be granted. The grant was made by Santiago Ulibarrí two days after the petition was filed,[96] but approval of the grant was not obtained from Governor Armijo until 1842, three years later. Armijo ordered *juez de paz* Juan de Dios Maese to place the Ulibarrís in possession,[97] which he did in July 1842. At that time the landmarks were pointed out and the grantees were given the land as a private grant.[98]

During the Mexican Period the Sanguijuela grant was used by the Ulibarrís for grazing their cattle, which were said to number between two or three hundred head by 1848.[99] In 1844 José Francisco Ulibarrí was still living in San Miguel, for he sent another petition to the governor stating that the Sanguijuela grantees had lost their documents and requesting that new ones be issued. José Francisco said that the earlier grant had been solicited because the petitioners needed a permanent location where the grazing lands and waters were sufficient for their animals.[100] He claimed that although the land requested was within the boundaries of the Las Vegas grant the settlers there would not by injured by the grant but would actually benefit from increased protection from Indian raids. Apparently no action was ever taken on Francisco's petition.[101]

In any case, the Ulibarrís did receive a private grant within the Las Vegas community grant giving them exclusive rights to the pastures in that locality.[102] This is in contrast to other overlapping grants like Manuelitas, which was a community grant conferring no exclusive rights to common waters and pastures but only rights in common with those who had settled before. The 1844 petition of José Francisco Ulibarrí claimed that the Las

Vegas *pobladores* had made no objection to the Sanguijuela grant. However, it should be noted that there is no evidence that the Las Vegas authorities were ever asked whether they had an objection. This was not the case with the Manuelitas grant where the Las Vegas *juez de paz* was asked, did object to the grant, and was overruled.

The 1845 Manuelitas grant, the 1846 John Scolly grant, and the 1842 Santiago Boné grant, each affected the settlement of the northern parts of the Las Vegas grant, but since the new villages of Sapello, Los Alamos, and Manuelitas were located on the Sapello River they did not affect the water rights of settlements on the Gallinas. The Manuelitas grant was made to a group of settlers from Santa Cruz de la Cañada who complained in their petition about the shortage of land and water in that area.[103] Since the land requested overlapped both the Mora and Las Vegas grants, officials in each of those jurisdictions were consulted by the New Mexico *asamblea*.[104] Although the Las Vegas *juez de paz* protested the new grant saying that its overlap of the Las Vegas common lands would be prejudicial,[105] he was overruled by the *asamblea*, which made the grant with the provision that the grantees would receive as private tracts only the amount of land they could cultivate, leaving the rest as common lands.[106] The Manuelitas grant documents reveal that the government of New Mexico recognized the Las Vegas grant because it consulted the *juez de paz* at Las Vegas about the advisability of making the Manuelitas grant. Moreover, even though the government overruled the *juez*, it protected the right of the residents living on the Las Vegas grant to use the common lands.

The grant to Irishman John Scolly also overlapped the Las Vegas grant, and was also objected to on the ground, among others, that it would prejudice the Las Vegas common lands. This time, however, the objection was made by a committee of two appointed in 1845 by Governor Mariano Martínez to investigate the John Scolly petition.[107] When Governor Manuel Armijo returned to office for the third time the grant was made despite this and other objections put forward in Santa Fe by the Martínez-Chavez committee report.[108] John Scolly and his associates were placed in possession of their grant by *Juez de Paz* Jesús María Montoya in May of 1846. Montoya told the grantees that the pastures and water on the grant would be held in common,[109] in accordance with Governor Armijo's earlier granting decrees. The Martínez-Chavez report of 1845 interpreted this to mean that the John Scolly commons would not be available to the Las Vegas grant settlers, making the Scolly grant closer in its effect to the Sanguijuela grant than to Manuelitas where common lands were to be shared with the Las Vegas settlers. The settlement of La Junta (later called Watrous), that grew up on the Scolly grant was outside the northern boundary of the Las Vegas grant, though about a third of the Scolly grant overlapped the Las Vegas grant as finally surveyed.

The Santiago Boné grant, the last of the Las Vegas overlaps, also overlapped the Scolly and Mora grants. The documents for this grant were lost and this was probably one of the reasons the petition for confirmation of the grant submitted to the Court of Private Land Claims was voluntarily dismissed by Boné's heirs. Another probable reason for the dismissal of the Boné petition was the assertion by the U.S. government that the 1842 document was not a separate grant but merely an allotment of land under a community grant to Santiago Boné and thirty other persons. According to the act of possession for this grant, known as the Estanislado Sandoval grant, the grantees were to establish a settlement there surrounded by a wall six *varas* high. The Santa Fe Trail passed through the area and the grantees were required to maintain the road and the ford over the junction of the Mora and Sapello Rivers.[110] It does not appear that this town was built according to these specifications, but a settlement called La Junta (Watrous) did grow up at the confluence of the two rivers. A diary of a lieutenant with Kearny's army mentions the settlement as the first one to be encountered in New Mexico, and also describes Santiago Boné (an Hispanicized version of James Boney), as "a generous and open-hearted adventurer, and in appearance what . . . Daniel Boone, of Kentucky, must have been in his day."[111] The Boné grant was not confirmed by the courts, but its history illustrates how the Las Vegas area became known in the 1840s. La Junta was a rendezvous site for travelers eastbound on the Santa Fe Trail waiting for enough people to form a caravan. Some of these travelers undoubtedly saw the possibilities for establishing settlements in the area. By 1855 there were 172 families in the Sapello area—a large enough settlement to provide a buffer zone against Indian raids on Las Vegas from the north.[112]

Besides these overlapping grants that were submitted to the Surveyor General and the Court of Private Land Claims for confirmation, several smaller grants were made within the Las Vegas grant by local officials and not submitted to United States officials for adjudication. Many of these grants were made by *Juez de Paz* Santiago Ulibarrí, and were the basis of new settlements at Ojitos Frios,[113] Agua Sarca,[114] and Salitre. Ojitos Frios is a settlement twelve miles southwest of Las Vegas. Agua Sarca is located at a gap in the high ridge through which one of the branches of the Santa Fe Trail passed. After General Kearny's troops of the Army of the West marched through this pass in 1846 it became known as Kearny's Gap, but previously it was known as the Puerto del Norte. It is likely that the proximity of the Santa Fe Trail and a water source from several intermittent streams that come together here is what made this a desirable place to settle. The Salitre grant is particularly interesting because it carried with it an exclusive water right. *Juez de Paz* Ulibarrí stated in the grant that since water was scarce at that place, Manuel de Herrera was the only one who could use the water for irrigation.[115]

 The settlement pattern on the Las Vegas community grant and surrounding area discussed here was similar to settlement in other areas of northern New Mexico where a base settlement was first established (in this case, San Miguel del Bado), from which further settlements could branch out. Similar patterns developed in the Chama and Taos Valleys. In the Taos valley, Taos Pueblo became the focal point of Spanish settlement as Hispanics settled around the Pueblo, often encroaching on its lands, and sometimes retreating to the confines of the fortified Pueblo when Comanche raids made it impossible for them to stay on their scattered *ranchos*. Actual settlement often occurred either before or after the making of the land grants that spread across the available land surrounding the Pueblo.[116] In the Chama valley, the base community of Abiquiú became the administrative headquarters for the surrounding area, with an *alcalde* and then an *ayuntamiento*, providing local governmental functions. Again, establishment of permanent settlements were not necessarily contemporaneous with the making of land grants in the area.[117]

Similarly, San Miguel del Bado became the administrative center for the area surrounding that community as settlements were projected out from there to the north and east. When the interests of large scale ranchers who needed land to graze their flocks of sheep and herds of cattle came into conflict with the interests of small-scale subsistence farmers who needed farm land as well as grazing land, two contradictory land policies pursued by the Spanish and Mexican governments of New Mexico also collided. The policy most often expressed in writing was the liberal one of encouraging new settlements in order to improve agriculture, to have a place to settle an overflowing population, and to protect interior settlements from Indian incursions. The other policy was a more restrictive one from the standpoint of small holders — it protected the interests of large landowners.

In the early 1700s, the government favored the restrictive elitist land grant policy giving priority in granting of land to the citizen-soldiers who helped Diego de Vargas reconquer New Mexico. This was a carry-over of the seventeenth-century policy which encouraged the grants of *encomiendas*; a grant of land that carried with it the right to receive tribute from the Indians living on that land. Initially this tribute was sufficient to meet the needs of a relatively small Spanish population, but as that population increased and the Pueblo Indian population decreased, it became increasingly necessary for the Spanish to engage in subsistence farming to feed themselves.[118] A government policy emphasizing the improvement of agriculture led to an increased importance of community land grants, which increased in number during the early nineteenth century.[119] The first Las Vegas grant to Cabesa de Baca was fashioned from the eighteenth century mold of the private grant to a privileged few, but the Las Vegas community grant emerged clearly from the nineteenth-century community grant model.

As the settlement of Las Vegas area demonstrates, an increase in population coupled with greater protection from Plains Indian hostilities, swung the balance toward the first settlements on the Las Vegas and Tecolote community land grants. These changes were part of a gradual process of land grant settlement often influenced by local politics. First the San Miguel del Bado authorities tried to obstruct the granting of land to Antonio Ortiz and Luis María Cabesa de Baca, although the governor of New Mexico had approved both grants. Other San Miguel *alcaldes* tried to prevent the settlement of the Tecolote grant. Finally the pattern changed somewhat when certain San Miguel del Bado officials themselves became settlers and part owners of the Las Vegas grant instead of trying to block its settlement. After Tecolote and Las Vegas were settled permanently by 1838, a battle ensued over control of the Las Vegas common lands.

The Ulibarrí family in general, and Santiago Ulibarrí in particular, were major players in that struggle. The Sanguijuela grant was made by Santiago to members of his family and purported to give them exclusive use rights to approximately 20,000 acres of common lands of the Las Vegas grant. One witness testified in the Court of Private Land Claims that when he tried to herd sheep on the grant in 1845, he was ordered to leave by Jose Ulibarrí and Juan Griego.[120] Thus the Ulibarrí family was apparently successful in gaining control, at least for a time, of a large portion of the Las Vegas common lands, although their grant was later rejected by the Court of Private Land Claims. Of all the conflicts and overlaps in this region, Sanguijuela and Santiago Boné are examples of a community grant followed by a private grant. In the other cases, the Las Vegas community grant was required to share its common resources with later overlapping community grants, as happened with the Manuelitas and John Scolly grants.

When two community grants overlapped, the struggle for control of common lands was often reflected as a conflict between the central government in Santa Fe and the local governments in Las Vegas and Mora. For example, the *asamblea* in Santa Fe made the Manuelitas grant over the objection of the Las Vegas *juez de paz*, though the Mora *juez de paz* agreed to the grant as long as residents of the Mora grant could use Manuelitas common lands. It is probable that Las Vegas objected because Manuelitas overlapped that grant more than it did the Mora grant. Also, the Sanguijuela grant had already been made without consulting the local officials at Las Vegas, and presumably they did not want that to happen again.[121] When the authorities in Santa Fe overruled the *juez de paz* at Las Vegas, they were exercising a kind of eminent domain power, but they mitigated the effect on the Las Vegas settlers by allowing a sharing of the common lands between the Las Vegas and Manuelitas settlers.

From the early 1820s a precarious balance was sought by local officials at San Miguel del Bado. They encouraged new settlements on the edge of the frontier to protect their communities against Indian raids, but they did not want those communities so close to existing settlements as to crowd their use of the common lands. The settlement pattern described here is typical of northern New Mexico in the manner in which new settlements were attempted on the edge of the frontier, then temporarily abandoned before permanent settlement was finally effected. These permanent settlements were generally not compact municipalities clustered around a central plaza, but were strung out up and down the rivers upon which the settlers were dependent for irrigation water. This was the pattern for the early Las Vegas settlements.

The nature of population growth on the Las Vegas grant and adjacent areas is currently being considered by New Mexico courts in the determination of water rights in the area. The pueblo rights doctrine currently being asserted by the municipality of Las Vegas as a claim to water from the Gallinas River, assumes a settlement pattern on the Las Vegas grant unlike that which has been described above. The doctrine as laid down by California courts and applied to Las Vegas by the New Mexico Supreme Court, holds that a community described by the court as a colonization pueblo could have an "expanding right to all the waters of a particular river by virtue of the town's prior founding."[122] In fact, there was no such thing under Spanish and Mexican law as a pueblo rights doctrine. Historians have examined the doctrine and found it to be unsupportable.[123]

Not only did the pueblo rights doctrine not exist under the laws of Spain or Mexico, but Daniel Tyler has pointed out after a comprehensive examination of New Mexico's judicial and administrative system of water distribution, that such a doctrine would be inconceivable at the time it is claimed to have been in effect in New Mexico. Rather than a "prior and paramount right" of one community to take water at the expense of nearby communities and individuals, Tyler finds the New Mexican documents to reveal a system of sharing under which the water needs of all communities and individuals on a river were recognized, so that no water user would be denied agricultural water.[124]

The foregoing review of the settlement of the Las Vegas grant discloses several other reasons why any pueblo water right, if such a doctrine existed,[125] would not be applicable to the Las Vegas settlement pattern. There was no discrete municipality to which a prior and paramount water right could attach, and there is no reference in the documents to a preferential municipal water right.[126]

This analysis of the pueblo rights doctrine as inapplicable to Las Vegas is made extremely difficult by the mysterious nature of the doctrine itself.

While legal writers have argued about the viability of the pueblo water right, no historian has found it to exist. Thus we have the following absurd situation that is similar to others that have arisen throughout the history of the adjudication of Hispanic land and water rights. An erroneous interpretation by Anglo courts of an Hispanic legal/historical concept becomes encapsulated in the decision of the court of last resort, like the *Sandoval* decision by the U. S. Supreme Court. Then that incorrect legal holding is repeated by both lawyers and historians as if it were historically accurate. Once New Mexican judges held that the pueblo rights doctrine existed, lawyers began debating whether that decision was correct, and if it was, what its implications were.[127] As the body of this literature continues to grow, the pueblo rights doctrine assumes more solidity and substance than is warranted by its ephemeral underpinnings. At the intersection of law and history, then, an invisible enemy has been created.

To perform the task of showing that the pueblo rights doctrine does not apply to Las Vegas, it is necessary to know what the pueblo looks like that, for the sake of this discussion, is said to have this prior and paramount water right.[128] The *Cartwright* opinion says that a municipality that was founded as a Mexican pueblo has the right "to the waters flowing to and through the boundaries of the pueblo." By showing that the boundaries of the municipality of Las Vegas at the time of the *Cartwright* decision bear little relationship to the settlements in the Las Vegas area from the late 1830s to the mid 1840s, it is hoped that this invisible enemy known as the pueblo rights doctrine can finally be laid to rest.

The *Cartwright* court viewed the settlement of Las Vegas as follows:

> A new, undeveloped, and unoccupied territory was being settled. There were no questions of priority of use when a colonization pueblo was established because there were no such prior users. Water formed the life blood of the community or settlement, not only in its origin but as it grew and expanded. A group of fifty families at the founding of a colony found it no more so than when their number was multiplied to hundreds or even thousands in an orderly, progressive growth.[129]

The court apparently assumed that the initial settlers listed in the grant documents were the beginning of the orderly growth of a compact community that resulted in the present day town of Las Vegas. This was not the case. Instead the growth of settlements on the Las Vegas grant was haphazard, based more on the availability of water and protection from Indian raids than on a colonization plan conceived by the Mexican central government and faithfully followed by local governments and by the individual *pobladores.*

As we have seen, the first permanent settlements on the Las Vegas grant occurred in 1838, both at Las Vegas and at San Gerónimo. The local *juez de paz* could not get the first allottees to settle Las Vegas until three years after the grant was made, partly because these *pobladores* wanted to settle at Tecolote instead. The settlements at San Gerónimo and Las Vegas were certainly not part of an orderly plan of settlement. The San Gerónimo settlers thought they were on the Tecolote grant. The local authorities did not know where the boundary between the Las Vegas and Tecolote grants was, and the two local officials involved with the Tecolote grant got into a jurisdictional dispute regarding the boundaries of their respective jurisdictions.

It appears that local officials were often competing for jurisdictional power instead of cooperating in a plan to establish "colonization pueblos." The problem of overlapping authority between local officials is also evident. *Juez de paz* Santiago Ulibarrí of San Miguel del Bado, made grants within the Las Vegas grant although Las Vegas was within the jurisdiction of other officials at the time the Ulibarrí grants were made.

Nor was there a coordinated land settlement policy between local authorities and the central government in Santa Fe. When a Las Vegas official objected to the Manuelitas grant, he was overruled by the *asamblea* in Santa Fe. Even successive governors in Santa Fe disagreed about land grants and the proper policy to be followed in their settlement. Although Governor Mariano Martínez and the committee he appointed recommended against the John Scolly grant, Governor Manuel Armijo later proceeded to make the grant anyway. None of this conjures up a vision of an orderly, consistent, government policy regarding the settlement of the Las Vegas grant and the surrounding area.

Therefore, even if there had been a pueblo rights doctrine under Spanish and Mexican law, it does not apply to the settlement pattern on the Las Vegas grant. The doctrine appears to be based on the compact Spanish municipality known as a *pueblo.* Spanish law provided for three types of formal municipalities: the *ciudad,* the *villa,* and the *pueblo.*[130] No *ciudad* was ever established in New Mexico, but there were four *villas:* Santa Fe, Albuquerque, Santa Cruz de la Cañada, and El Paso. Most other settlements in New Mexico after the Pueblo Revolt were small and scattered, lacking

the compact character envisioned by Spanish law for a *pueblo*.[131] Plans for formal municipalities show settlers living in a precisely laid out community, with parallel streets marking rectangular blocks around a central plaza. Lands on the edge of the community were reserved for cultivated fields, pasture lands, municipal lands, and *ejido* lands.[132] These municipalities had town councils that carried out municipal functions and exercised municipal rights to land and water. But nowhere on the Las Vegas grant was there such a formal Hispanic municipality or *pueblo*. Nor was there a municipal council exercising municipal rights to water for domestic use independent of rights to irrigation water. Rather, there were a number of settlements scattered along the Gallinas, and Sapello Rivers, including upper and lower Las Vegas, San Gerónimo, Lagunas, Ojitos Frios, Agua Sarca, Los Fuertes, San Agustín, Concepción, Cañada del Salitre, Lagunas, Los Ojos (Hot Springs), and Los Alamos.[133]

The policy mentioned repeatedly in government documents was the policy of encouraging new settlements as a means of increasing agriculture production and to provide more protection from Indian attacks. Any absolute water rights preference based on a priority in time among individual settlements would be entirely at odds with these oft-stated goals. No group of settlers would risk their lives at a settlement exposed to Indian raids if their efforts were rewarded with a status subordinate to settlements deriving protection from these attacks by the presence of the new settlement. Certainly the government of New Mexico could not expect to increase agricultural production by encouraging new settlements, if those settlements did not have a right to share existing irrigation water with older settlements.

If some community in the vicinity of present day Las Vegas had the benefit of a pueblo water right during the 1830s or 1840s there certainly would have been some mention of it in the documents. The *alcalde* who made the first allotments at Las Vegas would not have allowed the Sanguijuela grant upriver from Las Vegas without mentioning a municipal water right, if one existed. The Sanguijuela grant provided an opportunity for any pueblo water right to be exercised, but no protest was made against that grant by Las Vegas authorities. Moreover, when an agreement between irrigators on a Las Vegas *acequia* and a mill owner was formalized before the Las Vegas *juez de paz* in 1846, no mention was made by that official of any municipal water right that might be impaired by the new mill.[134] In short, no historical evidence has been found that would support a pueblo water right for Las Vegas.

Of all the officials who assumed authority to act in regard to the Las Vegas grant, Juan de Dios Maese seems to have acted the most consistently in administering local affairs on the Las Vegas grant. Maese is the official whom General Stephen Watts Kearney ordered to take an oath of allegiance to the United States when the Army of the West arrived in Las Vegas in August 1846. A year later he was tried by an American court in Santa Fe for treason. He was exonerated, but during the disturbances that led to his arrest, his mill was burned. He later helped found the community of La Liendre down river from Las Vegas on the Gallinas. Unfortunately, that community died out when water consumption increased upstream and La Liendre's *acequias* dried up.[135] If *Cartwright* remains the law, other *acequias* and the communities they serve could also go the way of La Liendre — sacrificed because of an erroneous rule of water distribution created by lawyers, and discredited by historians. It will take a decision by the Supreme Court of New Mexico reversing *Cartwright v. Public Service Company of New Mexico* to finally defeat the invisible enemy of the pueblo rights doctrine.

Nine

Not a Pepper, Not an Onion: The Battle for the Las Vegas Grant

On the fifteenth of August, 1846, Stephen Watts Kearny, the leader of the occupying Army of the West, was camped about a mile from the town of Las Vegas, the largest community on the Las Vegas land grant. Las Vegas was also the first sizeable community Kearny and his army of 1500 men had encountered since they set out from Fort Leavenworth, Kansas, in the latter part of June, following the Santa Fe Trail to New Mexico. Before marching into town that morning, Kearny was advised that just south of Las Vegas, at the place now known as Kearny's Gap (then called *El Puertecito* or Puerto del Norte),[1] a force of 600 men was waiting to do battle with his army. That battle never materialized, much to the disappointment of General Kearny's troops. But the general's coming to Las Vegas signaled the beginning of another kind of battle, one fought in courtrooms, not at a narrow pass south of Las Vegas. The battle recounted here is the struggle for the nearly half million acres of common lands of the Las Vegas grant.[2]

Kearny's arrival in New Mexico turned out to be a peaceful one: not a shot was fired, either in Las Vegas, or five days later when his army entered Santa Fe. But Kearny's speech to the assembled townspeople on the Las Vegas plaza was the opening salvo in a war of words that was to disrupt forever the relatively peaceful life of farming and livestock raising enjoyed by the settlers on the Las Vegas grant. In a short speech from the roof of what is now the Dice apartment building on the plaza, Kearny told the assembled townsfolk that he, and the government he represented, would protect the persons and property of Las Vegans. His words even showed a certain poetic flair:

> I now tell you that those who remain peaceably at home, attending to their crops and herds, shall be protected by me in their property, their persons, and their religion; and not a pepper, not an onion shall be disturbed or taken . . .[3]

As promised, the Las Vegas grant was confirmed by the U.S. Congress to the town of Las Vegas on 21 June 1860. But for the next forty years, a conflict raged on the grant over who owned the common lands.

One reason for this controversy was the vagueness of the confirming act of Congress regarding what land was confirmed and to whom. Congress confirmed the grant "as recommended for confirmation by the surveyor general," but Surveyor General Pelham had to rule on two conflicting claims, one by the heirs of Luis María Cabesa de Baca, the other by the town of Las Vegas.[4] Cabesa de Baca had been the first individual to attempt to settle the land within the Las Vegas grant. He had received a private grant for the same land in 1821, but his attempts to settle the grant were frustrated by Indian raids, and he finally abandoned the land around 1831.[5] Pelham ruled that both the Baca and the Town of Las Vegas claims were valid but did not decide between them. He left it up to "the proper tribunals" to sort it out. The obvious incongruity of two groups of claimants owning the same land was resolved by the agreement of the Baca heirs to accept an equivalent amount of land from the public domain in lieu of their claim to the land within the Las Vegas grant.[6] But no one would know how much land the Baca heirs were entitled to until the Las Vegas grant was surveyed. So the General Land Office directed the surveyor general to give the surveying of the Las Vegas grant a high priority.[7]

A survey of the Las Vegas grant during the months prior to December 1860 showed that the grant contained 496,446 acres, and that it conflicted with the Town of Tecolote grant, the Antonio Ortiz grant, and the John Scolly grant.[8] It took some forty years before the Las Vegas grant was finally resurveyed to adjust its southern boundary for the Tecolote and Antonio Ortiz overlaps, reducing its size by almost 65,000 acres. During this forty year period, conflicts occurred on several levels over the ownership of the common lands of the Las Vegas grant: in the surveyor general's office and in the office of the secretary of the interior where surveying the common lands was the issue; in the territorial courts where the question of common land ownership was argued and decided, and on the land itself, where individuals tried to fence portions of the common lands.

The initial conflict arose over the extent of the Las Vegas grant. If federal officials had their way, the grant would have been reduced to the allotted private lands (first estimated at about 20,000 acres, later at 6,000 acres), in which case there would have been no common lands to fight about. The proponents for this position attempted to have the 1860 survey changed to include only the private, occupied lands. On the other side, the group representing the land grant argued strenuously that a patent should be issued immediately for the 496,446 acres surveyed in 1860. The paper trail of this conflict followed a seemingly endless path back and forth between the General Land Office in Washington and the surveyor general's office in Santa Fe.

The numerous written exchanges between the surveyor general and the General Land Office were commenced by the prodding of Joab Houghten, the attorney for the Las Vegas grant during the 1870s. Houghten had been appointed to the bench by General Kearny, even though he had no legal training. After being the subject of intense criticism during his tenure as a judge, he finally challenged his severest critic to a duel. Houghten escaped unscathed without firing a shot, however, because his deafness prevented him from hearing the command to "fire," and luckily for him his opponent was not a very good shot.[9] Having lived through this battle for his honor, Joab Houghten was retained by the Las Vegas grant to fight a battle for its common lands.

In April of 1875 Houghten urged the government to issue a patent to the Las Vegas grant.[10] In response to his inquiry the Land Office stated that a reexamination of the grant boundaries was necessary because "the exterior limits of the survey are so extensive."[11] Here for the first time, the Land Office revealed its desire to reduce the size of the Las Vegas grant by changing the 1860 survey, because the grant was too large. The Land Office directed the surveyor general to take testimony and make a field examination, if necessary, to locate the grant boundaries and explain the conflict with the Tecolote and Scolly grants.[12] Three affidavits were taken in October of 1875,[13] and attorney Houghten filed a brief on the boundaries,[14] but no further action was taken on the Las Vegas patent application until 1878. In that year the Land Office directed the surveyor general to determine the proper location of the western boundary of the grant, which was also the eastern boundary of the San Miguel del Bado grant. Since San Miguel del Bado had not been surveyed, the surveyor general was told to determine the location of the Agua Caliente, which marked the northeast corner of the San Miguel del Bado grant and the western boundary of the Las Vegas grant. The Land Office learned of hot springs some eight miles east of the western boundary of the Las Vegas grant as established by the 1860 survey, and asked the surveyor general to determine if this was the real Agua Caliente. If it was, the common lands would be substantially reduced.[15] Again affidavits of witnesses were taken,[16] and Francisco Baca y Sandoval, the secretary of the commissioners of the Las Vegas grant, stated that he deemed this testimony sufficient to submit the matter to the Department of the Interior.[17] It soon became clear from the witnesses' testimony that the Hot Springs referred to by the General Land Office were those located near present-day Montezuma, which had always been known as Ojos Calientes. The Aguas Calientes referred to a small stream called the Rito Agua Caliente that empties into the Pecos River a little north of the village of San José. Accordingly, the matter of changing the western boundary of the Las Vegas grant was dropped.

The General Land Office then directed that the southern boundary line on the 1860 Las Vegas survey be amended to conform to the existing survey of the Antonio Ortiz grant and to the proposed survey of the Tecolote grant.[18] The General Land Office was apparently satisfied that the other boundaries as located on the 1860 survey were correct. It was not clear, however, that the Land Office was prepared to recommend the issuance of a patent based upon that survey.

The Tecolote survey was performed and sent to the General Land Office,[19] but no amended survey of the Las Vegas grant was forthcoming despite numerous letters from the General Land Office in Washington to Surveyor General Atkinson in Santa Fe between 1878 and 1884.[20] By this time, Joab Houghten's initiative in trying to get a patent for his clients had lost momentum. A new surveyor general of New Mexico would soon question whether the common lands of the Las Vegas grant should be recognized by the United States government at all.

In 1885 George Washington Julian became surveyor general and the attack on the Las Vegas grant survey took on a new dimension. Julian was charged with reexamining all grants whose approval by his predecessors was questionable,[21] and he undertook the task with a reformer's zeal. The surveyor general told the General Land Office that he could save four million acres of claimed land grant land for the public domain if he received sufficient funds from Congress. He hoped that the Las Vegas grant's common lands would make up part of those lands.[22]

The 1876 decision in the *Tameling* case held that once Congress had confirmed a grant the courts could not look behind that confirmation — even an erroneous confirmation passed title to the grant.[23] So Julian was limited to questioning the amount of land Congress and the surveyor general had meant to confirm for the Las Vegas grant. This entailed construing the 1860 Act of Congress, he argued, not attacking it. This was a very fine distinction, but one upon which almost half a million acres of common lands was riding.

In March of 1887 Surveyor General Julian recommended to the General Land Office that the Las Vegas grant be resurveyed to include only the allotted private tracts, arguing that the grant was for agricultural purposes and that the Mexican government did not intend to convey the common lands as part of the grant. Citing no historical or legal authority for this proposition, Julian apparently based his argument on the size of the grant's common lands (then thought to be approximately 475,000 acres) rather than on Mexican law.[24] The General Land Office approved Julian's recommendation in November 1887, and in a scathing report the same year, the Secretary of the Interior not only repeated Julian's argument about the common lands, but also suggested that the Baca heirs and the Las Vegas grantees had been in collusion, and were not in fact rival claimants. In this atmosphere of controversy and conspiracy, the impetus for a resurvey of the Las Vegas grant had begun, but several attempts would be made in the courts to stop it.[25]

The job of surveying the private allotments within a land grant was in many ways more difficult than the task of surveying the exterior boundaries, and Julian chose Will Tipton for the job.[26] Tipton, the chief translator and custodian of the Spanish and Mexican archives for the surveyor general,[27] was not a surveyor, but he had undertaken similar investigations before this.[28] However, the Las Vegas survey turned out to be particularly daunting. In a report to Julian in July 1887, Tipton described some of the problems he had encountered, providing valuable information on the location of the initial allotments.

Tipton told Julian that the lands allotted under the Las Vegas grant were not in a solid body, but were scattered along the Gallinas River for several miles. He mentioned the settlements of Agua Sarca, west of Las Vegas; Lower Puertecito, five miles to the south; Upper Town, two and a half miles to the north; and Hot Springs as places where lands had been allotted. The exact location of these allotments was difficult to ascertain, however, because of the vague boundary descriptions in the original documents. Most of the allotments fronted on the Gallinas River, and it was only this frontage that was measured and listed in the act of possession. The length of the allotments varied, and the only way to accurately locate the tracts was by finding deeds describing later transfers of the same land in the county deed records and through interviewing landowners. Tipton found a few such deeds, but noted that many deeds had not been recorded. Among the deeds he did discover, some described tracts extending from the river to the

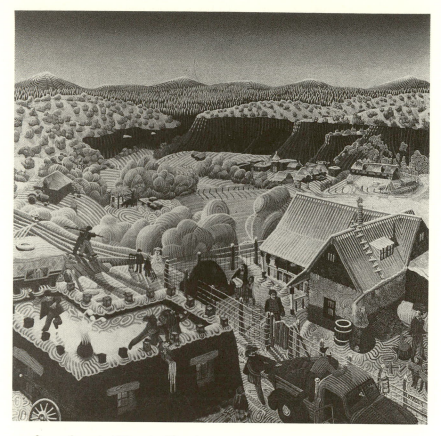

9.2. Scene of a typical Hispanic village in winter. Painting by Glen Strock

irrigation ditch, while others showed parcels running west from the river to a ridge called the *crestón*, a mile or more from the river.[29]

Tipton learned of seven of the original grantees that were still living, and secured an affidavit from one of them. Tomás Ulibarrí stated that he had received 100 *varas* of land from *Alcalde* José Ulibarrí in 1837 but had left Las Vegas for a few years to work in the placer mines (probably Real de Dolores southwest of Santa Fe).[30] Tipton also took affidavits from Juan Aragón[31] and Ramón Ulibarrí[32] and reported that a survey of the allotted lands would take much longer than had been anticipated, if it could be done at all.[33]

The actual surveying of the allotted lands was done, not by Tipton, but by Russell B. Rice, Special Agent for the surveyor general's office. Rice,

who had also served as county surveyor for San Miguel County, began his
work in November 1887, and over the next six years rendered numerous
reports to Surveyor General Julian and his successors. Special Agent Rice
encountered the same problems that Julian did — unrecorded deeds, poorly
organized and indexed county records — and some new problems such as
individuals who tried to obstruct his investigation.[34] Although Rice was
never able to complete his survey because of lack of funds,[35] his reports also
shed light on the location of settlements where allotments were made. He
mentions the settlements of Sapello, Los Alamos, and Las Dispensas along
the Sapello River, in addition to Lagunitas, Jacales, San Agustín, Sanguijuela, La Liendre, and San Gerónimo.[36]

While the surveyor general's Office was attempting to reduce the size of
the Las Vegas grant, conflicts were raging on the grant itself and in the
territorial courts. To understand the reasons for these physical and legal
disputes one needs to put them in context with the three different views
regarding the ownership of the Las Vegas common lands. The first view
was the one championed by Surveyor General Julian and Special Agents
Tipton and Rice: that the common lands were not owned by the grant at all
but by the United States government as its public domain. Under this view
anyone could acquire a piece of the former common lands as private
property. This theory benefitted the outsider filing a homestead entry to
the detriment of the heirs of the land grant. Under the second view of
common lands ownership, the original grantees and their successors owned
the common lands as private property. Under this view, a speculator purchasing one of these interests would own a fractional share of the common
lands, and if combined with the other shares the entire common lands could
be sold. A weakness of this theory was the difficulty of ascertaining who the
original grantees were. The petition refers to twenty-five individuals in
addition to the four named petitioners, but thirty-six names were listed on
the document purporting to be the act of possession. In fact, none of these
individuals settled at Las Vegas in 1835. In any case, this theory benefitted
the speculator to the detriment of the land grant heirs. The third theory
held that the Las Vegas grant was a community grant whose common lands
were owned by the owners of private tracts of land within the grant and
could not be sold under Hispanic law. This view is the one that benefitted
the average grant resident, and is the historically correct view.[37]

After the United States' occupation of New Mexico, Las Vegas rapidly
developed into the largest city and the leading commercial center in the

territory. This growth was encouraged by the establishment of Fort Union in 1851 and the coming of the railroad to Las Vegas in 1879. The commercial boom in and around Las Vegas made land more valuable there, and several lawsuits were generated over ownership of the common lands. The three theories of common land ownership were pitted against one another in two of these lawsuits in the New Mexico territorial courts.[38]

The first of these cases began in 1873 when a complaint was filed seeking to enjoin three prominent merchants and ranchers, May Hays, Juan Romero, and Miguel García y Chávez, from distributing forty to eighty acre farm tracts from the common lands to various individuals. Hays, Romero, and García had been elected as commissioners of the grant at a public meeting of land grant inhabitants, but the complainants challenged their authority to partition the common lands. Attorney Thomas Catron represented the complainants and Joab Houghten represented the defendants. The San Miguel County District Court judge agreed with the complainants and enjoined the defendants from any further land partitions, but did not make clear the reason for his decision.[39] As was true in several subsequent cases, the issue of ownership of the common lands was complicated by the additional question of who should receive the patent for the Las Vegas grant. In 1873 the District Court did not clarify either of these issues.

The next lawsuit was the 1887 case of *Milhiser* v. Padilla. The *Milhiser* case grew out of the practice of fencing portions of the common lands, often by outsiders claiming a portion of these lands through deeds from grant heirs or because of homestead claims. It was opposition to this type of fencing that spawned the Gorras Blancas Hispanic protest movement of the 1880s and 1890s.[40] But the *Milhiser* case involved the reverse situation. There the fences were put up by locals — the three Padilla brothers, José, Francisco, and Pablo — at a place called La Monilla some thirteen miles east of Las Vegas. This portion of the common lands was especially desirable because of its abundant grasses enabling the defendants to harvest large amounts of hay. Each Padilla had fenced a 160 acre parcel, basing their claims on adverse possession, the Homestead laws, and on deeds from the original grantees or their heirs.[41]

The plaintiffs also claimed through original grantees of the Las Vegas Grant. Pablo Ulibarrí and Eulogio Segura. Their descendants had sold their interest in the grant to Louis Sulzbacher, who in turn transferred his interest to the plaintiffs. These plaintiffs were asking the court to enjoin the

9.3. Dry-farmed field near Las Vegas, New Mexico, ca. 1909. Photograph by Jesse L. Nusbaum, neg. no. 61298. Courtesy Museum of New Mexico.

defendants from fencing the common lands on the ground that, the grant having been made to the initial twenty-nine grantees alone, the plaintiffs had an interest in the common lands as purchasers of two of these shares. The case was heard by Judge Elisha V. Long, a man who was to have a tremendous influence on the Las Vegas grant as secretary of the Board of Trustees later appointed for the grant. Judge Long, then chief justice of the New Mexico Supreme Court but serving as District Court judge, referred the *Milhiser* case to Referee R. M. Johnson to take evidence and make a report. Johnson's report recommended a decision in favor of the Padillas, denying the relief sought by the Milhisers.

It took Judge Long a year to render his written decision, and when the plaintiffs heard that he would concur with the referee's report they attempted to dismiss their suit. By doing so they hoped to blunt the effect of the decision as a precedent by making the case moot. Thus a formal decision would not be necessary and the *Milhiser* case would not affect future cases. But Judge Long not only included his written decision as part of the record of the trial, he had it privately printed along with summaries of the testimony of witnesses and a translation of the grant documents. Judge Long's opinion agreeing with the referee's report had a far-reaching effect at the time it was rendered and is still a source of controversy.[42]

Judge Long's reasoning bears close scrutiny because his view of the common lands was diametrically opposed to the views held by land speculators and by government officials like Surveyor General Julian. Long's forceful statement of his view of common land ownership undoubtedly had some effect in turning the tide which had been running in favor of shrinking the Las Vegas grant.[43] But it also had unforeseen consequences. The judge examined all the documents connected with the grant, in order to answer the question: was the grant owned by the first twenty-nine individual grantees and their heirs or by all individuals in need of land who settled on the grant? Long then put another question in his attempt to answer the first one: would one of the first twenty-nine settlers have been successful in compelling the Mexican authorities to exclude other needy settlers from the grant in the 1840s? If Pablo Ulibarrí, one of the plaintiffs' predecessors in title, could not have enforced a claim during the Mexican Period of exclusive right to possession (along with his twenty-eight co-grantees), then neither could the *Milhiser* plaintiffs.[44]

Judge Long answered these questions in the negative, holding that the Mexican authorities would not have recognized a claim by the twenty-nine initial grantees to exclusive rights in the grant. First the judge looked at the petition for the grant which specified that "the development of agriculture" was one of the reasons why the land was solicited. Long reasoned that a withdrawal from settlement of such a large body of land for the exclusive use of twenty-nine individuals would hardly have been an act designed to promote agriculture. Then he examined the grant itself and found that it was made not only to the petitioners, but to all those who needed land to cultivate. Since the petitioners had agreed to comply with the conditions imposed by the Mexican government, they could hardly contend that this condition was not binding upon them. Judge Long also pointed to the fact that at least 100 additional settlers were given possession of land on the Las Vegas grant without any protest from the twenty-nine initial grantees. Long concluded that if these twenty-nine individuals had claimed exclusive title from the Mexican government prior to 1846, that claim would have been rejected.[45]

Judge Elisha V. Long's opinion in *Milhiser* was celebrated as a victory by poor Hispanic farmers and ranchers on the Las Vegas grant, but it was an empty victory. The decision did demolish the theory that the common lands were owned exclusively by the original grantees, and for this reason it infuriated speculators like Thomas B. Catron and Stephen B. Elkins. Catron was worried that the decision would serve as a precedent calling into question his ownership of other community grants he had purchased from original grantees.[46] Long's decision was also a cogent answer to Surveyor General Julian's view, adopted by the General Land Office, that the Las Vegas grant was comprised solely of the allotted private lands and not the common lands. Long made it clear that the common lands were owned by the town of Las Vegas, even if it was not evident what legal entity constituted the town of Las Vegas. This matter was left open and took another decade to sort out. But the common lands were certainly not public domain owned by the United States and available for settlement under the homestead laws. Having made it clear who didn't own the common lands, the judge did not decide who did own them and under what conditions they could be utilized. This was due in part to the fact that the posture of the case called for a decision only as to the extent of the Plaintiff's title to the contested land. Under the legal rule still followed today, the plaintiffs had to win or lose on the strength of their own title, not on the weakness of the defendant's title. Judge Long did not rule on the Padilla's claim, but if he had it would probably have been upheld simply because they got there first. This is where the judge's reasoning went astray.[47]

Since the *Milhiser* decision accepted Mexican law as the basis for its result, the question must be asked whether fencing and building structures upon a part of the common lands as the Padillas had done, would have been countenanced under Mexican law and custom. The clues to arriving at the answer are to be found in the documents. Judge Long had read the documents to mean that "the lands within the boundaries of the Las Vegas grant, not occupied or set apart to some actual settler, should be open to settlement and actual occupancy for agricultural purposes to any citizen destitute of land." The key words are "open to settlement and actual occupancy for agricultural purposes."[48] Under Mexican law it was the private allotted lands that were used for settlement and farming. The resources of the common lands were used by all, and no one person could appropriate any part of the common lands for themselves. But Judge Long was saying that on the Las Vegas grant, the common lands could be occupied, farmed, and fenced by one person.

One reason why Judge Long arrived at this incongruous result is that he was personally opposed to the activities of Las Gorras Blancas. By seeming to uphold the fencing by the Padilla brothers he was striking a blow against Las Gorras Blancas who were opposed to such fencing.[49] To understand the background of these legal maneuverings it is necessary to understand Las Gorras Blancas and the political realities surrounding that protest movement.

Las Gorras Blancas was a protest group sympathetic with one of the three views of the common lands mentioned earlier. They certainly did not agree with the government's position that the common lands belonged to the United States as public domain. As a result of this view the Department of the Interior declared in the 1880s that the open lands within the grant should be available for homesteading. Consequently, the number of homestead entries on the Las Vegas grant began to increase dramatically, though it was soon discovered that many of these entries were fraudulent. The key person involved in this activity was Max Frost, head of the land office in Santa Fe, who was alleged to have been a silent partner with Las Vegas attorney Miguel Salazar. Eventually Frost was forced to resign, and many prominent Las Vegas citizens were indicted in connection with these schemes, including Charles Ilfeld, who later became a member of the Board of Trustees of the Las Vegas grant. These were some of the people who tried to benefit from the first view of common land ownership — and it was these people whom Las Gorras Blancas opposed.[50]

Nor did Las Gorras Blancas agree with the second view of the common lands — the position that the descendants of the original grantees owned these lands as private property. This point of view was supported by land speculators and merchants like the Milhisers and members of the wealthy Romero family: Eugenio, Cleofas, and Margarito Romero, among others. The Romeros had for years been involved in extensive timber cutting on the common lands. They then converted land grant timber to railroad ties, which they sold to the railroad at a handsome profit. This exploitation of the grant's resources by unauthorized individuals continued well after the grant board was established in 1902. One of the worst offenders was Margarito Romero, who in 1903 was arrested by the grant board for cutting timber in the Gallinas Canyon, and who later took the board to court to challenge its authority. Margarito's brother, Eugenio, and his son Cleofas had been the target of Las Gorras Blancas when thousands of their freshly cut railroad ties were destroyed by the vigilantes.[51] It is therefore ironic that another member of the first board of trustees of the Las Vegas Grant was Eugenio Romero. The actions of individuals who saw the common lands as a means of advancing their own personal interests were forcefully opposed by Las Gorras Blancas.

The third view of the ownership of the common lands was the only one that stood to benefit the occupants of the grant who were descendants and successors of the original grantees. These occupants were the true owners of the common lands, the ones who should have gotten the benefits of using the land or received the proceeds from its sale, but they received little benefit from their patrimony. The strongest representatives of these owners of the grant were Las Gorras Blancas and "the coterie of young Mexicano businessmen and *políticos*" who supported them. But the movement eventually lost its effectiveness when the focus of the common land issue shifted to the courts and to local politics.[52]

After Judge Long's opinion in *Milhiser,* Las Gorras Blancas were at the height of their power. They had gained widespread sympathy for their activities—mainly the cutting of barbed-wire fences erected to enclose large sections of the common lands. Las Gorras Blancas was an extension of the White Caps of southern Indiana, one of the protest groups active during the range wars of the 1880s.[53] In the midwest the battle was between farmers and cattlemen, a struggle that had been going on in the southwest since the two tried to coexist in sixteenth century Mexico. But in northeastern New Mexico land grant ownership was an additional factor to be dealt with.[54]

With the invention and perfection of barbed wire by 1874[55] increased areas of Las Vegas grant common lands began to be fenced in by the mid 1880s, sometimes exceeding ten thousand acres in size. As the number of fences increased during the time that *Milhiser v. Padilla* was being heard, retaliatory actions against the fences began to occur. In June 1889 José Ignacio Luján's fences, crops, and farm equipment near San Ignacio were destroyed, and earlier that spring the house of Surveyor General Edward F. Hobart was burned. Twenty-one individuals were indicted for fence cutting, but when the first one brought to trial in November 1889 was acquitted by a jury, the charges against the other twenty were dropped. A week later Judge Long's decision in *Milhiser* was released. As protest activities reached their peak over the next year, the ownership of the Las Vegas grant's common lands still had not been resolved.[56]

Various factions began maneuvering to establish a legal entity called the town of Las Vegas in order to obtain a patent to the grant from the government. In 1889 Julian was replaced by Edward Hobart as surveyor general of New Mexico, and the policy of resurveying the Las Vegas grant began to change. Hobart was in favor of issuing the patent for the entire half million acres of the Las Vegas grant to the Town of Las Vegas, in direct opposition to surveyor general Julian's policy. Hobart's reversal is not surprising when one learns that the surveyor general claimed part of the common lands himself! As surveyor Russell B. Rice wrote to Secretary of the Interior John W. Noble: "It is difficult to understand how the interests of the United State need expect much protection from a surveyor general whose personal interest are directly opposed to it."[57]

Nevertheless, Julian's crusade to protect the public domain by reducing the common lands of the Las Vegas grant continued to have a life of its own even after his departure. When Interior Secretary Noble ruled in 1891 that the patent should cover only the allotted lands, a suit was filed in the District of Columbia to block the resurvey of the grant. Although the petitioners were successful, the decision was reversed by the U.S. Supreme Court on a technicality. Meanwhile, Russell B. Rice was still writing reports supporting Julian's theory as late as 1893, but by that time his funds had run out and his work was abandoned.[58] The momentum for the resurvey of the Las Vegas grant had petered out, and it became evident that someone was entitled to receive a patent to the approximately 400,000 acres of the Las Vegas grant common lands.

Congress had confirmed the grant to the *town* of Las Vegas, as it had done with many other community land grants it confirmed. When the Department of the Interior finally decided that it was indeed the town of Las Vegas that was entitled to receive the patent, various factions began maneuvering to establish a legal entity that could hold the patent.[59] In addition, a last ditch attempt was made by the proponents of the second view of common lands ownership (title in the heirs of the original grantees), to block the issuance of the patent.

The heirs of the original grantees filed suit in Federal court to enjoin the issuance of the patent to the town of Las Vegas, because there was no legally incorporated town of Las Vegas. However, when the case reached the U.S.

Supreme Court, the justices sidestepped the issue. The high court refused
to be put in the position of guessing where the legal entity called the town
of Las Vegas could be found. Instead, the court simply directed the General
Land Office to issue the patent to the town of Las Vegas, and left it to other
tribunals to determine what and where the town of Las Vegas really was.[60]

The final part of the battle for the common lands of the Las Vegas Grant
started in the early 1900s with the circulation of two opposing petitions,
each proposing a different method of managing the land grant. One petition evolved out of a series of community meetings held in April and May of
1902. After much discussion, the group led by Ezequiel C. de Baca proposed that West Las Vegas be incorporated as the town of Las Vegas and
that it request delivery of the patent. This would solve the problem which
had been baffling the courts for over a decade, since there would then be a
legal entity capable of receiving the patent. In an attempt to avoid the
dangers of political factionalism in running the land grant, the town officials would appoint a land commission composed of land grant residents to
manage the grant. The group appointed a temporary board of directors
headed by Eugenio Romero. In fact, the incorporation plan lacked protection from municipal politics since the board would be appointed by town
officials not elected by grant members. What was needed was a democrat-
ically elected board of trustees to run the entire grant as was soon to be the
case with other community land grants. But this was not to be.[61]

The opposing petition, supported by Republican businessmen from East
Las Vegas, called for the district court to appoint a board of trustees.
Among the leaders of this group was banker Jefferson Raynolds, who had
been the plaintiff in the federal suit to enjoin the resurveying of the grant. A
lawsuit was filed in state district court by Charles Spiess and the Veeder law
firm, which asked that a board of trustees take charge of the grant, be given
the power to borrow money, and sell common lands, among other things.
Judge William J. Mills, son-in-law to land speculator Wilson Wadding-
ham, granted the petition and appointed a seven man board of trustees. The
members of this first board were: Jefferson Raynolds, a prominent Las
Vegas banker; Charles Ilfeld, one of New Mexico's leading merchants who
had earlier been indicted for land fraud; Elisha V. Long, attorney and the
judge who had decided *Milhiser v. Padilla;* Eugenio Romero, the wealthy
merchant who had taken so much timber from the common lands; F. H.
Pierce, manager of the Agua Pura Water Company; Felix Esquibel, a
prominent rancher; and Isidoro Gallegos, a wealthy dealer in land and

livestock. It was apparent from the beginning, and was borne out in time, that this was not a people's board, but a board bent on realizing their own vision of progress on the Las Vegas grant. That vision consisted primarily of selling the common lands to questionable developers.[62]

Several attempts were made to challenge the authority of this board of trustees but none were successful. One reason was that the judge who heard the case that finally came to trial was William J. Mills, the same judge who had appointed the first board. Since he was reviewing his own actions it is not surprising that he dismissed the case.[63] Judge Mills' decision to appoint the board was protected from further challenge by a law passed by the New Mexico legislature in 1903. In fact it was Waldo Spiess, a state senator as well as a lawyer, who "scurried to Santa Fe, where the territorial legislature was in session, obtained a waiver of legislative rules and secured the passage of an act legalizing *ex post facto* the action of Judge Mills."[64] The statute gave the district court of San Miguel County authority to appoint and supervise a board of trustees to manage and control the common lands of the Las Vegas Land Grant.[65] That board is still in existence.

When Judge Long became the secretary and guiding spirit of the grant in the early 1900's, his policy of opening the grant for settlement was realized. The trustees entered into several transactions with land speculators who planned to colonize the grant with outsiders. For example, in 1906 the board sold 50,000 acres to A.W. Thompson who proposed bringing in settlers by rail from Chicago and Kansas City. The Las Vegas *Optic* was enthusiastic about the scheme: "Imagine what it will mean to Las Vegas itself to unload three or four hundred colonists in this town every Wednesday and Saturday morning." But like other such plans this one did not materialize.[66]

Management of the grant by a board of trustees led to the sale of most of the common lands with little benefit accruing to the residents of the grant. By 1931 the boards of trustees had sold over 300,000 acres of common lands, by 1942 there were approximately 29,000 acres of common lands left, and in 1990 only about 2400 acres remained. About half of the income received by the grant by 1931, went for attorney's fees, surveyor's fees, taxes, expenses, and salaries for board members. These salaries do not include substantial amounts of common lands deeded to board members in compensation for services rendered. The board of trustees did afford some protection to the communities of San Agustín, Concepción, Los Vigiles, and Gallinas when it deeded portions of the Las Vegas common lands to trustees elected by those communities. By so doing, the Las Vegas board of trustees created mini-community grants within the larger community grant, for these deeded lands surround each community and must be used by the inhabitants for grazing their livestock, and getting wood and timber for domestic use. But Las Vegas common lands outside these mini-grants were treated as available for development, as was apparent from the first letterhead of the board, which read: "Las Vegas Grant, over 400,000 acres of patented land."[67]

9.4. Letterhead of the board of trustees of the Las Vegas Grant. The language, "Owning Over 400,000 Acres of Patented Land," gives the impression that the common lands were for sale. Courtesy New Mexico State Records Center and Archives.

Here was a community land grant being run by an elite board of trustees many of whom had been trying for decades to impose their view of common land ownership on the grant. But this was not the traditional Hispanic idea of the common lands. Under the traditional common lands or *ejido* legal concept, these lands were to be managed for the benefit of the community. This meant that those lands capable of being farmed, which were the irrigable lands along the river, were available for allotment to future settlers, while the rest of the common lands were used in common by all the settlers. Historian Daniel Tyler has expressed it best:

New Mexicans who founded new communities believed that they were entitled to common lands for all the purposes specified by Spanish and Mexican laws over the centuries: recreation, grazing, cattle raising, cutting wood, watering animals, hunting, picking wild fruits and berries, etc. Because United States authorities failed to understand the Hispanic system of land tenure in which *ejido* lands were an essential part of community grants, Mexicans who chose to stay in the United States lost property which they thought was protected under the Treaty of Guadalupe Hidalgo.[68]

Looking back at the unique history of the Las Vegas grant it may be useful to compare its fate to that of other Northern New Mexico community land grants. First of all, the grant was confirmed to a community, in this case to the town of Las Vegas. The pitfall of confirmation of a community grant to an individual as was the case with the Tierra Amarilla grant, did not occur. Furthermore, the trap of the partition suit dividing the common lands and resulting in their sale, as happened with Las Trampas, did not take place either. This was because the government's relentless attack on the survey left the ownership of the common lands undecided. It is ironic that the governments' actions in this regard may have delayed the loss of the common lands by confusing the question of title to these lands. Judge Long's decision in *Milhiser v. Padilla* may have had a similar effect in the short term, but in the long run it was the *Milhiser* decision that contained the seeds that bore the bitter fruit of Judge Mills' takeover of the grant. Remember that Judge Long had decided that all the common lands should be open for settlement and actual occupancy. This implied development and sale of the common lands as well, which Judge Long proceeded to do when he was appointed to the grant board.

So what are we to make of the "not a pepper, not an onion" promise made that August morning in 1846 by General Kearny to the people of Las Vegas? Was their property—the common lands of the Las Vegas grant—protected by the United States? I think not. Rather the United States devoted its substantial resources in trying to reduce the size of the Las Vegas grant and even went so far as to declare the common lands open for homestead entry. That is not to say that the United States government was entirely responsible for the loss of the common lands of the Las Vegas grant. The state courts and the New Mexico legislature sealed the fate of the Las Vegas grant by appointing a nondemocratic board of trustees who systematically sold off the common lands, thus administering the final coup de grace to the grant. It was the average grant resident and land grant heir that was the loser, as different political factions fought for control of the common lands.

But for a brief period during the early 1890s the interests of the heirs and successors to the Las Vegas grant were really protected. Las Gorras Blancas had the sympathy of most of the grant residents as they temporarily stopped the carving up of the common lands. But the phenomenal growth of the town of Las Vegas in the late 1800s, where mercantile capitalism replaced the growing of peppers and onions, made it virtually inevitable that these lands would become just another resource from which the board of trustees could make a profit.[69]

Ten

The Ramón Vigil Grant:
An Undetected Forgery

At first glance, the history of the Ramón Vigil grant looks ordinary enough. It was among the first grants to be confirmed by the surveyor general of New Mexico, and it soon became the object of land speculation.[1] But a closer examination reveals the elements of a fascinating story—even a mystery. The grant documents were forgeries that remained undetected by the Federal officials charged with the investigation of the grant. Who forged them and why the forgery was not discovered are elements of that mystery. Beyond this puzzle, we have a most unusual land speculator as a primary actor in this history. His business acumen was keen and his success in turning a tidy profit from the grant exceeded that of the other speculators involved with the grant. In fact this man was probably more successful than anyone in the Santa Fe Ring, including the notorious Thomas B. Catron himself. This man's name was Thomas Aquinas Hayes and he was a Catholic priest.

The history of the Ramón Vigil grant raises questions concerning other land grant forgeries, and about the relative skill of the surveyor general compared with the Court of Private Land Claims, in detecting forgeries and in combing the archives for documents otherwise bearing on the validity of land grants.

The grant was made, not to Ramón Vigil, but to Pedro Sánchez in 1742. Over a hundred years later, in 1851, Ramón Vigil purchased the grant from one of the heirs of Pedro Sánchez.[2] But the documents purporting to be the 1742 grant to Pedro Sánchez, are all written in the same handwriting, and contain letter-patching and ink-pooling probably caused by a writer who is slowly drawing the words rather than spontaneously writing across the page. This indication of a forgery is corroborated by a comparison of the forged signatures and rubrics of Pedro Sánchez and of the government officials involved in the grant with genuine examples of their handwriting. None of the signatures and rubrics in the document are genuine. Since the grant documents were forged, the next inquiry is whether the events described in the documents took place at all.[3]

The answer to this question depends on who forged the documents, what their motive was, and what independent evidence there is of the events described in the documents. Marjorie Bell Chambers first noted the forgery and suggested that the forger was the original grantee, Pedro Sánchez.[4]

10.2. *Petition for land later known as the Ramón Vigil Grant. The title papers for the grant were forged. Courtesy New Mexico State Records Center and Archives.*

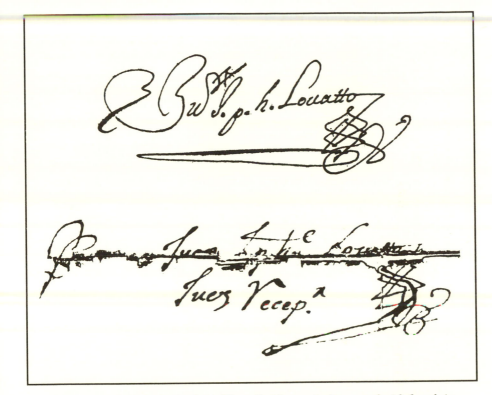

10.3. Genuine signature and rubric of Juan José Lovato (top) compared with forged signature and rubric (bottom) found on the second page of the Pedro Sánchez/Ramón Vigil title papers.

However, a comparison of the Sánchez signature and rubric on the grant documents with a genuine Sánchez signature and rubric shows that the Sánchez signature also was forged — and not very skillfully.[5] Since by definition one does not forge ones own signature, this eliminates Pedro Sánchez as the forger. In addition, there is independent evidence of the grant: a reference to the Pedro Sánchez grant in a 1763 lawsuit filed by the Indians of the Pueblo of San Ildefonso.[6] So the forgery must have taken place later in the history of the grant. To follow this lead we must begin with the persons, places, and events described in the documents and search for a motive on the part of one of the principal players who might have had something to gain from a forgery. The grant to Pedro Sánchez is the starting point. But who was Pedro Sánchez?

The documents provide only clues, but we do know these basic facts. Pedro's father, Pedro Sánchez de Iñigo, was the natural son of Juana López,[7] who was heavily involved in land in the Santa Fe area.[8] Pedro's uncle was Jacinto Sánchez, *alcalde* for Santa Cruz de la Cañada in 1713. Pedro married Micaela Quintana in 1718 and started raising a family. By 1742, Pedro Sánchez was apparently a captain at the Santa Fe garrison.[9]

In his 1742 petition to Governor Gaspar Domingo Mendoza,[10] Sánchez requested a tract of land west of the Rio Grande to support his large family, which then consisted of his wife, twelve children, three orphaned nephews, and three female servants. Sánchez stated that he had to borrow lands from his neighbors to plant his crops because the land he had acquired by purchase was not sufficient to support his large family. Even with the additional borrowed land, he told Governor Mendoza in his petition, he was only able to keep a few sheep, four cows, and some horses. The land he sought was described as being bounded on the north by the lands of the Indians of the Pueblo of San Ildefonso, on the south by the lands of Captain Andrés Montoya, on the east by the Rio Grande and on the west by the Sierra Madre.[11] Governor Mendoza made the grant to Sánchez in 1742, directing the *alcalde* of the villa of Santa Cruz de la Cañada to place him in possession of the land, following the form used in similar cases. The land was granted on the condition that Sánchez settle upon it within the period prescribed by the royal laws.[12]

Eight days later, the *alcalde* of Santa Cruz, Juan José Lobato, went to the land with Pedro Sánchez and two witnesses. According to Lobato's report, he notified the principal Indians of the Pueblo of San Ildefonso to appear and produce their title papers. As was true with most of the Pueblos, they had no title papers. However, to avoid future disputes, *alcalde* Lobato reported that he had extended the Pueblo's lands beyond those which they had cultivated, to include those lands that they considered the best. With the consent of both Pedro Sánchez and the Indians, a cross was erected to mark the boundary between them.[13] Sánchez was then placed in possession of the land described in his petition, with the usual ceremony of casting stones, plucking up grass, and shouting "Long live the King" to signify that the grantee was in undisputed possession of the land.[14]

This was apparently not the first grant made to Pedro Sánchez. When the Santa Cruz *alcalde* investigated the 1743 petition for the Black Mesa grant, he found that it had been granted to Pedro Sánchez or to his father-in-law, Miguel Quintana in about 1731. The *alcalde* learned that Sánchez

had planted a few fields of corn and squash, but had abandoned them after
about four months. Later he tried to pasture his sheep on the grant but gave
this up too when "wolves [attacked and] bit his shepards." Any claim that
Sánchez might have had to the Black Mesa grant was held forfeited by
Governor Mendoza in 1743 due to abandonment.[15] Another factor in
Mendoza's decision was probably his 1742 approval of the grant to Pedro
Sánchez, with which this chapter is concerned. Sánchez subsequently abandoned his 1742 grant, later known as the Ramón Vigil grant, but exactly
when is uncertain.

In the late 1840s Pedro Sánchez sought still another grant of land.
This was the Bartolome Trujillo claim near Abiquiú, which had been made
to Trujillo and nine others in 1734. Indian hostilities forced the abandonment of the Trujillo grant, and Governor Tomás Vélez Cachupín later
ordered the resettlement of this and other abandoned settlements north of
Santa Fe.[16] Since Pedro Sánchez had attempted to register the land for
himself, Bartolome Trujillo asked Governor Vélez Cachupín to revali-
date the grant to him, stating that he had not intended to abandon the
grant and promising to contribute sixty pesos worth of produce to the king.
This request, called a petition seeking an act of clemency, was granted, apparently influenced in large measure by the gift of produce.[17] Since Spanish law prohibited the granting of land to an individual who was already
occupying another land grant, Pedro Sánchez had probably abandoned
his 1742 grant before asking for the Bartolome Trujillo grant. In any
case, a 1763 lawsuit concerning San Ildefonso Pueblo indicates that the
Pedro Sanchez/Ramón Vigil grant had been abandoned at least by that
date.

San Ildefonso Pueblo started this lawsuit by asking Governor Tomás
Vélez Cachupín to measure the four square leagues to which the Pueblo was
entitled, claiming encroachments on their land by certain Spaniards.[18] On
the west side of the pueblo, the Indians claimed that some of the Pedro
Sánchez grant was within their boundaries.[19] Governor Vélez Cachupín
ordered the *Alcalde* of Santa Cruz to measure the Pueblo's league of 5,000
varas in each cardinal direction.[20] Measuring with a *cordel* 100 varas long,
the *alcalde* reached the house and corral of Pedro Sánchez with thirty-two
lengths of the cordel or 3200 varas. Thus Sánchez was 1800 varas within
San Ildefonso's league. Other Spanish families were also found to be within
the league, and all were given an opportunity to present their documents
and argue their side of the case to the governor.[21]

Pedro Sánchez had apparently abandoned his lands by this time, for he did not present his grant papers or file a petition. The other families within the Pueblo's league urged the governor not to evict them from their lands, arguing that the laws should not be enforced "with all their rigor." To do so, they said, would mean that the Spaniards would have to move to unoccupied lands more than forty leagues away. They argued that this dispersal of the Spanish population would prejudice the defense of the province. For if the Spaniards were evicted from the San Ildefonso league, the other Pueblos would also complain of Spanish encroachment, possibly resulting in a further scattering of the Spaniards. This was a weighty argument at a time when Spanish defense against Comanche and Apache raids was weakening.[22]

But pressure on the Pueblos by Spanish settlers seeking more land was increasing, and Governor Vélez Cachupín was pulled in both directions. Rather than make a difficult decision himself, the governor referred the case to the magistrate for the Villa of Chihuahua, Fernando de Torijay Leri.[23] In 1764 this attorney rendered an opinion, that represented a compromise. While recognizing the right of San Ildefonso to their four square leagues, the lawyer found some merit in the arguments of the Spaniards about opening the door to lawsuits by the other Pueblos if the Spanish were evicted. So the Chihuahua official suggested that the encroaching Spaniards on the south and the east be allowed to remain and that the Pueblo be given as much land as it had lost in those directions from the land available on the north and the west. Apparently the west side was chosen because the Sánchez grant had been abandoned.[24]

Governor Vélez Cachupín agreed with the Chihuahua attorney's recommendation and granted the Pueblo all the land they needed on the west side, including the land previously granted to Pedro Sánchez, for pasturing San Ildefonso's cattle. This land would also be available to pasture the horses of the Santa Fe presidio, according to the governor's order.[25] When this order was announced by the local *alcalde*, the heirs of Pedro Sánchez said that they would obey it, although they had not appeared earlier to contest the Indians' claim.[26]

These events would seem to have put an end to the Pedro Sánchez grant, but two documents appeared almost a hundred years later in the surveyor general's office, showing that Ramón Vigil claimed to have bought the grant. According to the first of these documents, dated in 1749, Francisco Sánchez, one of Pedro's sons, bought out the interests of his brothers and sisters in the grant. By this time, Pedro Sánchez and his wife must have been dead. Also presumed to be deceased were four of the twelve children Sánchez said he had in 1742, for the document shows that one of eight living heirs bought out the interests of the other seven. For the interests of his three sisters (Bárbara, María Teresa, and María), Francisco Sánchez paid forty varas of land in La Mesilla and a house of twenty-four vigas. In addition, he paid eight sheep each to brothers Miguel and Bernardo, eight pesos to his brother Julián, and a bull to his brother Pedro for their respective interests.[27]

In the second document, dated 1851, Antonio Sánchez, one of the heirs of Francisco Sánchez, sold his interest in the grant, and the interests of seven of his ten brothers and sisters, to José Ramón Vigil. This time the selling price was a yoke of oxen, thirty-six ewes, one ram, and twenty dollars.[28] The fact that three Sánchez heirs did not convey their interests to Vigil was to result in a later court claim by these heirs to a three-eleventh interest in the grant.[29]

Armed with the 1749 and 1851 sale documents and with "the original grant document," Ramón Vigil was in a position to seek confirmation of the grant in his name before the surveyor general of New Mexico, which he did on 9 May 1856. He was represented by J.S. Watts, an associate justice on the first New Mexico Territorial Supreme Court, who alleged in the petition that Vigil had acquired eight parts of the grant by the 1851 deed.[30] Surveyor General William Pelham recommended to Congress in 1859 that the grant be confirmed, and on 21 June 1860 the Ramón Vigil grant, as it was then known, was confirmed by Congress.[31] When the boundaries were surveyed in 1877, the grant was found to contain over thirty-one thousand acres.[32] The approval of a land grant of this size when the grant documents were forged was highly improper, but that questionable situation was compounded by certain irregularities in the deeds through which Ramón Vigil claimed to have acquired title to the grant.

The 1749 and 1851 deeds contain different descriptions of the grant from those contained in the forged Sánchez grant document. While the forged grant document referred to a tract bounded by the lands of San Ildefonso Pueblo on the north, the Rio Grande on the east, the Sierra Madre on the west, and by the lands of Captain Andrés Montoya on the south, the description in the two deeds had as a northern boundary the abrevadero (watering place) of the Rio de los Guajes to the hill of the Rito de los Frijoles. The 1749 deed adds a southern boundary call: the lands of

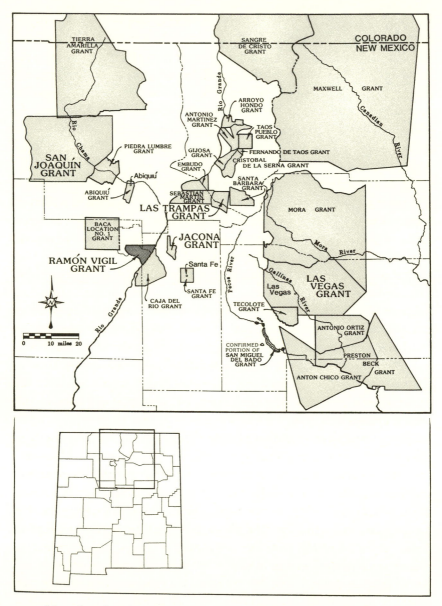

10.4. Map of northern New Mexico land grants with the Ramón Vigil grant high-lighted.

Montoya, the only one that agrees with the description in the forged Sánchez grant.

There are other suspicious circumstances connected with the documentation of the grant to Pedro Sánchez. It arrived at the surveyor general's office, not in the hands of Ramón Vigil, but in those of Manuel Alvarez, the unofficial American consul in Santa Fe. Alvarez filed the document on 9 March 1852 and it was recorded in the surveyor general's records. Right after the grant document the 1749 and 1851 deeds are recorded. The 1851 deed to Ramón Vigil, dated less than seven months before the forged Sánchez grant was filed, contains the statement that if the original grant document is found it should be delivered to the "proper owner," i.e. Ramón Vigil.[33] This was very strange! Did Ramón Vigil forge the grant in those seven months and then have it laundered by having the respectable consul, Manuel Alvarez, file it with the surveyor general?

This seems like a hypothesis worth investigating. Ramón Vigil served as the *alcalde* of Santa Clara in the 1840s, and in that capacity numerous documents were either written by him or at his direction. Vigil's act of possession for the Rio del Oso grant provides a handwriting sample with which to compare the forged Sanchez grant.[34] When such a comparison is made, one sees remarkable similarities between the handwriting in the two documents — enough to establish Ramón Vigil's culpability. But after the exhilaration of that discovery, the questions of method and motive still remain unanswered.

Trying to visualize what it was that the forger was copying, one comes to the realization that everything on the forged grant seems plausible — the petition, the grant, and the act of possession are all internally consistent, and the officals involved actually did hold office at that time. Since nothing seems to have been added to the forged document which would point to a motive, maybe something was subtracted from the document being copied. A clue is found in the fact that when several grants were revoked by Governor Cruzat y Gongora in 1735, the revocation was sometimes noted on the grant document itself. For example, the Barranca grant contains the following notation at the end: *"Esta merced de tierras con la posesion que le corresponde se mando recojer,"* (this land grant with its corresponding possession, is ordered revoked.[35]

Thus a probable scenario in this case is as follows: when Ramón Vigil was approached by the Sánchez heirs with an offer to buy the Pedro Sánchez grant he saw that the original grant had been revoked as a result of the 1763 San Ildefonso litigation. So Vigil or his secretary remedied the situation by copying the entire grant and omitting the notation that the grant had been revoked, thus breathing new life into the grant.

We may never know Ramón Vigil's motive, but what we do know is that the grant that bears his name should never have been confirmed by the United States government, especially when more deserving grants were rejected entirely. But it was confirmed, due to Ramón Vigil's efforts to put together a patchwork of documents and witness testimony to support his claim. To determine how this was possible it might help to see what we can learn about the character of Ramón Vigil, the man.

Little is known about the life of Ramón Vigil beyond the fact that he was married to Catarina Montoya and had seven children by her, five boys and two girls.[36] One revealing incident has survived from the Mexican archives, however, which gives us some intriguing information about him.

In 1828, Vigil and the prominent Santa Fe merchant Thomas H. Boggs had a number of beaver pelts confiscated from them by the *alcalde* of Jémez. Boggs was returning from Sonora where he allegedly planned to buy horses. Now he was accused of trapping beaver without a license. Depositions were taken before the *alcalde* of Taos and sent to *Alcalde* Juan Estevan Pino of Santa Fe, for decision. The crucial testimony in the case was a deposition given by Ramón Vigil which contains a clue to Vigil's character. In the deposition Vigil stated that he had met Boggs at the junction of the Gila and the Rio Grande Rivers. According to Vigil, Boggs did not have any traps with him — only horses, which he had bought in Sonora. As to the beaver skins, Vigil testified that they had been purchased from three Mexicans who were, according to David J. Weber, part of the James Ohio Pattie's California-bound party. On the basis of this testimony, Pino ordered the furs returned to Boggs and Vigil.[37]

Boggs was saved by Ramón Vigil's testimony, but it appears likely that he was guilty. Just two years before, Boggs had been suspected by Governor Armijo of trapping without a license on his way to California but Armijo was not able to apprehend him. Having Ramón Vigil along on his 1828 trip could have been a clever ruse. The Mexican authorities were much more likely to believe a Mexican citizen than an American. Furthermore, it appears that Vigil himself was trapping, as some of the confiscated furs were his. Claiming to have purchased furs that were actually trapped was not uncommon among the mountain men.[38] If Ramón Vigil was willing to engage in a cover-up for Boggs, as appears highly probable, it would not be out of character for him to have forged the grant that now bears his name. With all these suspicious circumstances, the question remains, how did this forged grant get past the surveyor general to be confirmed so quickly?

The answer lies in the adjudication process followed by the surveyor general and the Court of Private Land Claims and with the experts employed by the government as translators and as witnesses to the genuineness of documents. Surveyor General William Pelham, the first to hold the office, had two translators assisting him: David J. Miller and David V. Whiting. Whiting translated the Sánchez grant document for the land that Ramón Vigil was claiming, but evidently saw nothing in the document to raise his suspicions.[39]

In the early years the surveyor general's office did not have time to make a thorough examination of all the documents submitted to it, but in the case of the Ramón Vigil grant few documents were filed. Surprisingly, the Ramón Vigil petition, together with the forged Pedro Sánchez grant and Whiting's translation, were all that Surveyor General Pelham had before him when he wrote his cursory opinion approving the grant. There were not even any of the usual affidavits of witnesses supporting the claim. This perfunctory procedure was later replaced by the truly adversary proceedings of the Court of Private Land Claims. Most of the other eleven forgeries of land grant documents were uncovered by the Land Claims Court.[40]

The lead expert for the government concerning the genuineness of documents was William (Will) M. Tipton. He had been working for the surveyor general's office since 1876, and by 1884 was the office's chief translator, handwriting expert, and custodian of the Spanish archives.[41] His familiarity with the Spanish and Mexican archives made him a sought after expert witness who was often called upon to testify in cases of suspected forgery. It was probably due to Tipton that one of the few forgeries discovered by a surveyor general was exposed. In 1879 Surveyor General Atkinson pointed out several erasures, suspicious alterations, and anachronisms in the Orejas del Llano de los Aguajes grant documents and suggested that the signatures appeared to have been traced. Although he recommended that the claim be rejected, no action was taken by Congress and the claim was submitted to the Court of Private Land Claims. There

Tipton testified to additional factors pointing to forgery, such as the facts that the governor in 1826 never signed his name "A. Narbona," that the abbreviation "N.M." used in the document was of later American origin and hence was not used in 1826, and that all the documents had been written by one person. Despite these suspicious circumstances, the reason the court rejected the grant was not because of forgery but because the court claimed the governor of New Mexico did not have the authority to make the grant at that time.[42]

It is apparent from Tipton's careful analysis of this forgery, that if someone with his skill had been working for the surveyor general in 1856 when the Ramón Vigil forgery was submitted, the grant would never have been approved. In other Land Claims Court cases where the genuineness of grant documents was at issue, Tipton's testimony was often crucial. For example, he testified at length about the forgery of documents concerning the Santa Teresa de Jesús grant, comparing the genuine and the forged handwriting of Antonio de Armenta, and particularly two rubrics which he actually copied onto the record, showing how the forged rubric differed from the genuine one. Tipton also noted that the paper and the ink used for the forged document were different from those customarily used by Antonio Armenta.[43] The most spectacular forgery case in which Tipton testified was the Peralta-Reavis grant. Here the elaborate scheme of James Addison Reavis was exposed by the government with the help of chemical analyses of the ink and paper used and photographic analyses of document alterations. Tipton testified that the documents through which Reavis was claiming some twelve million acres of land were entirely forged because they were written with a steel pen and modern ink instead of a quill pen and the ink used in the third quarter of the eighteenth century when the documents were supposed to have been written. In addition the handwriting was a poor copy of the writing then in vogue.[44]

The U.S. attorney for the Court of Private Land Claims had more technical and expert witness resources than did the surveyor general, so he was more likely to detect forgeries and often produced documentary evidence demonstrating reasons for the rejection of a grant that had been overlooked by the surveyor general. This point is illustrated by comparing the Ramón Vigil adjudication with that of the neighboring grant to the south, the Rito de los Frijoles grant. Here we can also see the potential multiplier effect of one forgery on adjoining grants.

When the claimants of the Rito de los Frijoles grant presented their documents to the surveyor general, these papers did not contain a description of the boundaries. So when Surveyor General Henry Atkinson recommended in 1883 that the Rito de los Frijoles grant be confirmed, he relied on the southern boundary of the forged Pedro Sánchez grant to determine the northern boundary of the Rito de los Frijoles grant. Although unaware of Ramón Vigil's forgery, in hindsight his recommendation rested on a rather weak foundation.[45]

This potential injustice was corrected by the Court of Private Land Claims when the Rito de los Frijoles grant was submitted to that tribunal, after Congress's failure to confirm the grant. This time the government introduced Spanish Archive 1352 showing that governor Vélez Cachupín had ordered that the occupants of the grant be ejected. After the claimants disobeyed Vélez Cachupín's order and asked Governor Mendinueta for a hearing, Mendinueta held that the grant was void, because the adjoining landowners had not been notified and given a chance to object when the grant was made, and because the grant was not settled. The Court of Private Land Claims rejected the grant on the basis of Mendinueta's decree.[46]

If the Pedro Sánchez/Ramón Vigil grant had been adjudicated by the Court of Private Land Claims, the government would almost certainly have both detected the forgery and introduced Spanish Archive 1351 showing that the grant to Pedro Sánchez was abandoned in 1765. This would very likely have led the Court of Private Land Claims to reject the grant. But instead, the grant gained early confirmation by the surveyor general.

The balloon that was the Ramón Vigil grant soon became overinflated in regard to the amounts of money that changed hands during several more transfers of the grant. During this phase of the grant's history we meet a priest who was also an avid—and extremely successful—land grant speculator.

Thomas Aquinas Hayes came to New Mexico as one of Archbishop Lamy's recruits when Hayes was still a seminarian not yet ordained to the priesthood. He left St. Louis in 1856 with a group of soon to be priests escorted by the Right Reverend Joseph Machebeuf.[47] After ordination he was initially assigned to Santa Clara Pueblo in 1859, and then, from 1865 to 1867, served as parish priest for Bernalillo. Hayes was sent to the Jesuit parish of Conejos in Colorado in 1878, and must have gotten into some trouble there, for in September of 1881 he was arrested in Albuquerque on a warrant issued in La Junta, Colorado.[48] By that time he had acquired a poor reputation and was characterized in the Jesuit Diary for San Felipe parish in Albuquerque as being of highly questionable character.[49] Hayes escaped from the clutches of the law when the Albuquerque Jesuits took him in.[50]

Hayes's name, hispanicized to Tomás de Aquino, began appearing in the Santa Fe deed books by 1863 when he lent Gaspar Ortiz y Alarid and his wife eight thousand dollars and took a mortgage from Ortiz in return.[51] In 1879 Father Hayes purchased the Pedro Sánchez/Ramón Vigil grant from Ramón Vigil for four thousand dollars.[52] This probably seemed like a lot of money to Ramón Vigil who had paid only twenty dollars and some sheep and oxen for the grant twenty-eight years earlier. But Father Hayes had even greater speculative ambitions. Just over a month after Hayes bought the grant he sold it for sixteen thousand dollars.[53] And this was just the beginning of the priest's involvement with the Ramón Vigil grant.

The sale for sixteen thousand dollars to Edward Sorin from Indiana was probably designed to inflate the paper value of the grant, because within two years Father Hayes had bought the grant back from Sorin at the same price. That was in July 1881.[54] Hayes then set to work on two fronts in preparation for an even bigger deal. First he began to marshall evidence to support an attack on the government survey of the grant done in 1877. He also attempted to purchase the three Sánchez interests in the grant that Ramón Vigil had failed to acquire.

The official survey had found the grant to contain 31,802 acres, but Father Hayes thought it should be even larger. To prove his case he hired surveyors Thomas Gwyn and John C. Duval to retrace some of the lines of the government survey following the official field notes. Gwyn and Duval submitted a written report to Hayes that questioned the accuracy of that survey. They said that the topography they traversed following the bearings and distances of the official survey did not correspond with the land described in the field notes. Furthermore, they did not find any of the monuments called for in the field notes for the lines they traced, nor could they discover a single surveyor's blaze mark to indicate that Deputy Surveyors Sawyer and McElroy had actually surveyed the boundaries of the grant.[55]

Father Hayes filed the Gwyn/Duval report with Surveyor General Henry Atkinson in September of 1882, asking for a new survey of the Ramón Vigil grant.[56] He also filed with the surveyor general a formal protest of the Sawyer/McElroy survey[57] and attached seven affidavits to support it.[58] He based his protest on the claim that the western boundary of

the grant should have been run much further west, along the summit of the
Sierra Madre instead of along its base. When submitted to the General
Land Office in Washington D.C. the protest was overruled, because "the
rule is well settled in regard to cases like this, that where hills, mountains
and mountain ranges are named as boundaries, the foot or base is to be
taken as the boundary indicated, unless the top, ridge, or summit is clearly
indicated as such."[59]

This was indeed the rule established by the surveyor general's office, but
it was arbitrary—and wrong. Father Hayes accurately pointed out that
under Spanish and Mexican legal custom, when a mountain was a boundary
the summit was to be taken as the dividing line, unless otherwise indicated.
If this had not been true, two land grants bounded by the same mountain
range would not adjoin one another but would be separated by the land
comprising the mountain range. Since the mountainside was needed by
both the grants for summer grazing and for gathering wood, the granting
authorities intended to include the mountain lands within each grant.[60]

Although reason was on the side of Father Hayes, he did not appeal the
decision when notified of it by Surveyor General Atkinson in April 1883.
Instead he was preparing to sell the grant. First he tried once more to
acquire the interests of the three Sánchez heirs who had not conveyed to
Ramón Vigil, but was again unsuccessful. This failure was to lead to a
lawsuit by 1900.[61]

Having failed to get the grant enlarged or to acquire all the outstanding
interests in the grant, Father Hayes again put the grant on the market. In
1884 he sold the Ramón Vigil grant to Winfield Smith of Milwaukee and
Edward Sheldon of Cleveland for a whopping $100,000![62] To be sure,
Hayes had invested some money in the grant, but his $96,000 profit amply
repaid his investment of time and the $4,000 he paid for the grant many
times over. The priest's 2,400 percent profit on his initial investment
appears to set a record for successful land grant speculation.[63]

Although it would appear unseemly today for a priest to be so heavily
involved in land speculation, it was not such a stigma at the time Father
Hayes was operating. As a secular priest not a member of a religious order,
Hayes was not required to take a vow of poverty. However, canon law did
prohibit clerics from habitually engaging in business, defined as involvement in a continuity of several transactions.[64] It would appear that Father
Hayes had stepped over this line, but there is no evidence that he was ever
criticized by the archbishop for doing so. He was undoubtedly the benefici-

ary of an extremely lax attitude prevalent in New Mexico at the time, which viewed activities that today would be deemed fraudulent as merely commendable business enterprise. Nevertheless, as we have seen, Hayes was not highly thought of in Albuquerque and the surrounding area.

Father Hayes's poor reputation seems to have been based more on a drinking problem, than on business conduct unbecoming a priest. His speculative investments eventually benefitted the church, for at his death in 1892 he left thirty-five thousand dollars to the American College in Rome for four scholarships for young men who were U.S. citizens born in Great Britain.[65]

There is no evidence that Father Hayes had any connection with the forgery of the Ramón Vigil grant for he did not arrive in New Mexico until five years after the forged grant was filed, but his acquaintance with land speculator Gaspar Ortiz y Alarid raises some interesting connections with other forged grants. When Ortiz filed a claim for the Roque Lovato grant in 1871, the documents submitted were originals, not copies, and there was no grant document containing the boundaries of the claimed grant. Usually the original documents remained in the archives and the grantee received a copy called the *testimonio*. Gaspar Ortiz's possession of the original could be the result of the sale of some of New Mexico's archives by Governor Pile in 1870, for Ortiz is known to have purchased some of them.[66] In any event, the only mention of boundaries of the Lovato grant was in the deed by which Ortiz acquired the grant, and when this document was proven to be a forgery, the bubble of the Roque Lovato grant burst dramatically. The key testimony against Ortiz was that of Will Tipton, who testified that the deed was written with a steel pen, although the document was dated at a time when that writing instrument did not exist in New Mexico. Undaunted Ortiz filed a petition for confirmation of the alleged 100,000 acre Sierra Mosca grant two years later and testified as a witness in support of the Uña del Gato grant five years after that.[67] Both of these grants were clumsy forgeries. It is certainly a curious coincidence that Father Hayes and Gaspar Ortiz, who also gave generously to the church, were in some way connected with four of the twelve known land grant forgeries known in New Mexico and Arizona.

Thomas Aquinas Hayes sold the Ramón Vigil grant in time to avoid a couple of serious problems that would plague the new owners. Buyer Edward Sheldon had paid two-fifths of the purchase price and purchaser Winfield Smith three-fifths.[68] When Sheldon sold his interest in 1884 for

forty-four thousand dollars he made a small profit,[69] but after that, none of
the succeeding owners was able to get back what they paid for the grant.
Not only did they take a loss on their investments, most of the owners after
Father Hayes had to deal with time-consuming and expensive problems.
Two of these problems were the unsuccessful attempt in 1885 to have the
grant resurveyed, and the filing of a lawsuit in 1900 against the owners by
the Sánchez heirs whose interests in the grant had not been conveyed to
Ramón Vigil.

Although the 1882 protest by Father Hayes to the official survey was
overruled, the matter did not rest there. Instead, the new owners filed an
appeal in 1885 to the secretary of the interior of the earlier decision by the
commissioner of the General Land Office.[70] An interesting aspect of this
episode was the identity of the owner's attorney, the surveyor general who
had turned down the first protest, Henry M. Atkinson. Atkinson must have
advised the filing of the appeal, but it was foolish advice that only served to
line his pockets. The reasoning he used in his brief was convoluted and
rested largely on Atkinson the lawyer's interpretation of what Atkinson the
surveyor general had meant when he wrote a letter submitting the first
protest to the General Land Office for decision. Atkinson the attorney was
saying what Atkinson the surveyor general had thought about the case but
had never written down,[71] and which was contrary to what he had committed to writing as surveyor general. The Department of the Interior was
not taken in by this blatant attempt by the former surveyor general to
garner legal fees on the basis of his having held that office, and it turned
down the appeal on the ground that it was not filed within the required sixty
days of the decision.[72] Ironically, Atkinson himself had notified Father
Hayes of this requirement when he was surveyor general.[73]

This was not the only time that Henry Atkinson had abused his office, or
engaged in unethical or illegal practices. Surveys conducted under Atkinson's regime as surveyor general were often of substandard quality and were
frequently not done in the manner required by government regulations.
Additionally, as a speculator in land grants, Atkinson was an incorporator of
four cattle companies with a combined capitalization of five million dollars,
together with Thomas B. Catron and William H. McBroom, his own
deputy surveyor.[74] Probably the most outrageous example of Atkinson's
corruption was his decision as surveyor general concerning the controversy
over the Anton Chico grant discussed in Chapter 1.[75]

After their failure to expand the boundaries of the Ramón Vigil grant, the new owners were faced with the problem of claims by the Sánchez heirs who didn't sell to Ramón Vigil, culminating in the filing of a lawsuit in 1900. After volumes of testimony and extensive hearings and other proceedings, the plaintiffs lost the lawsuit, failing to secure a share of the property. Fortunately for the historian, however, the lengthy testimony in the case fills in some gaps concerning the use of the land comprising the Ramón Vigil grant.

It is doubtful that anyone settled permanently on the grant until the late 1880s when the owners brought in some Texans to run a cattle ranch.[76] At the beginning of the life of the grant we know that Pedro Sánchez had lived on the grant, for his abandoned house and corral were noted during the 1863 lawsuit with San Ildefonso Pueblo.[77] It is likely that parts of the grant were used for pasture by some of the Sánchez heirs, by members of San Ildefonso Pueblo, and perhaps by others, up until the purchase of the grant by Ramón Vigil. During the trial of the *Sánchez v. Fletcher* lawsuit, witnesses testified that Ramón Vigil had forbidden the pasture of animals on the grant, although he did make exceptions for a few individuals. There was also testimony that Ramón Vigil's wife lived in Española and that Vigil himself probably did not live on the grant very long, although he did have a house there.[78]

A portion of the testimony in the case also disclosed that Father Hayes had acknowledged to some of the Sánchez heirs that Ramón Vigil had told him that certain heirs had not sold their interests. Father Hayes had promised these heirs that he would not interfere with their rights,[79] so when he sold the grant to Sheldon and Smith, Hayes knew that he did not own the entire grant. It is unlikely that he informed his buyers of these outstanding interests, or he would not have received a purchase price of $100,000 from them. Although the owners ultimately defeated the lawsuit by the Sánchez heirs, it was probably an expensive victory in lawyers' fees, for the case dragged on for five years. Father Hayes's feat of making a ninety-six thousand dollar profit on the sale of the Ramón Vigil grant is all the more remarkable because he was selling the grant together with two lawsuits that would cost the new owners additional cash: the suit to enlarge the boundaries and the claim of the Sánchez heirs to a share of the grant.

After Father Hayes sold the grant, several attempts were made by the new owners to squeeze some kind of a cash return out of the land, but these operations were all short-lived. The cattle operation, involving a lease to Texan W. C. Bishop to run three thousand head of cattle on the land, lasted only two years; probably the grass available would not support such a large-scale operation. Another scheme looked to the timber as a source of income. For ten thousand dollars the owners sold H. S. Buckman the right to cut any timber on the grant over eight inches in diameter. Buckman, who had been cutting timber off the Petaca grant east of Tres Piedras, had made a practice of cutting timber on land grants after they came into Anglo hands. He had hoped to make a profit off the Ramón Vigil grant's two thousand acres of timber using the recently constructed "Chili Line" of the Denver & Rio Grande Railroad to ship the timber out. But the railroad was on the other side of the Rio Grande from the grant, so Buckman had to build a bridge across the river. Then the bridge washed out and had to be rebuilt. This, in addition to building a company town for his employees and constructing extensive logging roads, made the operation more costly than anticipated. The greatest cost, however, was to the environment. Today, the results of Buckman's heavy clear-cutting can still be seen. Ironically, it was the Buckman operation that moved the Sánchez heirs to file their lawsuit, for they claimed a share of the profits.[80]

But little in the way of profits were to be realized from the Ramón Vigil grant. Buckman left the scene prior to 1905 and by 1908 the Ramón Land and Lumber Company had purchased the grant and was trying to make a profit cutting timber on the land. The corporation purchased the grant for fifty-five thousand dollars, but by December 1910 it was hopelessly in debt. The company had paid twenty thousand dollars toward the purchase price and had cut timber valued at twenty to twenty-five thousand dollars. But a large amount of their timber was seized by the federal government when a dispute developed over the location of the northern boundary of the grant. As in the 1763 San Ildefonso lawsuit and the surveyor general's proceedings, no one could agree about where that boundary was, and now the government claimed that the company had been cutting timber on federal land. There followed an attempt to reorganize the Ramón Land and Lumber Company involving a transfer of its stock and an assignment of its debts to the U.S. Bank and Trust Company headquartered in Santa Fe. The purpose of this plan was to try to sell the grant, pay off Ramón Land and Lumber Company's creditors, and distribute any surplus to its stockholders — after the attorney for Ramón Land and Lumber had been paid and after U.S. Bank and Trust had received its commission.[81]

The president of U.S. Bank and Trust Company was no stranger to land grant matters — his name was Napoleon Bonaparte Laughlin. At first he hoped to sell the grant at three dollars per acre, pay off the creditors, and leave a surplus for the stockholders. The bank was to receive a 6 percent commission on whatever funds it paid out, so the higher the selling price the greater the profit for the bank. After the bank's failure to sell at $3 per acre within five months after the agreement was signed, Laughlin offered the grant at $2 per acre. Still no takers. By March of 1913 the bank was offering the grant for $1.75 per acre, and by September of that year it had gone down to $1.50. Then the self-dealing began. One of the bank's directors, Frederick Muller, obtained an option to purchase the grant for $50,000 (later raised to $53,500) on 25 October 1913, and on the same day Muller signed an option to sell the grant to Ashley Pond of Detroit for $80,000. It looked as if Muller might pocket $26,500 because of his position as a director of the bank. When Pond and a group of four associates exercised their option, they left Muller, Laughlin's bank, the attorney for Ramón Land and Lumber Company, and its creditors to fight over the money. In a complicated lawsuit, Muller was denied the money he claimed, because he had breached his duty as bank director. The bank got a commission of about $3,000, computed on only a portion of the sales price, and was denied its attorney's fees. The big winner was the attorney for Ramón Land and Lumber Company, Francis C. Wilson, who was awarded an attorney's fee of $8,000. In the end, Ashley Pond got the land and the lawyers ended up with most of the surplus money.[82]

Ashley Pond was the first owner of the grant since Pedro Sánchez who was not out to exploit it to the hilt. He was attracted to the land for its intrinsic scenic value, not for the profit that could be made by selling the grant or the timber on it. Pond's dream, when he came to New Mexico from Detroit, was to establish a school for boys based on the ideal of the rugged outdoor life that Teddy Roosevelt had popularized. His first attempt to found such a school at Watrous was thwarted when the Mora flood of 1904 washed away the buildings he planned to use for the school.[83]

Pond's first venture on the Ramón Vigil grant was not a school but a recreation club for sportsmen from the East. The two-story lodge built of corrugated sheet metal painted red became the headquarters of the Pajarito Club, which included a game preserve, as well as camping and hunting grounds. The affluent patrons of the club from Detroit and Boston were mostly executives in the fledgling automobile industry. They enjoyed the spectacular New Mexico scenery and the abundant hunting and fishing, and the club was a success. But it was a short-lived success, for in 1917, the

spring in Pajarito Canyon, which supplied the water for the dude ranch, dried up. This forced the Detroiters to leave their enchanted setting just as the Indian dwellers of the area had been forced to leave centuries before due to a similar drought. Then the Pajarito Land Company sold the Ramón Vigil grant to sheepman Frank Bond in 1918 for about what it had paid for it.[84]

Ashley Pond's dream did not die, however. He soon established the Los Alamos Ranch School on a neighboring homestead north of the Ramón Vigil grant, which operated continuously from 1918 until it was taken by the government for the Manhattan Project in 1942. Frank Bond, who owned several other land grants for his vast sheepherding enterprise, used the Ramón Vigil grant in connection with the neighboring Baca Location, which he had also acquired. The use of both grants gave Bond access to the sheep trails leading up the Jémez Mountains where his sheep grazed in the summer.[85]

After the time that Bond owned the grant and while the Ranch School was thriving, a visitor rode into the area on a pack trip from his summer home near Pecos. He, like Ashley Pond before him, had come to New Mexico to regain his health. He was also a dreamer. But his dream was to bring undreamed of change to the beautiful Pajarito Plateau. The man's name was J. Robert Oppenheimer and his dream was to combine his love of physics with his love of New Mexico. The result was the atomic bomb and the Los Alamos we know today.[86]

On 7 December 1942, just a year after Pearl Harbor, a letter to the head of the Los Alamos Ranch School from Secretary of War Henry L. Stimson was read to the assembled students and faculty. It began: "You are advised that it was been determined necessary to the interests of the United States in the prosecution of the War that the property of Los Alamos Ranch School be acquired for military purposes." These same military purposes led the U.S. government, which had already purchased the Ramón Vigil grant from Bond in 1934, to establish the city of Los Alamos north of the grant. But today, if you look on the General Land Office map where Los Alamos should be, it's not there, apparently for security reasons.[87]

Thus we have the story of the Ramón Vigil grant, made by the Spanish government and abandoned, then forged, revived, and confirmed by the American government. It's a story with ironies stretching across three centuries. The revocation of the grant occurred because of the eighteenth-century claims of the San Ildefonso Indians, who still live on their lands northeast of the Ramón Vigil grant. Ramón Vigil's speculation repeated itself in the nineteenth century when that unusual priest named after Saint Thomas Acquinas, Father Hayes, made a record amount of money for land speculation though he never lived on the land. Now a new kind of man-made power has made itself felt on the land with twentieth-century Los Alamos. But the land itself has persisted with its own quiet power, best described by Peggy Pond Church, whose father, Ashley Pond, was the first owner of the Ramón Vigil grant to understand, "that there are certain places in the earth where the great powers that move between earth and sky are much closer and more available than others, and . . . this region, this stretch of valley, plateau and circling mountain, was one of them."[88]

Eleven
The Jacona Grant:
A Success Story

All too often New Mexican land grant histories tell the same bleak story of legitimate Hispanic property rights lost under an American legal system that was supposed to protect those rights. Other chapters have pointed out some of the ways that these land grants were lost: the shenanigans of a surveyor general,[1] the unjust decisions of the Court of Private Land Claims,[2] the avarice and unethical conduct of lawyers taking up to half of a grant as their fee for getting a grant confirmed,[3] or the unfair operation of the partition statute.[4] Of those grants that got past these obstacles relatively intact, several more saw modern-day land developers appear on the scene with devastating consequences to the grant heirs. The Atrisco grant was converted into the Westland Development Corporation, and the grant heirs were given a few shares of stock for their land. The Tomé grant was sold to a large interstate land developer,[5] and the Chilili grant was converted to an agricultural cooperative in 1943, but then many of the heirs were excluded from the management of the grant and most of the common lands were sold without their consent.[6]

The Jacona grant is a partial exception to this rule. Although the grant heirs lost one-third of their land to attorney Napoleon Bonaparte Laughlin, they were able to escape the fate of many other grants and hold on to the balance of their land.

The Jacona grant gets its name from the Indian Pueblo of Jacona, which once existed on the present-day site of the grant. This small Tewa Pueblo on the south side of the Pojoaque River was abandoned for some unknown reason in 1696, when its inhabitants left and settled among the other Tewa Pueblos.[7] This left a choice piece of land available for Spanish settlement. The first Spaniard to ask for some of this land was Captain Jacinto Peláez,[8] who was given two *fanegas* of corn-growing land (enough land to plant about four bushels of seed corn) within the old pueblo.[9]

The first Spaniard to leave a lasting mark on Jacona was Ignacio Roybal, who in 1702, requested a grant of the remainder of the Jacona Pueblo, excluding the Peláez land. Governor Pedro Rodríguez Cubero granted Roybal's petition without even ordering the customary investigation by the local *alcalde*, and since no document evidencing the act of possession has survived, it is not clear whether this important ceremony ever took place.[10]

This caused some problems later when the grant was submitted to United States authorities for confirmation.

After he received the Jacona grant, Ignacio Roybal acted swiftly to consolidate and expand his holdings. In 1705 he purchased one and a half fanegas of corn growing land east of the Jacona grant from Captain Juan de Mestas for fifty pesos.[11] In addition, Roybal was given a grazing grant in 1704 that bounded San Ildefonso pueblo. San Ildefonso took Roybal to court to contest their mutual boundary in connection with this grazing grant, initiating a series of court battles over land and water that have not been fully resolved to this day.[12] The entrepreneurial spirit with which Ignacio Roybal settled, defended, and expanded his land holdings around the Jacona grant was impressive. This spirit was repeated in the early 1900s in the manner by which Roybal's descendants held on to what was left of the Jacona grant.

Roybal came to New Mexico at the request of don Diego de Vargas, who went to Spain in 1693 and recruited him from his native province of Galicia, to help in the reconquest of New Mexico after the 1680 Pueblo Revolt. Only twenty-one years old at the time, Roybal married into the socially prominent, but controversial, Gomez Robledo family a year after he left Spain. He took Francisca, one of the three Gomez Robledo sisters, as his wife, making him a brother-in-law of his Jacona neighbor Jacinto Peláez, who married Margarita Gomez Robledo. The four Gomez Robledo sisters had returned to New Mexico after the Pueblo Revolt and married well. Their father and uncles were socially prominent in spite of the fact that their uncle Francisco had been tried by the inquisition in Mexico City for "judaical tendencies." He was acquitted, but the allegation that he and his brothers actually had little tails branded them with the name "*las colitas.*" This did not affect the Gomez Robledo sisters' status as eligible brides, however. In addition to Francisca and Margarita Gomez Robledo, a third sister, María, was married to *rico* Diego Arias de Quiros, another member of the elite group of soldier-citizens to which Ignacio Roybal belonged.[13]

In addition to his land holdings and socially prominent position, Ignacio Roybal exercised substantial political power. He was *Alcalde* of Santa Fe by 1708, achieved the military rank of *alférez* within ten years of his arrival in New Mexico, and was often asked by the governor for his opinion on political and military matters. In addition, he served most of his life as High Sheriff of the Inquisition.[14]

11.2. *The Ignacio Roybal house, one of the oldest residences in the Pojoaque Valley, is an excellent example of New Mexico's traditional Spanish Colonial architectural style. Historic Santa Fe Foundation #37591. Courtesy New Mexico State Records Center and Archives.*

Although he kept a house and servants in Santa Fe for most of his life, by 1702 Ignacio Roybal had settled at Jacona.[15] He built a house there that is still standing, one of the oldest residences in the Pojoaque Valley.[16] Roybal's family grew steadily; Ignacio and Francisca had four daughters and five sons: María Manuela, María, Juana, Elena, Santiago, Bernardo, Mateo, Ignacio, and Pedro. The wealth of the Roybal family is indicated by the fact that they were able to afford an education in Mexico City for Santiago Roybal, the family's most illustrious member, who after ordination as a priest, was sent to Santa Fe by Bishop Crespo of Durango as his vicar.[17]

Settlement on the Jacona grant also grew. After Ignacio Roybal's death in 1756, the grant was partitioned between his sons by the executor of his estate, Santiago Roybal. In 1782 another of Ignacio's sons, Mateo Roybal, asked Governor Juan Bautista de Anza to give him possession of that part of the Jacona grant that he had received under the earlier partition. Anza complied with the request, and by so doing the governor was in effect acknowledging the validity of the 1702 grant to Ignacio Roybal.[18] It would later be argued in court that this act cured whatever defect may have existed in the original grant due to the absence of an act of possession. In any case, the 1782 confirmation and the earlier partition of the grant to Roybal's heirs, showed that the grant was still being treated as a private grant.

By the early 1800s the population on Jacona grant had grown slowly but surely. By 1833 there were enough people in the Jacona, San Ildefonso, Pojoaque, Nambé, and Cuyamungue area to warrant the establishment of an *ayuntamiento* at San Ildefonso.[19] Jacona irrigators and their ditch association, the Acequia Madre de los Señores Roybales de Jacona, were still fighting with San Ildefonso in 1836.[20] Things had not changed much. By 1874 there were said to be fifty families living on the grant, twenty-five of them living at the place called Jacona, or Los Roybales, on the south bank of the Nambé river.[21]

After the United States occupation of New Mexico, attorney Samuel Ellison[22] asked the surveyor general of New Mexico to confirm the Jacona grant to the heirs and legal representatives of Ignacio de Roybal and Jacinto Peláez.[23] Surveyor General James K. Proudfit partially obliged, recommending to Congress that the grant be confirmed to the heirs of Ignacio Roybal only.[24] Congress did not act on the surveyor general's recommendation, however, so the grant was filed with the Court of Private Land Claims a year after that court was established.[25]

Again the petitioners claimed to be the heirs and assignees of Ignacio Roybal and asked the court to confirm the grant to them. When the two original attorneys hired by the petitioners both died before the trial, three of the local grant residents acting for the grant, hired attorney Napoleon Bonaparte Laughlin to represent the Jacona heirs.[26] This may have been their first mistake. Laughlin got the grant confirmed, but his actions after the confirmation were certainly not in the best interests of the grantees.

Although the attorney for the government argued that the grant should not be confirmed because the act of possession had never been produced, the Court of Private Land Claims held that if this was a defect, it was cured in two ways. First, the 1702 grant itself, which was listed in the Book of the *Cabildo* of Santa Fe, conveyed title to Ignacio Roybal, who, through his possession of the land for forty years, perfected his title by prescription.[27] The second basis for confirmation was the 1782 proceedings before Governor Anza. Since these proceedings were based on the initial grant to Ignacio

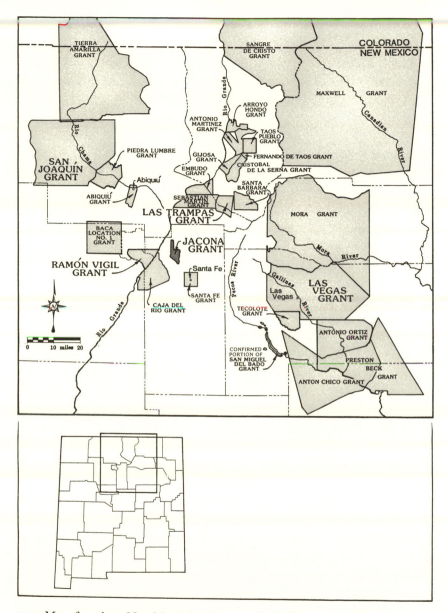

11.3. Map of northern New Mexico land grants with the Jacona grant highlighted.

Roybal, the governor's favorable action on the petition of Mateo Roybal assumed the validity of the original grant, according to the court's opinion.[28]

After confirmation by the Land Court the grant was surveyed. This was the second survey of the Jacona grant, the first having been made in 1878 after the grant was approved by the surveyor general. This time instead of some forty thousand acres as shown in the earlier survey, the Jacona grant was found to contain only about seven thousand acres after deducting almost five thousand acres for overlaps with the pueblos of Tesuque, San Ildefonso, and Pojoaque.[29] The overlaps still do not account for the great discrepancy between the 1898 and 1878 surveys. One explanation for the difference might be the inclusion of Ignacio Roybal's grazing grant along with the Jacona grant in the 1878 survey.

In any case attorney Laughlin did not challenge the survey that so drastically shrunk the Jacona grant—instead he prepared a lawsuit that would yield him one-third of the grant, or its equivalent in money. But when Napoleon Bonaparte Laughlin filed suit to partition the grant, he could convince only three grant residents to join him in the suit as plaintiffs.[30] The suit was calculated to give as little notice as possible to the grant residents that their erstwhile attorney was now asking a court to partition, or more likely, to sell the Jacona grant. This was accomplished by naming as defendants only the unknown heirs of the original grantee, a favorite practice of the attorneys of the day. Since no living individuals were named as defendants, no one had to be served with papers concerning the lawsuit. Instead, notice of the suit was published in a local newspaper, which might have given notice of the existence of the lawsuit to a few people living on the land, except for the fact that it was published in English. Thus, most of the grant residents, who spoke and read only Spanish, would not have been able to read it, even if they were in the habit of regularly checking the legal notices. The New Mexico supreme court stopped this highly unfair practice five years later, when it held that persons in possession of land sought to be partitioned must be named in the complaint and served with a copy, or the court's decision would not be binding upon them.[31]

But in 1908 Laughlin freely indulged in the fiction that he had tried to locate the heirs of Ignacio Roybal, and anyone else who might have a claim to the Jacona grant. It was not surprising that no one answered Laughlin's complaint. He asked the court for a default judgement, and the judge granted his request to partition or sell the grant.[32] The next step was the appointment of a referee to prepare a genealogy for Ignacio Roybal and his wife.[33] The person appointed was probably Laughlin's secretary.[34] Her report (most likely prepared by Laughlin) found that there were about 170 individuals with interests in the grant ranging from 579 acres to less than one-half acre. Most important to Laughlin was the finding that Laughlin himself was entitled to one-third of the grant (about 2,300 acres) as his fee for securing confirmation and for handling the partition suit.[35] This even though the fee arrangement with the grant's original attorneys had called for one-fourth of the grant as the fee, and Laughlin's "services" in connection with the partition suit were hardly beneficial to the grant.[36]

From this point on, the judicial machinery produced a series of legal papers that seemed to be heading toward another forced transfer of a major portion of a land grant into the hands of its attorney. First, the judge in this uncontested partition and quiet title suit approved the referee's report and quieted title to the Jacona grant to those named in the genealogy.[37] Then, after appointing commissioners to determine whether the grant should be sold or physically divided, Judge McFie accepted their recommendation that the grant must be sold.[38] It is noteworthy that in other partition suits the same conclusion was always reached — not surprising since the commissioners were generally chosen from a small coterie of individuals friendly to the land grant lawyers.[39] Finally Judge McFie ordered the Jacona grant sold to the highest bidder.[40]

 This seemingly inexorable movement toward another land grant loss would have reached the usual ending of an uncontested sale to the attorney or his proxies, had not a certain resident of the Jacona grant been rehearsing his unique part in this legal drama — a part that would irrevocably change the final scene. Cosme Herrera found out about the Laughlin lawsuit and organized people on the grant by notifying them of the consequences if they did not take some action. He was able to convince 110 other grant residents to contribute fifteen dollars each toward their purchase of the grant. Cosme Herrera then purchased the grant and deeded it to these individuals. On 18 June 1909 the group signed an agreement, in Spanish, reciting their respective rights and obligations.[41] It is not known whether Cosme Herrera and his 110 allies consulted a lawyer, but it is probable that they did, for the

1. Nicolás Casados
2. Estanislado Gallegos
3. José Domingo Gallegos
4. Pablo Gallegos
5. Perfeto Gallegos
6. Cosme Garcia
7. Marcos García
8. Nestor García
9. Teodoro García
10. Anastacio Gómez y Roybal
11. Desiderio Gómez
12. Juan de Jesus Gómez
13. Pedro Gómez y Gonzales
14. Balentín Gonzales
15. Benino Gonzales
16. Eleuterio Gonzales
17. Guermio Gonzales
18. José Urban Gonzales
19. Nicolás Gonzales y Duran
20. Nicolás Gonzales y Roybal
21. Pedro Gonzales
22. Cosme Herrera
23. Emiliano López
24. Nestor López
25. Benito Luján
26. Salome Luján
27. Canuto Martínez
28. Juan Francisco Martínez
29. Sotero Martínez
30. Esquipula Montoya
31. Jacobo Montoya
32. José de la Luz Montoya
33. Juan Montoya
34. Antonio Ortiz y Rivera
35. Desiderio Ortiz
36. José de la Luz Ortiz
37. Manuel Ortiz

38. Rafael Ortiz y Benavidez
39. Rafael Ortiz y Romero
40. Severo Ortiz
41. Tomás Ortiz
42. Daniel Quintana
43. Efren Quintana
44. José Lonjino Quintana
45. Librado Quintana
46. Abrán Romero
47. Antonio Eulalio Romero
48. Antonio Romero y Valdez
49. Atoche Romero
50. Celilio Romero
51. Emelecio Romero
52. Estevan Romero
53. Felipe Romero
54. Juan Bautista Romero
55. Juan Romero y Valdez
56. Juan R. Romero
57. Librado Romero
58. Matias Romero
59. Pablo Romero
60. Pedro A. Romero
61. Ramón Rodarte Romero
62. Simón Romero
63. Vidal Romero y Ortiz
64. Teofilo Romero y Trujillo
65. Vidal Romero y Trujillo
66. Andrés N. y Roybal
67. Antonio Jose Roybal
68. Cosme Roybal
69. Elisio Roybal
70. Emiliano Roybal
71. Esquipula Roybal
72. Eutimio Roybal
73. Felipe Roybal
74. Felipe Roybal y Quintana

75. Florensio Roybal
76. José A. Roybal
77. José Ines Roybal
78. Juan Roybal
79. Juan Bautista Roybal
80. Juan Isidro Roybal
81. Juan Roybal y Romero
82. Julián Roybal
83. Manuel Roybal y López
84. Manuel Roybal y Luján
85. Manuel Sabino y Roybal
86. María Dolores Roybal
87. María Manuelita Roybal
88. Martín Roybal y Luján
89. Maximiano Roybal
90. Merejillo Roybal
91. Paula Roybal y Jirón
92. Pedro Roybal y Roybal
93. Rafael Ortiz Roybal
94. Ramón N. Roybal
95. Remedios Roybal
96. Reyes Roybal
97. Ricardo Roybal y Romero
98. Santiago Roybal
99. Tomás Roybal
100. Vicente F. Roybal
101. Encarnacion Salazar
102. Evaristo F. Trujillo
103. Guadalupe Trujillo
104. Juan Trujillo
105. Juan de la Cruz Trujillo
106. Luis R. Trujillo
107. Ramón S. Trujillo
108. Telesforo Trujillo
109. Elias Valdez
110. Nepumuseno Valencia
111. Manuel Vigil

11.4. List of individuals who purchased the Jacona grant's common lands in 1909 after taking up a collection to save the grant from sale to an outsider.

agreement bears the mark of some kind of legal assistance, though the inconsistencies and flaws in the document point to a non-lawyer as its ultimate author.

The agreement is remarkable in the annals of land grant history for it reveals the heirs and members of a land grant taking control of their own destiny. By purchasing their grant, this group avoided some of the pitfalls that have hampered other land grants. In contrast, residents on grants such as Las Trampas and Tierra Amarilla, delayed their efforts to get their grants back, often receiving faulty legal advice and losing their common lands.[42]

After saving their grant, the members established a three-man commission to manage the grant's affairs.[43] Among its duties, the commission determined the property taxes on the common lands, assessed the members for their proportionate shares of the tax, and then paid the tax to the county. As happened on other grants, more and more members failed to pay their share of the taxes, and the commission reached the point where it did not have the funds to pay the annual property tax bill on the common lands. Faced with another crisis, the grant again exhibited remarkable resourcefulness. First, in 1919, the grant executed a deed under which 110 individual members agreed to partition the common lands among themselves. This was not a partition like the one Napoleon Bonaparte Laughlin requested — one designed to destroy the grant. Under this arrangement each member received 60½ acres of the common lands and had to declare the land to the county tax assessor and pay the taxes on it.[44]

Eventually the Santa Fe County authorities changed their records to reflect this ownership change, but the partition did not entirely solve Jacona's tax problem.[45] So in 1928 the grant took another innovative step. Some of the parties to the 1909 agreement filed suit against forty-six other parties to the agreement claiming that the defendants had not paid their share of taxes and asking the court to declare that the forty-six had forfeited their interest in the grant.[46] Only one of the defendants appeared in the lawsuit and he was allowed to retain his part of the grant. The interests of the remaining forty-five were declared forfeited[47] and these interests were conveyed to the remaining one hundred and two members of the grant by deed.[48]

A basic question present throughout the Jacona grant's history was the nature of the grant: was it a private or a community grant? At the outset Jacona was clearly a private grant made to Ignacio Roybal and Francisca Gomez Robledo, and later confirmed as a private grant by the Court of

Private Land Claims. However, the 18 June 1909 agreement, taken together with the deed from Cosme Herrera to the same 111 signatories of that agreement, demonstrates an intent that Jacona be organized and run as a community grant. But this was a community grant with a difference. The grant owners, who had purchased the land at the partition sale and thus owned the land outright, had established a community grant *as between themselves*, but as between the grant owners and outsiders like the state and federal government, the grant was owned privately. The government had no jurisdiction to establish rules for the operation of the grant, as it did for true community grants, confirmed as such by the United States.[49] The Jacona grant started as a private grant, was confirmed as a private grant, and was saved from extinction when 111 individuals purchased it and then converted it to a community grant as between themselves. Later, they were to convert it back to a private grant when this seemed the best way to avoid the loss of the common lands from another scourge of the Anglo occupation of New Mexico — taxes.

What is it about the Jacona grant that made it a survivor? Here are a few suggestions. Most private land grants in New Mexico eventually evolved into community grants as more people settled on the grant lands.[50] These grants were often operated as community grants, though under American law they were considered as private land grants. Whether the common lands of these grants were lost, as happened with the Juan José Lobato grant, or were saved, as with Jacona and with the Cundiyó grant, greatly depended on the initiative of grant members. The story of Jacona is a prime example of such individual initiative.

The Cundiyó grant is another example of a grant with a unified community acting effectively to protect its interests. In 1926 when an erroneous tax assessment threatened to cause the loss of its common lands, a committee from the grant negotiated a lower tax assessment with the county.[51] Then in 1975, Cundiyó was chosen for a title clearance project that eventually cleared the title to the private lands within that land grant. Cundiyó was chosen because the grant's land base was compact and its social structure was tight-knit and relatively unified.[52]

That both Jacona and Cundiyó were private grants run as community grants suggests that status as a true community grant may have some disadvantages. Many community grants have been battlegrounds for factional fighting; the history of these skirmishes is written in the New Mexico appellate court reports. No matter which side wins, the land grant members suffer because the cost comes out of their pockets and out of their land base. The most successful grants have handled their disputes internally. Following the example of the Penitente brotherhood, these land grants provided for their needy and disciplined their wrongdoers, all without help from the outside world. They often found that when the outside world got involved in their problems, someone in the outside world benefitted, not the land grant. Official community land grant status has not always been the protective shield it could be. Land grant boards have sometimes operated in a partisan manner, keeping their dealings hidden from the general membership, engendering litigation between the members and the land grant boards.

This is not to say that a true community land grant cannot take control of its destiny as Cundiyó and Jacona have done. What is needed is the unity of purpose those grants have demonstrated. Jacona in particular has shown how to use the New Mexico court system to its advantage. The descendants of Ignacio Roybal and Francisca Gómez Robledo have followed in the footsteps of their prominent forebears, demonstrating similar business acumen, which has made it possible for present day grant members to retain their land and reap substantial benefits from it at the same time. With the continual ups and downs of New Mexico land grant history, it is important to know that some grants, like Jacona, have not only survived but have also flourished.

Conclusion:
Common Lands, Common Law,
and Uncommon Controversy

On a chilly day in late November 1990, spectators gathered in a small courtroom on the second floor of the old Federal Building in Santa Fe to witness a lawsuit that contained many of the same land and water issues that had frequently been litigated in New Mexico under three sovereigns. The State Engineer of New Mexico as plaintiff had filed a huge water rights adjudication lawsuit asking the court to establish priority dates for each of the *acequias* in the Taos area. The court's decision would mean that *acequias* with later priority dates could be denied irrigation water during times of shortage in favor of those with earlier dates. Although Taos Pueblo was not involved at this stage of the proceedings, the Pueblo would have a chance to dispute the findings of Judge Frank Zinn as to Hispanic water rights when the Pueblo's water rights were established at a later date.[1]

The issues that Judge Zinn was charged with resolving are the issues that New Mexico's *alcaldes*, *ayuntamientos*, and governors had struggled with for the past four centuries: how are contradictory Indian and non-Indians claims to be resolved, what is the effect to be given to custom, and who has the burden, as between the government and the claimant, of proving matters as to which there is little or no archival evidence. But the fundamental question lurking behind these water rights hearings is the extent to which water will be privatized in New Mexico. Privatization of land and Hispanic land loss have steadily increased in the state as communal lands and the communities that use them have been reduced to near extinction.[2] Now the conflict between privatization and common use, between strict technical rules of law and customary practice, and between New Mexico's Pueblo Indian and Hispanic population competing with each other and with land speculators for scarce water resources was coming to a head.

The rights of Indian and non-Indian claimants have been settled in traditional ways in the past, with both groups sharing available water, though the Indians' rights were not always adequately protected. Now however, the system of water adjudication tends to encourage competition between Indian and non-Indian in battles fought in the courtroom instead of interactions on the land.[3] The importance of custom in determining land and water rights is likewise still an issue. In the 1890s land titles were unfairly adjudicated partly because the courts did not recognize customary law, and in the 1990s there still exists the danger that water rights will be similarly reduced or lost completely unless the court recognizes customary arrangements for sharing water between *acequias*.[4] When rights to land grants were adjudicated by the Court of Private Land Claims in the 1890s and early 1900s, claimants had to shoulder the burden of proving that their land claims were valid even though the records they needed to make their case were often lost, destroyed, or inaccessible while in official custody. Now water rights claimants have the burden of proving water usage prior to the Pueblo Revolt although the records of such usage were destroyed during that 1680 revolution.[5]

In the century that has passed since the Court of Private Land Claims determined the validity of New Mexico's land grants, Hispanic land and water rights have been steadily eroded, though public awareness of the situation has been clouded until recently. Writers like John Nichols, Stanley Crawford, and others, have eloquently pleaded the case for the connection between Hispanic land and water rights and the survival of Hispanic culture in northern New Mexico.[6] In Judge Zinn's Santa Fe courtroom, John Nichols testified as a landowner in Taos and as an irrigator from three different *acequias*, that it seemed absurd on a practical level that each of those *acequias* would have a different priority date. Stanley Crawford has written about a similar case where the legal process had taken something vital, like the ineffable combination of earth, sun, water, and seed and distilled it into legal briefs containing arcane technicalities making the magic of water something that can be bought and sold.[7] The same thing was happening again, but it would not go unreported. Unfortunately in the 1890s there was no one willing and able to witness unfair land grant adjudications and report that an injustice was being done.

Perhaps the greatest irony remaining after some four hundred years of land grants and lawsuits in New Mexico is that, recent land and water rights litigation itself has caused much of the most valuable research to be accomplished. Several of the land grants referred to in these chapters have been the subject of recent litigation. A suit concerning use rights to part of the Carson National Forest by settlers on the Las Trampas grant was decided by the federal district court in Santa Fe in 1982.[8] Water rights on the Gallinas and Pecos Rivers and the question of the pueblo rights doctrine on the Las Vegas grant are presently the subject of another massive adjudication suit filed by the New Mexico State Engineer's Office,[9] and a quiet title suit in Santa Fe County recently decided land titles on the Jacona grant.[10] The reports of expert witnesses in the Aamodt (Rio Pojoaque), L. T. Lewis

(Pecos River), and Taos water rights adjudication cases have added significantly to our knowledge of land and water rights in New Mexico.[11] Much research remains to be done however, in order to obtain a complete picture of Hispanic land tenure and society in New Mexico prior to the United States invasion. While one scholar has pointed out the pitfalls of relying on experts whose reports are prepared for litigation to fill the gap in land grant studies,[12] other scholars have relied heavily on these reports,[13] and the experts themselves have expanded upon and published their reports to favorable reviews.[14] As studies of land and water rights in New Mexico are beginning to catch up with similar studies in Latin America, the emphasis should be on the encouragement of a high level of scholarship, imaginative new approaches, and open debate.

 The state of land grant studies in New Mexico and the Southwest can be compared to the historiography of Mexican land tenure and the agrarian aspects of the Mexican revolution. François Chevalier painted the broad sweep of Mexican colonial land tenure, taking much of his documentation from northern Mexico and emphasizing the *hacienda* as the dominant form of land-holding in his pioneering work.[15] Later, some historians of the Mexican revolution explained that event as an uprising of the Mexican peasant against the abuses of the *hacienda* system.[16] Recently however, a number of local and regional studies have led to revisionist viewpoints concerning the Mexican revolution. Rather than landless peasants being the primary actors, middle class *rancheros* owning relatively small tracts of land, were also found to have played a crucial role in the revolution.[17] This new emphasis on regional history in Mexico is radically changing the conventional wisdom about land tenure in Mexico and elsewhere in Latin America.[18]

When one compares studies of land tenure in Mexico to the historiography of the land grants in the Southwestern United States it is apparent that no one has approached the latter field with the breadth of a Chevalier. Hispanic land grants existed in the present states of California, Texas, Louisiana, and Florida, as well as New Mexico, and all were adjudicated in different ways with different results. No one except J. J. Bowden has attempted a detailed study of this broad field.[19] Even when the field is narrowed to New Mexico the gaps in the published studies are large, though a more complete understanding of the history and adjudication of

New Mexico land grants is beginning to emerge as regional studies of specific land grants are published. The Maxwell grant was the first land grant to be the subject of individual treatment by William Kelleher in 1942,[20] and later by Jim Berry Pearson,[21] Lawrence R. Murphy,[22] and Morris F. Taylor.[23] Leading the way with more recent studies of northern New Mexico land grants are G. Emlen Hall and Anselmo Arellano with their works on the Pecos Pueblo and Las Vegas grants respectively.[24] Paul Kutsche and John Van Ness have published a study of the village of Cañones which is connected with the Juan Bautista Valdez, Piedra Lumbre, and Polvadera grants.[25] Each land grant merits in-depth treatment amounting to a regional study of a part of New Mexico. Preliminary indications reveal a wide variety of land tenure, political, and social patterns in the different regions. When more studies are completed we may have more revisionist history similar to the revisionist history of the Mexican Revolution that is now being written.

This book contains several conclusions that can also be seen as revisionist in nature. These include a dismal assessment of the fairness of land grant adjudication in New Mexico and the opinion that unethical practices by lawyers who were members of the Santa Fe Ring were widespread. As to the latter point, Victor Westphall and other scholars have expressed some skepticism that lawyers like Thomas B. Catron were engaged in unethical or fraudulent practices.[26] In the Las Trampas and Juan José Lovato grant partition and quiet title suits, however, we see clear evidence of such conduct, not only on the part of Catron, but also by lawyers Alois B. Renehan, Charles Catron, and Alonzo McMillan. As more study is done of these and other lawyers' involvement in other land grant partition and quiet title suits, we may learn of other instances of unethical or fraudulent conduct.[27] Enough evidence has been unearthed so far, however, to establish that the activities of these lawyers resulted in the privatization of much of the common lands that survived the effects of the *Sandoval* decision. In addition, the partition statute itself must also be blamed for Hispanic common land loss.

Another major cause of Hispanic land loss was unfair adjudication of land grants due in part to the conflict between the Hispanic and Anglo legal systems. In Chapter 2, the differences in procedure and the differences in social and legal values that underlie the conflict between the two systems are discussed. In chapters 1, 2, 3, and 6 the different emphasis on custom in the two legal systems is explored, and in chapters 1, 5, and 9 the failure of the Anglo-American legal system to understand the common lands is analyzed. Although the United States Supreme Court was decidedly un-sympathetic toward common land ownership in the *Sandoval* case, this form of land tenure was well known to the English common law. In fact a system of common ownership of land and common use rights in the land of others existed in England and throughout Europe that was remarkably similar

12.2. Surveyors at work on calculations for the enclosure at Henlow, Bedfordshire, England (1798). From The Land Question and European Society, *Frank E. Huggett (London: Thames and Hudson, 1975).*

to the Spanish system of commons found in Spain and New Mexico.[28] Thus, the mistaken interpretation by the courts of common lands in New Mexico was not due to an historical absence of this form of land tenure in England or the United States.

The English common lands concept goes back to the era when most land ownership was common and private land ownership existed hardly at all.[29] This situation developed into a system of mixed private and common ownership in feudal England, with two main types of common ownership and use rights: the rights of landowners in an agricultural community to use woods and pasture lands owned by the community, and the rights of such citizens to make use of privately owned lands. The loss of the commons in England began in the early 1700s and continued through the end of the century as land was privatized under the notorious enclosure acts.[30] Almost a century before the historic *Sandoval* decision, the 1801 Enclosure Act set up a commission to fence the common lands so that newly privatized land could be brought under cultivation.[31] The *Sandoval* decision was a judicial rather than a legislative enclosure, based more on a policy favoring privatization to encourage economic development than on the legal authorities cited by the court.

By the time *Sandoval* was decided American judges often looked with suspicion on the concept of common lands and common use-rights, as can be seen in a 1833 New York case where the judge stated:

> these common rights which were at one time thought to be essential to the prosperity of agriculture, subsequent experience, . . . has shown to be prejudicial. In this country such rights are uncongenial with the genius of our government, and with the spirit of independence which animates our cultivators of the soil.[32]

This ethnocentric viewpoint was also expressed by Americans toward the entire system of Hispanic Civil law.[33] Since the common lands concept was out of favor in United States law, American judges were also unsympathetic toward Hispanic common lands ownership as defined by Spanish and Mexican law. Thus the United States Supreme Court was prepared to adopt the argument made by United States Attorney Matthew Reynolds against common lands and in favor of U.S. government ownership of those lands. Thereafter, Forest Service administration of former common lands in northern New Mexico has been like that of a private entrepreneur, selling timber and grazing rights despite a professed policy of multiple use.[34]

One scholar has argued that the *Sandoval* decision did not in itself cause such a massive loss of common lands. Using records concerning the common lands of the San Miguel del Bado grant, with which the *Sandoval* case was concerned, G. Emlen Hall shows that most of what had been grant common lands was acquired as private property by grant residents under the Federal Small Holding Claim and Homestead laws in the late 1890s and early 1900s. Hall concludes that approximately two-thirds of San Miguel del Bado's common lands were recovered by its residents as private property that they still own today.[35] However, most northern New Mexico common lands, like the Las Trampas and San Joaquín grants, became National Forest land not available for small holding or homestead claims.[36] Since it was only the portion of the San Miguel del Bado grant not set aside as National Forest that the grantees were able to reclaim, Hall's conclusions appear to be limited to the land grant in question.[37]

Hall suggests, however, that the evidence he adduces for San Miguel del Bado may have broader implications, and implies that perhaps *Sandoval* was not wrong in its holding that New Mexico's community land grants did not own their common lands. Although in one place Hall calls the *Sandoval* holding "probably erroneous,"[38] in another he characterizes the argument that "the United States deprived the community grants of something that 'belonged' to them" as primitive.[39] Hall's more sophisticated reasoning makes a dangerous leap in logic, however. He says that "the United States did not so much expropriate the common lands of the San Miguel del Bado grant as alter the nature of their ownership from municipally owned commons to individually owned private tracts."[40] This gives the sense of a beneficent government not really taking land but simply giving it a different ownership. But the government did take the common lands under *Sandoval.* The fact that a few families were able to regain title to some of this land within the San Miguel del Bado grant does not change that fact. Nevertheless, this kind of regional study tracing the chain of title to grant common lands is extremely valuable, and needs to be done on other New Mexico land grants to determine the extent to which Hall's conclusions might have a wider application.

A look at a map of northern New Mexico reveals that most of the land that once comprised the common lands of community land grants is now owned by the government. Some of this land was privatized — often into the hands of a lawyer representing the grant — and then purchased by the United States government in an avowed effort to assist rural Hispanic villagers.[41] Probably the larger portion became public domain of the United States under *Sandoval* and is administered by the Forest Service. One can argue, as do William deBuys and Alvar Carlson, that under federal ownership things did not change that much on the land grants and that often government regulations were actually beneficial.[42]

William deBuys has met the problem head on in his excellent book *Enchantment and Exploitation: The Life and Hard Times of a New Mexico Mountain Range.* DeBuys suggests that possibly the best approach for dispossessed land grant heirs to take is to become involved in the land management process of the National Forests. He believes that the Forest Service has done a better job managing these lands than have the land grants themselves. While some would point out that Forest Service stewardship has not always benefitted the forests,[43] de Buys observes that "at the heart of every argument over resources and every discussion of how best to conserve the integrity of village culture lies the question of who, by rights, owns the land."[44] This is true. Accordingly, one could argue that if the land grants once owned these lands, it follows that the villagers within those grants should, at a bare minimum, be the major beneficiaries of current resource management.

Alvar Carlson has recently sounded a more fatalistic note regarding the preservation of the land-based Hispanic culture of Northern New Mexico:

"Spanish Americans will continue then gradually to forsake, voluntarily and involuntarily, aspects of their rural culture and homeland as they lose their land base and sense of traditional communities. . . ." This scholar believes that the causes of Hispanic land loss that he cites — "Anglo-American surveyor-generals (sic), the Court of Private Land Claims, the U.S. Forest Service, Santa Fe Ring lawyers, and land grabbers," — are merely scapegoats. Rather, he implies, blame should be placed on the Spanish and Mexican governments of New Mexico "for noncompliance with procedures or [on] the Spanish Americans themselves, who in many cases grossly exaggerated their claims to land grants, necessitating long legal disputes."[45]

Certainly there is evidence of exaggerated and fraudulent land grant claims[46] and it is also true that the Spanish and Mexican governments were not always consistent in regard to the granting of land. Governor Manuel Armijo in particular made grants in violation of the laws and procedures of Mexico long before Surveyors General Henry Atkinson, James Proudfit, and T. Rush Spencer had perfected the art of using public office for their own private benefit. Moreover, individual New Mexican citizens had engaged in land speculation long before the arrival of Thomas B. Catron, Charles Catron, Alonzo McMillan, and A. B. Renehan on the New Mexico scene. But present-day concerns regarding land and water in New Mexico will not disappear by blaming the victims, as does Carlson, be they Hispanic or Indian. Few would disagree with the proposition that the United States promised more by the Treaty of Guadalupe Hidalgo than it delivered.

Some say that past and present injustices would better be left forgotten since it is neither proper nor possible to remedy them. To do so, according to this argument, would cast doubt on existing titles.[47] Other experts have suggested solutions to the problem of Hispanic land loss in scholarly publications[48] or at congressional hearings.[49] It may be that the cycles of privatization will come full circle sometime in the future and local control of common resources will again be encouraged in Northern New Mexico. Environmentalists have suggested the common lands concept as a means of protecting resources where private or public owners interests have not treated them with due respect for the environment.[50]

 The loss of common resources through the manipulation of the concept of title is what was happening in Judge Zinn's Santa Fe courtroom with water rights, not so much because of the decision he would make, but because of the context within which he was forced to make it. Traditionally in Hispanic New Mexico water was shared by all water-users so that no one was ever completely deprived of water.[51] Absolute title with the right to sell water is an Anglo concept imposed on New Mexico water-users fairly recently, and like the imposition of the partition suit, it will inevitably lead to the loss of water rights just as the partition suit resulted in the loss of common lands. Communal control of irrigation water by *acequia* associations has helped the communities that use those resources to survive, but with privatization both water rights and the communities themselves are in jeopardy.[52]

Many of the case studies in this book have revealed injustice in the adjudication of Northern New Mexico's land grants. The San Joaquín grant lost its common lands because of the *Sandoval* decision and those lands are now part of the Santa Fe National Forest. The Embudo grant was rejected entirely because of a failure to recognize the reality of custom in New Mexico. The common lands of the Las Trampas grant were lost to speculators with the aid of the court-sanctioned partition suit. By documenting the unfairness and injustices that accompanied land loss in New Mexico, history can be made to bear witness to current policy and legal decisions affecting New Mexico's land and water resources. When Bureau of Land Management policy required the Embudo grant residents to buy back their homes from the government after the same government had unfairly acquired most of that grant, then at least let these facts be known.[53] When, in Tierra Amarilla, a community-based weaving and sheep-raising cooperative is not able to use state government land for grazing its sheep, at least let it be known that the same land was once communal grazing land of the Tierra Amarilla grant, lost due to the unfairness of the Surveyor General system.[54] And when residents of the Las Trampas grant are arrested and convicted for cutting trees without a Forest Service permit, let us recall that this land was once grant common lands acquired by the U.S. government with knowledge that the settlers had rights to the timber which the government is now unwilling to recognize.[55]

Whether or not the government or the courts ever correct past injustices, at least let it be known that they occurred. It would be well to recall the land grants and lawsuits of northern New Mexico's past as current litigation continues to decide the ownership of precious land and water resources in the state. Even Niccoló Machiavelli, that Renaissance political advisor with no more regard for the rights of the people than was expedient, advised the princely rulers of his day that "a prince should . . . refrain from [taking] the property of others, for men are quicker to forget the death of a father than the loss of a patrimony."[56]

Notes

Abbreviations

CFR	Code of Federal Regulations
HAHR	*Hispanic American Historical Review*
MANM	Mexican Archives of New Mexico
MASF	Minutes of the Ayuntamiento of Santa Fe
NM	New Mexico Reports
NMHR	*New Mexico Historical Review*
NMLG-PLC	New Mexico Land Grants Private Land Claims (microfilm records of the Surveyor General of New Mexico, 1987 ed.)
NMLG-SG	New Mexico Land Grants Surveyor General (microfilm records of the Court of Private Land Claims, 1987 ed.)
NMLG-PLCD	Microfilm records based on the Díaz guide
SANM I	Spanish Archives of New Mexico, series 1
SANM II	Spanish Archives of New Mexico, series 2
SRCA	State Records Center and Archives, Santa Fe, New Mexico
UNM-SC	University of New Mexico — Special Collections
US	United States Reports
USC	United States Code
USFL-LS	United States Forest Service — Land Status Division

In the rendering of Spanish names of individuals, I have followed the spelling used in Fray Angelico Chavez's *Origins of New Mexico Families*, even though variant spellings were used in the documents.

Introduction

1. The following books deal with the courthouse raid and Reies Lopez Tijerina, the best known land grant activist: Patricia Bell Blawis, *Tijerina and the Land Grants* (New York: International Publishers, 1971); Richard Gardner, *Grito: Reies Tijerina and the New Mexico Land Grant War of 1967* (Indianapolis and New York: The Bobbs-Merrill Company, 1970); Peter Nabokov, *Tijerina and the Courthouse Raid* (Albuquerque: University of New Mexico Press, 1969); Nabokov, "Reflections on the Alianza," *New Mexico Quarterly* 37 (Winter

1968): 343–56; Clark S. Knowlton, "Land-Grant Problems Among the State's Spanish-Americans," *New Mexico Business*, June 1967; Knowlton, "Reies Lopez Tijerina and the Alianza: Some Considerations," unpublished manuscript, and Knowlton, "Reies L. Tijerina and the Alianza Federal de Mercedes: Seekers after Justice," unpublished manuscript.

2. White, Koch, Kelley and McCarthy and New Mexico State Planning Office, *Land Title Study* (Santa Fe, 1971).

3. Attorneys Benjamin Phillips and John McCarthy also participated in the interviewing for and the writing of the *Land Title Study*.

4. A pioneering six-volume masters thesis by J. J. Bowden summarizes the history and adjudication of each of the land grants in New Mexico and Arizona, relying primarily on the records of the Surveyor General and the Court of Private Land Claims; Myra Ellen Jenkins, "The Baltasar Baca 'Grant': History of an Encroachment," *El Palacio* 68 (Spring 1961): 47–64; (Summer 1961): 87–105; Jenkins, "Spanish Land Grants in the Tewa Area," *NMHR* 47 (April 1972): 113–34; Jenkins, "Taos Pueblo and Its Neighbors, 1540–1847," *NMHR* 41 (April 1966): 85–114; Jenkins, "New Mexico Land Grants," paper presented at New Mexico Highlands University, March 4, 1970.

5. The University of New Mexico Press has published four volumes in its New Mexico Land Grant Series and Sunflower University Press has published two volumes, John R. and Christine M. Van Ness, eds., *Spanish and Mexican Land Grants in New Mexico and Colorado* (1980) and Malcolm Ebright ed., *Spanish and Mexican Land Grants and the Law* (1989).

6. A recent book that makes this argument in a telling fashion is, Richard Griswold del Castillo, *The Treaty of Guadalupe Hidalgo: A Legacy of Conflict* (Norman and London: University of Oklahoma Press, 1990); see also, Donald C. Cutter, "The Legacy of the Treaty of Guadalupe Hidalgo," *NMHR* 53 (October 1978): 305–15.

7. See Daniel Tyler, "The Role of Custom in Defining New Mexican Land and Water Rights," report filed in *U.S. and State of New Mexico v. Abeyta*, U.S. District Court cases No. 7896 and 7939, as well as Tyler's testimony in that case on 20 May 1991.

Chapter 1: Land Grants and the Law

1. Javier Malagón-Barceló, "The Role of the Letrado in the Colonization of America," *The Americas* 18 (1961–1962): 1–17; E. N. Van Kleffans, *Hispanic Law Until the End of the Middle Ages* (Edinburgh: Edinburgh University Press, 1968), passim.

2. J. H. Parry, *The Spanish Theory of Empire in the Sixteenth Century* (Cambridge: The University Press, 1940), p. 2.

3. Van Kleffans, *Hispanic Law*, pp. 34, 122.

4. Gustavus Schmidt, *The Civil Law of Spain and Mexico* (New Orleans, Thomas Rea 1851), p. 15.

5. Richard L. Kagan, *Lawsuits and Litigants in Castile: 1500–1700* (Chapel Hill: University of North Carolina Press, 1981), p. 23; Colin M. MacLachlan, *Criminal Justice in Eighteenth Century Mexico* (Berkeley: University of California Press, 1974), p. 22, note 8.

6. MacLachlan, *Criminal Justice*, p. 5.

7. Betty Eakle Dobkins, *The Spanish Element in Texas Water Law* (Austin: University of Texas Press, 1959), p. 69; Roque Bárcia, *Primer Diccionario General Etimológico de la Lengua Española* (Madrid: Establecimiento Tipográfico de Alvarez Hermanos, 1883), p. 632 (zanja). Other Spanish words of Arabic derivation connected with irrigation are *aljibe* (reservoir), *albanal* (drain or canal), *alema* (allotment of irrigation water), *alberca* (pool or pond), *alamin* (irrigation judge), *almoceda* (irrigation right for certain days), and *alfarda* (irrigation tax). Michael C. Meyer, *Water in the Hispanic Southwest: A Social and Legal History 1550–1850* (Tucson: University of Arizona Press, 1984), p. 20.

8. Kagan, *Lawsuits and Litigants*, pp. 23, 28–32; Van Kleffans, *Hispanic Law*, pp. 123–31, 208–10.

9. Ramón Gutiérrez, *When Jesus Came the Corn Mothers Went Away: Marriage, Sexuality, and Power in New Mexico, 1500–1846* (Stanford: Stanford University Press, 1991), p. 178.

10. J. M. Ots Capdequi, *España en América; El Régimen de Tierras in la Epoca Colonial* (México: Fondo de Cultura Económica, 1959), p. 50; Dobkins, *Texas Water Law*, p. 71.

11. J. Richard Salazar, "Nuestra Señora del Rosario, San Fernando y Santiago del Rio de las Truchas: A Brief History," unpublished manuscript, p. 8; SANM I No. 771, the Truchas grant; NMLG-PLC, Roll 45, Case 107, frames 9 and 14, the San Joaquín grant; Plan of Pitic, SANM I, No. 1265, sec. 6; Daniel Tyler, "Ejido Lands in New Mexico," in Ebright, ed., *Spanish and Mexican Land Grants*.

12. Elizabeth A. H. John, *Storms Brewed in Other Men's Worlds: The Confrontation of Indians, Spanish and French in the Southwest 1549–1795* (College Station: Texas A&M University Press, 1975), p. 9.

13. G. Michael Riley, *Fernando Cortés and the Marquesado in Morelos, 1522–1547* (Albuquerque: University of New Mexico Press, 1973), pp. 19–20.

14. John, *Other Men's Worlds*, pp. 9–10; David H. Snow, "A Note on Encomienda Economics in Seventeenth-Century New Mexico," in Marta Weigle et

al. (ed.) *Hispanic Arts and Ethnohistory in the Southwest* (Santa Fe: Ancient City Press, 1983), pp. 354–56.

15. MacLachlan, *Criminal Justice*, pp. 8–9.

16. Cecil Jane, trans. *The Journal of Christopher Columbus* (1960; reprint ed., New York: Bonanza Books, 1989), p. 23. Constance Carter, "Law and Society in Colonial Mexico: Audiencia Judges in Mexican Society from the Tello de Sandoval Visita General, 1543–1547" (Ph.D. diss., Columbia University, 1971), pp. 8–9.

17. Colin M. MacLachlan, *Spain's Empire in the New World: The Role of Ideas in Institutional and Social Change* (Berkeley: University of California Press, 1988), p. 13.

18. John Leddy Phelan, *The Kingdom of Quito in the Seventeenth Century: Bureaucratic Politics in the Spanish Empire* (Madison, Milwaukee and London: The University of Wisconsin Press, 1967), pp. 324–25. The *audiencia* of Mexico City was the only government in the region from 1528, when it was established, until the arrival of the viceroy in 1535. Carter, "Law and Society in Colonial Mexico," p. 13.

19. C. H. Haring, *The Spanish Empire in America* (New York and London: Harcourt Brace Jovanovich, 1975), pp. 110–27; Phelan, *The Kingdom of Quito*, pp. 328–29; Carter, "Law and Society in Colonial Mexico," pp. 11–14.

20. Norman F. Cantor, *Medieval History: The Life and Death of a Civilization* (New York: MacMillan, 1969), p. 341, quoted in Ralph Vigil, *Alonso de Zorita: Royal Judge and Christian Humanist, 1512–1585* (Norman: University of Oklahoma Press, 1987), p. 26.

21. *Recopilación de las Leyes de los Reynos de las Indias*, (Madrid, 1681), Libro 2, título 1, ley 1; Libro 2, título 1, ley 2.

22. Phelan, *The Kingdom of Quito*, pp. 327–28; Haring, *Spanish Empire in America*, p. 102.

23. *Recopilación*, Libro 4, título 5, leyes 1 and 2; título 7, leyes 1, 3, 4, 5, and 6; título 17, leyes 5 and 7; Marc Simmons, *Coronado's Land: Essays on Daily Life in Colonial New Mexico* (Albuquerque: University of New Mexico Press, 1991), pp. 70–71.

24. Weights and measures varied considerably throughout Spain and New Spain. The basic measurement — the vara — was for a long time the length of a specific staff kept in the town of Burgos to which all varas were supposed to correspond. The vara of Burgos measured 32.99 inches. Early Spanish kings and later the Mexican government tried to make the vara an even three feet, but the standard vara remained about 33 inches. Manuel Carrera Stampa, "The Evolution of Weights and Measures in New Spain," *HAHR* 29 (February 1949): 2–24; Mexican Colonization Law of 1823, SANM 1, No. 1107. Thomas C.

Barnes, Thomas H. Naylor, and Charles W. Polzer, *Northern New Spain: A Research Guide* (Tucson: The University of Arizona Press, 1981), p. 69, and Mariano Galván-Rivera, *Ordananzas de Tierras y Aguas...* published as a supplement to Joaquín Escriche's *Diccionario Razonado de Legislación y Jurisprudencia* (Paris: Rosa y Bouret, [1863]), pp. 202–4.

25. Ian Jacobs, *Ranchero Revolt: The Mexican Revolution in Guerrero* (Austin: University of Texas Press, 1982), p. 41. François Chevalier, *Land and Society in Colonial Mexico; The Great Hacienda* (Berkeley and Los Angeles: University of California Press, 1963), p. 54. Two New Mexico land grants where the settlers were required to have firearms within two years of the making of the grant were Arroyo Hondo (NMLG-SG, Roll 29, report 159, frame 197 et seq.) made in 1815, and the Rancho del Rio Grande grant (NMLG-SG, Roll 19, report 58, frame 49 et seq.) made in 1795.

26. Barnes, Naylor, and Polzer, *Northern New Spain*, p. 69, and Galván-Rivera, *Ordananzas de Tierras y Aguas...*, pp. 202–4.

27. Some of the regional studies that examine private and community landholdings of both the Spanish and the Indian populations as well as *encomiendas* are: William B. Taylor, *Landlord and Peasant in Colonial Oaxaca* (Stanford: Stanford University Press, 1972); José Cuello, "Saltillo in the Seventeenth Century: Local Society on the North Mexican Frontier" (Ph. D. diss., University of California, Berkeley, 1981); Elinore Magee Barrett, "Land Tenure and Settlement in the Tepalcatepec Lowland, Michoacán, Mexico" (Ph.D. diss., University of California, Berkeley, 1970); Charles H. Harris, III, *The Sánchez Navarros: A Socio-economic Study of a Coahuilan Latifundio 1846–1853* (Chicago: Loyola University Press, 1964), pp. 1–2, 7–8; Jacobs, *Ranchero Revolt*, p. 41.

28. Richard E. Greenleaf, "Land and Water in Mexico and New Mexico 1700–1821," *NMHR* 47 (April 1972): 104–7. G. Emlen Hall and David J. Weber, "Mexican Liberals and the Pueblo Indians, 1821–1829," *NMHR* 59 (January 1984): 5–32.

29. Chevalier, *Land and Society*, pp. 134–39. Case histories of the expansion of the twelve haciendas in the Valley of Saltillo are found in Cuello, "Saltillo in the Seventeenth Century," pp.112–35.

30. Chevalier, *Land and Society*, p. 142. For a description of the Aztec land tenure system at the time of the arrival of Cortés see, Charles Gibson, *The Aztecs Under Spanish Rule: A History of the Indians of the Valley of Mexico, 1519–1810* (Stanford: Stanford University Press, 1964), pp. 257–99; Chevalier, *Land and Society*, pp. 16–23; and George McCutchen McBride, *The Land System of Mexico* (1923; reprint ed., New York: Octagon Books, 1971), pp. 112–23.

31. William H. Dusenberry, *The Mexican Mesta: The Administration of Ranching in Colonial Mexico* (Urbana: University of Illinois Press, 1963), pp. 90–96.

32. Lesley Byrd Simpson, *Exploitation of Land in Central Mexico in the Sixteenth Century* (Berkeley: University of California Press, 1952).

33. David E. Vassberg, "The *Tierras Baldías:* Community Property and Public lands in 16th Century Castile," pp. 386–88; Barrett, "Land Tenure and Settlement in the Tepalcatepec Lowlands, Michoacán, Mexico," p. 120; and Emlen Hall, *The Four Leagues of Pecos: A Legal History of the Pecos Grant, 1800–1933* (Albuquerque: University of New Mexico Press, 1984), pp. 167–68.

34. Van Kleffens, *Hispanic Law*, p. 37.

35. The Cabildo of San Gabriel appointed Oñate's son Cristobal as governor instead of Martínez de Montoya. George P. Hammond and Agapito Rey, *Don Juan de Oñate: Colonizer of New Mexico, 1595–1628* (Albuquerque: The University of New Mexico Press, 1953), part II, pp. 1051–53. Frances V. Scholes, "Conquistador of New Mexico," *NMHR* 19 (1944): 340. David H. Snow lists the known *encomenderos* together with their *encomiendas* in "A Note on Encomienda Economics in Seventeenth-Century New Mexico," in Weigle et al., (ed.), *Hispanic Arts and Ethnohistory in the Southwest*, pp. 354–56.

36. Snow argues that *encomienda* tribute was not initially an onerous burden but that it gradually became so. Snow, "Encomienda Economics," pp. 353–34. Marc Simmons (ed. and trans.), *Father Juan Agustín de Morfi's Account of the Disorders in New Mexico* (Santa Fe, 1977), pp. 26–29. France V. Scholes, "Troublous Times in New Mexico," *NMHR* 12 (1937): 388.

37. France V. Scholes, "Civil Government and Society in New Mexico in the Seventeenth Century," *NMHR* 10 (April 1935): 105.

38. Charles Wilson Hackett, ed., *Revolt of the Pueblo Indians and Otermín's Attempted Reconquest, 1680–1682*, trans. by Charmion Clair Shelby, 2 vols. (Albuquerque: University of New Mexico Press, 1941), 1: xxi–xxiii cites religious grievances as the primary factor leading the Pueblos to revolt. For a summary of scholarly views as to the relative importance of religious persecution, forced labor, and tribute requirements as causes of the Pueblo Revolt, see David J. Weber, *The Spanish Frontier in North America* (New Haven: Yale University Press, 1992), pp. 415–16, n. 76. Although Vargas received a large *encomienda* grant as a reward for recolonizing New Mexico, the grant was never put into operation but was converted to money payments by his heirs. Lansing B. Bloom, "The Vargas Encomienda," *NMHR* 14 (October 1939): 371–72, 413.

39. Oakah L. Jones, Jr., "Pueblo Indian Auxiliaries and the Spanish Defense of New Mexico, 1692–1792" (Ph. D. diss., University of Oklahoma, 1964). Another reason for improved defense was the formation of presidial garrisons whose soldiers were supposed to be paid from the royal treasury. The Santa Fe presidio, established in 1693, was comprised of 120 men in 1783. Max L. Moorhead, *The Presidio: Bastion of the Spanish Borderlands* (Norman: University

of Oklahoma Press, 1975), pp. 66, 92. Max L. Moorhead, "Rebuilding the Presidio of Santa Fe, 1789–1791," *NMHR* 49 (April 1974): 124.

40. Marc Simmons, "Settlement Patterns and Village Plans in Colonial New Mexico," *Journal of the West* 8 (January 1969): 10–31; Simmons, *Morfi's Account of Disorders in New Mexico*, pp. 11–14.

41. The royal cedula appointing Domingo de Cruzate governor of New Mexico in 1684 contains the first record of written authority to make land grants. White et. al. and The New Mexico State Planning Office, *Land Title Study* (Santa Fe: State Planning Office, 1971), p. 10. A translation of this cedula is found at pp. 217–18.

42. The first mention of a land grant to a Spaniard that I have found is the Cerrillos grant made to Ensign Alonzo Rael de Aguilar by Governor Vargas in 1692. SANM I, No. 14.

43. A reference to the provision for regranting lands occupied before the Pueblo Revolt is found in decree of Juan Páez Hurtado, Santa Fe, 10 March 1713, SANM I, No. 491. See also, petition of Maria and Juana Griego to Governor Diego de Vargas, Santa Fe, 2 December 1703, SANM I, No. 294.

44. Francisco de la Maza, *Código de colonización y terrenos baldíos . . . publicado según acuerdo del Presidente de la República, 1541–1892* (Mexico: Secretaría de Fomento, 1893), pp. 237–40. For a translation see, Frederic Hall, *The Laws of Mexico* (San Francisco: A. L. Bancroft, 1885), pp. 150–53.

45. Marc Simmons, *New Mexico: A Bicentennial History* (New York: Norton, 1977; reprint, University of New Mexico Press, 1989), pp. 80–81 and pp. 97–100.

46. See, for example, the report of the *ayuntamiento* of Abiquiú concerning the Tierra Amarilla grant, NMLG-SG, Roll 12, report 3, frame 16, transcribed and translated in Malcolm Ebright, *The Tierra Amarilla Grant: A History of Chicanery* (Santa Fe: Center for Land Grant Studies, 1980), p. 34.

47. Governor Bartolome Baca made the report in both the Antonio Cháves and Tecolote grants. Roll 21, report 79, frames 209 et seq., SANM I, No. 218 (Antonio Cháves); Governor Baca to the *diputación*, Santa Fe, 19 November 1824, SANM I, No. 1009 (Tecolote).

48. When the Jacona grant was made to Ignacio Roybal in 1702, no opportunity was given to the adjacent San Ildefonso Pueblo to object to the grant. NMLG-PLC, Roll 36, case 35, frames 6–7. See chapter 11 on the Jacona grant at note 10.

49. The Picuris Indians objected to the Embudo grant and Alcalde Miguel José de la Vega y Coca settled the dispute, in favor of the Spanish, at the time of the delivery of possession. See chapter 6 on the Embudo grant at note 7.

50. Elizabeth Nelson Patrick, "Land Grants During the Administration of

Spanish Colonial Governor Pedro Fermín Mendinueta," *NMHR* 51 (January 1976): 11–12. A grant in which a rudimentary survey was performed, with distances measured along the boundaries, is the Guadalupe Miranda grant made by the governor of the state of Chihuahua in 1851. J. J. Bowden, *Spanish and Mexican Land Grants in the Chihuahuan Acquisition* (El Paso: Texas Western Press, 1971), p. 6.

51. Such an argument occurred in 1818 when Juan de Aguilar complained to Governor Facundo Melgares about the measurement of the Pecos league. Aguilar, whose land was found to have been within the league, said that a fifty vara *cordel* should have been used instead of a one-hundred-vara *cordel.* Alcalde Vincente Villanueva said that use of the shorter *cordel* would be prejudicial to the Indians because of the broken and irregular character of the ground. There is no record of how this dispute was settled. SANM I, No. 56; Hall, *Four Leagues of Pecos,* pp. 26–29.

52. During the Mexican Period the grantees would shout "Long live the president and the Mexican nation." Land grants were made to groups as well as individuals and sometimes to women. An example of a grant made to a woman is the Gijosa grant made in 1715 to Francisca Antonia de Gijosa. NMLG-SG, Roll 23, report 109, frames 595 et seq.; Bowden, "Private Land Claims," 4: 972–73, Myra Ellen Jenkins, "Some Eighteenth-Century New Mexico Women of Property," in Weigle, ed, *Hispanic Arts and Ethnohistory,* pp. 335–45.

53. See chapter 6 on the Embudo Grant, at notes 46–51 and accompanying text..

54. The adjudication of the Tierra Amarilla grant provides an example of the importance of the distinction between a private and a community grant. Ebright, *The Tierra Amarilla Grant,* passim.

55. Mariano Galván y Rivera, Ordenanzas de Tierras y Aguas . . . y Vigentes Hasta el Dia en la Republica Mejicana, published as a supplement to Joaquín Escriche's *Diccionario Razonado de Legislación y Jurisprudencia* [Paris, (1863)], p. 166, Section 19. Mesilla Colony Grant, NMLG-SG, Roll 21, report 86, frames 1132 et seq. (Reference courtesy Daniel Tyler).

56. See, for example, the Arroyo Hondo grant, NMLG-SG, Roll 29, report 159, frames 197 et seq.

57. The minimum four-year possession period is found in *Recopilación,* Libro 4, título 12, ley 1.

58. Galván y Rivera, *Tierras y Aguas,* p. 166, Section 19; p. 187, Capítulo 6.

59. Patrick, "Land Grants of Governor Mendinueta," pp. 10–11. See also, Governor Vélez Cachupín's detailed instructions concerning the building of Truchas when that grant was made in 1754, NMLG-SG, Roll 29, file 227, frames 906 et seq.; Richard Salazar, "Nuestra Señora del Rosario, San Fernando

y Santiago del Rio de las Truchas: A Brief History" (Paper presented at the Annual Meeting of the Western Social Science Association, Albuquerque, April 1980).

60. Provisions for laying out of Spanish municipalities are found in the *Recopilación*, Libro 4, título 7, leyes 1–12. See also, Simmons, "Settlement Patterns," pp. 12–13.

61. Marc Simmons, "Governor Cuervo and the Beginnings of Albuquerque: Another Look," *NMHR* 55 (July 1980): 189–207; Simmons, "Settlement Patterns," pp. 12–13.

62. The 1790 census for Santa Fe lists a total of 130 artisans out of a total population of 4,346 for the villa. Among the occupations listed are *zapatero* (shoemaker), *sastre* (tailor), *tornalero* (woodworker), *herrero* (blacksmith), *tejedor* (weaver), and *albañil* (mason). Janie Louise Aragon, "The People of Santa Fe in the 1790's," *Atzlan* 7 (Fall 1976): 392, 404.

63. Complaints by Pojoaque Pueblo against Captain Antonio de Salas for crop damage ca. 1660, Scholes, "Troublous Times," p. 389. See also SANM II, No. 361 for a complaint in 1731 by Taos Pueblo against Sebastian Martín, Baltazar Romero, and others, for crop damage.

64. Order of Governor Francisco Cuervo y Valdez, Santa Fe, 25 April 1705, SANM I, No. 1251; order of Lieutenant Governor Juan Páez Hurtado, Santa Fe, 27 March 1717. See chapter 4 on the Ciénega at Santa Fe, notes 10 and 11 and corresponding text.

65. For Ojo Caliente, see E. Boyd, "Troubles at Ojo Caliente: A Frontier Post," *El Palacio* 64 (November-December 1957): 347; for Abiquiú, see J. Richard Salazar, "Santa Rosa de Lima de Abiquiú," *New Mexico Architecture* 18 (September-October 1976): 16; for Las Trampas, SANM I, No. 975; for Ranchos de Taos, Declaration of Fray Miguel Menchero, Santa Bárbara, 10 May 1744, in Charles Wilson Hackett, *Historical Documents Relating to New Mexico, Nueva Vizcaya, and Approaches Thereto, to 1773* (Washington, D.C.: Carnegie Institution of Washington, 1937), p. 400: for Tomé, Frank D. Reeve, *History of New Mexico* (New York: Lewis Historical Publishing Company, Inc., 1961), 1: 319; for Valencia, Marc Simmons, *Albuquerque, a Narrative History* (Albuquerque: University of New Mexico Press, 1982), p. 104; for Belén, SANM I, No. 113.

66. Decree of Governor Tomás Vélez Cachupín, Santa Fe, 21 February 1750, SANM I, no. 1100; Boyd, "Troubles at Ojo Caliente," pp. 347–60.

67. Jack August, "Balance of Power Diplomacy in New Mexico: Governor Fernando de la Concha and the Indian Policy of Conciliation," *NMHR* 56 (April 1981): 141–60. For the increase in the Taos Valley population see Adams and Chaves, *Missions of New Mexico, 1776,* (Albuquerque: University of New

Mexico Press, 1956), pp. 112–13 for 1776, and SANM II, Roll 21, frame 545 for the 1796 census.

68. For a general survey of early population expansion, see Reeve, *History of New Mexico*, 1: 311–32.

69. Section 1, Regulations of 1828; David J. Weber, *The Mexican Frontier, 1821–1846* (Albuquerque: University of New Mexico Press, 1982), pp. 125–33 and Weber, *The Spanish Frontier in North America* (New Haven: Yale University Press, 1992), pp. 174–76. A good study of Anglo-Hispana intermarriage is Rebecca McDowell Craver, *The Impact of Intimacy: Mexican-Anglo Intermarriage in New Mexico, 1821–1846* (El Paso: Texas Western Press, 1982). Land grants are dealt with at pp. 31–36.

70. Lawrence R. Murphy, "The Beaubien and Miranda Land Grant, 1841–1846," *NMHR* 42 (January 1967): 29–32. Marianne L. Stoller, "Grants of Desperation, Lands of Speculation: Mexican Period Land Grants in Colorado," *Journal of the West* 19 (July 1980): 26; Harold H. Dunham, "New Mexico Land Grants with Special Reference to the Title Papers of the Maxwell Grant," *NMHR* 30 (January 1955): 5; Bowden, "Private Land Claims," 4: 850, 885.

71. See chapter 2, Land Grants, Lawsuits, and Custom; and chapter 3, Manuel Martinez's Ditch Dispute.

72. See chapter 3, Manuel Martinez's Ditch Dispute, at notes 35–41.

73. Luis María Cabesa de Baca received what was later to become the Las Vegas grant in 1821, but was not placed in possession until at least 1825 due to the delaying and obstructionist tactics of local alcaldes. Statement of Tomás Sena, Santa Fe, 13 January 1826, and Juan Antonio Cabesa de Baca to Governor Antonio Narbona, NMLG-SG, Roll 15, report 20, frames 44 and 30–31.

74. A few decisions were appealed to the Supreme Court in Mexico City. When in 1830 such an appeal was made, the Mexican high court refused to get involved, stating that the litigation should be resolved by the local authorities. SANM I, No. 1369. Appeals were also filed in Chihuahua and Guadalajara. Daniel Tyler, "Land and Water Tenure in New Mexico,: 1821–1846," p. 28.

75. Kearny's proclamation to the people of New Mexico delivered at Las Vegas on 15 August 1846 is reproduced in David J. Weber, *Foreigners in Their Native Land* (Albuquerque: University of New Mexico Press, 1973), pp. 161–62. Similar addresses were delivered at the Santa Fe plaza on August 19 and 22, according to Weber. See also, Proclamation of Brigadier General Stephen Watts Kearny, 22 August 1846, SANM I, No. 1113.

76. Nicolas Trist was appointed Commissioner of the United States to the Mexican Republic on 15 April 1847, and on that date was given written instructions together with a draft treaty. For a copy of these instructions and the draft treaty, see Hunter Miller, ed., *Treaties and Other International Acts of the United*

States of America, (Washington: Government Printing Office, 1937), 5: 261–67. The appointment of the Mexican commissioners was provided for in an armistice dated 24 August 1847. The Mexican commissioners were General José Joaquín de Herrera, José Bernardo Couto, Brigadier General Ignacio de Mora y Villamil, and Miguel Atristain. Miller, *Treaties*, 5 (1937): 279–80.

77. The instructions given to the Mexican commissioners and the Mexican draft treaty are found in Miller, *Treaties*, 5 (1937): 299–302. Article 9 of this draft treaty deals with land grants. Another Mexican draft treaty was presented to Trist on 9 January 1848 containing in its Article 11 a similar proposed land grant guarantee; its text is in Miller, *Treaties*, 5 (1937): 309–13. Trist's rejection of this article and his drafting of a substitute is chronicled in Geoffrey P. Mawn, "A Land-Grant Guarantee: The Treaty of Guadalupe Hidalgo or the Protocol of Querétaro?" *Journal of the West* 14 (October 1975): 52–53. Mawn includes the English text of Article 10 with the source of each portion at p. 53.

78. Luis G. Zorrilla, *Historia de las relaciones entre México y Los Estados Unidos de America, 1800–1958*, 2 vols. (Mexico: 1965), 1: 218, quoted in Weber, *Foreigners*, p. 141.

79. The phrase "manifest destiny" was coined by journalist John L. O'Sullivan who wrote in the New York Morning News for 27 December 1845 that "our manifest destiny is to overspread and possess the whole continent which Providence has given us for the development of the great experiment of liberty." Quoted in Frederick Merk, *Manifest Destiny and Mission in American History, a Reinterpretation* (New York: Knopf, 1963), pp. 31–32. This book provides an excellent discussion of the effect of American journalism of the period on public opinion in the United States. For a study of Mexican attitudes toward the United States during the two decades prior to the war, see Gene M. Brack, *Mexico Views Manifest Destiny, 1821–1846* (Albuquerque: University of New Mexico Press, 1975).

80. Buchanan to Trist, 25 October 1847, in Miller, *Treaties*, 5: 292. The Mexican commissioners were told on 22 January 1848 that further military occupation of Mexico would take place unless a treaty of peace was signed. Miller, *Treaties*, 5: 314.

81. For a discussion of the instruction to Trist recalling him from his mission and of Trist's decision to remain in Mexico, see Miller, *Treaties*, 5: 289–93, 296–97. For a review of the Senate proceedings leading to ratification, and President Polk's message to the Senate, see Miller, *Treaties*, 5: 246–53. A brief discussion of the reasons for the deletion of Article 10 is in Mawn, "Land-Grant Guarantee," p. 54. Secretary of State Buchanan's note of 18 March 1848 to the Mexican Minister of Foreign Relations, explaining the Senate amendments is found in Miller, *Treaties* 5: 253–57.

82. There was a precedent for revising rather than entirely deleting a treaty article in the treatment of Article 9; it was revised to eliminate certain objectionable parts while keeping other satisfactory portions with only slight revisions. Buchanan's explanation to the Mexican government of the revision of Article 9 is in Miller, *Treaties* 5: 254–55. Weber's *Foreigners* includes the text of Article 9 prior to amendment and as ratified, with comments on the reasons for the changes at pp. 162–68.

83. For the text of the Protocol in English and Spanish together with some of the extensive diplomatic correspondence concerning its validity, see Miller, *Treaties*, 5: 380–406. Miller includes excerpts from the Mexican and U.S. instruments of ratification at pp. 257–59.

84. Miller, *Treaties* 5: 401. Mawn discusses the political and diplomatic questions raised by the Protocol in his "Land-Grant Guarantee," pp. 59–60.

85. Article 5 of the Gadsden Treaty incorporated articles VIII and IX of the Guadalupe Hidalgo Treaty to apply to the territory ceded by Mexico in 1853. The provision in the Gadsden Treaty establishing the new boundary line was stated in Article 1 to supersede the boundary provisions in the Guadalupe Hidalgo Treaty with which it was inconsistent. Miller, *Treaties*, pp. 293–437; Bowden, "Private Land Claims," 1: 38–40, 47.

86. Miller, *Treaties*, 6: 293–437; see generally Paul Garber, *The Gadsden Treaty* (Gloucester, MA: Peter Smith, 1959); Odie Faulk, *Too Far North . . . Too Far South: The Controversial Boundary Survey and the Epic Story of the Gadsden Purchase* (Los Angeles: Westernlore Press, 1967); Richard Griswold del Castillo, *The Treaty of Guadalupe Hidalgo: A Legacy of Conflict* (Norman and London: University of Oklahoma Press, 1990).

87. Louisiana Purchase, Treaty of Paris, 30 April 1803, Miller, *Treaties*, 2(1931): 298–505. Florida Purchase, Treaty of 22 February 1819, Miller, *Treaties*, 3(1933): 3–64.

88. Most claims in Louisiana were confirmed by an Act of Congress that relinquished title to them, see Bowden, "Private Land Claims," 1: 106–18; adjudication of claims in the Florida Purchase is discussed in Bowden, "Private Land Claims," 1: 118–34; for the average size of these claims, see Bowden, "Private Land Claims," 1: 155, note 135.

89. Miller, *Treaties*, 3:10.

90. *Foster v. Nelson*, 27 U.S. 253 (1829).

91. *United States v. Percheman*, 32 U.S. 50, 87–88 (1833), emphasis added.

92. For land grant adjudication in California see Christian G. Fritz, *Federal Justice in California: The Court of Ogden Hoffman, 1851–1891* (Lincoln and London: University of Nebraska Press, 1991), pp. 134–209; Paul W. Gates, "Adjudication of Spanish-Mexican Land Claims in California," *The Huntington*

Library Quarterly 3 (May 1958): 213; Gates, "California's Embattled Settlers," *California Historical Society Quarterly* 41 (1962): 99; Bowden, "Private Land Claims," 1: 148–64 and William W. Morrow, *Spanish and Mexican Private Land Grants* (San Francisco and Los Angeles: Bancroft-Whitney, 1923).

93. Jones purchased the San Luis Rey and Pala grant encompassing twelve square leagues in San Diego. Fritz, *Federal Justice in California*, pp. 137–38; Report of William Carey Jones, S. Exec. Doc. No 18, 31st Cong., 2nd Sess., 1–136 (1851) cited and quoted in Bowden, "Private Land Claims," 1: 153–57.

94. Fritz, *Federal Justice in California*, pp. 137–38.

95. Senator Thomas Hart Benton made this argument in Congress. Cong. Globe, 30th Cong., 2nd Sess., 237–54 (1849) cited in Bowden, "Private Land Claims," 1: 149. See also, John Currey argues that requiring perfected claims to be submitted to the California land board violated both the Treaty of Guadalupe Hidalgo and the U.S. Constitution. Curry, "Treaty of Guadalupe Hidalgo and Private Land Claims," in Shuck, *History of the Bench and Bar of California* (Los Angeles: Commercial Printing House, 1901), pp. 57–71.

96. Miller, *Treaties* 5: 217–18.

97. Bowden, "Private Land Claims," 1: 161–62.

98. *Leese v. Clark*, 20 Cal. 387 (1862).

99. *Botiller v. Dominguez*, 74 Cal. 457 (1887).

100. *Botiller v. Dominguez*, 130 U.S. 238 (1888).

101. *U.S. v. Sutherland*, 60 U.S. 363, 365 (1856); *U.S. v. Auguisola*, 68 U.S. 352, 358 (1863).

102. *U.S. v. Kingsley*, 37 U.S. 476 (1838); *U.S. v Boisdore*, 52 U.S. 62 (1851).

103. *U.S. v. Fremont*, Ogden Hoffman, *Reports of Land Cases Determined in the District Court for the Northern District of California* (Reprint ed., 1975; San Francisco: Numa Hubert, 1862), p. 20 (1853); *U.S. v. Fremont*, 58 U.S. 541 (1855); *Dred Scott v. Sandford*, (1857); Fritz, *Federal Justice in California*, pp. 134–79.

104. For California, see Bowden, "Private Land Claims," 1: 162–63 and Morrow, *Spanish and Mexican Grants*, pp. 14–15. Between 22 December 1858 and 28 January 1879, Congress confirmed 8,636,673 acres of land in 46 grants in New Mexico. Grants not acted upon by Congress under the surveyor general system could be resubmitted to the Court of Private Land Claims. The Court of Private Land Claims confirmed 1,934,986 of the 34,653,340 acres of New Mexico land submitted to it. The resulting 6 percent confirmation percentage for the Land Claims Court and 31 percent for the Land Claims Court and the surveyor general is somewhat distorted by the inclusion of the notoriously fraudulent Peralta-Reavis grant (12,467,456 acres) which was rejected by the Court of Private Land Claims. If that acreage is subtracted from the total

acreage claimed, the confirmation percentages become 48 percent overall and 9 percent for the Court of Private Land Claims. For a list of the grants confirmed by Congress and the grants submitted to the Land Claims Court, see White et al., *Land Title Study*, pp. 222–23, pp. 228–34.

105. White et al., *Land Title Study*, p. 30. For a discussion of the public land survey system, see *Land Title Study*, pp. 94–96.

106. Victor Westphall, *The Public Domain in New Mexico: 1854–1891* (Albuquerque: University of New Mexico Press, 1965), discusses the Homestead Act of 1862, as well as the Donation Act of 1854, the Timber Culture Law of 1873, and the Desert Land Act of 1877, in chapters 3, 4, 6, and 7.

107. White et al., *Land Title Study*, pp. 30 and 70.

108. Westphall, *The Public Domain*, p. 19 and Victor Westphall, *Thomas Benton Catron and His Era* (Tucson: University of Arizona Press, 1973), p. 160.

109. On 18 January 1855 Surveyor General Pelham issued a notice to the inhabitants of New Mexico who claimed land under the Treaty of Guadalupe Hidalgo to submit their claims as soon as possible. By the end of September only fifteen claims had been filed. Bowden, "Private Land Claims," pp. 182–83.

110. "An Act to Establish the Surveyor General of New Mexico . . ." 22 July 1854. Chap. 103, 10 Stat. 308 (1854), Section 8.

111. Bowden, "Private Land Claims," pp. 176–84.

112. *American Jurisprudence*, 2nd Edition, 16: 935.

113. One of the most unfair confirmations under the surveyor general system involved the Tierra Amarilla grant. It was confirmed to one individual as a private grant when it was actually a community land grant. Ebright, *The Tierra Amarilla Grant*, passim. Due process requirements are discussed at p. 20.

114. For the Las Animas grant see NMLG-PLC, Rolls 46, 49, and 52, cases 128, 135, 154, and 216 respectively and for the Rio Don Carlos grant, see Bowden, "Private Land Claims," 6: 1794–1809.

115. *Tameling v. U.S. Freehold & Emigration Co.*, 93 U.S. 644 (1874).

116. The Juan José Lobato grant overlapped at least thirteen other grants, all but three of which were rejected because the Lovato grant had already been confirmed. Bowden, "Private Land Claims," 4: 1034. Another example is the Mora grant which partially overlapped five other grants, all of which were rejected. Bowden, "Private Land Claims," 4: 810.

117. Annual Report of the Surveyor General, 30 September 1855. H.R. Exec. Doc. No. 1, 34th Cong., 1st Sess., 301–7, cited in Bowden, "Private Land Claims," 1: 183.

118. H.R. Report No. 321, 36th Cong., 1st Sess., 1–2 (1860), cited in Bowden, "Private Land Claims," 1: 200–201.

119. Westphall, *The Public Domain in New Mexico*, pp. 21–32.

120. *Recopilación*, Libro 4, título 3, ley 24.

121. NMLG-SG Roll 16, report 29, frames 490 et seq.

122. The rule was established for California land grant adjudication, 9 Statutes 634 (1851), Section 14, and was followed by the surveyor general of New Mexico.

123. Michael J. Rock, "Anton Chico and Its Patent," in *Spanish and Mexican Land Grants in New Mexico and Colorado*, ed. Van Ness, pp. 88–89.

124. Rock, "Anton Chico," pp. 90–91; Bowden, "Private Land Claims," 3:689–97.

125. NMLG-SG, Roll 12, report 3, frames 564 et seq.; Ebright, *The Tierra Amarilla Grant*, passim.

126. Three of these cases were in the federal courts and two were decided by the New Mexico Supreme Court: *H.N.D. Land Co. v. Suazo*, 44 N.M. 547 (1940); *Flores v. Bruesselbach*, 149 F. 2d 616 (10th Cir., 1945); *Martinez v. Rivera*, 196 F. 2d. 192 (10th Cir., 1952); *Martinez v. Mundy*, 61 N.M. 87 (1956); and *Payne Land and Livestock Co. v. Archuleta*, 180 F. Supp. 651 (1960).

127. Rock, "Anton Chico," p. 91. In the case of the Juan José Lobato grant, George Hill Howard, as attorney for the grant claimants, received one-half of the grant as his fee for getting the grant confirmed. Hutchinson abstract of Lobato grant, pp. 9–10. Attorney J. B. Cessna was given a half interest in the John Heath grant in consideration for his services in seeking its confirmation. He was unsuccessful. Bowden, *Chihuahuan Acquisition Grants*, p. 30; *Cessna v. U.S.*, 169 U.S. 165 (1898).

128. New Mexico, *Laws* (1875–1876), chap. 3.

129. Galván y Rivera, *Tierras y Aguas*, p. 187.

130. Michael J. Rock, "Partition," unpublished manuscript, pp. 1–3. Among the grants that were partitioned were Cebolletta, San Cristobal, Santa Barbara, Mora, Sebastián Martín, and Las Trampas.

131. Howard Roberts Lamar, *The Far Southwest: 1846–1912* (New Haven and London: Yale University Press, 1966), pp. 146–48 and White et al., *Land Title Study*, p. 31.

132. The grant was made to another early Hispanic speculator, Domingo Fernández, and thirty associates in 1827. Victor Westphall, *Mercedes Reales: Hispanic Land Grants of the Upper Rio Grande Region* (Albuquerque: University of New Mexico Press, 1983), p. 232.

133. Antonio Joseph was of Portuguese descent. Hall, *Four Leagues of Pecos*, p. 128.

134. G. Emlen Hall, "Juan Estevan Pino, 'se les coma': New Mexico Land

Speculation in the 1820s," *NMHR* 57: 27 and Hall, "Giant Before the Surveyor General: The Land Career of Donaciano Vigil," in *Spanish and Mexican Land Grants in New Mexico and Colorado*, ed. Van Ness, pp. 64–73.

135. For articles by and about Julian, see Julian, "Land Stealing in New Mexico," *North American Review* 145: 20, and R. Hal Williams, "George W. Julian and Land Reform in New Mexico," *Agricultural History* 41: 72.

136. Julian wrote that President Cleveland "asked me if I would accept the office of Governor or Surveyor General of New Mexico and cooperate with him in breaking up the 'rings' of that Territory." Julian, "Land Stealing," *North American Review* 145: 17.

137. William A. J. Sparks to George Washington Julian, 11 December 1885, S. Exec. Doc. No. 113, 49th Cong, 2d Sess., 2(1887), cited in Bowden, "Private Land Claims," 1: 224–25.

138. Julian stated in 1887 that "the Surveyor-General [has] acted upon the principle that Spanish and Mexican grants are to be presumed, and all doubts solved in the interest of the claimant." Julian, "Land Stealing," *North American Review* 145:18. Julian's policies reversed this approach.

139. Russell B. Rice, San Miguel County Surveyor, to J. N. Lamoureaux, Commissioner, General Land Office, 8 April 1893, cited in Clark S. Knowlton, "The Town of Las Vegas Community Grant: An Anglo-American Coup d'Etat," *Journal of the West* 19: 18.

140. Bowden, "Private Land Claims," 1: 214–16 and 229–30.

141. Bowden, "Private Land Claims," 1: 230, note 108.

142. An act to establish a court of private land claims, 3 March 1891, 26 Statutes 854.

143. White et al., *Land Title Study*, pp. 34–38; Bowden, "Private Land Claims," 1: 230 n. 108.

144. The Act establishing the California Commission provided that in deciding on the validity of any claim, the commission "shall be governed by the Treaty of Guadalupe Hidalgo, the law of nations, the laws, usages, and customs of the government from which the claim is derived, the principles of equity, and the decisions of the Supreme Court of the United States," Act of March 3, 1851, chapter 41, 9 Statutes 631–34, Section 11.

145. Court of Private Land Claims Act, Section 13, clause 8, 26 Statutes 854.

146. Court of Private Land Claims Act, Section 13, clause 1, 26 Statutes 854.

147. 18 Cong. Rec. 2490 (1887), cited in White et al., *Land Title Study*, p. 38.

148. *Hayes v. U.S.*, 170 U.S. 637 (1898); this presumption was established in 1832 by the U.S. Supreme Court in the case of *U.S. v. Arredondo*, 31 U.S. 691 (1832).

149. See for example, *U.S. v. Chaves*, 159 U.S. 452 (1895).

150. Jennifer Davis, "Perceptions of Power: The Court of Private Land Claims and the Shrinking of the Santo Domingo de Cundiyó Land Grant," unpublished manuscript.

151. See for example, NMLG-PLC, Roll 54, case 282, frames 1095 et seq., Rancho de Galván grant.

152. *U.S. v. Sandoval*, 167 U.S. 278 (1897).

153. These were the villages of San José, Las Mulas, Puerticito, Gusano, Bernal, La Cuesta, and Pueblo. Bowden, "Private Land Claims," 3: 737–38.

154. See chapter 5 concerning the San Joaquín Grant.

155. Bowden, "Private Land Claims," 3: 743.

156. Emlen Hall, "San Miguel del Bado and the Loss of the Common Lands of New Mexico Community Land Grants," *NMHR* 66: 413; see also chapter 12, Conclusion, at notes 30 and 31.

157. Although the Arroyo Hondo grant was confirmed as a community grant in 1892, after the *Sandoval* decision the government asked the Court of Private Land Claims to reverse its decision in the Arroyo Hondo case as to the common lands. The land claims court refused, stating that the *Sandoval* decision was not retroactive. Bowden, "Private Land Claims," 4: 933–34; the Forest Service estimates that twenty-two percent of the Carson and Santa Fe National Forests were at one time common lands of community land grants. "Region 3 Policy on Managing National Forest Land in Northern New Mexico," Albuquerque.

158. *U.S. v. Pendell*, 185 U.S. 189 (1901), concerning the Santa Teresa grant.

159. *Whitney v. U.S.*, 181 U.S. 104 (1901), concerning the Estancia grant.

160. *U.S. v. Elder*, 177 U.S. 104 (1900), concerning the Cebolla grant; *Peabody v. U.S.*, 175 U.S. 546 (1899), concerning the Vallecito de Lobato grant, and *U.S. v. Bergere*, 168 U.S. 66 (1897), concerning the Bartolome Baca grant.

161. For example, the Mexican government decided that failure to record a grant in the archives did not make it invalid. Decision of Licenciado Antonio Barreiro, 26 April 1832, NMLG-PLC, Roll 45, case 107, frames 48–49, 262–63.

162. Ten non-Indian grants were found by the courts to be forged or were suspected of being forged: the Peralta-Reavis, Uña del Gato, Sopori, Oreja del Llano de los Aguajes, Corpus Christi, Sierra Mosca, Pueblo of San Cristoval, Medano Springs and Zapato, Ojita de Galisteo, and El Paso de los Algodones. Bowden, "Private Land Claims," 1: 305–6, n. 89. The Ramón Vigil grant (see chapter 10) must be added to this list.

163. In many cases, besides the absence of grant documents, there was no proof of settlement. See for example, Opinion of the Court of Private Land Claims, Chino Tejano Claim, NMLG-PLC, Roll 36, case 36, frame 82.

164. Rito de los Frijoles grant, SANM I, no. 1352; Bowden, "Private Land Claims," 5: 1230.

165. An example of a grant made on a specific condition was the Ocaté grant, made in 1837 to Manuel Alvarez by Governor Manuel Armijo on the condition that within three years Alvarez would settle the land and commence raising merino sheep. Alvarez did not fulfill this condition and the land claims court properly rejected the grant. NMLG-SG, Roll 26, report 143, frames 709 et seq.; Bowden, "Private Land Claims," 4: 827–35.

166. Examples of grants revoked by Spanish officials are a series of grants made by Lieutenant Governor Juan Páez Hurtado in the absence of Governor Gervasio Cruzat y Góngora from Santa Fe. On his return Governor Cruzat revoked the following grants: Barranca, Manuel García de Las Ribas, José Antonio Torres, Juan Estevan García de Noriega, and Antonio de Ulibarrí. Bowden, "Private Land Claims,", 4: 1090, 1118–19, 1131, 1133–34, and 1135–36. See also the John Heath grant, revoked in 1823 by the governor of New Mexico and the provincial deputation. Bowden, *Grants of the Chihuahuan Acquisition*, p. 79.

167. *Recopilación*, Libro 4, título 12, ley 1; SANM 1, no. 1352.

168. Under the acquired rights doctrine of international law, a land grant valid under Spanish and Mexican law must be respected by the U.S. Daniel Patrick O'Connell, *State Succession in Municipal Law and in International Law* 1: 239–50. For an excellent discussion of the acquired rights doctrine and its application to numerous specific situations in international practice, see John L. Walker, "The Treatment of Private Property in International Law After State Succession," pp. 40–73, in "Land, Law, and La Raza."

169. *U.S. v. Percheman*, 32 U.S. 50 (1833).

170. *U.S. v. Chaves*, 159 U.S. 452 (1895).

171. One exception was *U.S. v. Pendell*, 185 U.S. 189 (1902) where a grant was confirmed though no title papers were produced. There the Santa Teresa grant was confirmed based on continuous possession since 1790.

172. Supplemental Report of the United States Attorney in the Case of Numa Reymond et al. v. United States, Mss., Records of the General Services Administration, National Archives, Washington, D.C.; Record Group 60, Year File 9865–92, cited in Bowden, *Land Grants of the Chihuahuan Acquisition*, pp. 73–74.

173. Jill L. Marron, "The Court of Private Land Claims: Inviolate Protection or Inevitable Paternalism on the Frontier," unpublished manuscript.

174. Richard Wells Bradfute, *The Court of Private Land Claims: The Adjudication of Spanish and Mexican Land Grant Titles, 1891–1904* (Albuquerque: University of New Mexico Press, 1975), p. viii and pp. 222–23. Bowden, "Private Land Claims," 1: 310.

175. A. A. Simpson, Assistant Regional Forester, to Chief, Division of Watershed Management and Lands, Albuquerque, 17 March 1947.

176. Suzanne Forrest, *The Preservation of the Village: New Mexico's Hispanics and the New Deal* (Albuquerque: University of New Mexico Press, 1989), pp. 140–166.

177. Forrest, *Preservation of the Village*, pp. 164–166.

178. William deBuys, *Enchantment and Exploitation: The Life and Hard Times of a Mountain Range*, (Albuquerque: University of New mexico Press, 1985), pp. 245–47.

179. J. Paul Martinez, Acting Forest Ranger, Vallecitos, to Carson Forest Supervisor, 5 March 1947. Land Status Correspondence File, J. J. Lovato grant, Albuquerque.

180. A. A. Simpson, Assistant Regional Forester, Albuquerque, to Chief, Division of Watershed Management and Lands, Albuquerque, 17 March 1947.

181. deBuys, *Enchantment and Exploitation*, p. 251.

182. *Plessy v. Ferguson*, 163 U.S. 537 (1896); *Brown v. Board of Education*, 347 U.S. 483, 347 U.S. 497 (1953), 349 U.S. 294 (1954).

183. *Korematsu v. U.S.*, 323 U.S. 214 (1944); Public Law 100–383, 10 August 1988, 102 Stat. 903.

Chapter 2: Lawsuits, Litigants, and Custom

1. Testimony of Rafael Gallegos, *Quintana v. Leon*, Taos County Civil Cause No. 343 (1887), Transcript of Testimony, p. 11. Legal Files, Taos, Southern Pueblos Agency, Albuquerque.

2. Gabriel García Márquez has commented about the mythic and fantastic nature of much of the history of Latin America and has stated that "the first masterwork of the literature of magical realism is the 'Diary of Christopher Columbus.'" García Márquez, "The Solitude of Latin America (Nobel Lecture, 1982)", trans. Marina Castañeda; Michael Palencia Roth, "Intertextualities: Three Metamorphoses of Myth in 'The Autumn of the Patriarch'", in Julio Ortega, ed., *Gabriel García Márquez and the Powers of Fiction* (Austin: University of Texas Press, 1988), pp. 87–91 and p. 41.

3. Other sources that often help fill in historical gaps are deed records, wills, actions to probate wills or settle estates, as well as census and church records.

4. Rafael Sais testified on 3 April 1867 that Guadalupita was first settled in 1837. After occupying the land for five years the settlers moved to Taos because of Indian hostilities, and then in 1851 they returned to settle Guadalupita

permanently. *George Gold v. Felipe Tafoya*, Civil Cause No. 29, Mora County District Court Records, New Mexico State Records Center and Archives, Santa Fe.

5. J. A. Pitt–Rivers, *The People of the Sierra* (Chicago: University of Chicago Press, 1954) pp. 141–59.

6. In this instance one lawsuit provided enough material for an entire Ph.D. diss. John Bingner Owens, "Despotism, Absolutism, and the Law in Renaissance Spain: Toledo versus the Counts of Belalcazar," Ph.D. diss., The University of Wisconsin, 1972.

7. Alexandra Parma Cook and Noble David Cook, *Good Faith and Truthful Ignorance: A Case of Transatlantic Bigamy* (Durham: Duke University Press, 1991).

8. G. Emlen Hall, "Land Litigation and the Idea of New Mexico Progress," *Journal of the West* 27 (July 1988): 48; Daniel Tyler, "Land and Water Tenure in New Mexico: 1821–1846 (Unpublished report on file in *New Mexico v. Aamodt*, No. 6639, Federal District Court for New Mexico).

9. Janet Lecompte, "The Independent Women of Hispanic New Mexico, 1821–1846," *The Western Historical Quarterly* 12 (January 1981): 17–35.

10. Rosalind Z. Rock, "*Pido y Suplico:* Women and the Law in Spanish New Mexico, 1697–1763," *NMHR* 65 (April 1990): 145–59.

11. Gutiérrez, *When Jesus Came the Corn Mothers Went Away*, passim.

12. Robert J. Torrez, "Crime and Punishment in Spanish Colonial New Mexico," unpublished manuscript; Cutter, *The Protector de Indios in Colonial New Mexico, 1659–1821*, passim.

13. Meyer, *Water in the Hispanic Southwest*, passim.

14. Taylor, *Landlord and Peasant in Colonial Oaxaca*, passim.

15. John O. Baxter, *Spanish Irrigation in Taos Valley* (Santa Fe: New Mexico State Engineer Office, 1990). Baxter, *Spanish Irrigation in the Pojoaque and Tesuque Valleys During the Eighteenth and Early Nineteenth Centuries* (Santa Fe: New Mexico State Engineer Office, 1984).

16. See chapter 7, The San Joaquín Grant, note 69 and accompanying text.

17. Jerónimo Castillo de Bobadilla, *Politica para Corregidores* (Madrid, 1597), Libro 2, Cap. X, p. 34, cited in Kagan, *Lawsuits and Litigants*, p. 28.

18. Ibid.

19. Kagan, *Lawsuits and Litigants*, pp. 52, 60

20. Kagan, *Lawsuits and Litigants*, pp. 53–56.

21. Cited in Richard L. Kagan, *Lawsuits and Litigants*, p. 60.

22. Lansing Bartlett Bloom, "New Mexico Under Mexican Administration," *Old Santa Fe* 1 (1913): 271.

23. The first *asesor* appointed to New Mexico was licenciado J. Eleuterio

María de la Garza. The salary authorized for *asesores* was three thousand pesos annually. Tyler, "New Mexico in the 1820's," pp. 243–44; Bloom, "New Mexico Under Mexican Administration," p. 271.

24. Statement of Alcalde Juan García, Santa Fe, 14 August 1832. *Manuel Sena vs. Miguel and Felipe Sena*, SANM I, No. 905.

25. Daniel Tyler, "Land and Water Tenure in New Mexico, 1821–1846," unpublished ms., p. 28, note 85. Lansing Bartlett Bloom, "New Mexico Under Mexican Administration," *Old Santa Fe* 1 (1913): 270–71.

26. Woodrow Borah, *Justice by Insurance: The General Indian Court of Colonial Mexico and the Legal Aides of the Half-Real* (Berkeley, Los Angeles, London: University of California Press, 1983), pp. 1–5.

27. The office of *Protector de Indios* was vacant from 1717 to 1810. Charles R. Cutter, *The Protector de Indios in Colonial New Mexico, 1659–1821* (Albuquerque: University of New Mexico Press, 1986), p. 109

28. BIA documents, Southern Pueblo Agency, in Museum of New Mexico manuscript collection, No. 126, B–1, cited in Daniel Tyler, "Land and Water Tenure in New Mexico: 1821–1846," historical evidence in *New Mexico v. Aamodt*, note 66.

29. See, *Manuel Sena vs. Miguel and Felipe Sena*, SANM I, No. 905 (1837), *Maria and Juana Griego vs. Diego Arias de Quiros*, SANM I, No. 294 (1703).

30. David J. Langum, *Law and Community on the Mexican California Frontier* (Norman and London: University of Oklahoma Press, 1987), p. 98.

31. Maria and Juana Griego vs. Diego Arias de Quiros, SANM I, No. 294 (1703).

32. Don Pedro Bautista Pino, "*Exposicion Sucinta y Sencilla de la Provincia del Nuevo Mexico*," and Lic. Antonio Barreiro, "*Ojeada Sobre Nuevo Mexico*," in H. Bailey Carroll and J. Villasana Haggard, ed. and trans., *Three New Mexico Chronicles* (Albuquerque: The Quivera Society, 1942), pp. 94–96.

33. Manuel Dublan y José María Lozano, *Legislación Mexicana* (Mexico: Imprenta del Comercio de Dublan y Lozano, hijos, 1876), 1:384–95; David J. Weber, *The Mexican Frontier, 1821–1846: The American Southwest Under Mexico* (Albuquerque: University of New Mexico Press, 1982), p. 37.

34. SANM I, No. 1317.

35. Joseph W. McKnight, "Lawbooks on the Hispanic Frontier," *Journal of the West* 27 (July 1988): 80.

36. Petition of Domingo Fernandez to the *alcalde* of Santa Fe. Santa Fe, 16 September 1828. SANM I, No. 286.

37. Objection to grant of land to Luis Robidoux, MANM, Legislative proceedings, Roll 28, frame 84 (cited in Tyler, "Land and Water Tenure in New Mexico"); Domingo Fernandez to *alcalde* of Santa Fe, Santa Fe, 26 September

1828, SANM I, No. 286; grant by *asamblea* of Ojo de la Cabra land to Juan Otero, Santa Fe, 15 March 1845, SANM I, No. 676; Tyler, "Land and Water Tenure," pp. 32–36; Manuel Dublan y José María Lozano, *Legislación Mexicana* (Mexico: Imprenta del Comercio, a cargo de Dublan y Lozano, hijos, 1876).

38. David Langum found a reference to a Mexican lawbook on the organization and powers of the courts in late Mexican Period California. Langum, *Law and Community on the Mexican California Frontier*, pp. 125–26; Estate of Francisco Trébol Navarro, SANM I, No. 646, and Estate of Manuel Delgado, SANM I, No. 252, cited in Bernardo P. Gallegos *Literacy, Education, and Society in New Mexico, 1693–1821* (Albuquerque: University of New Mexico Press, 1992), pp. 57–59.

39. Ward Allen Minge, "Frontier Problems in New Mexico Preceding the Mexican War, 1840–1846," (Ph.D. diss., University of New Mexico, 1965), pp. 128–29. MANM, Roll 33, frames 1043–1499, Roll 36, frames 452–533, Roll 39, frames 270–358, Roll 41, frames 562–585.

40. A system of *alcalde* courts was also used in California during this period, but there appears to have been greater consistency in the procedures used there than was true in New Mexico. Langum, *Law and Community*, pp. 97–122.

41. Petition of Jose Francisco Lujan, Taos, April 11 1815. SANM I, No. 1357.

42. When settlement negotiations between the Spanish settlers and Taos Pueblo failed to bear fruit, the *alcalde* referred the matter back to Governor Maynez stating only that if the Spanish settlers were dispossessed it might "excite them to desperate actions." Governor Maynez and Alcalde Tafoya attempted to effect a compromise whereby the Spanish would compensate the Pueblo for the land they had settled on. Maynez again urged compromise and admonished the *alcalde* to refrain from veiled threats of violence. Statement of Jose Romero, Taos, 15 May 1815; Decree of Governor Maynez, Santa Fe, 22 May 1815. SANM I, No. 1357.

43. Decree of Governor Maynez, Santa Fe, 22 May 1815. SANM I, No. 1357.

44. The Chihuahua magistrate's solution was a creative one: recognize the Indians' right to their league of land, but measure it in such a way that it does not conflict with the Spanish settlement. The reason why this would not work at Taos was that Spanish settlements so surrounded the Pueblo that there was no comparable land available for the trade. SANM I, No. 1351.

45. Rock, "Women and the Law," p. 157.

46. This was the case, for example, when the governor knew the petitioner, as when he referred to Juan Jose Lucero of Los Corrales as "an honest and honorable man." Decree relating to petition of Juan Jose Lucero of Los Corrales, Santa Fe, 4 September 1840. SANM I, No. 1317.

47. Decree relating to petition of Francisco Ortiz y Delgado, Santa Fe, 6 May 1841. SANM I, No. 1317.

48. Decree relating to petition of José Ignacio Silva, Santa Fe, 11 June 1841. SANM I, No. 1317.

49. Decree relating to dispute of the *estranjero* Branch(e), Santa Fe, 21 October 1840. SANM I, No. 1317; see also dispute between Javier Mares and *alcalde* José Miguel Montoya, Santa Fe, 25 May 1841. SANM I, No. 1317

50. Decree relating to petition of Pedro Leon Lujan of Abiquiú, Santa Fe, 23 January 1841. SANM I, No. 1317.

51. *SANM* I, No. 1245.

52. *Las Siete Partidas*, Partida I, título 2, leyes 4, 5 and 6, Joaquín Escriche, *Manuel del Abogado Americano* (Paris, 1863), pp. 8–9.

53. Decree of governor, Santa Fe, 21 April 1833, SANM I, No. 1245.

54. Decree relating to petition of Jesus María Bernal of Jémez, Santa Fe, 25 December 1841. SANM I, No. 1317; decree relating to petition of Josefa Lucero of Taos, Santa Fe, 24 December 1840. SANM I, No. 1317.

55. Decree relating to petition of Tomas T. against her husband, 9 June 1841. SANM I, No. 1317.

56. Unsigned decision of Governor Francisco Sarracino, 21 April 1833. SANM I, No. 1245; Opinion of Miguel de Olaechea, Real Presidio de Paso del Rio del Norte, 1 May 1791, SANM I, No. 31. Since Governor Vélez Cachupín requested the *abogado's* opinion in 1750, he had to wait forty-one years for an answer, by which time he was out of office.

57. The documents comprising the Ojo de la Cabra litigation are found in SANM I, No. 676 (22 January 1845–18 March 1845), SANM I, No. 1381 (27 March 1845–7 July 1845), SANM I, No. 677 (14 March 1846–16 April 1846), and SANM I, No. 1383 (29 April 1846).

58. Manuel Alvarez to Powhattan Ellis, Santa Fe, December 1840, cited in Minge, "Frontier Problems in New Mexico," pp. 31–32, note 51. Langum, *Law and Community*, pp. 144–45. For more on the differences between civil and common law systems, see John Henry Merryman, *The Civil Law Tradition: An Introduction to the Legal Systems of Western Europe and Latin America* (Stanford: Stanford University Press, 1969), passim, and Rudolf B. Schlesinger, Hans W. Baade, Mirjan R. Damaska, and Peter E. Herzog, *Comparative Law* (Mineola, New York: The Foundation Press, 1988), pp. 229–766. For a translation of a portion of an 1813 murder case in Tucson that was appealed first to Durango and then to Guadalajara, see Kieran McCarty, *Desert Documentary* (Tucson: Arizona Historical Society, 1976), pp. 93–110.

59. Langum, *Law and Community*, pp. 131–44.

Chapter 3: Manuel Martinez's Ditch Dispute

1. MANM, Roll 15, Frames 171–96.

2. Ebright, *The Tierra Amarilla Grant*, pp. 10–11 and 36–37.

3. Thomas F. Glick, *Irrigation and Society in Medieval Valencia* (Cambridge: Harvard University Press, 1970), pp. 69–70. Glick refers to specific instances in medieval Valencia where violence surfaced in conflicts over water, especially when tensions were high during periods when water was scarce.

4. See chapter 2, note 1 and accompanying text.

5. John Nichols, *The Milagro Beanfield War* (New York: Holt, Rinehart and Winston, 1974). The mythical village of Milagro bears close resemblance to a village near Taos, New Mexico.

6. France V. Scholes, "Civil Government and Society in New Mexico in the Seventeenth Century," *NMHR* 10 (1935): 92.

7. An example of such a jurisdictional dispute appears in the history of the Rio del Pueblo grant in Taos County, made in 1832. The first petition for the grant in 1829 was referred to the *Ayuntamiento* of Santa Cruz, which recommended in favor of the grant. But before the grant was made, a protest was filed objecting to the making of the grant for several reasons, one of which was that the land was under the jurisdiction of the *Ayuntamiento* of Taos. Three years later a new petition was filed, complaining that the jurisdictional dispute between the two *ayuntamientos* was working a hardship on the petitioners because they did not know which one had authority. This time the territorial deputation referred the petition to the *Ayuntamiento* of Taos, which also recommended in favor of the grant. Governor Santiago Abreu made the grant on 22 July 1832, after a special three man committee appointed by the territorial deputation also recommended that the grant be made. NMLG-PLC, Roll 41, case 65, frame 6 et seq.; Bowden, "Private Land Claims," 4: 997–1000.

8. Glick, *Irrigation in Medieval Valencia*, p. 40.

9. See chapter 4, notes 22–24 and accompanying text regarding the Ciénega litigation for another example of the use of experts.

10. *"ser abundante de todas semillas y ser benefica al diezmo."* *Ayuntamiento* of Abiquiú to Governor Abreu, Abiquiú, 4 July 1832. MANM, Roll 15, Frames 172–73.

11. *"dictamen y parecer de los dos hombres peritos . . . que las acequias pasaban a regar atravesando tierras de varios individuos."* Ayuntamiento of Abiquiú to Governor Abreu, Abiquiú, 4 July 1832. MANM, Roll 15, Frames 172–73.

12. Martínez to Governor Abreu, Santa Fe, 3 July 1832. MANM, Roll 15, frames 171–72. Manuel Martínez was sometimes called Martín and Ramón

Martin was sometimes called Martinez; I have used Manuel Martinez and Ramón Martín because these are the names most frequently used in the documents.

13. "*tan demeritados, vejecidos y cansados, que ya el esmero mas esquisito; y el trabajo mas laborioso no basta para cosechar siquiera lo muy preciso.*" Martínez to Governor Abreu, Abiquiú, 23 April 1832. NMLG-SG, Roll 12, case 3, frame 15 (the Tierra Amarilla grant); Martínez to Governor Abreu, Santa Fe, 3 July 1832. MANM, Roll 15, frame 172. For land measurements see David Snow, "Review of Agrarian and Linear Land Measurement from 17th Century Documents in Colonial New Mexico," in Linda Tigges, ed., *Santa Fe Historic Plaza Study* I (Santa Fe: City Planning Department, 1990), pp. 90–95.

14. Governor Abreu to the *Ayuntamiento* of Abiquiú, 3 July 1832, MANM, Roll 15, frame 172.

15. *Ayuntamiento* of Abiquiú to Governor Abreu. MANM, Roll 15, frame 173.

16. Martín to Governor Abreu; Order of Governor Abreu. MANM, Roll 15, frames 174–75.

17. Martínez to *Alcalde* Gallegos, Abiquiú, 16 July 1832. MANM, Roll 15, frames 176 and 195.

18. Martínez to *Alcalde* Gallegos, Abiquiú, 17 July 1832. MANM, Roll 15, frame 191.

19. Frances Leon Swadesh, *Los Primeros Pobladores* (Notre Dame and London: University Press of Notre Dame, 1974), p. 51.

20. Martínez to Governor Abreu, Abiquiú, 16 July 1832. NMLG-SG, Roll 12, report 3, frames 18–19 (the Tierra Amarilla grant).

21. Grant by *diputación territorial*, Santa Fe, 20 July 1832. NMLG-SG, Roll 12, report 3, frames 18–19 (the Tierra Amarilla grant).

22. The Tierra Amarilla grant was confirmed by Congress in 1860 and patented for almost six hundred thousand acres. Chap. 167, 12 Stat. 71 (1860); Bowden, "Private Land Claims," 4: 1055–56.

23. Martínez to Alcalde Gallegos, Abiquiú, 17 July 1832. MANM, Roll 15, frame 193.

24. Juan Rafael Ortiz was *alcalde* of Santa Fe as early as 1802. Deed from Rafael Martín to Manuel Delgado, Catron Collection, Box 38, case 214, Cieneguilla grant. In 1814 he was elected as the New Mexico representative to the provincial assembly of the *Provincias Internas de Occident*. Marc Simmons, *Spanish Government in New Mexico* (Albuquerque: University of New Mexico Press, 1968; 1990), p. 209. By 1825 he was an alternate deputy to the first New Mexico territorial deputation, and in 1830 he was a full deputy in the fourth territorial deputation. Bloom, "New Mexico Under Mexican Administration,"

242, 271–72. He was constitutional *alcalde* of Santa Fe and a member of the Santa Fe *ayuntamiento* in 1829. Translation of *Diario, Ayuntamiento* of Santa Fe, Bancroft Collection, Berkeley.

25. *"la fuerza de la costumbre de esta Juridiccion que todas las acequias que estan fundadas antiguamente hasta la epoca presente, van rompiendo tierras de diferentes dueños y ninguna toma de agua se haya ubicada en terreno propio."* Alcalde Gallegos to Martínez. MANM, Roll 15, frames 193–94.

26. Pedro Ignacio Gallegos was a member of the second territorial deputation elected in 1826. Bloom, "New Mexico Under Mexican Administration," p. 246.

27. *"Es publico que hace años que su rancho esta inculto por la imposibilidad, irremediable, de no tener ni en remotas esperanzas de acequia para labrarlo."* Martínez to *Ayuntamiento* of Abiquiú, Abiquiú, 18 July 1832. MANM, Roll 15, frames 177–179.

28. Decree of the Spanish Cortes, 23 June 1813. Dublan and Lozano, *Legislación Mexicana,* 1:397–99. The law remained in effect until 1837 though it was suspended with the return of Ferdinand VII to the Spanish throne. Bloom, "New Mexico Under Mexican Administration," p. 48.

29. Statement of Marcos Delgado, MANM, Roll 15, frame 192.

30. Alcalde Gallegos to Martín, Abiquiú, July 1832. MANM, Roll 15, frame 196.

31. Alcalde Gallegos to Martínez, Abiquiú, 18 July 1832. MANM, Roll 15, frame 196.

32. Martín to Alcalde Gallegos, Abiquiú, 18 July 1832. MANM, Roll 15, frame 187.

33. *"pues de este paso resultaria el completo desengaño de que el dicho Ramón Martin engano a V.S. en todo cuanto le espuso."* *Ayuntamiento* of Abiquiú to Governor Abreu, Abiquiú, 19 July 1832. MANM, Roll 15, frames 181–184.

34. *"tener la menor conección con una nueva toma de agua, que el ayuntamiento de este pueblo en vista de sus atribuciones dió y pudo dar . . .que por el tiempo, diversidad de lugar y sircumstancia, no tiene la menor relación con lo que resolvio el Ayuntamiento."* *Ayuntamiento* of Abiquiú to Governor Abreu, Abiquiú, 19 July 1832. MANM, Roll 15, frames 181–84.

35. *"deseoso de vindicarme como hombre de bien sobre la imputacion que se me hace . . ."* Martínez to Governor Abreu, Abiquiú, 20 July 1832. MANM, Roll 15, frame 190.

36. Governor Abreu to Martínez, Santa Fe, 22 July 1832. MANM, Roll 15, frame 190.

37. Martínez to Governor Abreu, Abiquiú, 27 July 1832. MANM, Roll 15, frame 185.

38. *"resuelva lo que crea mas arreglado a justicia . . . y segun los usos y costumbres que en tales casos se han observado en esa juridiccion."* Governor Abreu to *Ayuntamiento* of Abiquiú, Abiquiú, 28 July 1832. MANM, Roll 15, frames 185–86.

39. Simmons, *Spanish Government in New Mexico*, p. 189.

40. Bowden, "Private Land Claims," 4:1017–18. Also involving the Taos *Ayuntamiento* were two attempts (one in 1827 and the other in 1837) to obtain a farming grant on land previously given as a grazing grant (the Rancho del Rio Grande grant) for benefit of the Cristóbal de la Serna grant. When asked by the governor for its report, the *ayuntamiento* recommended that the petition be denied because the first grant was still valid and it was necessary to protect the water supply of the settlement of San Francisco de las Trampas by preventing irrigation of land immediately upstream. The governor followed the *ayuntamiento's* recommendation each time. Rancho del Rio Grande grand, NMLG-SG, Roll 19, report 58; NMLG-PLC, Roll 34, case 10; Bowden, "Private Land Claims," 4: 986–89.

41. Report of Commission appointed by Governor Abreu regarding the Tierra Amarilla grant. NMLG, Roll 12, report 3; transcribed and translated in Ebright, *The Tierra Amarilla Grant*, pp. 38–39. See also, Bowden, "Private Land Claims," 4: 986–89, Rancho del Rio Grande grant.

42. Bloom, "New Mexico Under Mexican Administration," p. 271.

43. Lansing B. Bloom, ed. *Antonio Barreiro's Ojeada Sobre Nuevo Mexico* (Historical Society of New Mexico Publications in History, No. 5, 1928), p. 39. See chapter 2 for an overview of the administration of justice in Mexican Period New Mexico.

44. Joaquín Escriche, *Manuel del Abogado Americano* (Paris, 1863). pp. 8–9.

45. *"la fuerza de la costumbre de esta Juridiccion."* Alcalde Gallegos to Martínez. MANM, Roll 15, frames 193–94. As to the right under Hispanic law to conduct water through property of others to irrigate one's own property, see Michael C. Meyer, *Water in the Hispanic Southwest* (Tucson: University of Arizona Press, 1984), p. 154, n.42.

Chapter 4: The Ciénega of Santa Fe

1. No one word describes the legal status of the Ciénega throughout its history, unless it be community property, and that is potentially confusing with the current term for marital property in New Mexico and other Southwestern states. I have used the term *municipal commons* to describe the legal status of the Ciénega, although at times it was treated as *propio* property. The Spanish word *ciénaga* is spelled with an "a" according to the dictionary, but in New Mexico

and throughout New Spain, ciénega with an "e" was the more common usage. Francisco J. Santamaria, *Diccionario de Mejicanismos* (Mexico City, 1974), p. 241 (reference courtesy of David Weber).

2. David E. Vassberg, "The *Tierras Baldías:* Community Property and Public Lands in 16th Century Castile," *Agricultural History* 48 (July 1974): 383–89. See also, Joaquín Escriche, *Diccionario Razonado de Legislación y Jurisprudencia* (Paris: Librería de Rosa y Bouret, [1863]), passim.

3. Vassberg, *Tierras Baldías*, p. 391. The *ejido* was used for keeping stray animals and as a threshing floor. *Montes* were mountainous lands valued chiefly for their timber. The *dehesas* were enclosed pasture land, and the *prado* was high quality pasture land, often irrigated and sometimes cultivated. For detailed definitions of these terms, see Escriche's *Diccionario*.

4. *Recopilacion de leyes de los reynos de las Indias*, Libro IV, título 7, leyes 7 and 14.

5. Lansing B. Bloom and Ireneo L. Chavez, "Ynstruccion a Peralta por virey" *NMHR* 4 (April 1929): 180–81.

6. The plan of Pitic issued by Manuel Merino, Chihuahua, 20 January 1800, paragraphs 4 and 14. AGN, Tierras, vol. 2773, exp. 22 as cited and discussed in Meyer, *Water in the Hispanic Southwest*, pp. 30–37. SANM I, no. 1265, State Records Center and Archives, Santa Fe.

7. Cuello, "Saltillo in the Seventeenth Century," pp. 329–30; MANM, Roll 14, frames 996–97.

8. Vassberg, *"Tierras Baldías,"* pp. 388 and 390. For examples of both kinds of grants of common lands to municipalities, see David E. Vassberg, "The Sale of *Tierras Baldías* in Sixteenth-Century Castile," *Journal of Modern History* 47 (December 1975): 632, note 13.

9. *Old Santa Fe Today*, (Albuquerque: University of New Mexico Press, 1972), p. 56; Linda Tigges, "Soils, Tests, the Ciénega, and Spanish Colonial occupation in Downtown Santa Fe," in Linda Tigges, ed. *Santa Fe Historic Plaza Study* I (Santa Fe City Planning Department, 1990), pp. 75–84. Personal interview with David H. Snow, Santa Fe, 31 January 1992.

10. *"no pisen ni coma el sacate que en ella se cria pues el que lo necessitare y hubiere menester para dar de comer a sus cavalles pueden cortarlo o segar lo . . ."* Bando of Governor Francisco Cuervo y Valdez, Santa Fe, April 25, 1705, SANM I, No. 1251.

11. *"Por quanto es llegado el tiempo en que todos los años, se premulque Vando para que se recoxan el ganado de zerda que anda expersso en esta Villa de Santa Fe para que no aga daño alguno assi en los sembrados que se hizieren, como en la Sienega de esta dha Villa y asi mismo los caballos y demas vestias y ganados mayores y menores para que estos no pissen ni coman sus pastos para que . . . se pueda segar y mantener los cavallos de los presidiales que salen de escolta para el seguro de los que ban a el monte a traer leña y madera y para que lo referido . . . por redundar en bien comun de los vecinos desta dha*

villa," Bando of Lieutenant Governor Juan Páez Hurtado, Santa Fe, March 27, 1717. SANM I, no. 1251.

12. ". . . *para la fabrica de la SSta yglesia* . . ." Bando of Lieutenant Governor Juan Páez Hurtado, Santa Fe, March 27, 1717. The church referred to is the Parroquia, commenced by 1712, upon whose foundations Archbishop Jean Baptiste Lamy built the present day Cathedral of Saint Francis. Bruce Ellis, *Bishop Lamy's Santa Fe Cathedral* (Albuquerque: University of New Mexico Press, 1985), pp. 10 and 55.

13. "*a son de los instrumentos militares en las partes a costumbradas y se fixsen las puertas del cuerpo de guardia* . . ." *Bando* of Lieutenant Governor Juan Páez Hurtado, Santa Fe, 27 March, 1717. SANM I, no. 1251.

14. Vassberg, "*Tierras Baldías,*" pp. 386–88. The custom of stubble-grazing is documented in Mexican Period New Mexico in a community grant to Santiago Boné when the *alcalde* ordered that: "The justice shall fix the time for the gathering of the crops and for the loosing of the animals in the stubblefields. Should anyone gather corn, or turn [any] animals loose before the day fixed by the justice, he shall pay a fine of five pesos.""*el Juez determinara el tiempo de agarrar mais en la cosecha y la soltura de animales en los rastrojos, si alguno arranca mais o suelta animal antes del dia determinado por el juez pagara la multa de cinco pesos.*" Act of Possession by the *alcalde* of Mora, Juan Antonio García, NMLG-PLC, Roll 40, Case 62, frame 237. The Santiago Boné community grant was never settled.

15. Fray Angelico Chavez, *Origins of New Mexican Families* (Santa Fe: William Gannon, 1975), p. 134. Arias de Quiros died in 1738. *Old Santa Fe Today,* p. 56.

16. SANM I, no. 294 and *Old Santa Fe Today,* p. 56.

17. The Cabildo's decree of 23 July 1715 is not included in this archive but is referred to in Petition of Arias de Quiros to Governor Flores Mogollón, Santa Fe, n.d., SANM I, No. 8 and 169.

18. Petition of Arias de Quiros to Governor Flores Mogollón, Santa Fe, n.d., SANM I, No. 8 and 169. These archives are essentially the same for 1715 except that archive 169 is a copy by Roque de Pinto, secretary to Governor Flores Mogollón, of the original documents in archive no. 8. The 1716 documents are contained in archive 169 only.

19. Order of Governor Flores Mogollón, Santa Fe, 24 July 1715, SANM I, nos. 8 and 169.

20. Cabildo of Santa Fe to Governor Flores Mogollón, Santa Fe, 24 July 1715, SANM I, nos. 8 and 169.

21. *Para propios de la villa . . . para que goze el comun el beneficio que [h]asta aqui.* Order of Governor Flores Mogollón, Santa Fe, 27 July 1715, SANM I, nos. 8

and 169. The grant of the Ciénega to the *Villa* of Santa Fe was used by the U.S. government in the 1890s as evidence that the *Villa* of Santa Fe did not receive title to four square leagues of land at the time of its founding. The Court of Private Land Claims held that the city of Santa Fe was entitled to the four square leagues, but this decision was reversed by the U.S. Supreme Court. Ralph Emerson Twitchell, *The Spanish Archives of New Mexico* (Glendale, CA: The Arthur H. Clark Company, 1914), Vol. 1, p. 227, *U.S. v Santa Fe*, 165 U.S. 675 (1897).

22. Order of Governor Flores Mogollón, Santa Fe, 27 July 1715, SANM I, nos. 8 and 169.

23. SANM II, no. 172 cited in Stanley M. Hordes, "The History of the Santa Fe Plaza, 1610–1720," in Linda Tigges ed., *Santa Fe Historic Plaza Study* I (Santa Fe: City Planning Department, 1990), pp. 15–16, and Robert J. Torrez, "Crime and Punishment in Spanish Colonial New Mexico," unpublished manuscript, p.9. Diego de Velasco also helped survey the streets of the Villa in connection with another dispute litigated at the same time as the Ciénega dispute. Declaration of Governor Flores Mogollón, 29 July 1715, SANM I, nos. 8 and 169.

24. Declaration of Roque Madrid, Miguel Moran, Diego Velasco, and Juan Lorenzo de Medina, Santa Fe, 29 July 1715, SANM I, nos. 8 and 169.

25. Glick, *Irrigation and Society in Medieval Valencia*, p. 40.

26. See chapter 3, "Manuel Martinez's Ditch Dispute," notes 9–12 and accompanying text.

27. Order and grant by Governor Flores Mogollón, Santa Fe, 30 July 1715. SANM I, nos. 8 and 169.

28. For example, at the time of the founding of Santa Fe, it was provided that residents who abandoned their property for three months or more without permission from the municipal council would lose their property. Bloom and Chavez, "Ynstruccion a Peralta," *NMHR* 4 (April 1929): 180–81.

29. *Recopilación*, Libro 4, titulo 12, ley 1.

30. See, the Arroyo Hondo grant, New Mexico Land Grants Surveyor General (NMLG-SG), Roll 29, report 159, frames 44 et seq. and the Rancho del Rio Grande grant, NMLG-SG, Roll 19, report 58, frame 2 et seq.

31. Bowden, "Private Land Claims in the Southwest," 4: 827–30

32. *Recopilación*, Libro 4, titulo 12, ley 9. William B. Taylor, "Land and Water Rights in the Viceroyalty of New Spain," *NMHR* 50 (July 1975): 196, note 23. William Taylor's research in Mexico has disclosed many examples of grants to Spaniards later annulled because they infringed on Indian property rights.

33. Requerimiento of Captain Diego Arias, Santa Fe, 1 August 1715. SANM I, nos. 8 and 169.

34. *"y por que con dba seis varas en quadro no es dable el que pueda regar me guerta. . ."*

35. Petition of Arias de Quiros to Governor Flores Mogollón, Santa Fe, 3 August 1715. SANM I, nos. 8 and 169.

36. Order and grant by Governor Flores Mogollón, and Measurement of Pond by Diego Velasco and Roque de Pinto, Santa Fe, 3 August 1715. SANM I, nos. 8 and 169.

37. Petition of the Santa Fe *cabildo* to Governor Félix Martínez, Santa Fe, 1716. SANM I, no. 169.

38. Order of Governor Martínez, Santa Fe, 16 June 1716. SANM I, no. 169. Declaration of Diego Velasco, Andrés Gonzales, Juan Lorenzo de Medina, Miguel Durán, and Miguel Tenorio de Alba, Santa Fe, 16 June 1716. SANM I, no. 169.

39. *"poco o ningun vigor . . ."*

40. Declaration of Diego Velasco, Andres Gonzales, Juan Lorenzo de Medina, Miguel Durán, and Miguel Tenorio de Alba, Santa Fe, 16 June 1716. SANM I, no. 169.

41. Declaration of Lorenzo Madrid, Santa Fe, 17 June 1716. SANM I, no. 169.

42. Order of Governor Félix Martínez, Santa Fe, 11 August 1716. SANM I, no. 169.

43. Vassberg, *"Tierras Baldías,"* pp. 389–90, note 22.

44. Prior to the 1830s, treasury records for 1826–28 show that the Ciénega was leased intermittently. MANM, Hacienda Records, Comisaria Substituta, Accounts and Account Book, 1826–28.

45. In November 1830 the Santa Fe *ayuntamiento* notified the *diputación* that it had no secretary due to lack of funds for salaries. Bloom, "New Mexico under Mexican Administration," p. 273. The minutes of the *ayuntamiento*'s meeting of 12 April 1832 also refer to the meager resources of the *ayuntamiento*. MANM, Roll 14, frames 990–92.

46. Members of the Santa Fe *ayuntamiento* were fined for missing meetings. *Ayuntamiento* meeting in May 1833. MASF, p. 27. This rule seems to have generated a fair amount of revenue since absenteeism was a problem with the Santa Fe *ayuntamiento*. *Ayuntamiento* meeting of 28 April 1830. MANM, Roll 14, frames 996–97. At the meeting of 9 June 1832, First Alcalde Francisco Rascón paid 38 pesos 5 reales in fines presumably for missing meetings. MANM, Roll 15, frames 1003–5.

47. Licenses were required for holding *bailes* or games of *canuto*. Bloom, "New Mexico under Mexican Administration," p. 239; Municipal ordnances passed by the departmental assembly to be observed in all settlements. Santa Fe, 22 February 1846, SANM No. 1106, chapter 5, Article 31, no. 3–4.

48. *Ayuntamiento* of Santa Fe meeting, 28 April 1832. MANM, *Comisaria Substituta* Account Book, September 1826. Minutes of the Ayuntamiento of Santa Fe, 28 April 1832, MANM, Roll 14, frames 996–97.

49. John Langham arrived in New Mexico in 1825 and resided in Santa Fe from 1827 until his death in 1838. He was part of the caravan that left Santa Fe for Missouri in April 1838, and he was seized by a "fit of apoplexy" while assisting with the crossing of Ocate Creek 135 miles northeast of Santa Fe. Josiah Gregg, *Commerce of the Prairies*, ed. Max L. Moorhead (Norman and London: University of Oklahoma Press, 1954), p. 214. In 1831 Langham was paid $2,000.00 by William Sublette, on behalf of William Ashley, for beaver furs. David J. Weber, *The Taos Trappers: The Fur Trade in the Far Southwest, 1540–1846* (Norman: University of Oklahoma Press, 1980), p. 206.

50. Petition of John Langham to Governor Albino Pérez, Santa Fe, 3 May 1837. SANM I, no. 472.

51. Order of the *Ayuntamiento* of Santa Fe, Santa Fe, 5 May 1837. SANM I, no. 472.

52. Order of the *Ayuntamiento* of Santa Fe, Santa Fe, 5 May 1837. SANM I, no. 472. Fray Angelico Chavez questions whether Padre Manuel Gallegos had graduated from seminary and returned to New Mexico until 1840. *Trés Macho, He Said: Padre Gallegos of Albuquerque* (Santa Fe: William Gannon, 1985), p. 9. The documents would be consistent with this theory, however, for they usually refer to the *representative* of Señor Gallegos, implying Gallegos himself was not in Santa Fe. The Gallegos family owned land north of the Ciénega during this period. SANM I, No. 472.

53. Petition of John Langham, Santa Fe, 10 May 1837. SANM I, no. 472.

54. Order of Governor Pérez, Santa Fe, 17 May 1837. SANM I, no. 472.

55. Decision of *Ayuntamiento* of Santa Fe, Santa Fe, 18 May 1837. SANM I, no. 472.

56. Ramón Abreu to *Alcalde* Felipe Sena, Santa Fe, 28 June 1837, SANM I, no. 1216.

57. Chapter 3, Ditch Dispute, notes 34, 35, 39 and accompanying text.

58. For example, in 1832 Santiago Abreu was both governor, president of the *diputación*, and president of the *ayuntamiento*. Minutes of meetings of the Santa Fe *ayuntamiento*, 9 June 1832. MANM, Roll 14, frames 1003–5.

59. SANM I, no. 228.

60. Daniel Tyler, "New Mexico in the 1820s," pp. 101–5 gives a summary of the fiscal situation from 1827 through 1829, concluding that: "the total amount of liabilities invariably exceeded assets . . ." Ibid., p. 104. In 1828 Ramón Abreu was serving as secretary of the *diputación* and his salary was being paid by the

members of the *diputación* themselves, who hoped to be reimbursed when there was money in the treasury. Tyler, "New Mexico in the 1820s," p. 91. In 1839 the *junta departamental* stood in adjournment for most of the year, subject to the call of the governor, because of insufficient funds to pay their salaries. Bloom, "Mexican Administration," 2 (July 1914): 131. See also, Ward Allen Minge, "Frontier Problems in New Mexico Preceding the Mexican War," (Ph.D. diss., University of New Mexico, 1965), pp. 105–19.

61. In 1828 the *diputación* borrowed 2,000 pesos from the collector of tithes to meet expenses for three months. Tyler, "New Mexico in the 1820s," p. 92.

62. In 1828 the *diputación* did not have enough money to pay the salaries of the *regidores* in the Santa Fe *ayuntamiento*. Tyler, "New Mexico in the 1820s," pp. 91–92.

63. Bloom, "Mexican Administration," 1 (January 1914): 238–40.

64. The full text of this law is found in the Benjamin M. Read papers, NMSRCA. The law is summarized in Benjamin M. Read, *Illustrated History of New Mexico* (New York: Arno Press, 1976, reprint ed.), note on pp. 373–74.

65. Governor Narbona to Agustin Duran, Santa Fe, 4 June 1826. SANM I, no. 228. Narbona states that the Ciénega "has been declared as (property) belonging to the *fondo de arbitrios: sea declarado ser perteneciente al fondo de advitrios. Arbitrios* (literally tariffs) is often used with *propios* to denote municipal property. SANM I, No. 1106, chapter 5, article 31, no.2; *Decreto de 4 de Enero de 1813*, Dublán y Lozano, *Legislación Mexicana* (Mexico: Imprenta del Comercio, 1875–1890); Joaquín Esriche, *Diccionario Razonado de Legislación y Jurisprudencia* (Paris: Rosa y Bouret, [1863]), p. 1396.

66. Manuel José de Zuloaga to the *comisaria substituta* of New Mexico (Agustín Durán the territorial treasurer), Chihuahua, 31 July 1828. For a description of the office of *comisaria substituta*, see Tyler, "New Mexico in the 1820s," p. 97.

67. Santa Fe *ayuntamiento* to *diputación*, Santa Fe, 8 February 1844. SANM I, no. 228 and Tyler, "New Mexico in the 1820s," pp. 121–22. The *junta departamental* at first demurred to Armijo's request but then went along. For a loan of 1600 pesos from José Chavez on November 20, 1838, they mortgaged not only the Ciénega but also "the house of the Nation situated on the corner of the plaza in the street facing the Parroquia." Bloom, "Mexican Administration," 2 (October 1914): 133, nn. 481, 482. For the Vera Cruz Squadron, see Janet Lecompte, *Rebellion in Rio Arriba* (Albuquerque: University of New Mexico Press, 1985), pp. 67–75.

68. "... *una cosa tan seguro haiga pasado a propiedad aguesa...*" Ayuntamiento of Santa Fe to *junta departamental*, Santa Fe, 8 February 1844, SANM I, No. 228.

69. ". . . *resultado hubiera impedimentado una tropelia y sonasojo . . .*" Ayuntamiento of Santa Fe to *junta departmental*, Santa Fe, 8 February 1844, SANM I, No. 228.

70. ". . . *y la [virtud] no haver fondos por ahora con Qe cubrir la cantidad en que fue enagenada . . .*" *Asamblea departmental* to *ayuntamiento* of Santa Fe, 27 February 1844. SANM I, No. 228.

71. On 6 August 1846 it was announced to the departmental assembly that the departmental treasury was empty. Minge, "Frontier Problems," p. 303.

72. Bloom, "Mexican Administration," 2 (October 1914): 159–60.

73. Marianne Stoller, "Grants of Desperation, Lands of Speculation: Mexican Period Land Grants in Colorado," *JW* 19 (July 1980): 22–39; Janet Lecompte, "Manuel Armijo and the Americans," *JW* 19 (July 1980): 57–61.

74. Petition of Antonia de Moraga to Governor Flores Mogollón, n.d., SANM I, No. 491; Order of Governor Flores Mogollón, Santa Fe, 24 July 1715. SANM I, Nos. 8 and 169.

75. Vassberg, *Tierras Baldías*, p. 390.

76. Cordelia T. Snow, "A Hypothetical Configuration of the Early Santa Fe Plaza Based on the 1573 Ordenances or the Law of the Indies," in Tigges, ed., *Santa Fe Historic Plaza Study*, p. 56.

Chapter 5: San Joaquín

1. *Rio Arriba Land and Cattle Company v. United States*, 167 U.S. 298 (1897).

2. Pitt-Rivers, *The People of the Sierra*, pp. 14–33.

3. David E. Vassberg, *"Tierras Baldías,"* 383–90, and Dobkins, *The Spanish Element in Texas Water Law*, p. 71.

4. Vassberg, *"Tierras Baldías,"* p. 391.

5. Ots Capdequi, *España en America*, p. 50; Gustavus Schmidt, *The Civil Law of Spain and Mexico* (New Orleans: Thomas Rea, 1851), p. 63. "The municipal community was a land-owning democracy. It reached a considerable development, particularly in Castile, where it became a kind of small republic, with its own army and flag. This was the municipal spirit which the Spaniards transferred to the New World, where it struck root . . ." Salvador de Madariaga, *Latin America Between the Eagle and the Bear* (New York: Frederick A. Praeger, 1962), p. 60.

6. Ralph Emerson Twitchell, *The Spanish Archives of New Mexico*, 2 vols. (Cedar Rapids, Iowa: Touch Press, 1914), 1:208–9, item 771.

7. NMLG-PLC, Roll 45, case no. 107, frames 9, 14. These terms were also used in the Tierra Amarilla grant. Ebright, *The Tierra Amarilla Grant*, pp. 4–5, 40.

8. The Petaca Grant, NMLG-PLC, Roll 44, case 99, frames 21–22.

9. *Recopilación*, Libro 4: título 12, ley 1. This period was sometimes changed in specific grant documents. For example, the period was five years in the Petaca grant, NMLG-PLC Roll 44, case 99, frames 21–22).

10. *New Mexican*, 1 February 1979.

11. *New Mexican*, 1 February 1979.

12. *New Mexican*, 27 March 1981.

13. *New Mexican*, 9 July 1979.

14. U.S. Congress, House, Report 5963, 96th Cong., 1st sess., 1980.

15. For a summary of the history and adjudication of the San Joaquín grant see Bowden, "Private Land Claims in the Southwest," 4:1058–64.

16. The title papers for the San Joaquín grant are found in NMLG-SG, Cañón de Chama Grant, Roll 20, report 71, frames 577–582.

17. A *cuartilla* was probably one forty-eighth of a *fanega*. When used as a measurement of agrarian land, it meant the amount of land capable of being planted with that amount of grain (in this case, wheat). Thomas C. Barnes, Thomas H. Naylor, and Charles W. Polzer, *Northern New Spain: A Research Guide* (Tuscon: The University of Arizona Press, 1981), p. 69; and Manuel Carrera Stampa, "The Evolution of Weights and Measures in New Spain," *HAHR* 29 (February 1949): 15.

18. An *almud* was a measure of grain equaling one-twelfth of a *fanega*. Barnes, Naylor, and Polzer, *Northern New Spain*, p. 69. It is clear from the San Joaquín grant documents that all the allotted tracts capable of being irrigated were intended to carry water rights. Michael Meyer, however, has concluded that only one-third of the San Joaquín allotments carried water rights and two-thirds did not. Meyer apparently assumed, based on his reading of Galván Rivera's *Ordenanzas de tierras y aguas*, that only land planted in wheat carried water rights. Meyer, *Water in the Hispanic Southwest* (Tucson: University of Arizona Press, 1984), p. 128 and "The Legal Relationship of Land to Water in Northern Mexico and the Hispanic Southwest," *NMHR* 60 (January 1985): 71–72, note 70. This is an example of a mistaken interpretation, which if followed by the courts, could have a devastating effect on Hispanic water rights. It was arrived at because only codified law and its commentaries were consulted, not the documents themselves. The *alcalde*'s report makes clear the intent to provide full water rights to the allotments when he refers to the availability of about two leagues of irrigable land ("*como dos leguas, poco mas o menos, de [tierras de] lavor*"). NMLG-SG, Roll 20, report 71, frame 578. If only land planted in wheat carried water rights, then about 96 percent of each three-acre allotment would lack such water rights, a clearly erroneous conclusion when tested against New Mexico custom and practice as embodied in land grant and other archival documents.

19. Francisco Salazar was an *alférez* in the Abiquiú Militia, NMLG-PLC, Roll 45, case 107, frames 8, 13. The *alférez* was the standard bearer and is often translated as ensign although his functions were closer to those of a second lieutenant, Jones, "Pueblo Indian Auxiliaries and the Spanish Defense of New Mexico, pp. 147–48, n. 112.

20. A *poblador principal* (principal settler) was the leader of the group receiving a land grant, *Recopilación* Libro 4, título 3, ley 24.

21. NMLG-SG, Roll 20, report 71, frame 579.

22. For the history of the Piedra Lumbre grant, see Bowden, "Private Land Claims," 4:1077–82, and John R. Van Ness, "The Piedra Lumbre Grant and Hispanic Settlement in the Cañones Region" (Paper presented at the Nineteenth Annual Conference of the Western Social Science Association, Denver, 21 April 1977). For a discussion of the geographical meaning of *piedra lumbre*, see Frank D. Reeve, "Early Navajo Geography," *NMHR* 31 (October 1956): 290–98.

23. Petition for confirmation, NMLG-SG, Roll 20, report 71, frames 592–93; sketch map, frames 612–13.

24. NMLG-PLC, Roll 45, case 107, frames 18–18a.

25. When Julian was appointed surveyor general of New Mexico in 1885 by President Cleveland, his primary objective was to break up the Santa Fe Ring. Julian, "Land Stealing in New Mexico," p. 17. As a former chairman of the Committee of Private Land Claims in the House of Representatives, Julian had acquired some knowledge of New Mexico land grants. Bowden, "Private Land Claims," 1:222. He was prejudiced against New Mexico even before he arrived there however, for often in his journal he referred to the "stagnation of the natives" and the "prevailing tendency here to degenerate into barbarism." Williams, "George W. Julian and Land Reform in New Mexico, 1885–1889," p. 84.

26. NMLG-PLC, Roll 45, case 107, frames 85–104.

27. NMLG-SG, Roll 20, report 71, frames 622–24. Proudfit estimated that the grant contained 184,320 acres based on the sketch map submitted by the petitioners.

28. Bowden, "Private Land Claims," 4:1062.

29. Bowden, "Private Land Claims," 4:1062.

30. U.S., Congress, House, Report No. 131, 47th Cong., 1st sess., 1882, pp. 1–2.

31. Bowden, "Private Land Claims," 1:225.

32. Act of 3 March 1851, chapter 41, 9 *U.S. Statutes at Large*, 631–34, section 14 (1851).

33. U.S. Congress, Senate Exec. Doc. No. 21, 50th Cong., 1st sess., 1887, p. 5.

34. After reciting the boundaries, Alcalde García de la Mora stated that the unallotted land was *"para pastos, abredaderos, y por si se ofrese nuebos colonos y anmento de familias de hijos,"* "for pastures and watering places, with a view to the coming of new settlers and the increase of the families of their descendants." NMLG-PLC, case 107, Roll 45, frames 9, 14.

35. The Court of Private Land Claims rejected 32,718,354 acres of the 34,653,340 acres claimed before it. Of the rejected acres, 12,467,456 are represented by the notoriously fraudulent Peralta-Reavis grant. Of the remaining 20,250,898 rejected acres, an estimated 50 percent is comprised of the common lands rejected under the doctrine established in the cases of the San Joaquín and San Miguel del Vado grants, White, et al, *Land Title Study*, pp. 228–34.

36. Russell B. Rice, San Miguel County Surveyor, to J. N. Lamoreaux, Commissioner, General Land Office, 8 April 1893, cited in Clark S. Knowlton, "The Town of Las Vegas Community Grant: An Anglo-American Coup d'Etat, *Journal of the West* (July 1980): 18.

37. Protest Against Survey, 26 November 1885, Rio Arriba County, NMLG-SG, Roll 20, report 71, frames 658–63.

38. Statement of Will M. Tipton, Santa Fe, n.d. Thomas B. Catron Collection, Box 22, folder 107(2), Special Collections Department, University of New Mexico Library (UNM-SC), Albuquerque.

39. Amado Chaves to Will M. Tipton, Santa Fe, 28 July 1894; U.S. Attorney's summary of witness testimony. Catron Collection, box 22, folder 107(2), UNM-SC. Herbert O. Brayer, *William Blackmore: The Spanish and Mexican Land Grants of New Mexico and Colorado, 1863–1878* (Denver: Bradford Robinson, 1949), pp. 253–338.

40. Transcript of Trial, Catron Collection, box 22, folder 107(2), UNM-SC.

41. NMLG-PLC, Roll 45, case 107, frame 300; José María Chavez's son Patricio did testify, but the failure to call General Chavez himself was a serious mistake, either by Catron or by Frank Clancy who handled most of the trial. Transcript of Trial, pp. 74–84.

42. The government did claim in its answer to the claimants' complaint that only the allotted lands should be confirmed, but no mention was made of this contention at the trial. NMLG-PLC, Roll 45, case 107, frames 224–226.

43. *United States v. Sandoval*, 167 U.S. 278 (1897).

44. *Rio Arriba Land and Cattle Company v. United States*, 167 U.S. 298, 307–8 (1897). Opinion by Chief Justice Melville W. Fuller.

45. Twitchell's discussion of the ownership of property in a *villa* or other settlement in the nature of a community grant paraphrases or quotes at length (without quotation marks) from *United States v. Santa Fe*, 165 U.S. 675, 683 ff. (1897), which in turn is quoted in United States v. Sandoval, pp. 295–97; Ralph

Emerson Twitchell, *Old Santa Fe* (1925; reprint ed., Chicago: The Rio Grande Press, 1963), pp. 37–38.

46. Vassberg, "The *Tierra Baldías*," p. 400. The distinction between the *tierras baldías* and the *tierras concegiles* was not always clear in practice. Because of this, sixteenth-century Castilian monarchs were sometimes able to exact payment from municipalities for land used by them. Presumably, however, the *tierras concegiles* that had been granted to a municipality were exempt from such payments. Vassberg, "The Sale of *Tierra Baldías* in Sixteenth-century Castile," *Journal of Modern History* 47 (December 1975): 631–33, 637–38.

47. David E. Vassberg, "The Spanish Background: Problems Concerning Ownership, Usurpations, and Defense of Common Lands in 16th Century Castile," in Malcolm Ebright, ed., *Spanish and Mexican Land Grants and the Law* (Manhattan, Kansas: Sunflower University Press, 1989), and Vassberg, "Tierras Baldías," p. 400.

48. John L. Walker, "The Treatment of Private Property in International Law After State Succession," pp. 65–68, 74, in "Land, Law and La Raza" (A collection of papers presented for Professor Theodore Parnall's seminar in comparative law, UNM School of Law, Fall Semester, 1972), and Daniel Patrick O'Connell, *State Succession in Municipal Law and International Law*, 2 vols. (London: Cambridge University Press, 1967), 1:200.

49. *Apartada damente son del comun de cada una Ciudad o Villa . . . ejidos . . . los montes, e las dehesas, e todos los otros lugares semejantes destos, que son establecidos, e otorgados para pro comunal de cada Ciudad, o Villa. Las Siete Partidas del sabio rey don Alfonso el X, glosadas por el lic.* Gregorio Lopez, 4 vols. (Madrid: Oficina de d. Leon Amarita, 1829–1831), and Samuel Parsons Scott, trans. *Las Siete Partidas* (Chicago: Commerce Clearing House, 1931).

50. *Recopilación*, Libro 2: título 1, ley 2.

51. *Son objeto de esta ley aquellos terrenos de la nación, que no siendo de propiedad particular, ni pertenecientes a corporación alguna ó pueblo, pueden ser colonizados.* Decreto del 18 de Agosto de 1824, sobre colonization, Manuel Dublán and José María Lozano, *Legislación Mexicana*, 19 vols. (Mexico: Imprenta del Comercio, 1876–1890) 1: 712, translated in Frederic Hall, *The Laws of Mexico* (San Francisco: A. L. Bancroft, 1885), p. 148.

52. "*. . . tuvieron por bien SS. MM. ceder á las poblaciones de América y á los concejos de ellas, . . . cierta porcion de terrenos, para que acudiesen á su subsistancia y mejoramiento, usufructuándolas en pastos y labores, . . . Estos terrenos se denominaron inmediatamente conforme á sus clases, pertenencia y usos, concejiles ó de propios . . .*" Mariano Galván-Rivera, *Ordenanzas de Tierras y Aguas . . . Dictadas Sobre la Materia y Vigentes Hasta el Dia en la Republica Mejicana*, published as a supple-

ment to Joaquín Escriche's *Diccionario Razonado de Legislación y Jurisprudencia* (Paris: Librería Rosa y Bouret, [1863]), p. 187.

53. Simmons, *Spanish Government*, pp. 176–77; see also, chapter 2, "Lawsuits, Litigants, and Custom in Spanish and Mexican Period New Mexico."

54. For an example of such litigation see chapter 3, Manuel Martinez's Ditch Dispute.

55. In 1828, the Ministry of Justice in Mexico City provided for the first independent judicial system for New Mexico. The following positions and salaries were authorized: clerk of the district judge — 1,000 pesos; *asesor* (attorney general) — 500 pesos; clerk of the district judge — 500 pesos; and constable of the district judge — 500 pesos. None of these positions was filled except that of *asesor*, which was filled in 1831 by *licenciado* Antonio Barreiro *Old Santa Fe* 1 (January 1914): 271.

56. O'Connell, *State Succession* 1: 239–50. For a comprehensive discussion of the acquired rights doctrine and its application to numerous specific situations in international practice, see Walker, "The Treatment of Private Property," pp. 40–73.

57. Pedro Ignacio Gallegos to Licenciado Barreiro, 6 April 1832, NMLG-PLC, Roll 45, case 107, frames 42, 257. A handwritten copy of the original Spanish documents covering this litigation is found beginning at frame 24.

58. *Repartimiento de tierra*, 10 May 1932, NMLG-PLC, Roll 45, case 107, frames 49, 264.

59. "*qe conose muy de serca a los Alcaldes del Territorio y qe estos muchas veces puratuos de la ynorancia qe . . .hacer harbitreriades.*" Petition of Juan de Jesus Chacón to Governor Santiago Abreu, 2 April 1832, NMLG-PLC, Roll 45, case 107, frames 40–41, 255–56.

60. Governor Abreu to Licenciado Barreiro, 2 April 1832, NMLG-PLC, Roll 45, case 107, frames 41, 256.

61. Licenciado Barreiro to Governor Abreu, 2 April 1832, NMLG-PLC, Roll 45, case 107, frames 41, 256.

62. Governor Abreu to *Alcalde* Gallegos, 2 April 1832, NMLG-PLC, Roll 45, case 107, frames 41–42, 256.

63. *Alcalde* Gallegos to *Licenciado* Barreiro, 6 April 1832, NMLG-PLC, Roll 45, case 107, frames 42, 257.

64. *Licenciado* Barreiro to *Alcalde* Gallegos, 9 April 1832, NMLG-PLC, Roll 45, case 107, frames 43, 257–58.

65. Statement of José María Chavez, José Pablo Salazar, Miguel Velarde, and Santiago Salazar, 11 April 1832, NMLG-PLC, Roll 45, case 107, frames 43–44, 258.

66. "... *por querer gozar de nuestras propiedades sin consto de cautibar aquellas tierras tan remotes qe hemos fomentado con la sangre de nuestras venas y la de nuestras familias a pesar de ser unos infelises qe para conseguir una acha y un asadon nos aquilamos nosotros mismos . . .*" Statement of Juan de Jesus Chacón, José Antonio Durán, and Mateo García, 13 April 1832, NMLG-PLC, Roll 45, case 107, frames 44–45, 259.

67. "... *no ha sido otro mas de uncir una llunta de bueyes y ir sembrando sus semillas . . .*" Statement of José María Chavez, José Pablo Salazar, Miguel Velarde, and Santiago Salazar, 17 April 1832, NMLG-PLCD, Roll 45, case 107, frames 45–46, 260–61. *Alcalde* Gallegos had asked Governor Facundo Melcares for military protection so that the San Joaquín settlers could return. The possibility that the governor's denial of this request might be considered as a forfeiture of the original grant could explain why Gallegos was defending the San Joaquín settlers so vigorously. SANM I, No. 1282.

68. Statement of Juan de Jesus Chacón, José Antonio Durán, and Mateo García, 22 April 1832, NMLG-PLCD, Roll 45, case 107, frames 46–47,261.

69. "... *la posecion dada en el cañon de S. Joaq. in del Rio de Chama, pues aun quando ella caresca de algun requisito este no es requisito esencial y si de pura formalidad; . . .*" Decision of Licenciado Barreiro, 26 April 1832, NMLG-PLCD, Roll 45, case 107, frames 48–49, 262–63.

70. The *ayuntamiento* was the local governing body or town council authorized for villages having a population of at least 1,000. It was generally composed of two councilmen (*regidores*), two magistrates (*alcaldes constitucionales*), a secretary, and an attorney. The latter post was usually omitted as there were few attorneys in New Mexico at this time. Simmons, *Spanish Government*, pp. 206–7.

71. Nine of the eighteen individuals receiving allotments in 1832 had received allotments in 1808 at San Joaquín.

72. *Repartimiento de tierra,* 10 May 1832, NMLG-PLCD, Roll 45, case 107, frames 49, 264.

73. "... *y habiendo echo leer en presencia de todos la merced dada por el Senor Gobernador D. Joaquín del Rial Alencaster se encontre qe las tierras del Rio de la Gallina estaban vajo la posecion de dha merced y dice qe las tierras qe no fueron repartidas en el tiempo qe se dio la posecion quedaban pa aumento de los hijos de los pobladores . . .*" *Repartimiento de tierra,* 10 May 1832, NMLG-PLCD, Roll 45, case 107, frames 49, 264.

74. Report of Committee appointed by the territorial deputation, Santa Fe, 6 March 1833. SANM I, no. 1241.

75. Catron Collection, Box 22, folder 107, UNM-SC.

76. See the Cristóbal de la Serna Grant, NMLG-SG, Roll 29, report no. 158, frames 113, 117–18, and the Gijosa Grant, NMLG-PLCD, Roll 34, case 16,

frames 48–49, 52–53. The Serna grant was actually a quasi-community grant. It began as a private grant, but with the coming of additional settlers using the unallotted lands in common, it came to be treated as a community grant.

77. Las Huertas grant, NMLG-SG, Roll 26, report 144, frame 8; Refugio Colony grant, NMLG-SG, Roll 22, report 90; Daniel Tyler, "Ejido Lands in New Mexico," in Malcolm Ebright, ed. *Spanish and Mexican Land Grants and the Law* (Manhattan, Kansas: Sunflower University Press, 1989), pp. 24–35.

78. Tyler, "Ejido Lands in New Mexico," p. 26.

79. "*a todos juntos y en particular en su pertenencia y para lo demas anexo.*" NMLG-SG, Roll 16, report 27, frames 259–62.

80. "*con sus aguas pastos y abrevaderos,*" NMLG-SG, Roll 16, report 27, frames 259–62.

81. "*las cuales varas de tierra quedan con el derecho a los Pasteos, Aguas, Leñas, Maderas, Caminos, libres y comunes.*" A transcription and translation of this document is found in Malcolm Ebright, *The Tierra Amarilla Grant: A History of Chicanery* (Santa Fe: Center for Land Grant Studies, 1980), p. 26; see also *Martínez v. Mundy*, 61 N.M. 87 (1956).

82. Additional Brief on Behalf of the United States in the Supreme Court of the United States, case no. 195, October term, 1896. University of New Mexico School of Law Library. Reynolds does cite *U.S.v Pico*, 5 Wall 538–89, the same case cited by the claimants for the proposition that the boundaries called for in the act of possession were a conclusive determination of the boundaries of a land grant.

83. Frederick Hall, *The Laws of Mexico: A Compilation and Treatise Relating to Real Property, Mines, Water Rights, Personal Rights, Contracts, and Inheritances* (San Francisco: A. L. Bancroft and Company, 1885). The *Sandoval* court did cite passages from Elizondo's *Practica Universal Forense*, a commentary on Spanish law, but the references were ambiguous, and lacked any reference to Hispanic law. *U.S. v Sandoval*, 167 U.S. 278, 295–96 (1897).

84. *United States v. Sandoval*, 167 U.S. 278, 297 (1897).

Chapter 6: The Embudo Grant

1. Bradfute does point out that none of the justices fully understood the Hispanic law relating to land grants, and therefore his study of the opinions of the Land Claims Court is not necessarily an accurate reflection of Spanish and Mexican land tenure. Richard Wells Bradfute, *The Court of Private Land Claims, The Adjudication of Spanish and Mexican Land Grant Titles, 1891–1904* (Albuquerque, University of New Mexico Press, 1975), viii. See also White, Koch, Kelley and McCarthy and The New Mexico State Planning Office, *Land Title*

Study (Santa Fe, 1971), 27–46. In addition to the three states mentioned, the Land Claims Court's jurisdiction also embraced the states of Utah, Nevada, and Wyoming, but no claims were confirmed from the latter states.

2. For all quotes from the Embudo title papers see New Mexico Land Grants-Surveyor General (NMLG-SG), Roll 31, report 91, frames 285–88 (original documents), frames 299–304 (translations), State Records Center and Archives, Santa Fe.

3. The Sebastian Martín grant was first made in 1705 by Governor Cuervo y Valdez and revalidated in 1712. Bowden, *Private Land Claims*, 4, 1202.

4. Another version of the derivation of the name Embudo is based on the resemblance of certain hills in the area to an overturned funnel. T. M. Pearce, ed., *New Mexico Place Names* (Albuquerque: University of New Mexico Press, 1965), pp. 47 and 53.

5. This is probably the same man mentioned as Miguel de la Vega y Coca in Fray Angelico Chavez, *Origins of New Mexico Families* (Santa Fe, William Gannon, 1975), pp. 307–308. He was born in Mexico City and came to New Mexico in 1693 when he was 16. Later in life he was referred to simply as Coca, which became the family name since the double surname did not survive.

6. Picuris was one of the strongest northern pueblos with 3,000 inhabitants in 1680. Popé, the leader of the Pueblo Revolt, relied heavily on the Picuris for both warriors and leaders. The leader of the Picuris braves was Luis Tupatu, who was chosen to succeed Popé after his death. In 1705 the entire *pueblo* moved to another site, called Quartelejo, on the plains 350 miles north of Santa Fe. Two years later the Picuris were induced to return by Sergeant-Major Juan de Ulibarrí. Mrs. Edward E. Ayer, trans. *The Memorial of Fray Alonso de Benavides; 1630* (Albuquerque: Horn and Wallace, 1965), note 33, pp. 245–46. Note by Frederick W. Hodge.

7. NMLG-SG, Roll 31, report 91, fr. 288. *"y lo qe resulto de este buen medio fue entronisarse y yo cada rato estendiendo mas la vista abrasar mas tierras, en qe clarante manisfestaban ympedir la Poblason de los Españoles."* NMLG-SG, Roll 31, report 91, frame 288. *tiraron piedras arrancaron sacate, y dieron voces como suio propio y en senal de posesion.*

8. The name of the village was changed from Embudo to Dixon in 1900 when the U.S. post office was established and named after the local school master, Collin Dixon. Pearce, *New Mexico Place Names*, p. 47. This is an example of the loss or confusion of traditional Spanish community names which occurred when U.S. post offices took on names different from the villages where they were located. The name of the post office often became associated with the community. To add to the confusion in this case, another post office was later established at La Ciénega and named the Embudo post office.

9. Decree of Governor Tomás Velez Cachupin, Santa Fe, 21 February 1750. SANM I, No. 1100.

10. Adams and Chavez, ed., *Missions of New Mexico*, p. 91. Information on the Embudo settlements was kindly provided by Estevan Arellano on April 9, 1977.

11. See, for example, an entry of a marriage in 1823 at Embudo. Fray Angelico Chavez, *Archives of the Archdiocese of Santa Fe* (Washington, D.C.: Academy of American Franciscan History, 1957), p. 91, no. 13.

12. Adams and Chavez, *Missions of New Mexico*, p. 286. This expedition sought to open an overland trail from Santa Fe to the newly founded missions in California. Fray Angelico Chavez (translator) and Ted J. Warner (editor), *The Dominguez-Escalante Journal* (Provo, Utah: Brigham Young University Press, 1976), xiv.

13. *Sabras (sobres) de las tierras del Embudo*. Town of Cieneguilla grant, NMLG-SG, Roll 19, report 62; Bowden, "Private Land Claims," 4: 1015.

14. Cieneguilla opinion by Justice Reed, 19 August 1896, NMLG-PLC, Roll 42, case 84, frame 837; Embudo opinion by Justice Murray, 5 July 1898, NMLG-PLC, Roll 50, case 173, frames 268–70.

15. NMLG-SG, Roll 31, report 91, frames 283–309. The only documents in this file are the original grant documents, with transcriptions and translations. Bowden, "Private Land Claims," 4: 1199.

16. Petition of Antonio Griego, Albino Lopez, Manuel Valdez, and Juan Córdova for confirmation of the Embudo grant, NMLG-PLC, Roll 50, case 173, frames 250–51.

17. Laughlin's file on the Cieneguilla case in his papers at the NMSRCA had only one item in it: the printed report to Congress on the grant by the Surveyor General. The attorney who did most of the work on the case was Eugene A. Fiske. He had a more extensive file, but was apparently not well informed about it, for at the trial he stated: ". . . I really don't know anything about this case. This is Judge Laughlin's case and he had just handed me the papers." NMLG-PLC, Roll 42, case 84, frame 845.

18. NMLG-PLC, Roll 50, case 173, frame 273.

19. The court did not refer to any specific Spanish or Mexican law on the subject of admissibility of certified copies, and by this failure it violated a provision of the law which established the court. Section 7 of the 1891 Act of Congress provided that all decrees of the court must refer to the treaty, law, or ordinance under which the claim was rejected. An act to establish a Court of Private Land Claims . . . , 26 Statutes 854 (1891), Section 7.

20. See *Recopilación*, Libro 5, Título 8, De los Escrivanos de Govenacion. This *título* contains 40 laws regulating this profession in detail. See also, Scott, *Las Siete Partidas*, Partida III.

21. *Las Siete Partidas,* Partida 3, título 19 and Vance and Clagett, *A Guide to the Law and Legal Literature of Mexico* (Washington, D.C., 1945), p. 63.

22. The Secretary of Government and War for the province of New Mexico was an *escribano* and at one time the Cabildo (council) of Santa Fe had its own *escribano.* Simmons, *Spanish Government,* pp. 84–85.

23. NMLG-PLC, Roll 52, case 208, frame 21, (Town of Bernalillo grant).

24. *Las Siete Partidas,* Partida I, Título 2. For a good discussion of customary law, see John Leyba and Joseph Sena, "Customary Law in Spain and Mexico: 1848," in *Land, Law and La Raza,* papers presented for a seminar in comparative law, University of New Mexico School of Law, Fall Semester, 1972, under Professor Theodore Parnall.

25. Simmons, *Spanish Government,* p. 176. Richard Greenleaf has also emphasized the importance of custom: "Archival investigators often suspect that it was Spanish custom that conditioned legal practice in remote areas of the empire, especially in northern Mexico, rather than Hapsburg absolutist legal theories contained in the Recopilacion." Greenleaf, "Land and Water in Mexico and New Mexico, 1700–1821," *NMHR* 47 (1972): 86.

26. In his comprehensive study of the common lands of New Mexican land grants, Daniel Tyler placed his primary emphasis on actual practice as found in the land grant documents themselves. Daniel Tyler, "Ejido Lands in New Mexico," in Malcolm Ebright, ed. *Spanish and Mexican Land Grants and the Law* (Manhattan, Kansas: Sunflower University Press, 1989), pp. 24–35.

27. See for example, SANM I, No. 571, litigation in connection with the Polvadera grant before Governor Tomás Veléz Cachupín between Juan Pablo Martín and Miguel and Santiago Montoya. John R. Van Ness, "The Polvadera Grant: A History of Chicanery and Fraud," a paper presented at the annual meeting of the Western Social Science Association, 1975, p. 9.

28. See, for example, litigation in 1832 between two groups of settlers over the validity of the San Joaquín grant, decided by the Mexican *asesor* Antonio Barreiro. He upheld the validity of the grant, although a procedural requirement (depositing the original grant documents in the archives) had not been fulfilled. Cañon de Chama grant (so the San Joaquín grant was named by the Court of Private Land Claims), NMLG-PLCD, Roll 45, case 107, frames 47–48. See chapter 5, The San Joaquín Grant, note 69 and corresponding text. See also SANM I, no. 1352.

29. *United States v. Pendell,* 185 U.S. 189 (1902).

30. "The Town of Mora Grant," Bowden, 4: 814.

31. Decree of Governor Tomás Vélez Cachupín, Santa Fe, 21 February 1750, SANM I, no. 1100; Frances Leon Swadesh, *Los Primeros Pobladores, Hispanic Americans on the Ute Frontier* (Notre Dame, 1974), 38–39.

32. Embudo was within the jurisdiction of the *alcalata* of Santa Cruz de la Canada, yet it was two different *alcaldes* of Santa Fe who made the certified copy and who put the Embudo settlers in possession of the land.

33. Governor Bustamante had ordered the *alcalde* to put the Embudo settlers in possession if no one with a better right appeared to contest the proceeding. Once the Picuris protested, a hearing should have been held by the governor in which the Pueblos's rights would be protected. Under Spanish law the officer responsible for protecting the interests of the Pueblo Indians was the *protector de Indios*, but that office was vacant at this time. Simmons, *Spanish Government*, pp. 189–191. In the Embudo case, a good argument could have been made on behalf of the Picuris, that the Embudo grant encroached on their lands.

34. Bradfute, *Court of Private Land Claims*, p. 63.

35. Matthew Givens Reynolds, *Spanish and Mexican Land Laws; New Spain and Mexico* (St. Louis, 1895). *Hayes v. U.S.*, 170 U.S. 637, (1898) cites Reynolds's book as the only source for several points of Mexican law. For a book by Flipper about his experiences at West Point see Henry Ossian Flipper, *The Colored Cadet at West Point* (1969; reprint ed., New York: Homer Lee & Co., 1878).

36. *Las Siete Partidas*, Partida I, Título 2. *Las Siete Partidas*, Partida III, Título 29, Leyes 18 and 21 provide for acquisition of title by prescription (possession) after periods of possession of 10–30 years, depending on how possession was acquired.

37. Spanish law had its own rules of evidence and presumptions, which were based on Roman law. In *U.S. v. Chavez*, 175 U.S. 509, the U.S. Supreme Court cites Best, *Evidence* and Best, *Presumptions* for these rules, which should have been applied by the Court of Private Land Claims pursuant to Sec.7, Court of Private Land Claims Act, 26 Statutes 854 (1891).

38. Louisiana purchase: Treaty of Paris, 30 April, 1803, Hunter Miller, ed., *Treaties and Other International Acts of The United States of America* (Washington: U.S. Government Printing Office, 1931), 2, 498–505. Florida purchase: Treaty of February 22, 1819, Miller, *Treaties* (Washington: U.S. Government Printing Office, 1933), 3, 3–18.

39. *U.S. v. Percheman*, 32, U.S. (1833).

40. *Congressional Globe*, 30th Congress, 2nd Session, 1849, 237–254. John Currey, "The Treaty of Guadalupe Hidalgo and Private Land Claims," in Shuck, *History of the Bench and Bar of California* (Los Angeles: Commercial Printing House, 1901), 57.

41. *Botiller v. Dominguez*, 130 U.S. 238 (1889).

42. Act of March 3, 1851, chapter 41, 9 Statutes, 631–634, Section 14 (1851).

43. The following grants were made by *alcaldes:* Cañada de los Mestanos,

made in 1828 by the *alcalde* of Taos, NMLG-SG, Roll 31, file 82, frames 242 et seq. Bowden, "Private Land Claims," 4: 913; Guadalupita, made in 1837 by the *alcalde* of Taos, Bowden, "Private Land Claims, 4: 824.

44. The following grants were made by *ayuntamientos:* Cañon del Rio Colorado, made by the *ayuntamiento* of Taos in 1836, NMLG-PLC, Roll 49, case 166, frames 992 et seq., Bowden, "Private Land Claims," 4: 919; John Heath, made by the *ayuntamiento* of El Paso in 1823, NMLG-PLC, Roll 39, case 59, frames 697 et seq.; Bowden, *Spanish and Mexican Land Grants in the Chihuahuan Acquisition* (El Paso: Texas Western Press, 1971), pp. 77–84. The latter grant was one of the few whose rejection was proper, since it had been revoked by the governor of New Mexico, *Cessna v. U.S.*, 169 U.S. 165 (1898).

45. The San Antonio del Rio Colorado grant was made by the prefect of the first district of the department of New Mexico in 1842. It was rejected on the ground that a prefect did not have authority to make land grants. The office of prefect was established under the Mexican Constitution of 1837. NMLG-PLC, Roll 33, case 4, frame 521 et seq.; Bowden, "Private Land Claims," 4: 898–903.

46. *Hayes v. U.S.*, 170 U.S. 637 (1898).

47. *U.S. v. Arredondo*, 31 U.S. 691 (1832).

48. Act of March 3, 1891, chapter 539, 26 Statutes 854 (1891), Section 13, sub-section first.

49. Majority opinion of Justice Murray, 5 July 1898, NMLG-PLC, Roll 50, case 173, frames 268–270. Bradfute says of the decision in the Embudo and similar cases, "The copy was insufficient evidence and the grants had to be rejected." Bradfute, *Court of Private Land Claims*, p 139.

50. NMLG-PLC, Roll 50, Case 173, frame 277. Transcript of trial, testimony of Antonio Griego; Dissent of Justices Reed and Stone, 5 July 1898, NMLG-PLC, Roll 50, case 173, frame 271.

51. NMLG-PLCD, Roll 53, case 258, frame 20 (Town of Bernalillo grant).

52. 9 Statutes 922, Miller, *Treaties and Other International Acts of the United States of America* (Washington: U.S. Government Printing Office, 1937), 5: 218. (Article VIII). For another critical assessment of the fairness of the Court of Private Land Claims in relation to the Treaty of Guadalupe Hidalgo, see Richard Griswold del Castillo, *The Treaty of Guadalupe Hidalgo: A Legacy of Conflict* (Norman and London: University of Oklahoma Press, 1990), pp. 80–81.

53. An example of a grant revoked by the Mexican authorities was the John Heath grant made in 1823 by the *ayuntamiento* of El Paso and later revoked by the governor. *Cessna v. U.S.*, 169 U.S. 165 (1893), Bradfute, *Court of Private Land Claims*, pp. 210–211. If a grant with some procedural defect was not revoked by the Spanish or Mexican authorities, it should have been presumed by the U.S. to have been validated by these officials.

54. See chapter 1, notes 162–67 and corresponding text for a fuller discussion of the grounds for rejecting land grants under Hispanic law in New Mexico.

55. Other grants rejected by the court because the copies of the grant documents were made and certified by an *alcalde* were: Cieneguilla, Conejos, El Rito, Sanguijuela, and Sitio de Navajo. Bradfute, *Court of Private Land Claims*, p.139.

56. *U.S. v. Sandoval*, 167 U.S. 278 (1897) and *Land Title Study*, 43–44.

57. Map of the State of New Mexico, United States Department of the Interior, Bureau of Land Management, 1962.

58. *Rio Grande Sun*, 7 November 1974 and interview with Estevan Arellano, 9 April 1977 at La Junta, New Mexico.

59. Federal Color of Title Statute, 43 USC 1068. The percentage of applicants receiving patents is based on a sampling of fifty-three individuals represented by Northern New Mexico Legal Services who applied for clear title from the B.L.M. Only eight of this number have received patents, and six of those paid full market value. Of the remainder, six have been rejected and the rest are still pending. Written communication from NNMLS lawyer David Benavides, 5 January 1993.

60. The regulations interpreting 43 USC 1068 state that "a claim is not held in good faith where held with knowledge that the land is owned by the United States." 43 CFR 2540.0–5(b). This still begs the question of when the "knowledge of government ownership test" should be applied. Local B.L.M. officials are governed by the legal opinions of B.L.M. attorneys, who interpret the good faith requirement narrowly. Interview with Laura Yonemoto and Chet Granjean, BLM, Taos Resource Area, 14 January 1993. But the federal cases dealing with the question provide no basis for this interpretation. In both *Day v. Hickel*, 481 F. 2d 473, and *U.S. v. Wharton*, 514 F. 2d 406, knowledge of government ownership existed from the time the claimants moved onto the land and there was no good faith at purchase. In New Mexico, there is a presumption of good faith purchase, and knowledge of an adverse claim to land is not indicative of bad faith, *Thurmond v. Espalin*, 50 NM 737 (1946).

61. "What is Color-of-Title? . . . Requirements under the law to obtain a valid title include good faith *purchase*, a chain of title of twenty years, and valuable improvements and/or cultivation to the land." The Rio Grand Occupancy Resolution Program Brochure. Department of the Interior, Bureau of Land Management, Santa Fe, n.d. (emphasis added).

62. The Rio Grande Occupancy Resolution Program Brochure, Department of the Interior, Bureau of Land Management, Santa Fe, n. d.

63. The court rejected 32,718,354 acres of the 34,653,340 acres claimed. This is a 94 percent rejection rate of land claimed. The more conservative 91

percent rejection figure was reached by deducting the notoriously fraudulent Peralta-Reavis grant (12,467,456 acres) from the rejected acreage figure.

64. In a survey by the author of 48 grants adjudicated by the Land Claims Court, 17 were rejected entirely. Of those rejected, two were shown to be forgeries and in two cases there was no settlement on the land. One case was dismissed at the request of the claimants. The remaining rejections were based on technicalities of Anglo-American law bearing no relation to the requirements for land grant validity under Spanish and Mexican law.

65. Bradfute, *The Court of Private Land Claims*, viii and 223. J. J. Bowden states, "When . . . the Court of Private Land Claims ceased to exist on June 30, 1904, the United States could for the first time in half a century, relax, for it finally had fulfilled its treaty obligations respecting the recognition of private land claims in the Southwest." Bowden, "Private Land Claims," 1:310. But in a later book, Bowden says that the land grant problem has not been fully and satisfactorily settled. J.J. Bowden, *Spanish and Mexican Land Grants in the Chihuahuan Acquisition* (El Paso: Texas Western Press, 1971), p. 3.

66. Sandra Grisham and Jay Ortiz, "Methods of Proving Foreign Law in the Court of Private Land Claims," in Land, Law and La Raza, p. 37.

Chapter 7: The Las Trampas Grant

1. Documents in connection with the founding of the Villa of Santa Cruz de la Cañada. SANM 1, No. 882.

2. Richard Salazar, "Nuestra Señora del Rosario, San Fernando y Santiago del Rio de las Truchas: A Brief History," (unpublished manuscript), p. 4–5.

3. *Alcalde* Juan de Beytia to Governor Codallos y Rabal, Santa Cruz de la Cañada, 28 March 1748. The governor granted the request of the settlers of Pueblo Quemado, Ojo Caliente, and Santa Rosa de Abiquiú. Decree of Governor Codallos y Rabal, Santa Fe, 30 March 1748. SANM 1, No. 28.

4. Request of fourteen settlers to plant their lands at Pueblo Quemado. SANM 1, No. 718.

5. SANM 1, No. 766 and 767, cited in Salazar, "Truchas," p. 6.

6. Richard Salazar, "Santa Rosa de Lima de Abiquiú," *New Mexico Architecture* 18 (Sept.-Oct. 1976): 17.

7. Decree of Governor Tomás Vélez Cachupín, Santa Fe, 21 February 1750. SANM 1, No. 1100.

8. Governor Vélez Cachupín specified in the granting decree for the Nuestra Señora del Rosario, San Fernando y Santiago del Río de las Truchas grant that

the plaza be completely enclosed with only one gate large enough for *carretas* to pass through. SANM 1, No. 771.

9. Charles L. Briggs, "Our Strength is the Land: The Expression of Hierarchical and Egalitarian Principles in Hispano Society, 1750–1929," (Ph.D. diss., University of Chicago, 1980), pp. 229–232 and 236–237.

10. Marc Simmons, "Settlement Patterns and Village Plans in Colonial New Mexico," *Journal of the West* 8 (January 1969): 12–19.

11. *Los enemigos barbaros . . . el maior esfuerzo y valor en los Españoles.* Decree of Governor Tomas Velez Cachupín, Santa Fe, 21 February 1750. SANM 1, No. 1100.

12. Granting decree of Governor Tomás Vélez Cachupín, Santa Fe, 15 July 1751. NMLG-SG, Roll 16, report 17, frame 259.

13. Myra Ellen Jenkins, "Documentation Concerning San José de Gracia del Rio de las Trampas," (unpublished manuscript), pp. 5–6. Ramón A. Gutiérrez, *When Jesus Came, the Corn Mothers Went Away: Marriage, Sexuality, and Power in New Mexico, 1500–1846* (Stanford: Stanford University Press, 1991), p. 234.

14. Marc Simmons, "Tlascalans in the Spanish Borderlands," *NMHR* 39 (April 1964): 101–104.

15. Chavez, *Origins of New Mexico Families*, p. 270. Sebastian Rodriguez, a native of Angola, Africa, was one of no more than a dozen blacks in colonial New Mexico. Gutiérrez, *Marriage, Sexuality and Power*, p. 198; he was often given the job of announcing the governor's proclamations on the Santa Fe plaza, Twitchell, SANM, no. 882.

16. Jenkins, "Trampas Documentation," p. 5–8.

17. Marc Simmons, trans. and ed., *Father Juan Agustín de Morfi's Account of Disorders in New Mexico, 1778* (Isleta Pueblo: Historical Society of New Mexico, 1977), pp. 34–36; Gutiérrez, *Marriage, Sexuality, and Power*, pp. 188–190.

18. Deed from Sebastián Martín to twelve Las Trampas settlers. Certified by *Juez Receptor* Juan Joseph Lovato, Soledad, 1 July 1751. NMLG-SG, Roll 16, report 27, frames 263–64.

19. Granting decree of Governor Tomás Vélez Cachupín, Santa Fe, 15 July 1751. NMLG-SG, Roll 16, report 27, frames 259–62.

20. Act of possession by *Juez Receptor* Juan Joseph Lovato, Las Trampas, 20 July 1751. NMLG-SG, Roll 16, report 27, frames 256–57, 262.

21. Act of Possession. NMLG-SG, Roll 16, report 27, frame 256.

22. Thomas, *Forgotten Frontiers*, pp. 61–62. Since El Valle was not mentioned by Dominguez in 1776, either it had been temporarily abandoned or the El Valle referred to in 1773 was a different community.

23. Adams and Chavez, *Missions of New Mexico*, p. 99.

24. Bainbridge Bunting, "An Architectural Guide to Northern New Mexico," *New Mexico Architect*, 12 (September/October 1970): 38.

25. Adams and Chavez, *Missions of New Mexico*, pp. 100–101.

26. Marc Simmons, "New Mexico Smallpox Epidemic of 1780–1781," *NMHR* 41 (September, 1966): 319. Jenkins, "Trampas," p. 9.

27. Petition of Cristóbal Romero, Santa Fe, 21 June 1859. NMLG-SG, Roll 16, report 27, frames 18–19.

28. Affidavit of Juan Lorenzo Armijo, NMLG-SG, Roll 16, report 27, frame 25.

29. Affidavits of Mariano Sánchez and Juan Lorenzo Armijo, NMLG-SG, Roll 16, report 27, frames 24–25.

30. Decision of William Pelham, NMLG-SG, Roll 16, report 27, frame 53.

31. John Wilson (GLO) to Pelham, Sen. Misc. Doc. No. 12, 42nd Cong., 1st Sess., pp. 1–7 (1871), quoted in part in Bowden, "Private Land Claims" 1: 179–180.

32. An Act to confirm certain land claims in the territory of New Mexico, 167, 12 Stat. 71 (1860).

33. N.C. McFarland to Surveyor General H. M. Atkinson, Washington, D.C., 12 June 1884. NMLG-SG, Roll 16, report 27, frames 73–81.

34. Patent, United States of America to the Town of Las Trampas. Bowden, "Private Land Claims," 4: 1013–1014.

35. An Act Relating to Partition of Real Estate and for other purposes. New Mexico Laws (1875–1876), chapter III.

36. D. Martinez, Jr. to E. F. Hobart, Velarde, New Mexico, 26 November 1892. NMLG-SG, Roll 16, report 27, frame 179.

37. E. F. Best, Assistant Commissioner, GLO, to Surveyor General, Washington, D.C., 6 May 1896. NMLG-SG, Roll 16, report 27, frame 139.

38. William deBuys, "Fractions of Justice: A Legal and Social History of the Las Trampas Land Grant, New Mexico," *NMHR* 56 (January, 1981): 77–80.

39. *Martínez v. Rodríguez*. Taos County District Court Civil case no. 594, Complaint, Abstract of Title to the Las Trampas grant, pp. 139–41. Copy at the Land Status Section, U.S. Forest Service, Albuquerque. The copy of the abstract referred to in these notes differs in page numbering from the Forest Service copy. The Forest Service abstract has the 18 October 1900 complaint cited here at pages 31–33. Subsequent documents follow at successive pages.

40. *Martínez v. Rodríguez*. Taos County District Court Civil Case No. 594, complaint, Abstract, pp. 141–142.

41. *Rodríguez v. La Cueva Ranch Co.* 17 N.M. 246 (1912).

42. *Martínez v. Rodríguez*. Taos County District Court Civil Case No. 594, Proof of Publication, Abstract, p. 145.

43. Abstract, p. 146. Assisting Johnson was Amado Chavez, a silent partner with McMillan in buying up interests in the grant. deBuys, "Fractions of Justice," p. 80, note 34.

44. Abstract, pp. 146–147. The abstract describes the referee's report but does not include a copy of the report.

45. *Martínez v. Rodríguez*. Taos County Civil Case no. 594, Order of Partition, Abstract, pp. 148–152. The commissioners were Ireneo L. Chavez, Elias Brevoort and Henry W. Easton. Ireneo Chávez was Amado Chávez' brother.

46. Some interests were said to be less than 1/14,000 of the tract. *Martínez v. Rodríguez*, Taos County Civil Case No. 594, Report of Commissioners, 19 September 1901; Abstract, pp. 153–154; de Buys, "Fractions of Justice," p. 81.

47. *Martínez v. Rodríguez*, Taos County Civil Case No. 594. Final Judgment of Sale, 20 September 1901; Abstract, pp. 154–156.

48. Cause no. 840, Taos County District Court, State Records Center and Archives (SRCA), Brief, p. 12. Raynolds later became Secretary of the Territory of New Mexico, in which capacity he certified on 14 June 1907 the filing of the articles of incorporation of the Las Trampas Lumber Company which purchased the grant in 1907. Abstract, p. 175.

49. Cause no. 840, Taos County District Court, Brief, p. 11; deBuys, "Fractions of Justice," p. 82.

50. Memoranda, Folder no. 98, Renehan Gilbert Papers, SRCA; deBuys, "Fractions of Justice," p. 81.

51. Amado Chavez had numerous land grant related dealings. Some aspects of his life are discussed in Marc Simmons, *Charles Lummis and Amado Chaves* (Cerrillos: San Marcos Press, 1968; deBuys, "Fractions of Justice," p. 83. Cause no. 840, Brief, pp. 13 and 15.

52. Abstract, p. 157.

53. Frank H. Grubbs, "Frank Bond, Gentleman Sheepherder of Northern New Mexico, 1883–1915," *NMHR* 35: 169–99, 293–308; 36: 138–58, 230–43; 274–345; 37: 43–71; deBuys, "Fractions of Justice," p. 84.

54. Special Master's Deed from Ernest A. Johnston to Franklin Bond, 7 February 1903, recorded in Book 23, pp. 353–56, Taos County Deed Records; deBuys, "Fractions of Justice," pp. 84–85. Bond also purchased interests in the Piedra Lumbre grant, the Tome grant, the Ramón Vigil grant, and the Baca Location no. 1.

55. deBuys, "Fractions of Justice," p. 84.

56. Warranty Deed from Franklin and May A. Bond to Las Trampas Lumber Co., 20 June 1907, recorded in Book 28, pp. 511–13, Taos County Deed Records; deBuys, "Fractions of Justice," pp. 84–88; Grubbs, "Frank Bond, *NMHR* 36 (1961): 305–6.

57. *Priest v. Town of Las Vegas,* 16 N.M. 692 (1911).

58. Abstract, pp. 179–184 and Taos County District Court Case no. 840, Complaint, Amended Complaint, and Answer, SRCA.

59. Taos County District Court Civil Case no. 840, Reply, SRCA; deBuys, "Fractions of Justice," p. 88; deed from Franklin Bond and May A. Bond to Las Trampas Lumber Company, 20 June 1907, recorded in Book 18A, pp. 150–52, Rio Arriba County deed records; Demand to Frank Bond that he defend, Folder 99, Renehan Gilbert Papers, SRCA.

60. Cause no. 840, Complaint, Amended Complaint, and Consent to Judgement; Renehan to F. R. Frankenburger, [Santa Fe], 29 April 1918; Folder no. 98, Renehan Gilbert Papers, SRCA; deBuys, "Fractions of Justice," pp. 88–89.

61. Thomas A. Hayden, Map of the Occupied and Settled Lands Within Las Trampas Grant; Folder no. 98, Renehan Gilbert Papers, SRCA; deBuys, "Fractions of Justice," p. 89.

62. June 1913 Agreement, paragraph 1; Folder 98, Renehan-Gilbert Papers, SRCA.

63. June 1913 Agreement, paragraph 3; Folder No. 98, Renehan Gilbert Papers, SRCA, deed to Las Trampas Lumber Company for common lands signed by villagers, 26 November 1913, Folder No. 98, Renehan Gilbert Papers, SRCA.

64. Printed form of use-rights agreement, Renehan Gilbert papers, SRCA.

65. June 1913 Agreement; Folder No. 98, Renehan Gilbert Papers, SRCA.

66. Section 14–8–4, NMSA, formerly Laws 1901, chapter 62, Sec. 18.

67. Section 14–9–3, NMSA, formerly Laws 1923, chapter 11, Sec. 1.

68. Taos County District Court Civil Case, no. 840, Final Decree, 16 April 1914, SRCA; letter to the commissioners representing the people of Ojo Sarco, Las Trampas, Valle, Diamente [*sic*], Chamisal, and Llano, and to the people of said towns in general, Renehan Gilbert papers, SRCA; Record Book D, pp. 473–77, Taos County District Court Records, Taos.

69. deBuys, "Fractions of Justice," p. 89.

70. D. M. Lang, "Stumpage Appraisal Report," March 1926, Record Group 49, U.S. General Land Office, Land Exchange File, Carson, Las Trampas Grant, National Archives, Washington, D.C., pp. 1–2, reference courtesy Santiago "Jaime" Chávez; deBuys, "Fractions of Justice," pp. 89–90.

71. ". . . Attorney Renehan has brought the abstract down to date and it is being sent herewith by registered mail for advance consideration by the Department of the Interior . . ." District Forester, Albuquerque to The Forester, Washington, D.C., 24 February 1926, USFS-LS.

72. Abstract, pp. 63–64, USFS-LS.

73. D.M. Lang, "Stumpage Appraisal Report," March 1926, Record Group

49, U.S. General Land Office, Land Exchange File, Carson, Las Trampas Grant, National Archives, Washington, D.C.

74. An Act Providing for the acquirement [sic] by the United States of privately owned lands within Rio Arriba and Taos Counties, New Mexico, known as the Las Trampas grant, by exchanging therefor timber, within the exterior boundaries of any national forest situated within the State of New Mexico. Public Law No. 255, 68th Congress, S. 3024. Abstract, pp. 79–81, USFS-LS.

75. Congressman John Morrow to the Chief Forester, Washington, D.C., 5 March 1927. Correspondence file, USFS-LS.

76. House Joint Memorial No. 5, Record Group 49, Land Exchange File, National Archives.

77. The printed use-rights form runs to the named settler "and his heirs." Renehan Gilbert Papers, SRCA.

78. Renehan to F. R. Frankenburger, [Santa Fe], 29 April 1918. Renehan Gilbert Papers, SRCA.

79. Acting District Forester, Albuquerque, to The Forester, Washington, D.C., 30 March 1927, Record Group 49, Land Exchange File, National Archives.

80. Frank Bond's sheep were grazed under the *partido* system whereby the *partidario* (renter) grazed and otherwise cared for a flock of Bond's sheep and in return Bond paid the *partidario* a portion of the wool or of the lambs produced by the flock. Grazing permits were issued in Bond's name, and since prior use was a key factor in the granting of new permits under the more restrictive Forest Service policy, Bond continued to receive permits. Bond passed along the additional expense of grazing fees to his *partidarios*. Charles L. Briggs, "Our Strength Is the Land: The Expression of Hierarchical and Egalitarian Principles in Hispano Society, 1750–1929." (Ph. D. diss., University of Chicago, 1980), pp. 231, 235 and 237.

81. Briggs, "Our Strength is the Land," pp. 229–232 and 236–237; deBuys, "Fractions of Justice," p. 91. William deBuys traces the early growth of the Forest Service and its conflict with Hispanic villagers in chapter 15, "Bully Boys and Bureaucrats," in *Enchantment and Exploitation: The Life and Hard Times of a New Mexico Mountain Range* (Albuquerque: University of New Mexico Press, 1985).

82. William D. Hurst, Regional Forester, Albuquerque, "Region 3 Policy on Managing National Forest Land in Northern New Mexico," 6 March 1972.

83. The results of the study were published as White, et al., and State Planning Office, *Land Title Study* (Santa Fe, 1971).

84. M. J. Hassell, Forest Supervisor, to Keith M. Dotson, State Planning Officer, 7 May 1971. State Planning Office.

85. Although the Forest Service claimed that the abstract it examined did not contain any use-agreements (Quincy Raudles, Acting District Forester, Albuquerque, to The Forester, Washington, D.C., 30 March 1927), Renehan stated in his certificate to the updated abstract that it contained two use-agreements but that they were ineffective. Certificate of A. B. Renehan, 20 February 1926, Las Trampas Abstract, USFS-LS, Albuquerque.

86. "It is a well-settled general rule, in determining whether a purchaser had notice of . . . unrecorded interests so as to preclude him from being entitled to protection as a bona fide purchaser, that if he had knowledge of circumstances which, in the exercise of common reason and prudence, ought to put a man upon particular inquiry, he will be presumed to have made that inquiry, and will be charged with notice of every fact which such suggested investigation would in all probability have disclosed had it been properly pursued." *American Jurisprudence* 2nd. ed., 77: 767–68.

87. Transcript of Trial, Vol. V, p. 411.

Chapter 8: Settlement of the Las Vegas Community Grant

1. The Las Vegas, Tecolote, and Anton Chico grants are all currently operating as community land grants under the laws of New Mexico. See New Mexico Statutes Annotated (hereinafter N.M.S.A.) Sec. 49–6–1 to 49–6–14 for Las Vegas, Sec. 49–10–1 to 49–10–6 for Tecolote, and Sec. 49–1–1 to 49–1–21 for Anton Chico.

2. Other evidence submitted to the court includes reports by historians Daniel Tyler, Iris W.H. Engstrand, G. Emlen Hall, and Hans W. Baade.

3. *Cartwright v. Public Service Company of New Mexico*, 66 N.M. 64, 343 P. 2d 654 (1958).

4. For a detailed definition of *genízaro*, see Steven M. Horvath, "The Genízaros of Eighteenth Century New Mexico: A Reexamination," *Discovery*, XII (Fall 1977): 25–40.

5. A *vado* or *bado* is a place where one fords a river; a river ford. For the San Miguel del Bado grant see, NMLG-PLC, Roll 35, case 25, frame 664 et seq.; John L. Kessell, *Kiva, Cross and Crown: The Pecos Indians and New Mexico, 1540–1840* (National Park Service: Washington, D.C., 1979; reprint University of New Mexico Press, 1987), pp. 410, 415–416; J. J. Bowden, "Private Land Claims in the Southwest," 6 vols. (LLM thesis, Southern Methodist University, 1969) 3: 734–44; and G. Emlen Hall, "San Miguel del Bado and the Loss of the Common Lands of New Mexico Community Land Grants," *NMHR* 66 (October 1991): 413–32.

6. On 28 November 1798, the marriage of Juan de Dios Fernández, a Pecos Indian, to María Armijo, the daughter of grantee Juan Armijo, was recorded in the church records. Kessell, *Kiva, Cross and Crown*, p. 418.

7. Partition of land by *alcalde* Pedro Bautista Pino, San Jose del Bado, 14 March 1803, SANM I, No. 887. Kessell, *Kiva, Cross and Crown*, pp. 418–19 and G. Emlen Hall, *Four Leagues of Pecos* (Albuquerque: University of New Mexico Press, 1984), pp. 5–6.

8. Kessell, *Kiva, Cross and Crown*, pp. 426–27; Hall, *Four Leagues of Pecos*, p. 8.

9. For Los Trigos see NMLG-SG, Roll 13, report 8, frame 310 et seq.; for Alexander Valle see NMLG-SG, Roll 14, report 18, frame 675 et seq. See also, Hall, *Four Leagues of Pecos*, pp. 17–26.

10. John O. Baxter, *Las Carneradas: Sheep Trade in New Mexico, 1700–1860* (Albuquerque: University of New Mexico Press, 1987), pp. 92–93 and 125.

11. Antonio Ortiz Grant, NMLG-SG, Roll 17, report 42, frame 407 et seq.; see also Bowden, "Private Land Claims," 3:706–10.

12. Baxter, *Las Carneradas*, p. 125.

13. Preston Beck Grant, NMLG-SG, Roll 12, report 1, frame 6 et seq.; see also Bowden, "Private Land Claims," 3: 677–86. Pedro Bautista Pino was New Mexico's delegate to the *Cortes* or Spanish parliament held at Cádiz, Spain between 1810 and 1814. For Pino's report to the *Cortes*, see H. Bailey Carroll and J. Villasana Haggard, trans. and eds., *Three New Mexico Chronicles* (Albuquerque: The Quivera Society, 1942).

14. Baxter, *Las Carneradas*, p. 93.

15. Anton Chico grant, NMLG-SG, Roll 16, report 29, frames 490-et seq.; Bowden, "Private Land Claims," 3: 689–97; Michael J. Rock, "Anton Chico and Its Patent," *Journal of the West* 19 (1980): 86.

16. See *Stoneroad v. Beck*, 16 N.M. 754, and *Stoneroad v. Stoneroad*, 158 U.S. 240 (1895). *Jones v. St. Louis Land Co.*, 232 U.S. 355 (1913) deals with the conflict between the Beck and Perea grants and gives priority to the Beck grant. See also, Westphall, *Mercedes Reales*, pp. 222–24.

17. Tecolote grant, NMLG-SG, Roll 13, report 7, frame 6 et seq.

18. SANM, no. 1116. The village of San Gerónimo was actually on the Las Vegas community grant as it was later surveyed in 1899 and 1900. Map of the Las Vegas Grant in San Miguel and Mora Counties, New Mexico as resurveyed by Frank M. Johnson, Bureau of Land Management (BLM), Santa Fe. The earlier 1860 survey of the Las Vegas grant showed even the town of Tecolote to be on the Las Vegas grant, but this overlap between the two grants was later decided in favor of Tecolote. Plat of Las Vegas Grant as finally confirmed, surveyed under contract with the Surveyor General of New Mexico by Pelham and Clements, BLM, Santa Fe.

19. Ralph Emerson Twitchell, *The Spanish Archives of New Mexico*, 2 vol., (Arthur Clark: Glendale, California, 1914), 1: 376.

20. Charles R. Cutter, *The Protector de Indios in Colonial New Mexico, 1659–1821*, (Albuquerque: University of New Mexico Press, 1986), pp. 88–93.

21. In this lawsuit, Luis María Cabesa de Baca was accused of exacting personal service without pay, administering excessive punishment, and interfering with the religious observances of the Santo Domingo Indians. SANM II, no. 1188, Twitchell, *Spanish Archives*, 2: 342.

22. Cutter, *Protector de Indios*, pp. 88–92. Cabesa de Baca was assessed with court costs of 192 pesos and 7 reales. Not having the cash to pay these expenses, he was allowed by Governor Facundo Melgares to give the government nine mules valued at 25 pesos each in payment. Melgares to Alejo García Conde, Santa Fe, 18 June 1820, SANM 1, no. 1284; Decree of the *Real Audiencia de Guadalajara*, 18 January 1817, SANM 1, no. 1361.

23. SANM 1, no. 1362, SANM II, no. 1188.

24. Allotment of land by *alcalde* Luis María Cabesa de Baca to Santiago de Jesús Aragón, San Miguel del Bado, 4 October 1820. Stein Collection, document 5, SRCA, Santa Fe.

25. Petition of Luis María Cabesa de Baca, New Mexico, 16 January 1821, NMLG-SG, Roll 14, report 20, frames 1105–06. It is not clear from this document that it was in fact directed to the Durango provincial deputation, but the next document in the surveyor general's file is a purported copy of a grant to Cabesa de Baca by the Provincial Deputation of Durango.

26. For an example of criticism of large landowners, see protest against landholdings of Juan Estevan Pino by *alcalde* Diego Padilla, 17 February 1824, and by Manuel Antonio Baca, 13 March 1824, both from Santa Fe. SANM I, no. 899; for Cabesa de Baca as *alcalde* see Luis María Cabesa de Baca *alcalde*, re land of Domingo Benavides, San José del Bado, 24 May 1820. Book 34, pp. 384–85, San Miguel County deed records, allotment of land by *alcalde* Luis Maria Cabesa de Baca to Santiago de Jesús Aragon, San Miguel del Bado, 4 October 1820. Stein Collection, document 5, SRCA, Santa Fe.

27. Petition of Luis María Cabesa de Baca, 16 January 1821. NMLG-SG, Roll 14, frames 1105–06. For the names of Baca's three wives and their children, see Twitchell, *Spanish Archives of New Mexico*, 1: 47–48.

28. Copy of grant by the provincial deputation of Durango, 29 May 1821, NMLG-SG, Roll 15, report 20, frames 33–34.

29. Governor Bartolomé Baca to Alcalde Manuel Antonio Baca, Santa Fe, 17 October 1823, NMLG-SG, Roll 15, report 20, frames 33–34.

30. Petition of Juan Antonio Cabesa de Baca to New Mexico territorial

deputation, Santa Fe, 15 February 1825. NMLG-SG, Roll 14, report 20, frames 1103–04.

31. Response of New Mexico territorial deputation to petition of Juan Antonio Cabesa de Baca, Santa Fe, 16 February 1825. NMLG-SG, Roll 14, report 20, frame 1109.

32. Juan Antonio Cabesa de Baca to Governor Narbona, Santa Fe, 16 February 1825, NMLG-SG, Roll 15, report 20, frames 30–31.

33. Statement of Tomás Sena, Santa Fe, 13 January 1826, NMLG-SG, Roll 14, report 20, frame 1118.

34. Order of Governor Narbona, Santa Fe, 13 January 1826, NMLG-SG, Roll 14, report 20, frame 1118.

35. Petition of Luis María Cabesa de Baca, 16 January 1821. NMLG-SG, Roll 14, report 20, frames 1105–06. Cabesa de Baca referred to the Sapello River as the Chapellote River, an earlier variation of the current place name. Chapellote apparently derived from the French-Kiowa proper name Chapalote. T.M. Pearce, ed., *New Mexico Place Names: A Geographical Dictionary* (Albuquerque: The University of New Mexico Press, 1965), p. 151.

36. The Baca heirs stated in their petition to the surveyor general of New Mexico that the two grants covered the same lands. NMLG-SG, Roll 14, report 20, frames 1125–28. House Exec. Doc. No. 14, 36th Cong., 1st Sess., p. 1.

37. The 1860 survey of the Las Vegas grant showed it to contain 496,446.96 acres. Plat of Las Vegas grant by Deputy Surveyors Pelham and Clements, 8 December 1860, BLM, Santa Fe. Bowden, "Private Land Claims," 3: 787–88.

38. Affidavit of José Francisco Salas, NMLG-SG, Roll 14, frames 1155–62; House Exec. Doc. No. 14, 36th Cong., 1st Sess., p. 2.

39. Cutter, *Protector de Indios*, p. 92, note 29.

40. Josiah Gregg, *Commerce on the Prairies*, pp. 76–77.

41. Mexican Archives of New Mexico (MANM), Roll 5, frame 560. Cited in Anselmo F. Arellano, "Through Thick and Thin: Evolutionary Transitions of *Las Vegas Grandes* and its *Pobladores* (Ph.D. diss., University of New Mexico, 1990), pp. 26–27, note 38

42. MANM, Roll 9, frame 641, Arellano, *"Las Vegas Grandes,"* p. 44, note 79.

43. MANM, Roll 9, frames 851–53, Arellano, *"Las Vegas Grandes"* p. 44–45, notes 80–81.

44. Although Mexican law provided that New Mexico should have three presidial companies, each with six officers and one hundred men, throughout the Mexican period Santa Fe was the only formal presidio in New Mexico. Law of 21 March 1826, cited in Daniel Tyler, "New Mexico in the 1820's: The First

Administration of Manuel Armijo" (Ph.D. dissertation, University of New Mexico, 1970), pp. 162–64.

45. Tyler, "New Mexico in the 1820s," pp. 169, 179 and 181.

46. Tyler, "New Mexico in the 1820s," pp. 99, 150–51.

47. Vicente Rivera to Governor Albino Pérez, Paraje del Puertecito de las Vegas, 27 June 1837, MANM, Roll 23, frames 392–93.

48. MANM, Roll 9, frame 377.

49. Other priests involved in governmental affairs in New Mexico at this time were Antonio José Martínez, José Manuel Gallegos, Francisco Ignacio de Madariaga, and the vicar Juan Felipe Ortiz. Fray Angelico Chavez, *Tres Macho — He Said: Padre Gallegos of Albuquerque* (Santa Fe: William Gannon, 1985), p. 12.

50. José Francisco Leyba to the *diputación*, San Miguel del Bado, 17 June 1831. MANM, Roll 13, frame 613–19. Arellano, *Las Vegas Grandes*, pp. 55–61.

51. Report of committee of Abreu, Martínez, and Sandoval to the *diputación*, Santa Fe, 4 August 1831. MANM, Roll 13, frame 589–90.

52. *Ayuntamiento* of San Miguel del Bado to the *ayuntamiento* of Santa Fe, San Miguel del Bado, 8 February 1832, SANM I, no. 1123.

53. Arellano, *Las Vegas Grandes*, p. 59–60.

54. An example of a settlement actually subsidized by the Spanish government is San Antonio de Bejar (San Antonio, Texas), settled by a group of families from the Canary Islands. These settlers were furnished with transportation and one year's subsistence, including food, household goods, horses, mules, oxen, and farming tools. Lota M. Spell, "The Grant and First Survey of the City of San Antonio," *Southwestern Historical Quarterly*, 66 (July 1962): 73–89.

55. Francisco Sena received 200 *varas*, José Flores, one allotment of 75 *varas* and another of 100 *varas;* and José Ulibarrí 125 *varas*. NMLG-SG, Roll 15, report 20, frames 17–21.

56. Even before Father Leyba's proposal, Juan Estevan Pino had proposed that a military fort be established on the Canadian River, which would have the effect of protecting his land holdings and the Las Vegas area. MANM, Roll 9, frames 1119–22. Arellano, *Las Vegas Grandes*, pp. 53–55.

57. In 1832 San Miguel del Bado's *ayuntamiento* was comprised of *regidores* Vicente Rivera, Juan Estevan Sena, Vicente Romero, and Matías Gómez, plus José Miguel Sánchez, secretary. In 1835 the members of that body were José Ulibarrí, president, Francisco Sena, Gerónimo Gonzales, José Candelario Flores, Lorenzo Lucero, *regidores,* Tomas Aragón, *procurador síndico,* and José Antonio Casaus, secretary. SANM I, No. 1123 and SANM I, No. 1096.

58. Petition of Juan de Dios Maese, Miguel Archuleta, Manuel Durán, and

Antonio Casados to the *ayuntamiento* of San Miguel del Bado, 20 March 1835. NMLG-SG, Roll 15, report 20, frames 7–8.

59. *"el aumento de la agricultura y acomodo en tanto familia desacomodada . . ."* Report of the *ayuntamiento* of San Miguel del Bado, San Miguel del Bado, 20 March 1835. NMLG-SG, Roll 15, report 20, frames 8–9. Although used in the report, the *sin perjuicio* phrase is not used in the act of possession and a variant is used in the grant itself.

60. *La merced de estos terrenos es sin perjuicio de pastos y abrebaderos comunes.* Grant by territorial deputation, Santa Fe, 23 March 1835, NMLG-SG, Roll 15, report 20, frames 9–10.

61. Order of Governor Francisco Sarracino, Santa Fe, 24 March 1835. NMLG-SG, Roll 15, report 20, frames 12–13.

62. Act of possession by José de Jesús Ulibarrí, Santa Fe, 24 March 1835. NMLG-SG, Roll 15, report 20, frames 14–16. Lynn Perrigo, "The Original Las Vegas," pp. 31–32, note 24, Carnegie Library, Las Vegas. There is a discrepancy between the three versions of the Las Vegas grant documents as to the number of settlers placed in possession on 1 April 1835. The original documents list 36 (NMLG-SG, Roll 15, report 20, frames 17–18); the version recorded in the San Miguel County Courthouse lists 36 (Book 1, pp. 124–25); and the version recorded in the Surveyor General's office lists 37 (Surveyor General's Journal, pp. 38–39). But the house executive document, considered by subsequent courts to be the official version of the grant documents, lists only 31 (House Exec. Doc. No. 14, 36th Congress, 1st Sess. (1860), p. 31). This is just one of several mistakes in the transcription and translation of the grant documents that must have affected later court decisions regarding the Las Vegas grant, including the *Cartwright* case.

63. Lynn Perrigo, "The Original Las Vegas," pp. 31–32, note 24, Carnegie Library, Las Vegas.

64. *Juez de primera instancia* Juan de Dios Maese to the governor, San Miguel del Bado, 14 March 1836, SANM 1, No. 1315.

65. *Cartwright v. Public Service Co. of New Mexico*, 66 N.M. 64, 343 P. 2d 654 (1958).

66. Most of the 1835 Las Vegas allottees stated in 1836 that they preferred to settle at Tecolote since it was closer to San Miguel (SANM I, no. 1315), but when Tecolote and San Gerónimo were settled in April 1838 by others (SANM I, no. 1116), that option was no longer open and the Las Vegas grantees began to occupy their allotments. Prior to 1838 there was probably some summer occupation of the Las Vegas area with settlers returning to San Miguel for the winter. The San Miguel baptisms begin to show parents from Las Vegas in substantial numbers by 1838. AASF, Roll 11, frames 333, 334, 344, 364, and

367), and most deed records showing transfers and allotments of land also begin in 1838. See for example, *Juez de paz* Manuel Antonio Baca to Ventura Martín, 7 September 1838, Book 1 (large), pages 212–213, San Miguel County Deed Records; *Juez de paz* Manuel Antonio Baca to Ambrosio Gonzales and José María Vigil, 4 December 1838, Book 11, page 210, San Miguel County Deed Records. When a protest was filed on behalf of the Cabesa de Baca heirs dated 20 September 1837, it was directed to "certain persons who *intended* settling on the Vegas Grandes." Testimony of Remigio Rivera in support of the Cabesa de Baca grant, NMLG-SG, Roll 14, report 20, frames 1167–68. For a different view as to the earliest permanent settlement of Las Vegas, see Stanley M. Hordes, "The Position of the Town of Las Vegas Relative to the Las Vegas Grant, 1835–1879," report submitted in *State ex. rel. Reynolds and Pecos Valley Artesian Conservation District v. L.T. Lewis, et al.*, Chavez County District Court cause nos. 20294 and 22600, consolidated.

67. Russell B. Rice, Survey of the Land Allotted by the Mexican Government in the Gallinas River Valley in the Town of Las Vegas Prior to 1848. National Archives, RG 49, NM-PLC 20.

68. Allotment of 275 varas by *Juez de paz* Manuel Antonio Baca to Ventura Martín, 7 September 1838, Book 1 (large), pages 212–13, San Miguel County Deed Records.

69. MANM, Roll 40, frames 461–78. Las Vegas and Upper Town were transcribed by Julián Josué Vigil in *1845 Census of Las Vegas, New Mexico* (Springer, N.M.: Editorial Teleraña, 1985).

70. "*el estado de hambre y miseria a que se hallan reducidos los habitantes de ese territorio por el desarreglo de los Ayuntamtos y falta de tierras en que sembrar a resultas de tenerlas acopiadas unas cuantos particulares.*" SANM I, No. 1188. Governor Armijo's request was based on a directive to him from the president of Mexico, transmitted through the *Ministro de Relaciones Interiores y Exteriores.*

71. Salvador Montoya to the alcalde constitucional del Bado, San Miguel del Bado, 8 October, 1824. NMLG-SG, Roll 13, report 7, frames 7–8.

72. "*cuya decadencia . . . no estriba en la falta de terrenos sino en la de manos laboriosas.*" Governor Bartolomé Baca to the *diputación*, Santa Fe, 19 November 1824. NMLG-SG, Roll 12, report 7, frame 69.

73. NMLG-SG, Roll 13, report 7, frames 7–17.

74. Rafael Benavides, José Miguel García and Rafael García to the *alcalde constitucional del Bado*, San Antonio, 1 January 1838, SANM I, no. 1116.

75. The boundaries sought in this petition were, on the north el cerro del Tecolote; on the south, below the boundary of Montoya to the camino de los carros; on the east, the boundary of the Las Vegas Grant; and, on the west, La Cañada de Tres Hermanos. Petition of Rafael Benavides, José Miguel García

and Rafael García to the *Alcalde Constitucional del Bado,* San Antonio del Pueblo, January 31, 1838, SANM I, No. 1116.

76. *Alcalde* Rivera to Governor Manuel Armijo, San Miguel del Bado, February 1, 1838, SANM I, No. 1116.

77. Governor Armijo to Prefect Juan Andrés Archuleta, Santa Fe, February 12, 1838. SANM I, No. 1116.

78. Prefect Archuleta to el Ayuntamiento del Bado, Santa Fe, February 12, 1838, SANM I, No. 1116.

79. *Juez de Paz* Manuel Antonio Baca and *Juez de Paz* Vicente Rivera to Prefect Archuleta, San Miguel del Bado, 26 February 1838, SANM I, no. 1116.

80. We do not know who the two individuals referred to by the second Tecolote petitioners were, but early deed records disclose the following: a.) on 30 May 1826, Alcalde José Ramón Alarid allotted a 550 *vara* tract of irrigable land at the new settlement of Rio del Tecolote to Santiago Narvaiz; this tract was bounded on the north by lands of Antonio Martín and on the south by lands of Rafael Sena. Book 14, p. 78, San Miguel County Deed records; b.) on 10 September 1826 Rafael Sena had Alcalde José Ramón Alarid confirm the 1,000 *varas* of land he received at the time of the 1824 grant—he was bounded on the south by Miguel Quintana. Book 24, page 374, San Miguel County deed Records; c.) on 25 July 1829, *alcalde* Santiago Ulibarrí granted 1025 *varas* of land to Pedro Esperanza—this tract was bounded on the south by lands of Javier Mendosa. Book 1 (large), p. 216, San Miguel County deed records.

81. Petition of Rafael Benavides, José Miguel García, Juan de Dios Padilla and Rafael García to Prefect Archuleta, San Miguel del Bado, 15 March 1838, SANM I, No. 1116.

82. Order of Prefect Archuleta, Santa Fe, 24 March 1838, SANM I, no. 1116.

83. *Juez de Paz* Baca to *Juez de Paz* Rivera, Bado, 2 April 1838; report of *Juez de Paz* Rivera, San Antonio, 4 April 1838, SANM I, no. 1116.

84. Report of *Juez de Paz* Rivera, San Antonio, 4 April 1838, SANM I, no. 1116. Judge Baca suggested that perhaps the land involved was within the Las Vegas grant, but Rivera replied that it was not within the Las Vegas grant because those settlers had not partitioned the land among themselves and had allowed other people's cattle to graze there.

85. Decision of Prefect Archuleta, Rio Arriba, 7 April 1838, SANM I, no. 1116.

86. *Repartimiento* by *Juez de Paz* Baca, Partido de San Miguel del Bado, 16 April 1838, SANM I, no. 1116.

87. See for example, petition of Fernándo Durán y Chávez and Baltazar Romero on behalf of the citizens of Albuquerque to the Santa Fe Cabildo, Albuquerque, 1708, asking that the squadron of soldiers withdrawn by the

governor be restored. Twitchell, *Spanish Archives*, 1: 350–53, SANM I, no. 1205.

88. For Tecolote see, *Juez de Paz* Manuel Antonio Baca to Juan García, 19 April 1838, Book 1, pages 23–24, San Miguel County deed records; for Las Vegas see *Juez de Paz* Manuel Antonio Baca to Ventura Martín, 7 September 1838, Book 1, pages 212–13, San Miguel County deed records.

89. Petition of Manuel Antonio Baca, Santiago Ulibarrí, and Josef Gregorio Vigil to the *ayuntamiento* of San Miguel del Bado del Rio de Pecos, San Miguel del Bado, 12 April 1825. SANM I, no. 1153.

90. The other double overlap was the John Scolly grant which partially overlapped the Santiago Boné grant.

91. Other members of the Ulibarrí family put into possession at San José were: José Antonio, José Armigo, José de Jesús, and Francisco Ulibarrí, SANM I, No. 887.

92. Deed from Manuel Durán to Santiago Ulibarrí, San José del Bado, 1820; deed from Antonio Estrada to Santiago Ulibarrí, San Miguel del Bado, 19 October, 1825; deed from Francisco Ulibarrí to Santiago Ulibarrí, San Miguel del Bado, 31 May, 1832; deed from Toribio Baca to Santiago Ulibarrí, San José del Bado, 3 November 1833; and deed from José Archibeque to Santiago Ulibarrí, San Miguel del Bado, 7 July, 1834, Joe and Diana Stein Collection, NMSRCA, Santa Fe.

93. Commission of Santiago Ulibarrí as captain, Fifth Cavalry Company, First Regiment by Governor José Antonio Viscarra, Santa Fe, 7 April, 1823, Stein Collection, NMSRCA, Santa Fe. For Pino, see Hall, "Juan Estevan Pino," *NMHR*, 57: 28.

94. Petition of José Francisco Ulibarrí, José de Jesús Ulibarrí, Juan Griego, and Jesús González to Governor Armijo, San Miguel del Bado, 17 September, 1844, SANM I, No. 1026.

95. Petition of José de Jesus Ulibarrí to *juez de paz* Santiago Ulibarrí, San José del Bado, 20 March 1839, NMLG-PLC, Roll 50, case 170, frame 13. All the Sanguijuela documents in this file, except SANM 1, no. 1026, are typescripts. These documents were recorded in Book 1 (large), pp. 138–40, San Miguel County Deed Records in 1855 and were copied in 1889 and submitted to the Surveyor General by Russell B. Rice. NMLG-SG, Roll 15, report 20, frames 401–05.

96. Grant by *juez de paz* Santiago Ulibarrí, San Miguel del Bado, 22 March 1839. NMLG-PLC, Roll 50, case 170, frame 13.

97. Approval of Sanguijuela grant by Governor Armijo, Santa Fe, 8 May 1842. NMLG-PLC, Roll 50, case 170, frame 13.

98. Act of possession by *juez de paz* Juan de Dios Maese, Las Vegas, 4 July

1842. NMLG-PLC, Roll 50, case 170, frames 13–14. The boundaries of the Sanguijuela grant are confused by the fact that the petition requested a league in each direction, while the act of possession refers both to a league in circumference and to natural landmarks as defining the boundaries.

99. Testimony of Juan A. Bernal, Santa Fe, 10 June 1898. NMLG-PLC, Roll 50, case 170, frame 173.

100. José Francisco Ulibarrí to the governor, San Miguel del Bado, 17 September 1844, SANM I, No. 1026.

101. The claimants of the Sanguijuela grant before the Court of Private Land Claims were not able to produce title papers acceptable to the court so the claim was rejected. NMLG-PLC, Roll 50, case 170, frames 195–96. It is strange that the Sanguijuela grant documents were recorded in the San Miguel County deed records (Book 1, pp. 138–40) after José Francisco Ulibarrí had said they were lost and before the grant claimants told the Court of Private Land Claims that they were missing.

102. Testimony at the Court of Private Land Claims indicated that José Ulibarrí and Juan Griego ordered others not to graze their sheep on the grant. Testimony of Juan A. Bernal, Santa Fe, 10 June 1898. NMLG-PLC, Roll 50, case 170, frame 173.

103. Petition of Pedro Alcantar Vigil and nineteen others to Governor José Chavez, Santa Fe, 9 April 1845, NMLG-PLC, Roll 53, case 242, frames 34–36. The sketch map submitted to the Court of Private Land Claims shows that the cardinal directions of each boundary in the petition need to be moved clockwise for them to make sense. Thus the eastern boundary of the town of Mora is shifted to the north on the sketch map and so forth.

104. *Asamblea* to the prefects of the first and second districts, Santa Fe, 10 April 1845. NMLG-PLC, Roll 53, case 242, frame 36. Prefect Antonio Sena to *juez de paz* of Las Vegas. NMLG-PLC, Roll 53, case 242, frames 36–37. Diego Lucero to the *juez de paz* of Mora. NMLG-PLC, Roll 53, case 242, frame 37.

105. Report of the Las Vegas *juez de paz* Hilario Gonzales, Vegas, 19 May 1845 and Report of Prefect Antonio Sena, Santa Fe, 9 June 1845. NMLG-PLC, Roll 53, case 242, frames 39–40.

106. Grant by the *asamblea*. NMLG-PLC, Roll 53, case 242, frame 40.

107. SANM I, no. 918.

108. Report of committee composed of José Chávez and Santiago Martínez investigating the John Scolly grant, Santa Fe, 2 January 1845. SANM I, no. 918.

109. Act of possession by *Juez de Paz* Jesús María Montoya, 13 May 1846. NMLG-SG, Roll 13, report 9, frames 524–26.

110. Act of possession by *Juez de Paz* Juan Antonio García, 26 October 1842. NMLG-SG, Roll 40, case 62.

111. Ross Calvin, ed., *Lieutenant Emory Reports: A Reprint of Lieutenant W. H. Emory's Notes of a Military Reconnoissance* (Albuquerque: University of New Mexico Press, 1951), pp. 46–47.

112. SANM I, no. 1095. Fort Union provided additional protection.

113. In 1839 Santiago Ulibarrí made a grant of land to Juan and Ignacio Lucero at the Cañada de los Ojitos Frios at the confluence of Tecolote Creek and Ojitos Frios Creek. Grant by *Juez de Paz* Santiago Ulibarrí at the Cañada de los Ojitos Frios, San Miguel del Bado, 4 May 1839. Stein Collection, document 22, frame 49.

114. In 1841 Santiago Ulibarrí made two grants at Agua Sarca, four miles southwest of Las Vegas, to Tomás Martín and to María Concepción Blea, the wife of José Antonio Ulibarrí. Grant by *Juez de Paz* Santiago Ulibarrí at the Aqua Sarca, San Miguel del Bado, 14 April 1841 and 12 August 1841. Stein Collection, documents 25 and 26, frames 55–58.

115. Grant by *Juez de Paz* Santiago Ulibarrí to Manuel de Herrera of a tract of land 2,000 varas in circumference at Cañada del Salitre. Book 1, p. 46, San Miguel County deed records.

116. These grants include Cristóbal de la Serna, Francisca Antonio de Gijosa, Antonio Martínez, Los Luceros or Antoine Leroux, Antonio Martín, Don Fernando de Taos, and Arroyo Hondo. For a detailed study of the patterns of settlement and land ownership in the Taos Valley as they relate to irrigation there, see John O. Baxter, *Spanish Irrigation in Taos Valley*, (study prepared for the New Mexico State Engineer Office, Santa Fe, 1990).

117. For discussions of the settlement of the Tierra Amarilla grant north of Abiquiú see Robert J. Torrez," The San Juan Gold Rush of 1860 and Its Effect on the Development of Northern New Mexico, " *NMHR* 63 (July 1988): 257.

118. *Encomienda* tribute came in the form of one *fanega* of corn and one cotton blanket per Pueblo household. Mrs. Edward E. Ayer, trans., *The Memorial of Fray Alonso de Benavides* (Albuquerque: Horn and Wallace, 1965), pp. 23 and 105. Factors making Pueblo tribute more difficult to provide were drought, Apache raids, and forced labor required by corrupt governors. Snow, "Encomienda Economics," *Hispanic Arts and Ethnohistory*, pp. 350, 353–54.

119. The supplement to Frances Leon Swadesh, Julián Wilfredo Vigil, and Marina Baldonado Ochoa, *The Lands of New Mexico* (Santa Fe: Museum of New Mexico, 1975) lists 80 community land grants of which 37 percent were granted before 1800 and 63 percent between 1800 and 1853.

120. Testimony of Juan A. Bernal, Santa Fe, 10 June 1898. NMLG-PLC, Roll 50, case 170, frame 173.

121. When the Mora and Las Vegas officials were asked about the advisability of the Manuelitas grant, the question put to them was whether the land had any

owners or was vacant public land (*baldías*). When the Mora and Las Vegas officials both claimed the land, the issue became whether they would agree to the Manuelitas grant. NMLG-PLC, Roll 53, case 242, frames 36–39.

122. Iris Engstrand, "Introduction," to Daniel Tyler, *The Mythical Pueblo Rights Doctrine* (El Paso: Texas Western Press, 1990), p. 3. *Cartwright v. Public Service Co. of New Mexico*, 66 N.M. 64, 79–85.

123. The reasons why the "Pueblo Rights Doctrine" is false have been explored by Daniel Tyler and Iris Engstrand. Professor Engstrand traces the legal history of the doctrine back from the *Cartwright* case to several California cases which first recognized the supposed doctrine. Nowhere in these California cases is there a reference to the source of the doctrine under Hispanic law. The only authorities cited are Joaquín Escriche and the Plan of Pitic, but neither provides any basis for the Pueblo Rights Doctrine, which was apparently made up out of whole cloth by the California courts and then blindly applied to New Mexico and the Las Vegas grant by the New Mexico Supreme Court. Engstrand, "Introduction" to Tyler, *Mythical Pueblo Rights Doctrine*, pp. 1–20. Tyler, *Mythical Pueblo Rights Doctrine*, passim.

124. Tyler, *Mythical Pueblo Rights Doctrine*, pp. 41–45.

125. Although the conclusion of a line of reasoning based on an invalid premise is itself invalid, it is useful to view the historical development of Las Vegas in light of the erroneous "pueblo rights doctrine" in order to expose more fully the doctrine's errors. The first problem with the *Cartwright* analysis is that numerous settlements existed in the Las Vegas area, and it would have been inconceivable for he Mexican authorities to give a prior and paramount water right to one community at the expense of the other communities.

126. It has been assumed that the "pueblo rights doctrine" would apply to the *villa* of Albuquerque. Richard E. Greenleaf, "The Founding of Albuquerque, 1706: An Historical-Legal Problem," *NMHR* 39 (January 1964): 1–15. However, recent scholarship has pointed out that Albuquerque did not meet the requirements of the *Recopilación* and that its status as a *villa* was fraudulently obtained. Marc Simmons, *Albuquerque, A Narrative History* (Albuquerque: University of New Mexico Press, 1982), pp. 87–92.

127. Wells Hutchins, "Pueblo Water Rights in the West," *Texas Law Review* 38 (1960): 749; Robert Emmet Clark, "The Pueblo Rights Doctrine in New Mexico," *NMHR* 35 (October 1960): 275–83; Jefferson E. LeCates, "Water Law - The Effects of Acts of the Sovereign on the Pueblo Rights Doctrine in New Mexico," *Natural Resources Journal* 8 (October 1968): 727–37; and Anastasia S. Stevens, "Pueblo Water Rights in New Mexico," *Natural Resources Journal* 28 (Summer 1988): 535–83.

128. *Cartwright* says that the doctrine was derived from the Plan for the Villa

of San Pedro de la Conquista del Pitic, now Hermosillo, Sonora. *Cartwright v. Public Service Co. of New Mexico,* 66 N.M. 64, 82, 343 P. 2d 654 (1958).

129. Engstrand, "Introduction," to Tyler, *Mythical Pueblo Rights. Cartwright v. Public Services Co. of New Mexico,* 66 N.M. 64, 79–85, 343 P. 2d 654 (1958).

130. *Recopilación de Leyes de los Reynos de las Indios,* (1681), Book 4, title 7, law 1; Book 4, title 8, law 6; and Book 4, title 10, law 2.

131. Marc Simmons, "Settlement Patterns and Village Plans in Colonial New Mexico," *Journal of the West* 8 (January 1969): 7–21.

132. Zelia Nuttal, "Royal Ordnances Concerning the Laying out of New Towns," *Hispanic American Historical Review* 4 (November 1921): 743–53. For a specific town plan see, Lota M. Spell, "The Grant and First Survey of the City of San Antonio," *Southwestern Historical Quarterly* 66 (July 1962): 73–89.

133. This Los Alamos is not to be confused with the larger community in Los Alamos county.

134. Book 1 (large), p. 195, San Miguel County deed records; *Trambley v. Luterman,* 6 N.M. 15, 17–18.

135. Lynn I. Perrigo, *Hispanos: Historic Leaders in New Mexico* (Santa Fe: Sunstone Press, 1985), pp. 26–28.

Chapter 9: "Not a pepper, not an onion"

1. The Santa Fe Trail split into two branches just before it reached Kearny's Gap. One passed through the Puerto del Norte, the other negotiated the Puerto del Sur and then it also divided into two branches. Marc Simmons, *Following the Santa Fe Trail: A Guide for Modern Travelers* (Santa Fe: Ancient City Press, 1984), pp. 187–89.

2. Calvin, ed., *Lieutenant Emory Reports,* pp. 49–51; Lynn Perrigo, *Gateway to Glorieta* (Boulder: Pruett Publishing Company, 1982), pp. 12–13; Ralph Emerson Twitchell, *The Leading Facts of New Mexico History,* 2 vol. (Albuquerque: Horn and Wallace, 1963), 2: 199–205.

3. Kearny's proclamation in Las Vegas is quoted in Calvin, *Lieutenant Emory Reports,* pp. 49–51. Written proclamations were issued from Kearny's base at Bent's Fort on 31 July 1846 and later in Santa Fe on 22 August 1846, neither of which were as broad in their promises of protection of property and religion as was the oral proclamation in Las Vegas. Richard N. Ellis, *New Mexico Historic Documents* (Albuquerque: University of New Mexico Press, 1975), pp. 3–5. SANM I, no. 1113; David J. Weber, ed., *Foreigners,* p. 161. Perrigo, *Gateway to Glorieta,* pp. 12–13.

4. An Act to confirm certain private land claims in the Territory of New

Mexico, chapter 167, 12 Stat. 71 (1860). This was the only time in the annals of New Mexico's land grant adjudication that the same land was confirmed to two competing claimants.

5. Testimony of José Francisco Salas, House Exec. Doc. No. 14, 36th Cong.,1st Sess., p. 2.

6. Brief of Claimants by Watts and Jackson, Opinion of surveyor general William Pelham, Santa Fe, 18 December 1858, NMLG-SG, Roll 15, report 20, frames 75–82. Bowden, "Private Land Claims" 3: 797–98.

7. Bowden, "Private Land Claims," 3: 787–88.

8. The Town of Tecolote grant was confirmed by Congress on 22 December 1858 and was first surveyed in August 1859. Tecolote's north boundary of "*la cueva*" as surveyed in 1859, became the south boundary of the Las Vegas grant since the prior confirmation and survey of the Tecolote grant gave it paramount title. *Jones v. St. Louis Land Co.*, 232 U.S.355. The John Scolly grant also conflicted with a portion of the Las Vegas grant. Both were confirmed by the Act Congress of 21 June 1860, but the Scolly grant was recognized as being superior to Las Vegas to the extent that it conflicted with that grant. Bowden, "Private Land Claims," 3: 733 and 788, *Jones v. St. Louis Land Co.* The northern boundary of the Antonio Ortiz grant also determined a portion of the southern boundary of the Las Vegas grant because the Ortiz grant was given as a boundary call in the Las Vegas grant documents. The Ortiz grant was confirmed in 1869, surveyed in 1876, and patented in 1877. But it was not until 1893 that a controversy over the northern boundary was settled by a decision of Secretary of the Interior Hoke Smith. Bowden, "Private Land Claims," 3:708–10.

9. Ralph Emerson Twitchell, *The History of the Military Occupation of the Territory of New Mexico* (Chicago: The Rio Grande Press, 1963 reprint), pp. 174–75; Twitchell, *Leading Facts*, pp. 272–73.

10. Houghten's letter to the General Land Office (GLO) "urging issue of [the] patent . . ." is referred to in GLO Commissioner to Houghten, Washington, D.C., 4 May 1875, NMLG-SG, Roll 15, report 20, frames 90–91. Houghten's letter to Surveyor General James K. Proudfit enclosed the above letter and asked Proudfit for suggestions "to hasten the issue of this patent." Houghten to Surveyor General, Las Vegas, 14 May 1875. NMLG-SG, Roll 15, report 20, frames 92–93.

11. GLO Commissioner to Houghten, Washington, D.C., 4 May 1875, NMLG-SG, Roll 15, report 20, frames 90–91.

12. The boundaries that the GLO wanted located were, the Sapello River, the Aguaje de la Yequa, and the parts of the Antonio Ortiz and San Miguel del Bado grants that adjoined the Las Vegas grant. GLO to Surveyor General, Washington, D.C., 21 July 1875, NMLG-SG, Roll 15, report 20, frames 94–97.

13. Affidavit of Jesús Gonzales y Vigil, NMLG-SG, Roll 15, report 20, frames 99–100; affidavit of John B. Taylor, frames 101–103, and affidavit of Robert J. Hamilton, NMLG-SG, Roll 15, report 20, frames 105–7.

14. Brief or Statement of Joab Houghten, n.d., NMLG-SG, Roll 15, report 20, frames 109–21.

15. GLO to Surveyor General, Washington, D.C., 20 March 1878, NMLG-SG, Roll 15, report 20, frames 124–127.

16. Affidavit of Antonio Baca y Baca, NMLG-SG, Roll 15, report 20, frames 135–37, affidavit of Miguel Segura, NMLG-SG, Roll 15, report 20, frames 138–40 and affidavit of Pablo Montoya, NMLG-SG, Roll 15, report 20, frames 141–44, Santa Fe, 16 April 1878.

17. Francisco Baca y Sandoval to Surveyor General Atkinson, Santa Fe, 16 April 1878, NMLG-SG, Roll 15, report 20, frame 133.

18. GLO to Surveyor General, Washington, D.C., 31 May 1878, NMLG-SG, Roll 15, report 20, frames 108–24 (third series).

19. GLO to Surveyor General, Washington, D.C., 5 May 1884, NMLG-SG, Roll 15, report 20, frames 175–76.

20. GLO to Surveyor General, Washington, 3 December 1878, NMLG-SG, Roll 15, report 20, frames 166–67; 13 June 1881, NMLG-SG, Roll 15, report 20, frames 169–70; 10 August 1881, NMLG-SG, Roll 15, report 20, frames 172–73; 5 May 1884, NMLG-SG, Roll 15, report 20, frames 175–76; and 27 May 1884, NMLG-SG, Roll 15, report 20, frames 178–84.

21. U.S. Congress, Senate Exec. Doc. 113, 49th Cong., 2d sess., 1887, p. 2, quoted in Bowden, "Private Land Claims," 1: 224.

22. Julian was asking for an additional $27,000 to finance his work. Harold H. Dunham, *Government Handout: A Study in the Administration of the Public Lands, 1875–1891* (1941: reprint ed., New York: Da Capo Press, 1970), p. 256. R. Hal Williams, "George W. Julian and Land Reform in New Mexico, 1885–1889," *Agricultural History* 41 (January 1967): 84.

23. *Tameling v. U.S. Freehold and Emigration Co.*, 93 U.S. 644 (1876).

24. GLO to Julian, Washington, April 16, 1887, NMLG-SG, Roll 15, report 20, frames 188–92. This letter quotes Julian's letter of 22 March 1887.

25. GLO to Julian, Washington, April 16, 1887, NMLG-SG, Roll 15, report 20, frames 179–83 (third series).

26. Surveying private allotments within a land grant had never been attempted by 1887. Vague descriptions and lack of monuments on the ground made the task difficult. This was compounded by the fact that many of the original tracts had changed hands, deeds were often not recorded, and the county deed records were poorly organized, making it virtually impossible to

obtain a complete chain of title for any of the tracts. Will M. Tipton to Julian, Santa Fe, 18 July 1887, NMLG-SG, Roll 15, report 20, frames 228–38.

27. NMLG, Roll 35, case 23, frame 15.

28. Tipton was on the crew that surveyed the exterior boundaries of the San Joaquín grant in 1878. That survey was so controversial that Tipton later stated he did not agree with the location of the survey line, and charged that the affidavits of witnesses who had pointed out landmarks serving as boundaries were forged. See chapter 7, "The San Joaquín Grant," note 38 and corresponding text.

29. Tipton to Julian, Santa Fe, 18 July 1887, NMLG-SG, Roll 15, report 20, frames 228–38.

30. Affidavit of Tomás Ulibarrí, Las Vegas (Plaza Hotel), 24 June 1887, NMLG-SG, Roll 15, report 20, frames 199–205.

31. Affidavit of Juan Aragón, Las Vegas (Plaza Hotel), 28 June 1887, NMLG-SG, Roll 15, report 20, frames 207–15.

32. Affidavit of Ramón Ulibarrí, Las Vegas (Plaza Hotel), 5 July 1887, NMLG-SG, Roll 15, report 20, frames 217–26.

33. Tipton to Julian, Santa Fe, 18 July 1887, NMLG-SG, Roll 15, report 20, frames 228–238.

34. Rice to Julian, Las Vegas, 24 December 1887, NMLG-SG, Roll 15, report 20, frames 246–257.

35. Bowden, "Private Land Claims," 3: 790.

36. Rice to Julian, Las Vegas, 24 December 1887, NMLG-SG, Roll 15, report 20, frames 246–57.

37. Knowlton, "The Las Vegas Community Land Grant," pp. 16–17.

38. Chris Emmett, *Fort Union and the Winning of the Southwest* (Norman: University of Oklahoma Press, 1965), passim; William J. Parish, *The Charles Ilfeld Company: A Study of the Rise and Decline of Mercantile Capitalism in New Mexico* (Cambridge: Harvard University Press, 1961), p. 41; Perrigo, *Gateway to Glorieta*, pp. 15 and 17–19.

39. A summary of this case together with a full quotation of the court's order is found in John W. Noble, Secretary, Department of the Interior to the GLO, Washington, D.C., 5 December 1891, NMLG-SG, Roll 15, report 20, frames 306, 332–38. See also Knowlton, "The Las Vegas Community Land Grant," p. 17.

40. Robert J. Rosenbaum, *Mexicano Resistance in the Southwest: "The Sacred Right of Self-Preservation"* (Austin: University of Texas Press, 1981), pp. 104–24.

41. Elisha V. Long, *History of the Las Vegas Grant* (East Las Vegas: J. A. Carruth, 1890); the copy in the E. V. Long papers at the New Mexico State

Records Center and Archives bears the notation "This is my last copy — Please return. E. V. Long." Anthony White, *"Millhiser v. Padilla*: Litigation on the Las Vegas Land Grant, 1887–1889," (unpublished manuscript), pp. 15–16.

42. Anthony White, *"Millhiser v. Padilla,"* pp. 15–16.

43. Long, *History of the Las Vegas Grant*, refers to 25 instead of 29 grantees.

44. Long, *History of the Las Vegas Grant*, pp. 56–58.

45. The petitioners for the Las Vegas grant sought "the development of agriculture" (*el fomento de la agricultura*) and the *ayuntamiento* said it was "desirous of encouraging the advancement of agriculture" (*deseosa de protejer el aumento de la agricultura*), NMLG-SG, Roll 15, report 10, frames 8 and 58–59. Long, *History of the Las Vegas Grant*, pp. 59–62.

46. Rosenbaum, *Mexicano Resistance*, p. 103, note 13.

47. Long, *History of the Las Vegas Grant*, pp. 71–72. The Padillas did not seek to have their title to the common lands determined but merely asked the court to dismiss the complaint against them.

48. Long, *History of the Las Vegas Grant*, p. 73.

49. Rosenbaum, *Mexicano Resistance*, pp. 104–5.

50. Noble to the GLO, Washington, D.C., 5 December 1891, NMLG-SG, Roll 15, report 20, frame 344; Westphall, *The Public Domain in New Mexico*, pp. 105–8; Perrigo, *Gateway to Glorieta*, p. 107; Fraudulent homestead entries on the Las Vegas grant were part of a larger problem throughout the west. In April 1887 and investigation of selected townships in nine western states by the General Land Office revealed that out of 1416 entries under the Homestead and Preemption laws, in only 268 cases were all legal requirements met. Dunham, *Government Handout*, pp. 210–11.

51. Eugenio Romero was a vehement opponent of Las Gorras Blancas and is credited with a leading role in breaking up the organization. Eugenio and his property were frequently the object of White Cap attacks. Once three members of the organization entered his house at night to kill him but awoke him when they stumbled over a table. Romero scared them away when he fired into the air, and the trio were later arrested and convicted. Maurilio E. Vigil, *Los Patrones: Profiles of Hispanic Political Leaders in New Mexico History* (Washington, D.C.: University Press of America, 1980), p. 72, profiles of Trinidad Romero and Eugenio Romero are found at pp. 63–73. See also, Perrigo, *Gateway to Glorieta*, pp. 112, 116–17, and Arellano, *"Las Vegas Grandes,"* pp. 260–61.

52. Robert J. Rosenbaum and Robert W. Larson, "Mexicano Resistance to the Expropriation of Grant Lands in New Mexico," in Charles L. Briggs and John R. Van Ness, *Land, Water, and Culture* (Albuquerque: University of New Mexico Press, 1987), p. 289; Rosenbaum, *Mexicano Resistance*, pp. 137–38.

53. Parrish, *The Charles Ilfeld Company*, p. 176, note 24. The fencing of the

Las Vegas common lands had an earlier counterpart in the enclosure movement in England. G. M. Trevelyan, *English Social History* (New York: David McKay, 1942), pp. 116, 300, 576, 379, and 537.

54. One historian blames discontent on the Las Vegas grant with the corruption of wealthy merchants and speculators like the Romero family. He states that Las Gorras Blancas had a Robin Hood or Billy the Kid type image as champions of Hispanics who were being squeezed out of their traditional grazing lands. Parrish, *The Charles Ilfeld Company*, p. 176, notes 24 and 28.

55. Henry D. and Frances T. McCallum, *The Wire That Fenced the West* (Norman: University of Oklahoma Press, 1965), pp. 3–74.

56. Arellano, *"Las Vegas Grandes,"* pp. 305–311; Rosenbaum, *Mexicano Resistance*, pp. 103–9.

57. Rice to Noble, Las Vegas, 7 May 1890, NA, RG 49, NM PLC 20; Book 26, p. 528, and Book 27, p. 41, San Miguel County Deed Records.

58. In *Smith v. Raynolds*, 166 U.S. 717 (1896), the U.S. Supreme Court reversed the Court of Appeals of the District of Columbia for failure to name the proper parties, on the authority of *Warner Valley Stock Co. v. Smith*, 165 U.S. 28; Rice to Charles F. Easley, Las Vegas, 16 December 1893, NMLG-SG, Roll 15, report 20 frames 375–78; Noble to GLO, Washington, D. C., 5 December 1891, NMLG-SG, Roll 15, report 20, frames 306–49.

59. The Town of Las Vegas Grant, 27 L.D. 683 (1898).

60. *Maese v. Herman*, 183 U.S. 572 (1901).

61. Arellano, *"Las Vegas Grandes,"* pp. 339–47.

62. Acceptance of Appointment as Trustees, Cause No. 5545, San Miguel County District Court, E. V. Long Collection, 1902–1909, NMSRCA. Knowlton, "The Town of Las Vegas Community Land Grant," p. 20; Rosenbaum and Larson, "Mexicano Resistance," p. 293. Perrigo, *Gateway to Glorieta*, pp. 115–16.

63. Donald L. Craig, "Land, Water, and Education: An Administrative History of the Las Vegas Land Grant (M.A. Thesis, New Mexico Highlands University, 1990), pp. 23–25.

64. Knowlton, "The Town of Las Vegas Community Land Grant," p. 20.

65. Sec. 1, chapter 47, 1903 Laws; Anselmo F. Arellano, "People versus Trustees: Protest Activity on the Las Vegas Land Grant, 1902–1907," p. 8.

66. Arellano, *"Las Vegas Grandes,"* p. 353, Perrigo, *Gateway to Glorieta*, pp. 117–118.

67. E. V. Long received 2,560 acres for services rendered, while his law partner received 15,000 acres for securing the patent. Eugenio Romero was paid 1,920 acres to settle a claim his father had made against the board. Craig, "Administrative History of the Las Vegas Land Grant," pp. 21, 26–27; Perrigo,

Gateway to Glorieta, p. 123. An example of a mini-grant within the Las Vegas Community land grant is the deed of 3,296 acres to the trustees of the communities of San Agustín and La Concepción by deed dated 16 September 1929 and recorded in Book 163, pp. 186–88, San Miguel County deed book.

68. Daniel Tyler,"Ejido Lands in New Mexico," in Ebright, ed., *Spanish and Mexican Land Grants and the Law*, p. 34.

69. Clark S. Knowlton, "The Town of Las Vegas Community Land Grant," pp. 18–20. In the spring of 1890, Judge James O'Brien dismissed charges against Juan José Herrera and forty-six others charged with fence cutting, when the prosecution's witnesses failed to appear. Rosenbaum, *Mexicano Resistance*, pp. 103, 108–9.

Chapter 10: The Ramón Vigil Grant

1. The Ramón Vigil grant was one of several grants confirmed by Congress in 1860, the first land grant confirmations by that body. Chapter 167, 12 Stat. 71 (1860).

2. NMLG-SG, Reel 16, case 38, frames 1475, 1477–78. Surveyor General, Day Book C, Register of Land Titles, pp. 86–87, SRCA.

3. Report of Judith A. Housley, Forensic Document Examiner, 15 December 1992, Albuquerque.

4. Marjorie Bell Chambers, "Technically Sweet Los Alamos: The Development of a Federally Sponsored Scientific Community," (Ph.D. diss., University of New Mexico, 1974), pp. 15–16, n. 19.

5. Chambers was not able to find a document with a genuine Pedro Sánchez signature for comparison, "Los Alamos," p. 16, n. 19. With the help of Richard Salazar, New Mexico State Archivist, who discovered a document with a genuine Pedro Sánchez signature, it was possible to compare the authentic and the forged signatures. The document is an order by Governor Gervasio Cruzat y Góngora dated 12 June 1732, forbidding the sale of Apaches. Pedro Sánchez signed a certificate in 1733 stating that the decree had been read to the Spaniards and Indians in his jurisdiction. SANM II, No. 378.

6. Petition of Felipe Tafoya, (first document in the archive, n.d.), SANM I, No. 1351.

7. Fray Angelico Chavez, *Origins of New Mexico Families*, (Reprint ed.; Santa Fe: William Gannon, 1975) pp. 279–80.

8. Chambers, "Los Alamos," p. 17.

9. Fray Angelico Chavez, "Addenda to New Mexico Families," *El Palacio* 65 (1957): 184; Chavez, *New Mexico Families*, pp. 279–80.

10. Gaspar Domingo de Mendoza was governor of New Mexico from 1739 to 1743. Lansing B. Bloom, "The Governors of New Mexico," *NMHR* 10: 155.

11. Petition of Pedro Sanchez to Governor Gaspar Domingo de Mendoza, Santa Cruz, n.d., NMLG-SG, Reel 16, report 38, frame 1477.

12. Granting decree of Governor Gaspar Domingo de Mendoza, Santa Fe, 20 March 1742. NMLG-SG, Reel 16, report 38, frames 1477–78. The period within which the grantee was required to settle the grant was three months, though this period could be extended if the circumstances warranted it. *Recopilación*, Libro 4, titulo 12, ley 11. The three month requirement was extended to a year by Governor Cruzat in the case of the Bartolomé Trujillo grant. The grant was made in August and the settlers were not able to take possession until the next spring due to winter weather. Bowden, "Private Land Claims in the Southwest," 4: 1124.

13. As was true of the Picuris Pueblo when the Embudo grant was made, San Ildefonso was not represented at this important juncture. Later it was determined that Pedro Sánchez was encroaching on San Ildefonso land. See notes 18–21 and 24–26 and corresponding text (this chapter).

14. Act of Possession by *Alcalde* Juan José Lobato, Santa Cruz, 28 March 1742. NMLG-SG, Reel 16, report 38, frame 1475.

15. "*Mordieron los lobos a sus pastores. . . ,*" Act of possession and other documents of the Black Mesa grant, NMLG-PLC, Reel 39, case 56, frames 6–9.

16. Decree of Governor Tomás Vélez Cachupín, 21 February 1750. SANM 1, No. 1100.

17. Bartolomé Trujillo grant, SANM I, No. 976, NMLG-PLC, Roll 52, case 263, frames 490ff. Bowden, "Private Land Claims," 4: 1123–28.

18. The right of every New Mexican Indian Pueblo to four square leagues of land (the Pueblo league), was based more on custom than on formal law. However, the *Recopilación* does provide for a four square league settlement in the case of Spanish grants in Book 4, title 5, law 6, and in Book 4, title 5, law 10 where a group of at least ten married men agree to form a settlement. The Plan of Pitic refers to both these laws and indicates that they applied to settlements as large as Spanish villas. The 1789 Plan of Pitic provided for the founding of the Spanish villa of Pitic, now Hermosillo, Sonora. SANM I, 1265. While this document specifically applied to other settlements later established in New Mexico, some experts believe that it expresses the law in New Mexico for the seventeenth and eighteenth centuries also. Greenleaf, "Land and Water in Mexico and New Mexico," 103. William B. Taylor notes fourteen instances in New Mexico where the four square league standard is mentioned concerning Indian Pueblos. "Colonial Land and Water Rights of New Mexico Indian Pueblos," (unpublished manuscript), p. 44.

19. Petition of Felipe Tafoya (first document in the archive, n.d.), SANM I, No. 1351.

20. Order of Governor Tomás Vélez Cachupín, Santa Fe, 4 February 1763. SANM I, No. 1351.

21. *Alcalde* Carlos Fernandez to Governor Vélez Cachupín, Soledad, 21 February 1763. SANM I, No. 1351.

22. Statement of Juan Gómez del Castillo, n.d., SANM I, No. 1351.

23. Order of Governor Vélez Cachupín, Santa Fe, 12 November 1763. SANM I, No. 1351.

24. Opinion of *Licenciado* Fernando de Torijay y Leri, Chihuahua, 27 October 1764. SANM I, No. 1351.

25. Order of Governor Vélez Cachupín, Santa Fe, 12 April 1765. SANM I, No. 1351.

26. Report of *Alcalde* Antonio José Ortiz, San Ildefonso, 24 April 1765. SANM I, No. 1351.

27. Surveyor General, Day Book C, Register of Land Titles, p. 86, SRCA.

28. Surveyor General, Day Book C, Register of Land Titles, pp. 86–87, SRCA.

29. After the grant had been confirmed and sold several times, Victoria, Mariano, and Bárbara Sánchez filed a suit to quiet title to their three–eleventh interest and to partition the grant, claiming that they were the heirs who did not join in the conveyance to Ramón Vigil. *Manuel Sánchez v. George N. Fletcher,* New Mexico District Court Cause No. 4165, Santa Fe County. Prince Papers, SRCA.

30. Petition for confirmation, NMLG-SG, Reel 16, report 38, frames 1479–80.

31. NMLG-SG, Reel 16, report 38, frame 1486; chapter 167, 12 U.S. Statutes 71 (1860).

32. Bowden, "Private Land Claims," 4: 1219.

33. ". . . *merced que hallandose sera entregada al dueno que corresponde. . .*" Surveyor General, Day Book C, Register of Land Titles, SRCA, p. 87.

34. Rio del Oso grant, NMLG-SG, Reel 31, file 112, frames 672–73. Report of Judith A. Housley, Forensic Document Examiner, 15 September 1992, Albuquerque.

35. NMLG-PLC, Roll 43, case 97, frames 827–32.

36. Genealogy of Ramón Vigil prepared by Fred Vigil.

37. David J. Weber, *The Taos Trappers,* pp. 167–68; Robert Glass Cleland, *This Reckless Breed of Men,* pp. 213–14.

38. Weber, *Taos Trappers,* p. 159.

39. David Whiting Translation NMLG-SG, Reel 16, report 38, frames 1482–85.

40. The following grant documents were found to be or suspected of being forged: the Peralta-Reavis grant, the Uña del Gato grant, the Sopori grant, the Oreja del Llano de los Aguajes grant, the Corpus Christi grant, the Sierra Mosca grant, the Pueblo of San Cristobal grant, the Medano Springs and Zapato grant, the Ojita del Galisteo grant, the El Paso de los Algodones grant and the Pueblo of Laguna grant. Bowden, "Private Land Claims," 1: 305–6, n. 89.

41. NMLG-PLCD, Reel 35, case 23, frame 15.

42. Orejas del Llano de los Aguajes grant, NMLG-SG, Roll 24, report 117, frames 222 et seq.; NMLG-PLC, Roll 49, case 169, frames 1471 et seq.; Antonio Narbona was governor of New Mexico from 1825–1827. Bloom, "Governors of New Mexico," *NMHR* 10: 156. Bowden, "Private Land Claims," 4: 1022–31.

43. NMLG-PLC, Reel 35, case 23, frames 223–53, especially frame 228.

44. The proceedings in the Court of Private Land Claims for the Peralta-Reavis grant (PLC case 110) take up all of Rolls 62 and 63. Donald M. Powell, *The Peralta Grant*, (Norman: University of Oklahoma Press, 1960) discusses at pp. 90–99 the lapses in the documents presented by James Addison Reavis that alerted officials to their forgery. For Tipton's testimony see pp. 137–39. A popular account of the forgery of the Peralta grant is Clarence Budington Kelland, "The Red Baron of Arizona," *The Saturday Evening Post*, 11 October 1947, p. 97.

45. Rito de los Frijoles grant, NMLG-SG, Roll 25, report 133, frames 716–721; Bowden, "Private Land Claims," 4: 1227–28.

46. Rito de los Frijoles grant, NMLG-PLC, Roll 37, case 41, frames 348–50; Bowden, "Private Land Claims," 4: 1229–31.

47. W. J. Howlett, *Life of the Right Reverend Joseph P. Machebeuf* (Pueblo: Franklin Press, 1908), p. 213; Paul Horgan, *Lamy of Santa Fe*, (New York: Farrar, Straus and Giroux, 1975) p. 238.

48. Catholic directories for the years 1859 and 1865 through 1867; Diary of the Jesuit residence of our Lady of Guadalupe Parish, Conejos, Colorado, 31 July 1877.

49. Hayes is described as *"de caracter muy equivoco y de muy poco buen fama."* Jesuit Diary of San Felipe Neri Parish, Albuquerque, New Mexico, 20 September 1881, p. 306.

50. Thomas J. Steele, S. J., *Works and Days: A History of San Felipe Neri Church, 1867–1895* (Albuquerque: The Albuquerque Museum, 1983), pp. 57–58. The references in this note, and the preceding three notes are courtesy of Thomas J. Steele, S. J.

51. The debt was paid on 21 September 1864. Santa Fe County Deeds, Book C, p. 377.

52. Bernalillo County Deeds, Book O, p. 490. Reference courtesy Thomas Steele, S. J.

53. Santa Fe County Deeds, Book R2, p. 106. This deed was executed in Rome.

54. Santa Fe County Deeds, Book P1, pp. 249–50

55. Thomas Gwyn and John C. Duval to Thomas A. Hayes, Santa Fe, 16 September 1882. NMLG-SG, Reel 16, report 38, frames 1505–7.

56. Hayes to Henry M. Atkinson, Santa Fe, 16 September 1882. NMLG-SG, Reel 16, report 38, frame 1504.

57. Protest of Thomas A. Hayes. NMLG-SG, Reel 16, report 38, frames 1488–89.

58. Affidavit of Rafael Herrera, Manuel Luján, and Alejandro Gonzales, Affidavit of José Ramón Vigil, Affidavit of José Andrés Atencio, Affidavit of José María de Herrera, Affidavit of José Miguel Muñis, Affidavit of José Francisco Vigil, and Affidavit of José Benito Mestas. NMLG-SG, Reel 16, report 38, frames 1490–1503.

59. N. C. McFarland, Commissioner of the General Land Office to Surveyor General H. M. Atkinson, Washington, D.C., 10 April 1883, citing previous decision by that office in the case of the California Leavenworth grant on 24 April 1878. NMLG-SG, Reel 16, report 38, frames 1509–20.

60. The custom of granting mountain land for grazing and other uses was referred to in the affidavits of José Miguel Muñis, José Francisco Vigil, José Benito Mestas, and José María de Herrera. NMLG-SG, Roll 16, report 38, frames 1498, 1500, 1502, and 1496.

61. Surveyor General Atkinson to Thomas A. Hayes, Santa Fe, 16 April 1883. NMLG-SG, Reel 16, report 38, frame 1522; Sanchez v. Fletcher, Transcript of Hearing before E.P. Shield, Examiner, Prince Papers, NMSRCA.

62. Santa Fe County Deed Records, Book M, p. 572.

63. Most land grant speculators like Thomas B. Catron were unable to reap substantial profits on their investments. Catron, for instance, is said to have paid $200,000 for the Tierra Amarilla grant, which he eventually sold for $850,000 of which $495,000 was in cash. Even assuming Catron eventually got paid the total sales price, he would have made only 325 percent on his investment compared to the 2400 percent made by Father Hayes. Westphall, *Thomas Benton Catron*, pp. 46–60; Westphall, *Mercedes Reales*, p. 191.

64. William Conway, *Problems in Canon Law* (Westminster: Newman Press, 1956), p. 50 (reference courtesy Thomas J. Steele, S.J.).

65. Letter to author from Thomas J. Steele, S. J., 24 September 1984, and Hayes Folder, Archives of the Archdiocese of Santa Fe, Albuquerque.

66. Bruce T. Ellis, "Fraud Without Scandal: The Roque Lovato Grant and Gaspar Ortiz y Alarid," *NMHR* 57: 43–52 and n. 22.

67. Ellis, "Fraud Without Scandal," pp. 52–59.

68. Santa Fe County Deed Records, Book M, p. 572.

69. Edward Sheldon's profit, after paying $40,000 toward the purchase of the grant, was $4,000. Santa Fe County Deed Records, Book N, p. 423.

70. NMLG-SG, Reel 16, report 38, frame 1529.

71. Brief signed by Henry M. Atkinson, In the matter of the application for a resurvey of the Ramón Vigil grant. NMLG-SG, Reel 16, report 38, frames 1529–31.

72. NMLG-SG, Reel 16, report 38, frames 1533–39.

73. NMLG-SG, Reel 16, report 38, frame 1522.

74. Westphall, *The Public Domain in New Mexico, 1854–1891*, pp. 24–32.

75. See chapter 1, Notes 120–24, and corresponding text.

76. *Sanchez v. Fletcher*, Transcript, p. 21.

77. SANM I, No. 1351.

78. *Sanchez v. Fletcher*, Transcript, pp. 6, 13, 15 and 16.

79. The names of the heirs who were claimants represented by L. Bradford Prince in the lawsuit were Manuel Sánchez, Pedro A. Sánchez, María Concepcion Martínez, María Gertrudes Sánchez, María Faustina Rodríguez, Francisca Durán, Patrocinia Durán, Juliana Durán, Micaela Montes Vigil, Juan Montes Vigil, and Alejandro Montes Vigil. *Sanchez v. Fletcher*, Transcript, pp. 1A and 21.

80. Chambers, "Technically Sweet Los Alamos," pp. 30–33 and 36–37.; Cartwright v. U.S. Bank and Trust Co., 23 NM 82, 92–104; Rothman, "Pajarito Plateau," pp. 203–05.

81. *Cartwright v. U.S. Bank and Trust Co.*, pp. 99–106. For another example of a legal problem that was the recurring subject of litigation under three sovereigns, see G. Emlen Hall, "Land Litigation and the Idea of New Mexico Progress," in Malcolm Ebright, ed., *Spanish and Mexican Land Grants and the Law* (Manhattan, Kansas: Sunflower University Press, 1989), pp. 48–58.

82. The eight thousand dollar attorney's fee awarded to Francis C. Wilson was modest compared to the fee called for in an early version of the agreement with the U.S. Bank and Trust Co. Under that agreement, rejected because of the high fees, the attorneys would have received approximately twenty thousand dollars. *Cartwright v. U.S. Bank and Trust Co.*, pp. 99–145; Chambers, "Technically Sweet Los Alamos," p. 39.

83. Fermor and Peggy Pond Church, *When Los Alamos was a Ranch School*, (Los Alamos: Los Alamos Historical Society, 1974), p. 9.

84. Peggy Pond Church, "Trails Over Pajarito," unpublished manuscript, pp. 4–6; *Los Alamos: Beginning of an Era, 1943–1945*, p. 8; "Technically Sweet Los Alamos," pp. 38–39; Church, *Ranch School*, pp. 7–22.

85. Chambers, "Technically Sweet Los Alamos," p. 43; *Los Alamos: Beginning of an Era*, p. 9.

86. Church, *Ranch School*, p. 20–21; Rothman, *On Rims and Ridges*, pp. 214–25.

87. Church, *Ranch School*, p. 21; U.S. Department of the Interior, Geological Survey. Española Quadrangle.

88. Peggy Pond Church, *The House at Otowi Bridge* (Albuquerque: The University of New Mexico Press, 1959), p. 18.

Chapter 11: The Jacona Grant

1. See chapter 1, notes 105–24 and accompanying text.

2. See chapter 1, notes 140–68, and accompanying text.

3. See chapter 1, note 127 and accompanying text.

4. See chapter 1, notes 127–30, and accompanying text. For an excellent analysis of the ethical violations by New Mexico attorneys in connection with the partition statute, see David Benavides, "Lawyer-Induced Partitioning of New Mexican Land Grants: An Ethical Travesty," a paper presented for Professor Hall's seminar, UNM School of Law, Summer, 1990.

5. Charles T. DuMars and Malcolm Ebright, "Problems of Spanish and Mexican Land Grants in the Southwest: Their Origin and Extent," *The Southwestern Review of Management and Economics* 1 (Summer 1981): 195.

6. Chilili needed funds to redeem its common lands which had been lost to the state for delinquent taxes and the Farmers' Home Administration would loan the money only if the grant converted to an agricultural cooperative. DuMars and Ebright, "Problems of Spanish and Mexican Land Grants," *The Southwestern Review of Management and Economics*, 1 (Summer 1981): 196. Earlier cases involving the Chilili grant are *Merrifield v. Buckner*, 41 N.M. 442 (1937); and *Moya v. Chilili Cooperative Association*, 87 N.M. 99 (1974).

7. The Pueblo was a *visita* of the mission of Nambé in 1680. Hodge, *Handbook of American Indians North of Mexico* (1960), 1: 627.

8. Jacinto Peláez was a native of Villanueva in the Spanish province of Asturias. In 1691 he married Margarita Gomez Robledo, whose sister Francisca was wed to Ignacio Roybal. Fray Angelico Chavez, *Origins of New Mexico Families*, (Reprint ed.; Santa Fe: William Gannon, 1975), p. 256.

9. NMLG-SG, Roll 22, report 92, frame 354. About eighteen acres would be required to plant two fanegas of seed corn. A fanega was a measure of grain

ranging from 1.5 to 2.5 bushels, depending on the locality. Since the bulk measurement itself was not standard, the land measurement was quite inexact. Marc Simmons, *Spanish Government in New Mexico* (Albuquerque, 1968).

10. Petition of Ignacio Roybal and grant by Governor Pedro Rodriguez Cubero, Santa Fe, 2 October 1702. NMLG-SG, Roll 22, report 92, frames 354–56.

11. Deed from Juan de Mestas to Ignacio de Roybal, Santa Fe, 3 December 1705. SANM I, no. 735.

12. SANM I, no. 1339. See also G. Emlen Hall, "The Pueblo Grant Labyrinth", in Briggs and Van Ness, *Land, Water, and Culture.*

13. Chavez, *New Mexico Families*, pp. 36–37, John O. Baxter, "The Ignacio de Roybal House," *The Historic Santa Fe Foundation Bulletin*, vol. 6, no. 1 (January 1980).

14. SANM I, nos. 487, 488, and 1339. Alfred Barnaby Thomas, *After Coronado* (Norman: University of Oklahoma Press, 1935), pp. 106 and 253–54, Chavez, *New Mexico Families*, pp. xii, 273–75.

15. In that year Diego Brito, who had been banished from Santa Fe for being a scandalous and troublesome fellow — *un mozo escandoloso y ynquieto* — was ordered to serve Ignacio Roybal at Jacona for a year. Order of Alcalde Antonio Montoya, Santa Fe, 28 March 1702. SANM II, no 86. Reference courtesy of Richard Salazar.

16. The property was placed on the New Mexico State Register of Cultural Properties because of its historical importance. Baxter, "The Ignacio de Roybal House," passim.

17. Chavez, *New Mexico Families*, p. 275. Fray Angelico Chavez, "El Vicario Don Santiago Roybal," *El Palacio* 55 (August 1948): 231.

18. Governor Anza stated that he "granted . . . in the name of his majesty (whom God preserve) that portion of land which he [Mateo Roybal] possessed . . . which was made of the aforesaid Jacona to the Ensign Don Ignacio de Roybal . . ." SANM I, no. 1261.

19. MANM, Roll 42, frame 719.

20. Statement of Victor Garcia, Alcalde of San Ildefonso, 20 April 1836, Book A–1, Santa Fe County Deeds, p. 56.

21. Affidavit of Jesus María Ortiz before Surveyor General Proudfit, 5 June 1874. NMLG-SG, Roll 22, report 92, frames 362–63.

22. Samuel Ellison was appointed territorial librarian by 1881. He had custody of the Spanish and Mexican archives, many of which he translated, until they were turned over to the Surveyor General's office. J. Manuel Espinosa, "Memoir of A Kentuckian in New Mexico: 1848–1884," *NMHR* 13 (January 1937): 1.

23. Petition for confirmation of grant to Ignacio Roybal and Jacinto Peláez. NMLG-SG, Roll 22, report 92, frames 349–50.

24. It is not clear why the heirs of Jacinto Peláez were not included in the confirmation as requested in the petition. Opinion of Surveyor General James K. Proudfit, Santa Fe, 10 June 1874. NMLG-SG, Roll 22, report 92, frame 367.

25. Petition to Court of Private Land Claims for confirmation of the Jacona grant. NMLG-PLC, Roll 36, case 35, frames 472–75.

26. Bowden, "Private Land Claims," 3:536. Napoleon B. Laughlin was born at Grand Tower, Illinois, on 24 July 1844. After his graduation from the University of Missouri he moved to Texas, where he practiced law until he came to New Mexico in 1879. The following year he was elected to the lower house of the legislative assembly. In July 1894 he was appointed associate justice of the supreme court of New Mexico, and presided over the first judicial district. Ralph Emerson Twitchell, *Leading Facts,* 2:517, n. 435.

27. The Spanish code, *Las Siete Partidas,* supported this theory, which could have been used to confirm many other land grants that were rejected. *Las Siete Partidas,* Partida III, título 29, leyes 18 and 21.

28. Decree of Justice William Murray for the Court of Private Land Claims, 23 August 1893. NMLG-PLC, Roll 36, case 35, frames 539–42. Bowden, "Private Land Claims," 3:538–39.

29. Bowden, "Private Land Claims," 3:536, 539.

30. Complaint in cause no. 6323, Santa Fe District Court. Abstract, pp. 49–52. The plaintiffs in the lawsuit were Laughlin, Desiderio Gómez, Luis M. Ortiz, Camilo Martínez, and the heirs of Gaspar Ortiz y Alarid.

31. Affidavit of Publication in cause no. 6323, Santa Fe County District Court, Abstract, pp. 52–54. *Rodriguez v. La Cueva Ranch Co.,* 17 NM 246 (1912).

32. Motion for Default Judgement, and Default Judgement, action no. 6323, Santa Fe County District Court, Abstract, pp. 54–56.

33. Order of Reference, filed 23 January 1908, cause no. 6323, Santa Fe County District Court. Abstract, p. 57.

34. A. M. Leeson was appointed as referee and took testimony in "her office," at no. 23 Laughlin Building. Order of Reference, 23 January 1908 and Referee's Report, 26 March 1909, cause no. 6323, Santa Fe County District Court. Abstract, pp. 56–59.

35. Referee's Report, filed 26 March 1909, cause no. 6323, Santa Fe County District Court.

36. Authorization signed by Desiderio Gómez, Camilio Martín, and Anastasio Gómez, Santa Fe, 13 June 1893. NMLG-PLC, Roll 36, case 35, frame 515.

37. Decree Quieting Title, cause no. 6323, Santa Fe County District Court. Abstract, pp. 62–65

38. Report of Commissioners, cause no. 6323, Santa Fe County District Court. Abstract, pp. 65–66.

39. The commission appointed to divide or sell the Cañon de San Diego grant included several friends of the attorney involved in the case, A. B. McMillan. G. Taylor, "Notes on Community-Owned Land Grants in New Mexico," (Soil Conservation Service, 1937), pp. 7–8, U.N.M. Law Library.

40. Decree for Sale, cause no. 6323, Santa Fe District Court. Abstract, pp. 66–68

41. Agreement and Power of Attorney, 18 June 1909, recorded at Book Q–1 Santa Fe County Deeds, p. 184.

42. For Las Trampas, see chapter 3, Notes 55–56 and corresponding text. For Tierra Amarilla see, Ebright, *The Tierra Amarilla Grant*, pp. 25–27.

43. The commission was also referred to as the trustees of the Jacona grant or the board of directors of the Jacona grant. Quitclaim Deed to Nicacio Gallegos, 5 June 1952, recorded at Book 66, p. 94, Santa Fe County Deed Records; Lease to Manuel Roybal, 1 February 1954, recorded at Book 92, p. 289, Santa Fe County Miscellaneous Documents.

44. Partition Deed, 25 February 1919, recorded 27 February 1919 in Book C, Santa Fe County Contracts, p. 514.

45. The abstract of the Jacona grant contains numerous tax deeds beginning in 1934, whereby an interest in the Jacona grant was sold to the state for non-payment of taxes. The amounts involved were generally less than ten dollars, and many were less than one dollar. See, for example, tax deed no. 1289 from the Santa Fe County Treasurer to the State of New Mexico for delinquent taxes assessed to Aran Romero in the amount of fifty-six cents, 7 September 1937, recorded in Book 3, Santa Fe County Tax Deeds, p. 10. Abstract, p. 125.

46. Complaint, filed 7 May 1928 in Santa Fe County District Court cause no. 13032.

47. Final Decree filed 19 October 1928 in Santa Fe County District Court cause no. 13032.

48. Special Master's Deed, 9 February 1929, recorded on 19 November 1951 at Book 61, p. 89, Santa Fe County Deeds.

49. Chapter 49 of the New Mexico Statutes Annotated, set forth the rules for the operation of community grants recognized by the state of New Mexico.

50. Olen Leonard stated that, "with but few exceptions all grants in New Mexico eventually became community grants with. the addition of new families . . ." *The Role of the Land Grant in the Social Organization and Social*

Processes of a Spanish American Village in New Mexico (Albuquerque, 1970), p. 94, note 8.

51. Taylor, "Notes on Community Owned Land Grants," pp. 18–19.

52. Charles T. DuMars and Michael J. Rock, "The New Mexico Legal Rights Demonstration Land Grant Project — An Analysis of the Land Title Problems in the Santo Domingo de Cundiyo Land Grant," *New Mexico Law Review* 8 (Winter 1977–78): 1.

Chapter 12: Conclusion

1. *State ex rel. Reynolds and the U.S. and Taos Pueblo as Intervenor v. Eduardo Abeyta*, et al, U.S. District Court nos. 7896-SC and 7939-SC consolidated.

2. Emlen Hall, "San Miguel del Bado and the Loss of the Common Lands of New Mexico Community Land Grants," *NMHR* 66 (October 1991): 413–32.

3. Frances Levine, "Dividing the Water: The Impact of Water Rights Adjudication on New Mexican Communities," *Journal of the Southwest* 32 (Autumn 1990): 268–77; Frances Leon Quintana, "Land, Water, and Pueblo-Hispanic Relations in New Mexico," *Journal of the Southwest* 32 (Autumn 1990): 288–99.

4. For a discussion of the effect of local customs on Hispanic land and water rights see, Daniel Tyler, "The Role of Custom in Defining New Mexican Land and Water Rights," report filed in *State and U.S. v. Abeyta*, U.S. District Court causes no. 7896 and 7939, as well as Tyler's testimony in that case on 20 May 1991.

5. The state's expert historian in the Taos water rights adjudication implied that Spaniards were irrigating before 1680, but since any record of such irrigation had been destroyed, none of their *acequias* could have a priority date until after 1680. *State ex rel. Reynolds and the U.S. and Taos Pueblo as Intervenor v. Eduardo Abeyta, et al*, hearings 26 and 27 November, 1990; John O. Baxter, *Spanish Irrigation in Taos Valley*, (Santa Fe: New Mexico State Engineer Office, 1990), pp. 4–5.

6. John Nichols, *The Milagro Beanfield War* (New York: Holt, Rinehart and Winston, Inc., 1974); Stanley Crawford, *Mayordomo: Chronicle of an Acequia in Northern New Mexico* (Albuquerque: University of New Mexico Press, 1988).

7. Stanley Crawford, "Dancing for Water," *Journal of the Southwest* 32 (Autumn 1990): 265–67.

8. *U.S. v. Jose Paz Lopez et al.*, U.S. District Court cause nos. 81–180 and 81–181 consolidated.

9. *State ex. rel. Reynolds and Pecos Valley Artesian Conservation District v. L.T. Lewis, et al.*, Chavez County District Court cause nos. 20294 and 22600,

consolidated. This lawsuit aims at adjudication water rights on the Pecos River and its tributaries in New Mexico.

10. *Town of Jacona Land Grant Association v. Aamodt*, Santa Fe County District Court cause No. SF 85–575(C).

11. Reports in the Aamodt case (*State ex. rel. Reynolds v. R. Lee Aamodt, et al.*, U.S. District Court cause No. 6639), include Michael C. Meyer and Susan S. Deeds, "Land, Water, and Equity in Spanish Colonial and Mexican Law: Historical Evidence for the Court in the Case of State of New Mexico vs. R. Lee Aamodt et al."; John O. Baxter, *Spanish Irrigation in the Pojoaque and Tesuque Valleys during the Eighteenth and Early Nineteenth Centuries* (Santa Fe: New Mexico State Engineer Office, 1984); and Daniel Tyler, "Land and Water Tenure in New Mexico, 1821–1846." Reports in the L. T. Lewis case include, Iris H.W. Engstrand, "Water Rights of Municipalities under the Governments of Spain and Mexico," and Daniel Tyler *The Mythical Pueblo Rights Doctrine: Water Administration in Hispanic New Mexico* (El Paso: University of Texas at El Paso, 1990); reports in the Taos water rights adjudication include, John O. Baxter, *Spanish Irrigation in Taos Valley* (Santa Fe: New Mexico State Engineer Office, 1990), and Daniel Tyler, "The Role of Custom in Defining New Mexican Land and Water Rights." All of these reports are unpublished manuscripts except Tyler and Baxter.

12. Sylvia Rodríguez has argued that research for water rights litigation is narrow and skewed because it does not take into account archeological data, oral history, and ethnography, and that historical experts tend to be coopted by the adjudication system since they depend on it for their livelihood and affirmation as experts. *Journal of the Southwest* 32 (Autumn 1990): pp. 307–14.

13. See, for example, Charles T. DuMars, Marilyn O'Leary, and Albert E. Utton, *Pueblo Indian Water Rights: Struggle for a Precious Resource* (Tucson: The University of Arizona Press, 1984).

14. Michael C. Meyer, *Water in the Hispanic Southwest: A Social and Legal History, 1550–1850* (Tucson: The University of Arizona Press, 1984); Review of Tyler, *The Mythical Pueblo Rights Doctrine* by Alberto L. Hurtado, *NMHR* 67 (January 1992): 85.

15. François Chevalier, *La Formation des grands domaines au Mexique. Terre et société aux XVIᵉ–XVIIᵉ siécles* (Paris: Institut d'Ethnologie, 1952); translation of Chevalier (without notes), Alvin Eustis, trans., Lesley Byrd Simpson, ed., *Land and Society in Colonial Mexico* (Berkeley and Los Angeles: University of California Press, 1963). A major study of a particular hacienda or latifundio also came from the northern Mexican State of Coahuila. Charles H. Harris III, *The Sánchez Navarros: a Socio-economic Study of a Coahuilan Latifundio, 1846–1853* (Chicago: Loyola University Press, 1964.)

16. See, for example, John Womack Jr., *Zapata and the Mexican Revolution* (New York: Alfred A. Knopf, 1969).

17. According to regional studies in Mexico, there was not one revolution, but many. Resolution of ancient conflicts between communities and between families was also found to be as important a cause of the revolution as was social and economic reform. Ian Jacobs, *Ranchero Revolt: The Mexican Revolution in Guerrero* (Austin: University of Texas Press, 1982), pp. xiv–xxii; D.A. Brading, *Haciendas and Ranchos in the Mexican Bajío: León 1700–1860* (Cambridge, England: Cambridge University Press, 1978); Frans J. Schryer, "The Role of the Rancheros of Central Mexico in the Mexican Revolution (The Case of the Sierra Alta de Hidalgo)," *Canadian Journal of Latin American Studies* 4 (7) (1979), 21–41.

18. Two works published in 1972, one in the United States, the other in Mexico, have influenced the increased number of regional histories about Mexico. They are: William B. Taylor, *Landlord and Peasant in Colonial Oaxaca* (Stanford: Stanford University Press, 1972), and Luiz González's, *Pueblo en vilo: Microhistoria de San José de Gracia* (Mexico: El Colegio de México, 1972; second edition); for the English version see, Luis González, *San José de Gracia: A Mexican Village in Transition* (Austin: University of Texas Press, 1974). In Mexico these regional studies have been called microhistories. Luis González, *Invitación a la Microhistoria* (Mexico: Sepsetentas, 1973). A listing of other important regional studies is found in Jacobs, *Ranchero Revolt*, pp. xxi–xxii, notes 49–52.

19. J. J. Bowden "Private Land Claims in the Southwest," 6 vols. (Master's thesis, Southern Methodist University, 1969).

20. William A. Kelleher, *The Maxwell Land Grant* (Albuquerque: University of New Mexico Press, reprint edition 1984).

21. Jim Berry Pearson, *The Maxwell Land Grant* (Norman: University of Oklahoma Press, 1961).

22. Lawrence R. Murphy, "The Beaubien and Miranda Land Grant 1841–1846," *NMHR* 42 (1967): 27–47.

23. Morris F. Taylor, *O.P. McMains and the Maxwell Land Grant Conflict* (Tucson: University of Arizona Press, 1979). For a review of some of the literature on the Maxwell grant, see John R. Van Ness, Introduction to Keleher, *Maxwell Grant*, pp. vii–xvi.

24. G. Emlen Hall, *Four Leagues of Pecos* (Albuquerque: University of New Mexico Press, 1984), and Anselmo F. Arellano, "Through Thick and Thin: Evolutionary Transitions of Las Vegas Grandes and its *Pobladores* (Ph.D. diss., University of New Mexico, 1990).

25. Paul Kutsche and John R. Van Ness, *Cañones: Values, Crisis, and Survival in*

a Northern New Mexico Village (Albuquerque: University of New Mexico Press, 1981.)

26. Victor Westphall defends Thomas B. Catron from allegations that he engaged in fraudulent or unethical conduct, Westphall, *Catron*, pp. 97–99, and challenged anyone to present specific instances of land grant chicanery. Westphall, "Fraud and Implications of Fraud in the Land Grants of New Mexico," *NMHR* 49 (July 1974): 211. For additional examples of such chicanery, see David Benavides, "Lawyer-Induced Partitioning of New Mexican Land Grants: An Ethical Travesty," a paper presented for Professor Hall's seminar, UNM School of Law, Summer, 1990; and Malcolm Ebright, *The Tierra Amarilla Grant: A History of Chicanery* (Santa Fe: The Center for Land Grant Studies, 1980).

27. Robert Shadow and María Rodríquez-Shadow of Puebla, Mexico are currently studying the Mora grant's partition suit in connection with their work regarding the changing land ownership patterns on the Mora grant.

28. John R. Van Ness, "Hispanic Village Organization in Northern New Mexico: Corporate Community Structure in Historical and Comparative Perspective," in Paul Kutsche, ed. *The Survival of Spanish American Villages* (Colorado Springs: The Research Committee of The Colorado College, 1979); for an excellent study of common and private land ownership and agrarian life in medieval France see, Marc Bloch, *French Rural History*, trans. Janet Sondheimer (Berkeley and Los Angeles: University of California Press, 1966), especially pp. 167–234.

29. F. Pollock, *The Land Laws* (1896), p. 18, note 3.

30. E. C. K. Gonner, *Common Lands and Inclosure* (New York: Augustus Kelley, 1969); G. M. Trevelyan, *English Social History* (New York: David McKay Company, 1942), pp. 375–76.

31. Enclosure Act, 41 Geo. 3, c. 109.

32. *Van Rensselaer v. Radcliff*, 10 Wend. 639, 648–49 (N.Y. Sup. Ct., 1833), cited in Juergensmeyer and Wadley, n. 50, p. 370.

33. Iris H. W. Engstrand, Introduction to Tyler, *Mythical Pueblo Rights Doctrine*, p. 4.

34. David A. Clary, *Timber and the Forest Service* (Lawrence: University Press of Kansas, 1986), pp. xi–xii, 180–88, and passim.

35. Those who could show possession of a tract of the public domain were able to obtain title to the tract and many individuals took advantage of this law by filing affidavits declaring that they had used the land exclusively even though it had been common land. "Today perhaps ten prominent San Miguel del Bado families control the lion's share of the private land that represents the rejected common lands of the San Miguel del Bado grant." Emlen Hall, "San Miguel del

Bado and the Loss of the Common Lands of New Mexico Community Land Grants," *NMHR* 66 (October 1991): 413–32, n. 45.

36. The common lands of the Polvadera and Juan Bautista Valdez grants are also part of the National Forest. Paul Kutsche and John R. Van Ness, *Cañones: Values, Crisis, and Survival in a Northern New Mexico Village* (Albuquerque: University of New Mexico Press, 1981), p. 21.

37. It was because only 50,000 acres of San Miguel del Bado common lands ended up in the National Forest that the rest was available for privatization. Hall, "San Miguel del Bado," pp. 420–21, note 20.

38. Hall, "San Miguel del Bado," p. 416.

39. Hall, "San Miguel del Bado," p. 432.

40. Hall, "San Miguel del Bado," p. 416.

41. See chapter 1, notes 175–81 and corresponding text.

42. William deBuys, *Enchantment and Exploitation: The Life and Hard Times of a New Mexico Mountain Range* (Albuquerque: University of New Mexico Press, 1985). Alvar Carlson, *The Spanish-American Homeland: Four Centuries in New Mexico's Río Arriba* (Baltimore and London: The Johns Hopkins University Press, 1990).

43. Clary, *Timber and the Forest Service*, pp. 177–88.

44. DeBuys, *Enchantment and Exploitation*, pp. 271, 311–13, 277.

45. Alvar Carlson, *The Spanish-American Homeland*, pp. 210 and 216. Carlson's statement that "there will always be those, particularly academicians, who will tendentiously place the burden of accusation and guilt upon the U.S. government . . ." is not annotated nor does he cite any evidence for the statement, so the specifics of his charges can not be ascertained. Nevertheless Carlson does not refute the evidence cited by those unnamed academicians. Carlson, *Spanish-American Homeland*, pp. 210–11.

46. See chapter 10 regarding the Ramón Vigil grant, and chapter 1, note 162, and corresponding text.

47. William deBuys, *Enchantment and Exploitation*, p. 312–13.

48. Donald Cutter, "The Legacy of the Treaty of Guadalupe Hidalgo," *NMHR* 53, (October 1978): 305–15.

49. U.S. House of Representatives, Committee on Interior and Insular Affairs, *Status of Community Land Grants in Northern New Mexico*, 100th Congress, 2nd Session, Serial 100–65, 1989.

50. Juergensmeyer and Wadley, "The Common Lands Concept, 14 *Natural Resources Journal* 361 (1974).

51. Daniel Tyler, *The Mythical Pueblo Rights Doctrine*, pp. 40–45; Tyler, "Land and Water Tenure in New Mexico, 1821–1846," p. 64.

52. Frances Levine, "Dividing the Water: The Impact of Water Rights

Adjudication on New Mexican Communities," *Journal of the Southwest* 32 (Autumn 1990): 268–69.

53. See chapter 6 on the Embudo grant.

54. Donald Dale Jackson, "Around Los Ojos, sheep and land are fighting words," *Smithsonian* 22 (April 1991) 37–47. Malcolm Ebright, *The Tierra Amarilla Grant: A History of Chicanery* (Santa Fe: Center for Land Grant Studies, 1980).

55. See chapter 7 on the Las Trampas grant.

56. Niccoló Machiavelli, *The Prince*, Daniel Donno trans. (New York, Toronto, London, Sydney, Auckland: Bantam Books, 1966), p. 60. Reference courtesy Robert Torrez.

Selected Bibliography

This is not an exhaustive bibliography. While it deals primarily with New Mexico, I have also included materials relating to land, water, and society in California, Texas, Arizona, as well as Mexico, and other Latin American countries.

Adams, Eleanor B., and Fray Angelico Chavez. Translators and Annotators. *The Missions of New Mexico, 1776: A Description by Fray Francisco Atanasio Dominguez, with other Contemporary Documents*. Albuquerque: The University of New Mexico Press, 1956.

Almaráz, Félix D., Jr. *The San Antonio Missions and Their System of Land Tenure*. Austin: University of Texas Press, 1989.

Archibald, Robert. "Cañon de Carnué: Settlement of A Grant." *NMHR* 51 (October 1976): 313–28.

Arellano, Anselmo F. "Case Study: Sierra Acequias and Agriculture of the Mora Valley," unpublished manuscript.

———. "Through Thick and Thin: Evolutionary Transitions of *Las Vegas Grandes* and its *Pobladores*." Ph. D. dissertation, University of New Mexico, 1990.

Arellano, Anselmo F., and Julián Josué Vigil. *Las Vegas Grandes on the Gallinas: 1835–1985*. Las Vegas: Editorial Teleraña, 1985.

Aviña, Rose Hollenbaugh. *Spanish and Mexican Land Grants in California*. New York: Arno Press, 1976.

Barrett, Elinore Magee. "Land Tenure and Settlement in the Tepalcatepec Lowland, Michoacan, Mexico." Ph.D. dissertation, University of California, Berkeley, 1970.

Baxter, John O. *Las Carneradas: Sheep Trade in New Mexico, 1700–1860*. Albuquerque, University of New Mexico Press, 1987.

———. *Spanish Irrigation in Taos Valley*. Santa Fe: New Mexico State Engineer's Office, 1990.

———. *Spanish Irrigation in the Pojoaque and Tesuque Valleys During the Eighteenth and Early Nineteenth Centuries*. Santa Fe: New Mexico State Engineer Office, 1984.

Benavides, David. "Lawyer-Induced Partitioning of New Mexican Land Grants: An Ethical Travesty," a paper presented for Professor Hall's seminar, UNM School of Law, Summer, 1990.

Bishko, Charles Julian. "The Castilian as Plainsman: The Medieval Ranching Frontier in La Mancha and Extremadura." in *The New World Looks at its History*. Proceedings of the Second International Congress of Historians of the United States and Mexico. Archibald R. Lewis, ed. Austin: University of Texas Press, 1958.

——. "The Peninsular Background of Latin American Cattle Ranching." *The Hispanic American Historical Review* 32 (November 1952): 491.

Bloch, Marc. *French Rural History*. Berkeley and Los Angeles: University of California Press, 1966.

Bloom, Lansing Bartlett. "Albuquerque and Galisteo: Certificate of Their Founding, 1706." *NMHR* 10 (January, 1935): 48–50.

——. "New Mexico Under Mexican Administration." *Old Santa Fe* 1 (1913): 270.

——. "The Vargas Encomienda," *New Mexico Historical Review* 14 (October 1939): 366–417.

Bloom, Lansing Bartlett, and Ireno L. Chaves, "*Ynstruccions a Peralta por Vi-Rey*," with translation. *NMHR* 4 (April 1929): 178–87.

Borah, Woodrow. *Justice by Insurance: The General Indian Court of Colonial Mexico and the Legal Aides of the Half-Real*. Berkeley, Los Angeles, London: University of California Press, 1983.

Bowden J. J. *The Ponce de Leon Land Grant*. El Paso: Texas Western Press, 1969.

——. *Private Land Claims in the Southwest*. 6 vols. Master's thesis, Southern Methodist University, 1969.

——. *Spanish and Mexican Land Grants in the Chihuahuan Acquisition*. El Paso: Texas Western Press, 1971.

——. "Spanish and Mexican Land Grants in the Southwest," *Land and Water Law Review* 8 (1973): 467.

Brack, Gene M. *Mexico Views Manifest Destiny, 1821–1846*. Albuquerque: University of New Mexico Press, 1975

Bradfute, Richard Wells. *The Court of Private Land Claims: The Adjudication of Spanish and Mexican Land Grant Titles, 1891–1904*. Albuquerque: University of New Mexico Press, 1975.

Brading, D. A. *Haciendas and Ranchos in the Mexican Bajío: Leon, 1700–1860*. Cambridge: Cambridge University Press, 1978.

——. *Miners and Merchants in Bourbon Mexico, 1763–1810*. Cambridge: Cambridge University Press, 1971.

Brayer, Herbert O. "The Land Grants of Laguna." *Research* 1 (December 1936): 5–22.

——. "The Place of Land in Southwestern History." *Land Policy Review* 4 (December 1941): 15–20.

——. *Pueblo Indian Land Grants of the "Rio Abajo," New Mexico*. Albuquerque: University of New Mexico Press, 1939.

Briggs, Charles L. "Our Strength is the Land: The Expression of Hierarchical and Egalitarian Principles in Hispano Society, 1750–1929." Ph.D. dissertation, University of Chicago, 1980.

Briggs, Charles L., and John R. Van Ness. *Land, Water, and Culture: New Perspectives on Hispanic Land Grants*. Albuquerque: University of New Mexico Press, 1987.

Burkholder, Mark A., and D. S. Chandler. *From Impotence to Authority: The Spanish Crown and the American Audiencias, 1687–1808*. Columbia: University of Missouri Press, 1977.

Carlson, Alvar W. *The Spanish-American Homeland*. Baltimore and London: The Johns Hopkins University Press, 1990.

Carr, Ralph. "Private Land Claims in Colorado." *Colorado Magazine* 25 (January 1948): 10–30.

Carroll, H. Bailey, and J. Villasana Haggard, eds. and trans. *Three New Mexico Chronicles*. Albuquerque: The Quivera Society, 1942.

Carter, Constance. "Law and Society in Colonial Mexico: Audiencia Judges in Mexican Society from the Tello de Sandoval Visita General, 1543–1547." Ph. D. dissertation, Columbia University, 1971.

Chavez, Fray Angelico. *Archives of the Archdiocese of Santa Fe*. Washington D.C., 1957.

——. *Origins of New Mexico Families in the Spanish Colonial Period*. Santa Fe: William Gannon, 1954.

——. and Ted J. Warner. *The Dominguez-Escalante Journal*. Provo, Utah, 1976.

Chávez, Thomas E. *Conflict and Acculturation: Manuel Alvarez's 1842 Memorial*. Santa Fe: Museum of New Mexico Press, 1989.

——. *Manuel Alvarez, 1794–1856: A Southwestern Biography*. Niwot: University Press of Colorado, 1990.

Cheever, Frederico. "A New Approach to Spanish and Mexican Land Grants and the Public Trust Doctrine: Defining the Property Interest Protected by the Treaty of Guadalupe-Hidalgo." 33 *U.C.L.A. Law Review* 1364.

Chevalier, François. *Land and Society in Colonial Mexico: The Great Hacienda*. Berkeley and Los Angeles: University of California Press, 1963.

Clagett, Helen L. "Las Siete Partidas." *The Quarterly Journal of the Library of Congress* 22 (October 1965): 341–46.

Clark, Ira G. *Water in New Mexico: A History of its Management and Use.* Albuquerque: University of New Mexico Press, 1987.

Clary, David A. *Timber and the Forest Service.* Lawrence: University Press of Kansas, 1986.

Cline, Howard F. *Spanish and Mexican Land Grants in New Mexico, 1689–1848: A Technical Report.* New York: Clearwater, 1964.

Coan, Charles F. "Spanish and Mexican Land Grants, 1860–1911." In *A History of New Mexico.* Vol. 1. Chicago: American Historical Society, 1925.

Cook, Alexandra Parma, and Noble David Cook. *Good Faith and Truthful Ignorance: A Case of Transatlantic Bigamy.* Durham: Duke University Press, 1991.

Craig, Donald L. "Land, Water, and Education: An Administrative History of the Las Vegas Land Grant." Master's Thesis, New Mexico Highlands University, 1990.

Craver, Rebecca McDowell. *The Impact of Intimacy: Mexican-Anglo Intermarriage in New Mexico, 1821–1846.* The University of Texas at El Paso: Texas Western Press, 1982.

Crawford, Stanley. "Dancing for Water." *Journal of the Southwest* 32 (Autumn 1990): 265.

———. *Mayordomo: Chronicle of an Acequia in Northern New Mexico.* Albuquerque: University of New Mexico Press, 1988.

Crossland, Charlotte Benson. "Acequia Rights in Law and Tradition." *Journal of the Southwest* 32 (Autumn 1990): 278.

Cuello, José. "Saltillo in the Seventeenth Century: Local Society on the North Mexican Frontier." Ph. D. dissertation, University of California, Berkeley, 1981.

Currey, John. "Treaty of Guadalupe Hidalgo and Private Land Claims." In Shuck, *History of the Bench and Bar of California,* 1901, pp. 57–71.

Cutter, Charles R. *The Protector de Indios in Colonial New Mexico, 1659–1821.* Albuquerque: University of New Mexico Press, 1986.

Cutter, Donald C. "The Legacy of the Treaty of Guadalupe Hidalgo." *NMHR* 53 (October 1978): 305–15.

Davies, Keith A. *Landowners in Colonial Peru.* Austin: University of Texas Press, 1984.

deBuys, William. *Enchantment and Exploitation: The Life and Hard Times of a New Mexico Mountain Range.* Albuquerque: University of New Mexico Press, 1985.

———. "Fractions of Justice: A Legal and Social History of the Las Trampas Land Grant, New Mexico." *NMHR* 56 (January 1981): 71–97.

deBuys, William, and Alex Harris. *River of Traps: A Village Life*. University of New Mexico Press, 1990.

de la Peña, Guillermo. *A Legacy of Promises: Agriculture, Politics, and Ritual in the Morelos Highlands of Mexico*. Austin: University of Texas Press, 1981.

de la Peña, José F. *Oligarquía y Propiedad en Nueva España; 1550–1624*. Mexico: Fondo de Cultura Económica, 1983.

Díaz, Albert James. *A Guide to the Microfilm of Papers Relating to New Mexico Land Grants*. University of New Mexico Publications; Library Series No. 1. Albuquerque: University of New Mexico Press, 1960.

Dobkins, Betty Eakle. *The Spanish Element in Texas Water Law*. Austin: University of Texas Press, 1959.

Dorsey, Stephen W. "Land Stealing in New Mexico, A Rejoinder." *North American Review* 145 (October 1887): 396–409.

Dublán, Manuel, and José María Lozano. *Legislación Mexicana*. 19 vols. Mexico: Imprenta del Comercio, 1875–1890.

DuMars, Charles T., and Malcolm Ebright. "Problems of Spanish and Mexican Land Grants in the Southwest: Their Origin and Extent." *The Southwestern Review of Management and Economics* 1 (Summer 1981): 177.

DuMars, Charles T., Marilyn O'Leary, and Albert E. Utton. *Pueblo Indian Water Rights: Struggle for a Precious Resource*. Tucson: The University of Arizona Press, 1984.

DuMars, Charles T., and Michael J. Rock. "The New Mexico Legal Rights Demonstration Land Grant Project—An Analysis of the Land Title Problems in the Santo Domingo de Cundiyó Land Grant." *New Mexico Law Review* 8 (Winter 1977–78): 1–37.

Dunham, Harold H. "Coloradoans and Maxwell Grant." *Colorado Magazine* 32 (April 1955): 131–45.

———. *Government Handout: A Study in the Administration of the Public Lands, 1875–1891*. 1941. Reprint. New York: Da Capo Press, 1970.

———. "New Mexican Land Grants with Special Reference to the Title Papers of the Maxwell Grant." *NMHR* 15 (January 1955): 1–22.

———. *Spanish and Mexican Land Policies and Grants in the Taos Pueblo Region, New Mexico*. Pueblo de Taos v. United States. Docket no. 357. Indian Claims Commission, December, 1959.

———. "Spanish and Mexican Land Policies in the Taos Pueblo Region." In *Pueblo Indians*. 5 vols. 1: 151–311. New York: Garland Publishers, 1974.

Dusenberry, William Howard. *The Mexican Mesta: The Administration of Ranching in Colonial Mexico.* Urbana: The University of Illinois Press, 1963.

Eastman, Clyde, Garrey Carruthers, and James A. Liefer. "Contrasting Attitudes Toward Land in New Mexico." *New Mexico Business* (March, 1971): 3–20.

Eastman, Clyde, and James R. Gray. *Community Grazing: Practice and Potential in New Mexico.* Albuquerque: University of New Mexico Press, 1987.

Ebright, Malcolm. "The Embudo Grant: A Case Study of Justice and the Court of Private Land Claims." *Journal of the West* 19 (July 1980): 74–85.

——. "Introduction: Spanish and Mexican Land Grants and the Law. In *Land Grants and the Law.* Manhattan, Kansas: Sunflower University Press, 1989.

——. "Manuel Martínez's Ditch Dispute: A Study in Mexican Period Custom and Justice." *NMHR* 54 (January 1979): 21–34.

——. "The San Joaquín Grant: Who Owned the Common Lands? A Historical-Legal Puzzle." *NMHR* 57 (January 1982): 5–26.

——. *The Tierra Amarilla Grant: A History of Chicanery.* Santa Fe: The Center for Land Grant Studies, 1980.

——, ed. *Land Grants and the Law,* edited by Malcolm Ebright. Manhattan, Kansas: Sunflower University Press, 1989.

Elliott, J. H. *Imperial Spain, 1469–1716.* Reprint. London: Penguin Books, 1990.

Ellis, Bruce. *Bishop Lamy's Santa Fe Cathedral.* Albuquerque: University of New Mexico Press, 1985.

——. "Fraud without Scandal: The Roque Lovato Grant and Gaspar Ortiz y Alarid," NMHR 57 (Jan. 1982): 43–62.

Engstrand, Iris H. W. "An Enduring Legacy: California Ranchos in Historical Perspective." In *Spanish and Mexican Land Grants and the Law,* edited by Malcolm Ebright. Manhattan, Kansas: Sunflower University Press, 1989.

——. "Land Grant Problems in the Southwest: The Spanish and Mexican Heritage." *NMHR* 53 (October 1978): 317–36.

Escriche, Joaquín. *Diccionario Razonado de Legislación y Jurisprudencia.* Paris: Rosa y Bouret, [1863].

Espinosa, Gilberto. "About New Mexico Land Grants." *Albuquerque Bar Journal* 7 (September 1967): 5–15.

——. "New Mexico Land Grants." *State Bar of New Mexico Journal* 1 (November 1962): 3–13.

Faulk, Odie B. *Too Far North . . . Too Far South: The Controversial Boundary Survey and the Epic Story of the Gadsden Purchase,* Los Angeles: Westernlore Press, 1967.

Forrest, Suzanne. *The Preservation of the Village: New Mexico's Hispanics and the New Deal*. Albuquerque: University of New Mexico Press, 1989.

Freedman, David. "Land Reform and the New Mexico Land Grant Question" In Land, Law and La Raza" (A collection of papers presented for Professor Theodore Parnall's seminar in comparative law. UNM School of Law, Fall Semester, 1972).

Fritz, Christian G. *Federal Justice in California: The Court of Ogden Hoffman, 1851–1891*. Lincoln and London: University of Nebraska Press, 1991.

Galván Rivera, Mariano. *Ordenanzas de Tierras y Aguas*. Mexico, 1849.

Garber, Paul Neff. *The Gadsden Treaty*. Gloucester, Mass.: Peter Smith, 1959.

Gates, Paul W. *Land and Law in California: Essays on Land Policies*. Ames: Iowa State University Press, 1991.

Gibson, Charles. *The Aztecs Under Spanish Rule: A History of the Indians of the Valley of Mexico, 1519–1810*. Stanford: Stanford University Press, 1964.

Glick, Thomas F. *Irrigation and Society in Medieval Valencia*. Cambridge: Harvard University Press, 1970.

——. *The Old World Background of The Irrigation System of San Antonio, Texas*. El Paso: Texas Western Press, 1972.

Gómez, Fernando Chacón. "The Intended and Actual Effect of Article VIII of the Treaty of Guadalupe Hidalgo: Mexican Treaty Rights under International and Domestic Law." Ph. D. dissertation, The University of Michigan, 1977.

Gonner, E.C.K. *Common Land and Inclosure*. Frank Cass & Co. Ltd., 1966.

González, Luis. *Pueblo en vilo*. Mexico: Fondo de Cultura Económica, 1984.

——. *San José de Gracia, Mexican Village in Transition*. Translated by John Upton. Austin: University of Texas Press, 1974.

Greenleaf, Richard E. "Atrisco and Las Ciruelas 1722–1769." *NMHR* 42 (January 1967): 5–25.

——. "The Founding of Albuquerque, 1706: An Historical-Legal Problem." *NMHR* 39 (January 1964): 1–15.

——. "Land and Water in Mexico and New Mexico, 1700–1821." *New Mexico Historical Review* 47 (April 1972): 85–112.

Grisham, Sandra and Jay Ortiz. "Methods of Proving Foreign Law in the Court of Private Land Claims." In "Land, Law and La Raza" (A collection of papers presented for Professor Theodore Parnall's seminar in comparative law. UNM School of Law, Fall Semester, 1972).

Griswold del Castillo, Richard. *The Treaty of Guadalupe Hidalgo, A Legacy of Conflict*. Norman and London: University of Oklahoma Press, 1990.

Gutiérrez, Ramón A. *When Jesus Came, the Corn Mothers Went Away: Marriage,*

Sexuality, and Power in New Mexico, 1500–1846. Stanford: Stanford University Press, 1991.

Hackett, Charles Wilson, ed. *Historical Documents Relating to New Mexico, Nueva Vizcaya, and Approaches Thereto.* 3 vols. Washington, D.C.: Carnegie Institution, 1923–37.

——, ed. *Revolt of the Pueblo Indians and Otermín's Attempted Reconquest: 1680–1682.* Translated by Charmion Clair Shelby. 2 vols. Albuquerque: University of New Mexico Press, 1941.

Hall, Frederic. *The Laws of Mexico.* San Francisco: A.L. Bancroft, 1885.

Hall, G. Emlen. *Four Leagues of Pecos: A Legal History of the Pecos Grant, 1800–1933.* Albuquerque: University of New Mexico Press, 1984.

——. "Giant Before the Surveyor General: The Land Career of Donaciano Vigil." *Journal of the West* 19 (July 1980): 64–73.

——. "Juan Estevan Pino, 'se les coma': New Mexico Land Speculation in the 1820s." *NMHR* 57 (January 1982): 27.

——. "Land Litigation and the Idea of New Mexico Progress." In *Spanish and Mexican Land Grants and the Law.* Edited by Malcolm Ebright. Manhattan, Kansas: Sunflower University Press, 1989.

——. "San Miguel del Bado and the Loss of the Common Lands of New Mexico Community Land Grants." *NMHR* 66 (October 1991): 413.

——. "Shell Games: The Continuing Legacy of Rights to Minerals and Water on Spanish and Mexican Land Grants in the Southwest." Rocky Mountain Mineral Law Institute. New York: Matthew Bender and Company, 1991.

Hammond, George P. and Agapito Rey, eds. and trans. *Don Juan de Oñate: Colonizer of New Mexico, 1595–1628.* 2 vols. Albuquerque: University of New Mexico Press, 1953

Haring, C. H. *The Spanish Empire in America.* New York and London: Harcourt Brace Jovanovich, 1975.

Hoffman, Ogden. *Reports of Land Cases Determined in the United States District Court for the Northern District of California, 1853–1858,* 1862. Reprint. Yosemite Collections, 1975.

Horvath, Jr., Steven M. "The Social and Political Organization of the Genízaros of Plaza de Nuestra Señora de los Dolores de Belén, New Mexico, 1740–1812." Ph. D. dissertation, Brown University, 1979.

Hunt, Aurora. *Kirby Benedict: Frontier Federal Judge.* Glendale: Arthur H. Clark, 1961.

Hutchins, Wells A. "The Community Acequia: Its Origins and Development." *Southwestern Historical Review* 31 (January 1928): 261–84.

——. *The New Mexico Law of Water Rights.* Santa Fe: State Engineer of New Mexico, 1955.

Jacobs, Ian. *Ranchero Revolt, The Mexican Revolution in Guerrero.* Austin: University of Texas Press, 1982.

Jenkins, Myra Ellen. "The Baltasar Baca 'Grant': History of an Encroachment." *El Palacio* 68 (Spring 1961): 47–64; (Summer 1961): 87–105.

———. "Some Eighteenth-Century New Mexico Women of Property." In *Hispanic Arts & Ethnohistory in the Southwest.* Santa Fe: Ancient City Press, 1983.

———. "Spanish Land Grants in the Tewa Area." *NMHR* 47 (April 1972): 113–34.

———. "Taos Pueblo and its Neighbors, 1540–1847," *NMHR* 41 (April 1966): 85–114.

Jimenez, Petra F. "Methods of Obtaining Title to Property Under Spanish Law." In "Land, Law and La Raza" (A collection of papers presented for Professor Theodore Parnall's seminar in comparative law. UNM School of Law, Fall Semester, 1972).

Jones, Oakah L. *Nueva Vizcaya: Heartland of the Spanish Frontier.* Albuquerque: University of New Mexico Press, 1988.

———. *Los Paisanos: Spanish Settlers on the Northern Frontier of New Spain.* Norman: University of Oklahoma Press, 1979.

———. "Pueblo Indian Auxiliaries and the Spanish Defense of New Mexico, 1692–1792. Ph. D. dissertation, University of Oklahoma, 1964.

Julian, George W. "Land Stealing in New Mexico." *North American Review* 145 (July 1887): 17–31.

Kagan, Richard L. *Lawsuits and Litigants in Castile: 1500–1700.* Chapel Hill: The University of North Carolina Press, 1981.

Keleher, William A. *The Fabulous Frontier: Twelve New Mexico Items.* Albuquerque: University of New Mexico Press, 1982.

———. "Law of the New Mexico Land Grant." *NMHR* 4 (October 1929): 350–71.

———. *Maxwell Land Grant: A New Mexico Item.* Reprint. 1942, 1964. Albuquerque: University of New Mexico Press, 1984.

Kessell, John L., and Rick Hendricks, eds. *By Force of Arms: The Journals of don Diego de Vargas, New Mexico, 1691–93.* Albuquerque: University of New Mexico Press, 1992.

Kessell, John L., et al. eds. *Remote Beyond Compare: Letters of don Diego de Vargas to His Family from New Spain and New Mexico.* Albuquerque: University of New Mexico Press, 1989.

Knowlton, Clark S. "Land Grant Problems Among the State's Spanish Americans." *New Mexico Business* 20 (June 1967): 1–13.

———. "The Mora Land Grant: A New Mexican Tragedy." In *Spanish and*

Mexican Land Grants and the Law. Edited by Malcolm Ebright. Manhattan, Kansas: Sunflower University Press, 1989.

———. "The Spanish Americans in New Mexico."*Sociology and Social Research* 45 (July 1961): 448–54.

———. "The Study of Land Grants As an Academic Discipline." *Social Science Journal* 13 (October 1976): 3–7.

———. "The Town of Las Vegas Community Land Grant: An Anglo-American Coup d'Etat." *Journal of the West* 19 (July 1980): 12–21.

Kutsche, Paul, ed. *The Survival of Spanish American Villages.* The Colorado College Studies, No 15, Colorado Springs, 1979.

Kutsche, Paul, and John R. Van Ness. *Cañones: Values, Crisis, and Survival in a Northern New Mexico Village.* Albuquerque: University of New Mexico Press, 1981.

Lamar, Howard R. *The Far Southwest, 1846–1912: A Territorial History.* New Haven: Yale University Press, 1966.

———. "Land Policy in the Spanish Southwest, 1846–1891: A Study in Contrasts." *Journal of Economic History* 22 (December 1962): 498–515.

Langum, David J. *Law and Community of the Mexican California Frontier: Anglo-American Expatriates and the Clash of Legal Traditions, 1821–1846.* Norman and London: The University of Oklahoma Press, 1987.

———, ed. *Law in the West.* Manhattan, Kansas: Sunflower University Press, 1985.

Larson, Robert W. *New Mexico Populism: A Study of Radical Protest in a Western Territory.* Boulder: Colorado Associated University Press, 1974.

———. *New Mexico's Quest for Statehood, 1846–1912.* Albuquerque: University of New Mexico Press, 1968.

———. "The White Caps of New Mexico: A Study of Ethnic Militancy in the Southwest." *Pacific Historical Review* 44 (May 1975): 171–85.

Lecompte, Janet. "The Independent Women of Hispanic New Mexico, 1821–1846." *The Western Historical Quarterly* 12 (January 1981): 17–35.

———. *Rebellion in Río Arriba, 1837.* Albuquerque: University of New Mexico Press, 1985.

Leonard, Olen E. *The Role of the Land Grant in the Social Organization and Social Processes of a Spanish American Village in New Mexico.* Albuquerque: Calvin Horn, 1970.

Levine, Frances. "Dividing the Water: The Impact of Water Rights Adjudication on New Mexican Communities." *Journal of the Southwest* 32 (Autumn 1990): 268.

Leyba, John and Joseph Sena. "Customary Law in Spain and Mexico: 1848." In "Land, Law and La Raza"(papers presented for Professor Theodore Par-

nall's seminar in comparative law. University of New Mexico School of
Law, Fall Semester, 1972)

Lindley, Richard B. *Haciendas and Economic Development: Guadalajara, Mexico, at Independence.* Austin: University of Texas Press, 1983.

Lockhart, James. "Encomienda and Hacienda: The Evolution of the Great Estate in the Spanish Indies." *Hispanic American Historical Review* 49 (August): 413–29.

López, Gregorio. *Las Siete Partidas del sabio rey don Alfonso el IX.* Madrid: Oficina de d. Leon Amarita, 1829–1831.

López, Larry. "The Founding of San Francisco on the Rio Puerco: A Document." *NMHR* 55 (January 1980): 71–78.

Lunenfeld, Marvin. *The Council of the Santa Hermandad: A Study of the Pacification Forces of Ferdinand and Isabella.* Coral Gables: University of Miami Press, 1970.

MacLachlan, Colin M. *Criminal Justice in Eighteenth Century Mexico.* Berkeley: University of California Press, 1974.

———. *Spain's Empire in the New World: The Role of Ideas in Institutional and Social Change.* Berkeley: University of California Press, 1988.

MacLachlan, Colin M., and Jaime E. Rodriguez O. *The Forging of the Cosmic Race: A Reinterpretation of Colonial Mexico,* Berkeley: University of California Press, 1980, expanded 1990.

Madrid, Patricia A. "A Study of Spanish Prescription in Land Grant Claims." In "Land, Law and La Raza" (A collection of papers presented for Professor Theodore Parnall's seminar in comparative law. UNM School of Law, Fall Semester, 1972).

Margadant S., Guillermo F. "Mexican Colonial Land Law." In *Spanish and Mexican Land Grants and the Law.* Edited by Malcolm Ebright. Manhattan, Kansas: Sunflower University Press, 1989.

Martin, Cheryl English. *Rural Society in Colonial Morelos,* Albuquerque: University of New Mexico Press, 1985.

Mawn, Geoffrey P. "A Land Grant Guarantee: The Treaty of Guadalupe Hidalgo or the Protocol of Querétaro?" *Journal of the West* 4 (October 1975): 47–61.

McBride, George McCutchen. *The Land System of Mexico.* New York: Octagon Books, 1971.

McCarty, Frankie. *Land Grant Problems in New Mexico. Albuquerque Journal,* 28 September–10 October 1969.

McKnight, Joseph W. "Law Books on the Hispanic Frontier." In *Spanish and Mexican Land Grants and the Law.* Edited by Malcolm Ebright. Manhattan, Kansas: Sunflower University Press, 1989.

Merk, Frederick. *Manifest Destiny and Mission in American History.* New York: Vintage Books, 1963.

Metzgar, Joseph V. "The Atrisco Land Grant, 1692–1977." *NMHR* 52 (October 1977): 269–96.

Meyer, Michael C. *Water in the Hispanic Southwest: A Social and Legal History, 1550–1850.* Tucson: The University of Arizona Press, 1984.

Meyer, Michael C., and Susan M. Deeds. "Law, Water, and Equity in Spanish Colonial and Mexican Law: Historical Evidence for the Court in the Case of the State of New Mexico vs. R. Lee Aamodt, et al. Unpublished report on file in New Mexico v. Aamodt, No. 6639, Federal District Court for New Mexico

Miller, Hunter. Treaty of Guadalupe Hidalgo. In *Treaties and Other International Acts of the United States of America.* U.S. Government Printing Office, 1937.

——. Treaty of Spain 1819. In *Treaties and Other International Acts of the United States of America.* U.S. Government Printing Office, 1931.

Minge, Ward Alan. "Frontier Problems in New Mexico Preceding the Mexican War, 1840–1846." Ph. D. diss., University of New Mexico, 1965.

——. "The Last Will and Testament of Don Severino Martinez." *New Mexico Quarterly* 33 (1963): 33.

——. "Mexican Independence Day and a Ute Tragedy in Santa Fe, 1844." *El Corral de Santa Fe Westerners,* 1973, p. 107.

Montoya, Don and Bill Piatt. "The Treaty of Guadalupe-Hidalgo." In "Land, Law and La Raza" (A collection of papers presented for Professor Theodore Parnall's seminar in comparative law. UNM School of Law, Fall Semester, 1972).

Moorhead, Max L. *New Mexico's Royal Road.* Norman: University of Oklahoma Press, 1958.

——. *The Presidio: Bastion of the Spanish Borderlands.* Norman: University of Oklahoma Press, 1975.

——. "Rebuilding the Presidio of Santa Fe, 1789–1791." *NMHR* 49 (April 1974): 124.

Mosk, Sanford A. "The Influence of Tradition on Agriculture in New Mexico." *Journal of Economic History* 2 (December 1942): 34–51.

Morrow, Hon. William W. *Spanish and Mexican Private Land Grants.* San Francisco: Bancroft, Whitney Company, 1923; reprinted in *Spanish and Mexican Land Grants.* New York: Arno Press, 1974.

Murphy, James M. *The Spanish Legal Heritage in Arizona,* Tucson: Arizona Pioneers' Historical Society, 1966.

Murphy, Lawrence R. "The Beaubien and Miranda Land Grant, 1841–1846." *NMHR* 42 (January 1967): 27–47.

——. "Lucien B. Maxwell: The Making of A Western Legend." *Arizona and the West* 22 (Summer 1980): 109–24.

Nichols, Madaline W. "Las Siete Partidas." *California Law Review* 20: 260–85.

Nostrand, Richard. *The Hispano Homeland*. Norman and London: University of Oklahoma Press, 1992.

Nuttal, Zelia. "Royal Ordnances Concerning the Laying out of New Towns." *HAHR* 4 (November 1921): 743–53.

O'Connell, Daniel Patrick. *State Succession in Municipal Law and in International Law*. 2 vols. Cambridge: Cambridge University Press, 1967.

Oczon, Annabelle. "Land Grants in New Mexico: A Selective Bibliography." *NMHR* 57 (January 1982): 81–87.

Orozco, Wistano Luis. *Legislación y Jurisprudencia Sobre Terreno Baldíos*. Mexico: Imp. de El Tiempo, 1985.

Ortiz, Roxanne Dunbar. *Roots of Resistance: Land Tenure in New Mexico, 1680–1980*. Los Angeles: University of California Press, 1980.

Ots Capdequi, J. M. *España en América: El régimen de tierras en la época colonial*. México & Buenos Aires: Fondo de Cultura Económica, 1959.

Owens, John Bingner. "Despotism, Absolutism, and the Law in Renaissance Spain: Toledo Versus the Counts of Belalcazar (1445–1574). Ph. D. dissertation, University of Wisconsin, 1972.

Parrish, William J. *The Charles Ilfeld Company: A Study of the Rise and Decline of Mercantile Capitalism in New Mexico*. Cambridge: Harvard University Press, 1961.

Parry, J. H. *The Audencia of New Galicia in the Sixteenth Century: A Study in Spanish Colonial Government*. Cambridge: Cambridge University Press, 1948.

——. *The Spanish Seaborne Empire*. Berkeley, Los Angeles: University of California Press, 1966.

——. *The Spanish Theory of Empire in the Sixteenth Century*. Cambridge: Cambridge University Press, 1940.

Patrick, Elizabeth Nelson. "Land Grants During the Administration of Spanish Colonial Governor Pedro Feŕim de Mendinueta." *NMHR* 51 (January 1976): 5–18.

Pearce, T. M., ed. *New Mexico Place Names*. Albuquerque: University of New Mexico Press, 1965.

Pearson, Jim Berry. *The Maxwell Land Grant*. Norman: University of Oklahoma Press, 1961.

Perrigo, Lynn. *Gateway to Glorieta*. Boulder: Pruett Publishing, 1982.

———. *Hispanos: Historic Leaders in New Mexico*. Santa Fe: Sunstone Press, 1985.

———. "New Mexico in the Mexican Period, as Revealed in the Torres Documents." *NMHR* 29 (January 1954): 28–40.

———. "Some Laws and Legal Proceedings of the Mexican Period." *NMHR* 26 (July 1951): 244.

Phelan, John Leddy. *The Kingdom of Quito in the Seventeenth Century: Bureaucratic Politics in the Spanish Empire*. Madison, Milwaukee and London: The University of Wisconsin Press, 1967.

Phipps, Helen. *Some Aspects of the Agrarian Question in Mexico*. Austin: University of Texas, 1925 (University of Texas Bulletin No. 2515).

Pitt-Rivers, J. A. *The People of the Sierra*. New York: Criterion Books, 1954.

Poldervaart, Arie W. *Black-Robed Justice*. Historical Society of New Mexico, 1948.

Powell, Donald M. *The Peralta Grant: James Addison Reavis and the Barony of Arizona*. Norman: University of Oklahoma Press, 1960.

Poyo, Gerald E., and Gilberto M. Hinojoso, eds. *Tejano Origins in Eighteenth-Century San Antonio*. Austin: University of Texas Press, 1991.

Quintana, Frances Leon. "Land, Water, and Pueblo-Hispanic Relations in Northern New Mexico." *Journal of the Southwest* 32 (Autumn 1990): 288.

Quintana Frances Leon, and David J. Snow. "Historical Archeology of the Rito Colorado Valley, New Mexico." *Journal of the West* 19 (July 1980): 40–50.

Read, Benjamin M. *Illustrated History of New Mexico*. New York: Arno Press, 1976.

Read, Betty. "A Study of the 1851 and 1891 Acts to Settle Private Land Claims." In "Land, Law and La Raza" (A collection of papers presented for Professor Theodore Parnall's seminar in comparative law. UNM School of Law, Fall Semester, 1972).

Reynolds, Mathew. *Spanish and Mexican Land Laws: New Spain and Mexico*. St. Louis: Buxton and Skinner Stationery, 1895.

Riley, G. Michael. *Fernando Cortés and the Marquesado in Morelos, 1522–1547*. Albuquerque: University of New Mexico Press, 1973.

Rios-Bustamante, Antonio José. "New Mexico in the Eighteenth Century: Life, Labor and Trade in La Villa de San Felipe de Albuquerque, 1706–1790." *Aztlan* 7 (Fall, 1976): 357–89.

Rittenhouse, Jack D. *Disturnell's Treaty Map*. Santa Fe: Stagecoach Press, 1965.

Rock, Michael J. "An Annotated Bibliography of the New Mexico Land Grant Law Collection in the University of New Mexico Law Library." *New Mexico Law Review* 8 (Winter 1977–78): 39–54.

———. "Anton Chico and Its Patent." *Journal of the West* 19 (July 1980): 86–91.

———. "Catron's Quiet Title Suit." Unpublished manuscript.

———. "The Change in Tenure New Mexico Supreme Court Decisions Have

Effected Upon the Common Lands of Community Land Grants in New Mexico." *Social Science Journal* 13 (October 1976): 53–63.

Rock, Michael J., and Charles T. DuMars. "The New Mexico Legal Rights Demonstration Land Grant Project—An Analysis of the Land Title Problems in the Santo Domingo de Cundiyó Land Grant." *New Mexico Law Review* 8 (Winter 1977–78): 1–37.

Rock, Rosalind Z. " '*Pido y Suplico': Women and the Law in Spanish New Mexico, 1697–1763.*" *NMHR* 65 (April 1990): 145–59.

Rockwell, John A. *A Compilation of Spanish and Mexican Law in Relation to Mines and Titles to Real Estate, in Force in California, Texas and New Mexico.* New York: John S. Voorhies, 1851.

Rodríguez, Sylvia. "Applied Research on Land and Water in New Mexico: A Critique." *Journal of the Southwest* 32 (Autumn 1990): 300.

Rosenbaum, Robert J. *Mexicano Resistance in the Southwest: "The Sacred Right of Self-Preservation."* Austin: University of Texas Press, 1981.

Rothman, Hal. "Cultural and Environmental Change on the Pajarito Plateau." *NMHR* 64 (April 1989): 185–211.

Salazar, J. Richard. "The Bartolomé Fernández Grant: Another Grazing Grant in Navajo Country." Unpublished manuscript. SRCA.

———. "Blas de Hinojos: A Military Personality in Oblivion." Unpublished manuscript. SRCA.

———. "The Corpus Christi Grant: A Fraudulent Attempt at Acquiring a Land Grant in Northeastern New Mexico." Unpublished manuscript. SRCA.

———. "The Felipe Tafoya Grant: A Grazing Grant in West Central New Mexico." Unpublished manuscript. SRCA.

———. "Juan Andrés Archuleta: A Brief History of His Family and of His Role During the Mexican Period." Unpublished manuscript. SRCA.

———. "The Military Career of Donaciano Vigil." Unpublished manuscript. SRCA.

———. "Nuestra Señora Rosario, San Fernando y Santiago del Rio de las Truchas: A Brief History." (Paper presented at the Twenty-second Annual Conference of the Western Social Science Association. Albuquerque, 25 April 1980).

———. "The Role of the Land Grant and its Effect on Expansionism in Northern New Mexico, 1700–1821." Unpublished manuscript. SRCA.

———. "Santa Rosa de Lima de Abiquiú." *New Mexico Architecture* 18 (Sept.–Oct. 1976): 13–19.

———. "Spanish-Indian Relations in New Mexico during the Term of *Comandante General* Pedro de Nava, 1790–1802." Unpublished manuscript. SRCA.

Sandoval, David A. "Gnats, Goods, and Greasers: Mexican Merchants on the Santa Fe Trail." In *The Mexican Road: Trade, Travel, and Confrontation on the Santa Fe Trail.* Edited by Mark L. Gardner. Manhattan, Kansas: Sunflower University Press, 1989.

Scholes, Frances V. "Civil Government and Society in New Mexico in the Seventeenth Century." *NMHR* 10 (April 1935): 105.

———. "Conquistador of New Mexico." *NMHR* 19 (1944): 340.

———. "Troublous Times in New Mexico." *NMHR* 10 (1937): 388.

Scott, Samuel Parsons, translator. *Las Siete Partidas.* Chicago: Commerce Clearing House, 1931.

Sears, Louis Martin. "Nicholas P. Trist, A Diplomat with Ideals." *The Mississippi Valley Historical Review* 11 (June 1924–March 1925): 87–98.

Simmons, Marc. *Albuquerque: A Narrative History.* Albuquerque: University of New Mexico Press, 1982.

———. "Governor Cuervo and the Beginnings of Albuquerque: Another Look." *NMHR* 55 (July 1980): 189–207.

———. *The Little Lion of the Southwest: A Life of Manuel Antonio Chaves.* Chicago: Swallow Press, 1973.

———. "New Mexico's Colonial Agriculture." *El Palacio.* 89 (Spring 1983): 3–10.

———. "New Mexico's Smallpox Epidemic of 1780–1781." *NMHR* 41 (1966): 319–26.

———. "Settlement Patterns and Village Plans in Colonial New Mexico." *Journal of the West* 8 (January 1969): 7–21.

———. *Spanish Government in New Mexico.* Albuquerque: University of New Mexico Press, 1968.

———. "Spanish Irrigation Practices in New Mexico." *NMHR* 47 (April 1972): 135–50.

———, ed. and trans. *Father Juan Agustín de Morfi's Account of the Disorders in New Mexico.* Santa Fe: Historical Society of New Mexico, 1977.

Simpson, Lesley Byrd. *Exploitation of Land in Central Mexico in the Sixteenth Century.* Berkeley and Los Angeles: University of California Press, 1962.

Smith, Andrew T. "The Founding of the San Antonio de las Huertas Grant." *Social Science Journal* 13 (October 1976): 35–43.

Snow, David H. "A Note on Encomienda Economics in Seventeenth-Century New Mexico." In *Hispanic Arts and Ethnohistory in the Southwest.* Edited by Weigle, et. al.

———. *The Santa Fe Acequia Systems.* Santa Fe: National Park Service and New Mexico State Historic Preservation Division, 1988.

Spell, Lota M. "The Grant and First Survey of the City of San Antonio." *Southwestern Historical Quarterly* 66 (July 1962): 73–89.

Stampa, Manuel Carrera. "The Evolution of Weights and Measures in New Spain." *HAHR* 29 (February 1949): 15.

Stanley, F. "O. P. McMains, Champion of a Lost Cause." *NMHR* 24 (January 1949): 1–11.

Stoller, Marianne L. "A Study of Nineteenth Century Hispanic Arts and Crafts in the American Southwest: Appearances and Processes." Ph. D. dissertation, University of Pennsylvania, 1979.

———. "Grants of Desperation, Lands of Speculation: Mexican Period Land Grants in Colorado." *Journal of the West* 19 (July 1980): 22–39.

Swadesh, Frances Leon. *Los Primeros Pobladores: Hispanic Americans of the Ute Frontier.* Notre Dame, Indiana.: University of Notre Dame Press, 1974.

Swadesh, Frances Leon, Julian Wilfredo Vigil, and Marina Baldonado Ochoa. *The Lands of New Mexico.* Santa Fe: Museum of New Mexico, 1975.

Tannenbaum, Frank. *The Mexican Agrarian Revolution.* Archon Books, 1929.

Taylor, Morris F. "Captain William Craig and the Vigil and St. Vrain Grant 1855–1870." *The Colorado Magazine* 45 (Fall 1968): 301–21.

———. "The Leitensdorfer Claim in the Vigil and St. Vrain Grant." *Journal of the West* 19 (July 1980): 92–99.

———. "A New Look At An Old Case: The Bent Heirs' Claim in the Maxwell Grant." *NMHR* 43 (July 1968): 213–28.

———. *O. P. McMains and the Maxwell Land Grant Conflict.* Tucson: University of Arizona Press, 1979.

———. "The Two Land Grants of Gervacio Nolan." *NMHR* 47 (April 1972): 151–84.

———. "The Uña de Gato Grant in Colfax County." *NMHR* 51 (April 1976): 121–43.

Taylor, William B. "Colonial Land and Water Rights of New Mexico Indian Pueblos. Unpublished report on file in New Mexico v. Aamodt, No. 6639, Federal District Court for New Mexico.

———. "Land and Water Rights in New Spain." *NMHR* 50 (July 1975): 189.

———. *Landlord and Peasant in Colonial Oaxaca.* Stanford: Stanford University Press, 1972.

Thomas, Alfred Barnaby, trans. and ed. *After Coronado: Spanish Exploration Northeast of New Mexico, 1696–1727.* Norman: University of Oklahoma Press, 1935.

———, trans. and ed. *Forgotten Frontiers: A Study of the Spanish Indian Policy of Don Juan Bautista de Anza Governor of New Mexico 1777–1787.* Norman: University of Oklahoma Press, 1932.

Tigges, Linda, ed. *Santa Fe Historic Plaza Study I.* Santa Fe: City Planning Department, 1990.

Timmons, W. H. *El Paso: A Borderlands History*. El Paso: Texas Western Press, 1990.

Tittman, Edward D. "The First Irrigation Law Suit." *NMHR* 2 (October 1927): 363–68.

Torrez, Robert J. "Crime and Punishment in Spanish Colonial New Mexico." Unpublished manuscript. SRCA.

———. "'El Bornes': La Tierra Amarilla and T. D. Burns." *NMHR* 56 (April 1981): 161–175.

———. "The San Juan Gold Rush of 1860 and Its Effect on the Development of Northern New Mexico." *NMHR* 63 (July 1988): 257–72.

Twinam, Ann. *Miners, Merchants, and Farmers in Colonial Colombia*. Austin: University of Texas Press, 1982.

Twitchell, Ralph Emerson. *The Leading Facts of New Mexico History*. Albuquerque: Horn & Wallace, 1963.

———. *Old Santa Fe*. 1925. Reprint, Chicago: Rio Grande Press, 1963.

———. *The Spanish Archives of New Mexico*. 2 vols., 1914. Reprint, New York: Arno Press, 1976.

Tyler, Daniel. "Anglo-American Penetration of the Southwest: The View from New Mexico." *Southwestern Historical Quarterly* 75 (January 1972): 325–88.

———. "Dating the Caño Ditch: Detective Work in the Pojoaque Valley. *NMHR* 61 (January 1986): 15–25.

———. "Ejido Lands in New Mexico." in *Spanish and Mexican Land Grants and the Law*. Edited by Malcolm Ebright. Manhattan, Kansas: Sunflower University Press, 1989.

———. "Land and Water Tenure in New Mexico: 1821–1846." Unpublished report on file in New Mexico v. Aamodt, No. 6639, Federal District Court for New Mexico.

———. *The Mythical Pueblo Rights Doctrine: Water Administration in Hispanic New Mexico*. El Paso: Texas Western Press, 1990.

———. "New Mexico in the 1820s: The First Administration of Manuel Armijo." Ph. D. dissertation, University of New Mexico, 1971.

———. "The Role of Hispanic Custom in Defining New Mexican Land and Water Rights." Unpublished manuscript on file in State v. Abeyta, May 1991.

———. "Underground Water in Hispanic New Mexico: A Brief Analysis of Laws, Customs, and Disputes." *NMHR* 66 (July 1991): 287–301.

Vance, John Thomas, and Helen L. Clagett. *A Guide to the Law and Legal Literature of Mexico*. Washington, D.C.: Library of Congress, 1945.

Van Kleffans, Eelco Nicolaas. *Hispanic Law Until the End of the Middle Ages*. Edinburgh: Edinburgh University Press, 1968.

Van Ness, John R. *Hispanos in Northern New Mexico: The Development of Corporate Community and Multicommunity.* New York: AMS Press, 1991.

——. "The Juan Bautista Valdez Grant: Was it a Community Land Grant." In *Spanish and Mexican Land Grants in New Mexico and Colorado.* Edited by Van Ness and Van Ness. (Manhattan, Kansas: Sunflower University Press, 1980).

——. "Spanish American vs. Anglo American Land Tenure and the Study of Economic Change in New Mexico." *Social Science Journal* 13 (October 1976): 45–52.

Van Ness, John R., and Christine M. Van Ness, eds. *Spanish and Mexican Land Grants in New Mexico.* Manhattan, Kansas: Sunflower University Press, 1980.

Vassberg, David E. *Land and Society in Golden Age Castile.* Cambridge, England: Cambridge University Press, 1984.

——. "The Sale of the *Tierras Baldías* In Sixteenth-Century Castille." *Journal of Modern History* 47 (December 1975): 629–54.

——. "The Spanish Background: Problems Concerning Ownership, Usurpations, and Defense of Common Lands in Sixteenth-Century Castile." In *Spanish and Mexican Land Grants and the Law.* Edited by Malcolm Ebright. Manhattan, Kansas: Sunflower University Press, 1989.

——. "The *Tierras Baldías*: Community Property and Public Lands in 16th Century Castile." *Agricultural History* 48 (July 1974): 383.

Vigil, Julián Josué. "1845 Census of Las Vegas, New Mexico," 1985.

——. *Five New Mexican Eighteenth and Nineteenth Century Census Fragments.* Springer: Editorial Telaraña, 1984.

——. "Guide to the Archives of the Archdiocese of Santa Fe." SRCA.

——. *Mexican Archives of New Mexico, 1821–1846.* Springer: Editorial Telaraña, 1984.

——. "SANM I:10: [The] Vigil Index." Springer: Editorial Telaraña, 1984.

——. "San Miguel del Bado, 1830 Confirmations." 1985. SRCA.

——. "San Miguel del Bado, 1841 Census." 1984. SRCA.

——. *A Short Index to New Mexican Soldiers' Service Records and Enlistment Papers, 1821–1846.* Springer: Editorial Telaraña, 1984.

Vigil, Ralph H. *Alonso de Zorita: Royal Judge and Christian Humanist 1512–1585.* Norman: University of Oklahoma Press, 1987.

Voss, Stuart F. *On the Periphery of Nineteenth-Century Mexico: Sonora and Sinaloa, 1810–1877.* Tucson, The University of Arizona Press, 1982.

Walker, John L. "The Treatment of Private Property in International Law after State Succession." In "Land, Law and La Raza" (A collection of papers presented for Professor Theodore Parnall's seminar in comparative law. UNM School of Law, Fall Semester, 1972).

Warner, Louis H. "Conveyance of Property, the Spanish and Mexican Way." *NMHR* 6 (October 1931): 334–59.

——. "Wills and Hijuelas." *NMHR* 7 (1932): 75–89.

Weber, David J. *Foreigners in Their Native Land: Historical Roots of the Mexican Americans.* Albuquerque: University of New Mexico Press, 1973.

——. "Land and Water Rights of the Pueblos of New Mexico Under Mexican Sovereignty, 1821–1846." Unpublished report on file in New Mexico v. Aamodt, No. 6639, Federal District Court for New Mexico, 1979.

——. *The Mexican Frontier, 1821–1846: The American Southwest Under Mexico.* Albuquerque: University of New Mexico Press, 1982.

——. *The Spanish Frontier in North America.* New Haven: Yale University Press, 1992

——. "The New Mexico Archives in 1827." NMHR 61 (January 1986): 53–61.

——. *The Taos Trappers: The Fur Trade in the Far Southwest, 1540–1846.* Norman: University of Oklahoma Press, 1971.

——, ed. and trans. *Arms, Indians, and the Mismanagement of New Mexico: Donaciano Vigil, 1846.* El Paso: Texas Western Press, 1986.

Weber, David J., and G. Emlen Hall. "Mexican Liberals and the Pueblo Indians, 1821–1829." *NMHR* 59 (January 1984): 5.

Weisser, Michael R. *The Peasants of the Montes.* Chicago and London: The University of Chicago Press, 1976.

Westphall, Victor. "Fraud and Implications of Fraud in the Land Grants of New Mexico." *NMHR* 49 (July 1974): 189–218.

——. *Mercedes Reales: Hispanic Land Grants of the Upper Rio Grande Region.* Albuquerque: University of New Mexico Press, 1983.

——. *The Public Domain in New Mexico: 1854–1891.* Albuquerque: University of New Mexico Press, 1965.

——. Thomas Benton Catron: A Historical Defense." *NMHR* 63 (January 1988): 43–57.

White, Koch, Kelley, and McCarthy, and the New Mexico State Planning Office. *Land Title Study.* Santa Fe: State Planning Office, 1971.

Womack, John, Jr. *Zapata and the Mexican Revolution.* New York: Alfred A. Knopf, 1969.

Glossary

abogado. Lawyer; in Spain, the lawyer who researched the law that applied to a particular case, wrote the briefs required, and presented the legal arguments orally to the judge.

abrevaderos. Public access to water sources.

acequia. An irrigation ditch; from the Arabic as-saquiya.

alcalde. Local governmental official with judicial, executive, and police powers.

alcaldía. The area governed by an *akalde* or *ayuntamiento*.

alférez. Ensign, standard bearer.

asesor. Legal advisor.

asamblea. Legislative assembly; successor to the diputación.

atarque. diversion dam for an irrigation ditch.

audiencia. A judicial body, sometimes with legislative powers; the highest court of appeal in Mexico.

ayuntamiento. Town council.

bando. Proclamation, decree.

cabildo. Municipal council; also the meeting place of such a council.

caballería. Unit of agricultural land, about 105 acres.

caciques. Indian chief or local ruler.

caño. Conduit, culvert.

carreta. A two-wheeled cart.

casa consistorial. City hall; house where community meetings are held.

cédula. Order or decree, usually from the king.

ciénega. A swampy place; wetlands.

conciliación. An arbitration proceeding.

cordel. A rope for measuring land, usually 50 or 100 *varas* long.

cortés. Senate or congress of deputies in Spain.

comandante general. The official who administered the military-political district known as the *comandancia general*.

comisaría substituta. The territorial treasury.

dehesa. Common pasture land.

de novo. To start anew.

derrota de mieses. Stubble grazing.

dictamen. Judgement, legal opinion.

diputación. Territorial legislature.

ejido. Common land owned by a community.

encomienda. A grant of Indians.

escribano. Notary, judicial assistant; an official with legal training.

estancia. Ranch.

estanciero. Rancher, owner of an *estancia.*

expediente. A file of papers, as of a court case or the proceedings in a land grant.

extranjero. Foreigner.

fanega. Unit of dry measure from 1.5 to 2.5 bushels.

hijuela. A deed, often effecting the division of a larger tract.

fondas de advitrios.

hombre bueno. Advocate in a conciliation proceeding.

jefe politico. The governor.

juez comisionado. A judge specially assigned to a case.

juez de paz. Justice of the peace; successor to *alcaldes* during the Mexican Period.

juez de primera instancia. Judge of the first instance, lower court judge.

junta departamental. Departmental legislature.

latifundio. A large unit of land holding comprised of several *haciendas.*

leña. Firewood, generally for heating the home and cooking on a wood stove.

letrado. A lawyer; literally, a man of letters.

licenciado. Lawyer.

mayerdomo de propios. Administrator of municipal lands owned by a town or city.

merced. A grant of land or water.

monte. Mountainous common lands used primarily for wood-gathering.

noria. A well.

partido. A political subdivision; a sheep contract.

pastos. Common grazing land.

pobladores. Settlers.

portero. Gatekeeper, sergeant-at-arms.

prado. High quality pasture land, often irrigated.

prefect. Governmental official during the Mexican Period, subordinate to the governor, who administered a *prefectura.*

procurador general. Attorney general.

procurador síndico. Attorney or legal advisor of a municipal corporation.

propios. Municipally owned property.

puesto. An outpost.

regidor. Member of an *ayuntamiento.*

rúbric. Rubric, flourish at the end of a signature by which its authenticity is verified.

sala constitucional. The *ayuntamiento's* meeting place.

sin perjuicio de tercero. Without injury to third parties.

sitio de gañado major. Tract of land for grazing cattle.

sitio de gañado menor. Tract of land for grazing sheep.

solar de casa. Small tract of land for a dwelling; housesite.

suerte. Plot of farm land.

tanque. pond, often for irrigation.

teniente. Assistant.

testimonio. A copy of land grant or other proceedings given to the parties.

tierras baldías. Public land, vacant land.

tierras concegiles. Common lands of communities.

tierras eriasas. Uncultivated land.

tierras realengas. Public land of the sovereign.

tierras del pan llevar. Wheat-raising land.

torreón. Watchtower.

vara. Unit of measurement, approximately 33 inches.

vecino. A landowning resident of a community entitled to vote.

villa. The largest of the Hispanic municipalities in New Mexico; the four *villas* were Santa Fe, Santa Cruz de la Cañada, Albuquerque, and El Paso del Norte.

visita. A church that lacks a resident priest, but is visited by a priest who conducts services.

zanja. Feeder ditch.

INDEX